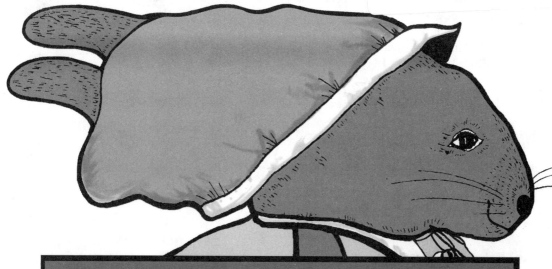

# THIRD GRADE TEACHER'S
## *Month-by-Month*
# ACTIVITIES PROGRAM

## ELIZABETH CROSBY STULL

*Illustrations by Deborah Wright*

**THE CENTER FOR APPLIED
RESEARCH IN EDUCATION**
Paramus, New Jersey 07652

**Library of Congress Cataloging-in-Publication Data**

Stull, Elizabeth Crosby.
    Third-grade teacher's month-by-month activities program / Elizabeth Crosby Stull.
      p.  cm.
    ISBN 0-13-041962-1
    1. Education, Primary—Activity programs—United States.   2. Third grade
(Education)—United States.   I.  Title.

LB1537 .S848 2002
372.24'1—dc21
                                   2001047342

Acquisitions Editor: *Susan Kolwicz*
Production Editor: *Mariann Hutlak*
Interior Design/Formatting: *Robyn Beckerman*

Printed in the United States of America

10  9  8  7  6  5  4  3  2  1

**ISBN 0-13-041962-1**

---

**Attention: Corporations and Schools**

The Center for Applied Research in Education books are available at quantity discounts with bulk purchase for educational, business, or sales promotional use. For information, please write to: Prentice Hall Career Special Sales, 240 Frisch Court, Paramus, NJ 07652. Please supply: title of book, ISBN, quantity, how the book will be used, date needed.

---

**THE CENTER FOR APPLIED RESEARCH
IN EDUCATION**
**Paramus, NJ 07652**

http://www.phdirect.com/education

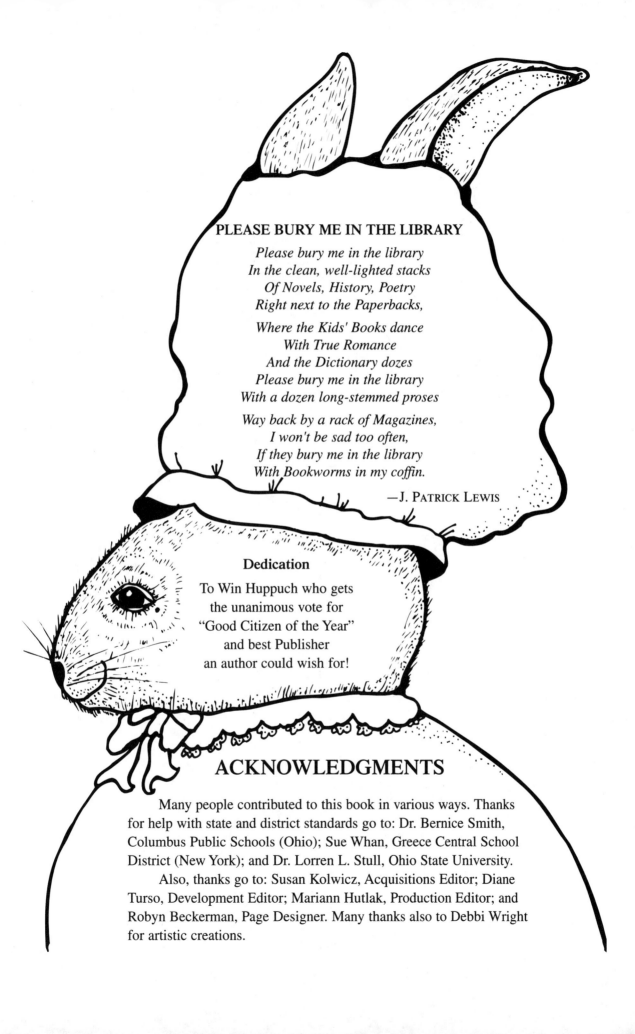

## PLEASE BURY ME IN THE LIBRARY

*Please bury me in the library
In the clean, well-lighted stacks
Of Novels, History, Poetry
Right next to the Paperbacks,*

*Where the Kids' Books dance
With True Romance
And the Dictionary dozes
Please bury me in the library
With a dozen long-stemmed proses*

*Way back by a rack of Magazines,
I won't be sad too often,
If they bury me in the library
With Bookworms in my coffin.*

—J. Patrick Lewis

### Dedication

To Win Huppuch who gets
the unanimous vote for
"Good Citizen of the Year"
and best Publisher
an author could wish for!

## ACKNOWLEDGMENTS

Many people contributed to this book in various ways. Thanks for help with state and district standards go to: Dr. Bernice Smith, Columbus Public Schools (Ohio); Sue Whan, Greece Central School District (New York); and Dr. Lorren L. Stull, Ohio State University.

Also, thanks go to: Susan Kolwicz, Acquisitions Editor; Diane Turso, Development Editor; Mariann Hutlak, Production Editor; and Robyn Beckerman, Page Designer. Many thanks also to Debbi Wright for artistic creations.

# ABOUT THE AUTHOR

Elizabeth Crosby Stull, Ph.D. (Ohio State University), has over 30 years of experience in education as a primary teacher and teacher educator. She began her career as a teacher in the public schools of Greece Central, Camillus, and Pittsford in upstate New York. She was an associate professor at Otterbein College, Education Department, and also taught in the Education Department for Ohio State University. Children's literature is a special interest.

Dr. Stull has published many articles in professional journals such as *Instructor* and *Teaching K–8*. She has written three other books for primary educators published by The Center for Applied Research in Education: *Kindergarten Teacher's Month-by-Month Activities Program* with co-author Carol Lewis Price (1987), *First Grade Teacher's Month-by-Month Activities Program* (1990), and *Second Grade Teacher's Month-by-Month Activities Program* (1992). In addition, Dr. Stull has written other educational resources for classroom teachers, including *Multicultural Discovery Activities for the Elementary Grades* (1994), *Kindergarten Teacher's Survival Guide* (1997), and *Let's Read! A Month-by-Month Activities Program for Beginning Readers* (2000).

Dr. Stull is a member of the National Association for the Education of Young Children (NAEYC) and the International Reading Association (IRA). In her spare time, she enjoys painting, antiquing, and traveling.

# ABOUT THIS BOOK

Many new teachers ask, *"How do I begin to teach third grade? What do I do first?"* This book addresses those questions and more. It begins by giving third-grade teachers a first-day plan that has worked effectively for many teachers over the years. Then it offers a wide variety of teaching suggestions and activities for each month of the school year. It includes over 135 full-page activity sheets that are charmingly illustrated and ready for immediate use. Most importantly, this practical resource helps you create an environment that motivates and invites students to learn throughout the school year.

Since classroom management is a key component for a successful teaching experience, you'll find many strategies and techniques to help you maintain control throughout the coming months. In addition, there are tips for setting up stimulating, hands-on learning centers where children are encouraged to engage in activities for practice and enrichment.

Nationally, there is a movement toward teaching basic skills and evaluating those skills through state testing in the curriculum areas. This book addresses grade-level performance expectations and gives suggestions for helping students achieve success, especially in the areas of reading and mathematics. Some attention is devoted to methods of testing students.

For your convenience, the activities in this program are organized into monthly sections that cover the following skill areas:

**Recommended Books (Literacy)**—Each month's list of ten recommended books with brief annotations gives you classic as well as current selections to stimulate your students' love of reading. You'll find books linked to the skills taught for the month as well as those meant for pure reading enjoyment. The last book in each list is a chapter book that can be read aloud to the entire class.

**Reading/Language Arts**—When children are given the strategies and tools they need to learn basic reading skills, then reading success is certainly achievable. Here you'll find many specific phonics suggestions plus numerous chants, jingles, and rhymes used to reinforce the ever-expanding letter-sound connections third graders need to master. Finding the main idea of a story, reading to locate specific information, using story maps, synthesizing information, spelling, becoming familiar with reference materials, understanding word paraphrasing, and using similes and metaphors are just a few of the topics covered in this area.

In addition, students gain an appreciation of our language through a monthly focus on a group of words and sayings by exploring how they originated or found their way into our language.

**Mathematics**—The basic operations of addition, subtraction, multiplication, and division contain suggested activities designed to help students learn these operations through rote memory. By the completion of third grade, mastery of these operations should be completed. Many other math concepts are also addressed, such as length, width, volume, fractions, geometry, estimation, and prediction. Tips are given for making charts, graphs, and Venn diagrams to enable students to gain practice in working with math concepts. Whenever possible, math concepts are related to real-life scenarios.

**Social Studies**—Each month offers a variety of different topics for study. There is an emphasis at grade three on acquiring knowledge about our country, past and present. Attention is paid to cities and states plus symbols that represent our country. Also included is coverage of colonial days that students compare/contrast to present-day history, map studies, and a list of holidays and celebrations with suggestions on how to integrate them into the third-grade learning experience.

**Science/Health**—Through the use of a learning center, students can be encouraged to "act like scientists" and investigate, use equipment, keep logs, make predictions, test hypotheses, and describe outcomes. This section presents a rich array of different topics along with ideas on incorporating them into the curriculum. For example, you'll explore birds and migration, dinosaurs, seasonal changes, weather charting, animal study, and much more.

**Author-of-the-Month**—Each month contains a well-known children's author or illustrator, carefully selected for third-grade interest level, to add spark to your reading program while encouraging further reading and library research. Provided is a brief summary of the author, an annotated bibliography of recommended books to be gathered for the classroom and read aloud, and a rich collection of ideas for developing these books for extended use in the classroom.

Art, music, and physical activity are not presented as separate sections, but the book does include a wide variety of suggestions for each of these areas presented in the content study. For example, many art and music ideas are given in the Author-of-the-Month section for each month, such as making and sharing books, interviewing techniques, retellings, book reporting, painting murals, and making designs and prints.

Above all, we must remember that average third graders are curious and want to learn new things. School needs to offer these children a variety of challenges, opportunities to ponder, and events to explore. Yet, they can be motivated to memorize facts that will serve them well for the rest of their years in school. Third grade marks the end of what we call the "primary" learning years—so make the most of your year with these exuberant and delightful children!

*Elizabeth Crosby Stull*

# CONTENTS

## SEPTEMBER

# OCTOBER

## FOCUS ON SCIENCE • 98

Set Up a Weather Station • Weather Affects People • Seeds Are "Going to the Dogs" • The Tumbling Tumbleweed • Collect Seeds for Projects • Musical Instruments With Seeds • Seeds Are Stored Food • Autumn Harvest and Markets • Speaking of Tasting • Problem Solving With Scarecrows • Sometimes Solving One Problem Creates Another • Have a Scarecrow Contest in Your School

## OCTOBER AUTHOR STUDY: ROBERT D. SANSOUCI • 103

## REPRODUCIBLE ACTIVITY PAGES FOR OCTOBER • 108

### READING/LANGUAGE ARTS

The Fiction vs. Nonfiction Witch • Parts of Speech for Lunch • My Mini Book of Resources (3 pages) • Letter-Writing Form • Spello • Story Vine (Web)

### MATH

Column Addition • Pumpkin Math • Make a Quilt Pattern • The Masked Money Bandit • Who Can Buy Pizza Today?

### SOCIAL STUDIES

Travel Poster—My Home Town • Gifts of Nature Memory Game • Join the Firefighters!

### SCIENCE

Our Sense of Taste • Make a Scary Scarecrow

### AUTHOR STUDY

Ingredients for a Fairy Tale/Folktale

# NOVEMBER

## NOVEMBER BOOKS • 130

## FOCUS ON READING • 131

What Is a Compound Word? • A Pictionary of Compound Words • Compound Words—Find Your Other Half • Compound Words—Fill in the Humming Blanks • A Fresh Approach to Compounding Words and Ideas • Sign Language • Working with Contractions (Have) • Working with Contractions (Not) • Chester Couldn't, Shouldn't, Wouldn't, and Didn't • More Contraction Groups • Contractions in Sentences • I'm a Major League "Contraction Sport" • Making Inferences • Inferring—Before Story Time • Inferring—After Story Time • Vocabulary Building Through Reading • Vocabulary Building—Guided Reading • Words Are Magnetic • Beginning Word Sorts • "Out of Sorts" • Compare and Contrast • Compare and Contrast—Differences • Compare and Contrast Actual Items (Realia)

# DECEMBER

## FOCUS ON LANGUAGE ARTS • 196

## FOCUS ON SPELLING • 207

## FOCUS ON MATH • 208

## FOCUS ON SOCIAL STUDIES • 211

# JANUARY

## FOCUS ON SCIENCE • 270

The Solar System • The Morning Star, the Evening Star • The Stars in Color • Energy from the Sun • Stargazing at Night • Make a Papier-Mâché Solar System • Space Adventure • A Rainbow Experiment • Telling Time by the Sun

## JANUARY AUTHOR STUDY: JEAN FRITZ • 273

## REPRODUCIBLE ACTIVITY PAGES FOR JANUARY • 278

### READING/LANGUAGE ARTS

My January Self-Assessment • Baxter and the Blender • Story Outline • Story Character Web • Author Checklist • Handwriting Skills

### MATH

Percy Penguin's Math Slide • Become a Division Star • Snowman Math

### SOCIAL STUDIES

The People's House • Famous Americans Album

### SCIENCE

Our Solar System • Science Tools

### AUTHOR STUDY

Become an Inventor with Jean Fritz

# FEBRUARY

## FEBRUARY BOOKS • 296

## FOCUS ON READING • 297

The KWL Approach • Declarative and Interrogative Sentences • Change the Sentence from Tell to Ask • More Work with Webs • Homophones • Homophone Guess • Rebus Stories Using Homophones • What's a Homograph? • Using Homographs • Homograph Sentences Strips

## FOCUS ON LANGUAGE ARTS • 303

### MORE READING OPPORTUNITIES . . . . . . . . . . . . . . . . . 303

Newspaper Cutups • Close Your Eyes and Visualize • Close Your Eyes, Visualize, and Draw • Some Trickster Tales for Black History Month • An Anasi Recipe for Good Eating • Tales of Presidents • Computer in the Classroom • World Wide Web • Writing for Information

# MARCH

## FOCUS ON MATH • 365

## FOCUS ON SOCIAL STUDIES • 369

## FOCUS ON SCIENCE • 374

## MARCH AUTHOR/ILLUSTRATOR STUDY: JOANNA COLE AND BRUCE DEGEN • 377

# APRIL

### MATH

Fraction Food • More Than, Less Than

### SOCIAL STUDIES

Colonial Days vs. Today • Patriotic Coins and Stamps

### SCIENCE

Classify Birds by Feet • Nature's Weavers

### AUTHOR STUDY

J. Patrick Lewis Writes Poetry that Sings

# MAY/JUNE

Spring Growth • Grass Seed/Bird Seed Letters • Vocabulary Flashcards • Articulation of Sounds • Formula of the Day • Experience Chart Stories • Book Jackets • Revisiting Stories • Revisiting Activity Pages • Compound-Word Challenge • Research and Reference Material Puzzlers • Vocabulary Building—From Simple to Complex • Vocabulary Building—From Complex to Simple • Am I Asking? I Am Telling! • Reading Road Signs • Find Little Words in Big Words • Test Taking: Multiple-Choice Variety • Test Taking: How Is This Test Different? • Test Taking: Finding the Main Idea • The Puppets Have the Answers • End-of-Year Wrap-Up Statements for Records

Making Story Characters • Revisit and Reteach Consonant Blends • Reading Cloths • Story Wall Hanging: Arpillera • Poetry Reading • Reading a Story vs. Watching a Videotape • Link Reading to All Subjects • Link Reading to Sports • Pull a Story Out of a Hat

School Pen Pals • Penmanship Awards • Story Starters from Well-Known Books and Writers • Read, Stop, and Write • Spring Writing Slogan

I Speak, You Listen. You Speak, I Listen. • Are You a Talking Machine? • Indoor/Outdoor Voices • Pleasant Speakers • Have a Debate, or a Pro/Con Presentation

### MATH

"Oh, Yes, You Do Need Math!" • Working With Weight • Baseball Math • Basketball Bears • Tennis Teddies

### SOCIAL STUDIES

Wants and Needs

### SCIENCE

Listen for Sounds of Spring • Let's Go Digging for a Graph • Write a Bird Report • Spring Tree Graph

### AUTHOR STUDY

Spin a Story With Matt Christopher

# APPENDICES

# SEPTEMBER

# SEPTEMBER BOOKS

**Chalk, Gary.** *Yankee Doodle, A Revolutionary Tail* **(New York: Dorling Kindersley, 1993).** A patriotic mouse named Yankee Doodle recounts his version of the major events of the Revolutionary War. In this version the soldiers have pop guns and hobby horses.

**Clement, Rod.** *Counting on Frank* **(Milwaukee, WI: Gareth Stevens Publishing, 1991).** A boy's dad says, "You have a brain. Use it!" So he does. He can't get math out of his head. His dog, Frank, takes up lots of space, so the boy calculates that 24 Franks could fit into his bedroom. At the end, the author gives the readers puzzlers and a chance to use their brain.

**Falwell, Cathryn.** *Word Wizard* **(New York: Clarion, 1998).** By way of a magic spoon, Anna can transform words by moving the letters about. For example, the word *canoe* becomes *ocean*. With this new-found skill, Anna helps a little lost boy.

**Norworth, Jack.** *Take Me Out to the Ballgame.* **Illustrations by Alec Gillman (New York: Four Winds Press, 1992).** Jack Norworth wrote the lyrics for "Take Me Out to the Ballgame" during a half-hour ride on the subway in New York City. The song became an American classic, and this book is a visual celebration of the game of baseball.

**Polacco, Patricia.** *Mrs. Katz and Tush* **(New York: Bantam, 1992).** An intergenerational story about an older Jewish woman and Larnel, a young African-American boy, who live in the same neighborhood. Mrs. Katz is all alone and Larnel has just the answer for her—a cat. She agrees on one condition, that he help her take care of it. A loving friendship blossoms.

**Prelutsky, Jack (selected by).** *The Random House Book of Poetry for Children.* **Illustrated by Arnold Lobel (New York: Random House, 1983).** What a treasury of poems for children to hold in their hands and read. Short poems, on every subject, by many poets. Enjoyable!

**Pringle, Laurence.** *Naming the Cat.* **Illustrations by Katherine Potter (New York: Walker and Company, 1998).** A family tries to find just the right name for its adopted cat and comes up with some amusing names. Text and illustrations of lively cats are in harmony.

**Schulson, Rachel Ellenberg.** *Guns: What You Should Know.* **Illustrated by Mary Jones (New York: Albert Whitman, 1997).** It's never too early to begin a gun-safety program. This book is a useful introduction to firearms and what they can do. (Recommended for grades K–3.)

**Young, Ed.** *Seven Blind Mice* **(New York: Philomel, 1992).** Seven different colored mice find a strange "something" by their pond. Each day a different mouse goes to find out what it is and comes back with a different conclusion. Finally on day seven, they make a grand discovery. (Good for a discussion of getting all the facts before making a decision.)

**(CHAPTER BOOK) Naylor, Phyllis R.** *Shiloh* **(New York: Simon & Schuster Books for Children, 1991).** Read aloud this touching story of a little boy from a poor family who wants a dog so badly that he will sacrifice and almost destroy his relationship with his father to get one. It's not just any dog, it's Shiloh, who is being mistreated and needs to be rescued.

# SEPTEMBER

Days are shorter, nights are cooler, and it's time for school once again. Third grade is a critical passage because it marks the last of the primary grades where skill building is important for future success. This grade provides a rich opportunity for students to review material that was presented in the early primary grades, to fill in the gaps, and also to broaden the learning experience. Students at this age are generally eager for the learning year to begin—they're at an inquisitive stage and are interested in how things work. They're alert to their environment and are eager to make connections and share findings with classmates. They're also "team players" at this stage of development and are interested in knowing the rules, which makes them pleasant companions during a day of learning. Let's make your September classroom interesting and challenging for them!

## GETTING READY FOR SEPTEMBER

### LEARNING CENTERS

Attractive Centers can be set up in various places around the classroom for Math, Science, Social Studies, Language Arts, Reading, Art, and other special activities. These can change and vary monthly. You need to make the area visually attractive so it appeals to students and draws them there. Plan to have a sign-up sheet, written directions, necessary materials, a place for finished products, a place for ongoing projects to be stored, and a method for maintaining the upkeep of the area. Introduce the Centers gradually, with one activity at a time. Go slowly in September until classroom management has been worked out. Determine how many students can work simultaneously at the Center, and if materials can be removed from the Center and taken elsewhere to complete activities. Make sure all of this has been planned before the introduction of the Center to the students.

It is generally the intent to have students gain experience at the Learning Center that will reinforce or extend content already taught in the various subjects. In this way, students can work independently and you are free to work with skill groups. New material is not introduced here, unless it's in the form of a group lesson. Learning Centers can run smoothly when students go there for remediation, reinforcement, skill-building, and enrichment activities. After new content material has been formally taught, it can appear in the appropriate Center with designated activities, and there will be less confusion.

Learning Centers may be used in a variety of ways. They can be in operation when assigned work is completed, during free time, and during recess time. They can also be built into the daily schedule as "Center Time."

Rules for behavior need to be established and enforced. If, for some reason, a Learning Center is not operating smoothly or becomes a problem in the classroom, then put up a "CLOSED" sign at the area until changes are made. For example, if the Learning Center has a large ship or sailing motif, the sign can read "Voyage Cancelled Tuesday and Wednesday—Stormy Weather." If famous American historical figures are in charge of the Learning Centers, make a large banner that would be appropriate for that person or time period. For example, at Benjamin Franklin's Science Center, the sign could read "Electrical Problems—Closed Until Further Notice" or "Thunder and Lightning—Closed Today." Favorite characters from children's books can also be used effectively for guiding students through the activities. For historical figures, directions written or printed on colored paper cut into patriotic shapes of the flag, Liberty Bell, stamps, eagle, Uncle Sam hat, and so on, add an inviting visual component to the Centers. For storybook characters, written directions can be put on cutouts of appropriate symbols taken from the story.

A life-size replica of the book character in charge of each Learning Center can be made by students. Use heavy poster paper, construction paper, or kraft paper and felt pens. This artwork can be done during recess time or during project time. Students can work in teams and vote on a name for each Learning Center. In order to promote a serious learning environment in these areas, avoid the use of commercial figures and comic-page characters.

Make sure equipment necessary for carrying out the activities is in place at the Center so that it is a self-contained unit. Baskets, coffee tins, or juice cans that are covered with construction paper and labeled can house scissors, rulers, pencils, and other necessary equipment.

## CHECKING PERMANENT RECORDS

You need to check the permanent records for each student. These records are usually housed in the main office. Third graders have had three years of formal schooling up to this point, and the aca-

demic achievement record to date should provide valuable information. Although achievement will change throughout the grades, the records provide an excellent starting point. Having knowledge of standardized test scores and aptitude scores is also important. If the records are written objectively and professionally, they should be valued. If you choose not to read these records until the year has begun, you have lost valuable time. When a child has health problems or a unique home situation, you must know this immediately.

## GETTING THE CLASSROOM READY

You need to get the classroom ready for learning *prior* to the arrival of the students. Welcoming the students into an environment already set up and ready to go sends a clear nonverbal signal that learning is a top priority in this classroom. The following are some things that need attention:

- Put backing paper or cloth material, such as burlap, on bulletin boards to give the environment some warmth.

- Arrange the desks in an order that is conducive to learning (single rows, double rows, groups of four, horizontal rows, etc.).

- Secure tables or put desks together for Learning Center areas.

- Decide which bulletin boards you will be in charge of and which ones will be a collaborative effort with students working together.

- Complete your bulletin boards (for example, weekly schedule, large calendar, room assistant's chart, classroom rules and consequences, newspaper articles, an incomplete board to be worked on the first day, etc.).

- Make student nametags for the desks.

- Have oaktag shapes available at each desk so students can make their own nametag to be worn the first day and for special classes.

- Display the alphabet (cursive) in the classroom.

- Secure at least 30 books from the public library for the classroom library area.

- Set up your desk (stapler, large scissors, tape, and so on).

- Fill in the planbook for the first day (minimum).

- Cut out a large bus shape and place self-stick notes inside it with a bus number written on each one. On the first day students can sign their name on the appropriate bus slip (hang by the door).

- Make sure supplies are available for the first day. These include books, writing paper, pencils, scissors, rulers, paste or glue, chalk, erasers, etc.

- Check with the custodian for an ample supply of paper toweling and cleaning items, including a wastebasket.

- Locate the large scissors and a designated place to store them (your desk).

- Make sure to gain practice with the intercom system so that you can send and receive messages from the office.

- Buy a bag of kitty litter and place it under the sink. Throughout the year when a student has an upset stomach and gets sick in the classroom, cover the area liberally with the kitty litter and call for custodial help with cleanup, even if it means the class has to leave the room and go outdoors. (Always take a packet of kitty litter with you when you go on a field trip.)

- Check to see if the classroom computer/printer is in working order.
- Check the TV/VCR controls.
- Check the cassette recorder in the Listening Center.
- Have a flashlight available in the classroom.
- Secure a radio that is run on batteries. (This is good for checking weather reports, hourly news for student reports, emergencies, etc.)
- Have a cell phone available for emergency use only by the teacher or an aide.

# THE VERY FIRST DAY OF SCHOOL

You have written the daily plans in your planbook *prior to the first day*. In other words, these are done, and in the book, when you walk into the classroom. In addition, you may wish to record the first day's plans on a 4- by 6-inch card to keep at the desk, or carry in a convenient pocket, so that you can check to see what's next on the agenda. During the first hour, especially, there are so many distractions and things to which you must attend, that a written reminder right at hand is helpful. It gives students a feeling of confidence in you when transitions are made effortlessly and smoothly.

## WHAT DO I DO FIRST?

These are essential practices for setting up an organized classroom and for establishing a firm foundation. *The first day is critical.* These procedures can be done sequentially.

- Greet students at the door and check off their names from your class roster.
- Students can take any seat, or an assigned seat if you've chosen to put their nametags on desks or tables. These can always be changed later.
- When all students have arrived, call out their names and have them raise their hand so you can locate them in the classroom and begin to put together names with faces.
- Send attendance cards to the office. If there is a question about a name on the list (e.g., student is not there, or the student is there but the name is not on your list), check with the office immediately.
- Take the lunch count and send to the office. (This varies with schools.)
- Check to see who rides a bus and who walks. Then, make sure students know their bus number and record their name on the bus shape that you have hung by the door.
- Print or write your name on the chalkboard and introduce yourself.
- Lead students in Pledge of Allegiance and a patriotic song.

# WHAT DO I DO NEXT?

After the "housekeeping" portion is accomplished—and this may take from 20–45 minutes—you can then introduce students to the curriculum materials, the weekly schedule, and the classroom environment. This is where you also present them with the list of rules and consequences. The rules may be changed later, but you need a set that is ready to go on the first day.

**The Curriculum Materials.** Put texts and workbook materials along the chalkboard. Then, from left to right, introduce students to the materials and some of the things they will be studying. Do this in such a way that it sounds interesting and exciting to the students. Include reading texts, if the school is using texts, the spelling workbook, math text, social studies resource books, science and health resource books, cursive handwriting workbook, and so on. At this time, it is appropriate to distribute some of this material. If it is your policy to have students put their name inside, or on the cover, of some of the individual workbooks, now is the time to do so. If you do not want students to use felt pens or pencils to draw, doodle, or scribble on the outside covers of commercial workbooks, now is the time to make that clear. Encourage them to save that energy for their handmade journal covers, portfolio covers, and project covers.

**The Weekly Schedule.** Students will be eager to know the weekly schedule, so have it posted in the classroom. Make up a set of colored paper plates to resemble clocks, and display them on the wall, in a row from Monday–Friday, showing the appropriate day, time, and subject on each clock. Call attention to them at this time. Refer to materials or supplies that may be needed for the special subjects, such as a smock for art class, gym shoes, and the responsibility for returning library books weekly.

**The Classroom Environment.** Feel free to move around the room to show the various areas of interest. These may include an aquarium, a tree with beanbag chairs underneath for cozy reading time, the classroom library nook, the computer area, the Learning Centers, paper and supply storage areas, and materials that are stored on the shelves for free-time or recess use. Point out the information that you have on the bulletin boards and also note that responsibility for some of the bulletin boards will be shared by them.

**The School Tour.** Students have now met you, the teacher, and have seen who their classmates are. They've heard what their weekly schedule will be. They have a general idea of the books they will start off with, and a sketch of the activities that will take place. Now let's stretch and get some exercise by moving out of the classroom for the building tour. At this point, you become the equivalent of a tour guide, and students will catch your excitement of being in this environment. Make sure you have your plans and information in order. It will make the trip more interesting and successful.

## THE GUIDED TOUR

Decide, in advance, how you want the class to line up at the door. Will there be a double or single line, or a boys' line and a girls' line? It's up to you, as the classroom management "engineer," to move the group from point A to point B with as little commotion as possible. Remember, you are now setting the tone for the year. If you have high expectations for behavior in the hallway, and you should have, now is the time to express them. Some teachers have used the analogy of an honor guard walking silently and at attention down the hallway. Some have used the analogy of the marching band that looks straight ahead, shoulders squared, head up, back straight, high steps. Make it a learning experience, a time to work on a healthy posture and self discipline, and a time to instill pride in their appearance and to build character. Compare them to an orderly formation one would find in an honor guard. We're looking for a quiet, orderly transition—*not* a meandering line and scuffling feet. Remember that you lead the line—you can control the speed and stop as often as necessary in order to inspect the line, praise the line, and discipline the line. Students at this age are still young enough to get into the spirit of a drum-and-bugle corps lineup, and will like the idea of being thought of as the "best" when it comes to moving in the hallways. Later, they can take turns being the line leader, but first they have to learn the behavior from your example.

Move to the cafeteria and have students walk through the lunch line area so that it will be familiar to them. Hopefully, the tables will be set up for lunch and, if so, have them sit down where the class will eat lunch. This will eliminate confusion later in the day.

Next, go past the library, the office, the nurse's office, the art room, the gym, and so on, in an effort to introduce new members to the school and to reacquaint students who are returning. Then return to the classroom.

## KEEP STUDENTS BUSY ALL DAY LONG

After this bit of exercise, you can have students do any number of things:

- Go over the set of rules/consequences with the class so that they understand it. Then have them retell it in their own words.
- Introduce themselves to their classmates, telling about their summer highlight(s).
- Decorate their writing folders.
- Write about their summer vacation or what they hope grade three will be like for them.
- Decorate the nametags to be worn around their necks, or pinned on, for special classes.

By now it may be time for a snack if you decide that you are going to have snack time in the morning. Here's where you can get student input. Many third graders still look forward to snacks in the morning, especially if they're on a later lunch schedule, so don't rule it out. Have a box of crackers available on the first and second day.

After lunch and recess, begin reading a chapter book to the entire class to settle the group down, and to begin a bonding process with the students. (See the Author-of-the-Month and Picture Book list for suggestions.) This book should be on your desk and ready to go. Show students the cover, read the title, author (and illustrator if pertinent), and tell them the genre of the story (mystery, adventure, and so on). If a student or students are already familiar with your choice, encourage them to listen and not divulge any story information to others. Explain that a good story can be read aloud many times and that we always learn something we missed the first time around.

There's still work to be done during the remainder of the day:

- Go over the fire drill routine with the class and conduct a drill.
- Have students engage in independent reading time.
- Present a math lesson.
- Have students write their signature on a sheet of paper that will be kept in their individual writing portfolio.
- Have students do a worksheet and correct it in class so that they have a paper to take home the first day.
- Play an indoor game.

## FIRST DAY WRAP-UP

- Review at the end of the day all of the things that have been accomplished.
- Explain something that they will learn the next day so they have something to look forward to (make it exciting, like a preview).
- Practice your line up—busses first, then walkers after busses have departed.

## REFLECTIONS FOR THE FIRST DAY AND THROUGHOUT SEPTEMBER

Have a firm but fair demeanor throughout each day. A teacher is not a "buddy." *Students at this age will like you. Your challenge is to get them to respect you.*

The main work during September is to establish and maintain classroom management and discipline. Work on this daily, even if it means that some of the lessons you planned don't get taught. They will get done later, and with ease, if you set the ground rules early and see to it that they are carried out. An excellent third-grade teacher must have good leadership skills, a business attitude, self-discipline, good planning skills, classroom management ability, good recovery and coping skills, and a love of students and the learning process.

You will work your heart out—and win theirs!

# FOCUS ON READING

## READING ASSESSMENT

If you are working with a formal reading program, an assessment package often accompanies the manual for teachers. This will be extremely helpful and an excellent starting point.

If you are not working with a formal reading program, check with the principal, the district reading specialist, special program specialist (remedial reading teacher, Title I coordinator), or an experienced grade-three teacher to see if help is available to you for assessment purposes.

You need to determine individual student progress, and how a student performs in relation to the group as a whole. Some students will have lost ground over the summer, but may move ahead quickly. Others may have been reading during the summer and could score at a high point and then level off. Therefore, remember that a reading assessment score is not fixed, but will vary throughout the year as you assess and reassess student progress.

You can determine what types of skill groups you will need for individuals and for the group as a whole.

## READING ASSESSMENT SKILLS

The following is a list of some of the reading skills to check:

### Phonics (Letter/Sound Relationship)

- Ask students to point to something in the room that begins with the same sound as door /d/, table /t/, floor /f/, etc. Use flashcards for this exercise.
- Give students a blank sheet of paper and have them number it from 1–10. Say a word and have them print the letter that is at the beginning of the word. This can also be done for ending sounds.
- Give students a worksheet and have them circle the correct beginning letter under a picture.
- Give students a worksheet with ten lines of various alphabet letters and have them circle the correct beginning sound for the word you say for line one, line two, etc.

### Reading Level

- Check the permanent records for information.
- Form small groups, and have students read aloud from several selections in grade-three reading books.
- Have students read independently on a one-to-one basis with you or the aide. (A rule of thumb is that if the student misses five words on a page, the material is too difficult.)
- Remember that most picture books are written on at least a third-grade level, but the vocabulary is not controlled and it is not a reliable measure.

### The Main Idea

- The student can verbalize what the story or paragraph is about.
- The student grasps the primary focus of the story.

### Making Predictions

- The student can relate to the action in a story and make reasonable statements about what may come next.
- The student is able to give a statement regarding a reasonable outcome for a story.
- The student is able to assess the feelings of a particular character and determine what action this could lead to.

### Reading Fluency

- The student still reads word by word.
- The student is able to read phrases.
- The student's reading voice is well paced so that meaning is not lost.

### Punctuation

- The student can identify the more familiar punctuation marks and knows the function of each.
- The student puts this knowledge to work when reading aloud.

### Root Words

- The student has the ability to locate the root word in order to help with the decoding process.
- The student can verbalize the proper ending (suffix) to a particular root word when listening to you reading aloud. For example, you say, "I am *go* to the store." Student can supply the "ing" sound and say, "I am *going* to the store." You say, "She already *plan* for the day." Student can supply "ed" and say, "She already *planned* for the day."

## MATCH WITS WITH A PROFESSIONAL READER AND WRITER

Sharpen the skills of organization and comprehension. Cut a short article from a section of the student newspaper. Make two or three photocopies of the article and put them in your desk drawer. Next, cut up the article and rearrange the paragraph order on another page. Tape it. Now photocopy that page and give one to each student. Students can read it and, with the cut-and-paste process, put it in order on another sheet so that it makes sense (with a beginning, middle, and ending). At the end of the day, retrieve the copies of the article from the desk drawer and students can check with the news article as it was printed in the paper to see if they put it in the same order.

Do this weekly. Sometimes the student has a different order, particularly in the middle, and it may be perfectly acceptable. Discuss the order of the finished product in the paper and try to determine why it was written in that manner. What was the focus? What was the person trying to stress? Perhaps that's why the order differed from that of students.

This particular exercise develops the skill of critical reading. Students read for meaning and clarity, and, in time, their own writing is influenced by this experience. If students are working with an article that is written by a columnist, often the e-mail address is given at the end of the article and they can interact with the journalist if appropriate.

## INTEGRATE READING INTO SUBJECT AREAS WHEN POSSIBLE

At each Learning Center and in the classroom library, have information books available that pertain to a subject being addressed in the content areas of Social Studies, Science, Health, and so on. Also, picture books and poetry books on particular topics provide an opportunity for reading enjoyment, reading rhythmically, and attaching visual stimuli to words. See the suggested reading list at the beginning of each month, as well as books that are recommended throughout this text.

## READ ALOUD DAILY

Check the Author-of-the-Month sections for chapter books, author information, and activities to carry out in the classroom. Then make time to read aloud to the students every day. Have them incorporate the story into their own journal writing; make predictions about what will happen next; and draw sketches of objects and places mentioned in the text. A good time to read aloud is just after lunch and recess. It brings the group together and sets the tone for the afternoon.

## BOOK INTRODUCTIONS

Even though students have been handling books for quite some time now, they haven't been doing this as a group in this particular classroom. Review the ground rules for the classroom library. Students may not take these books home; they are for school use. Students need to make sure their hands are clean when working with books. To mark their place in a book, use a bookmark. Do not write in a book. Convey the message that books are to be treasured and handled carefully while they are enjoying them.

## PARTS OF A BOOK

Review or teach the parts of a book as follows:

- cover with name of book, author, and illustrator
- end papers (mainly in picture books)
- title page
- dedication
- titles of chapters (and pages)
- index
- glossary

## ELMER'S ELEGANT READING CHART

If students don't remember Elmer, the colorful checkerboard elephant from the book entitled *Elmer* by David McKee, obtain a copy from the library and read it aloud. Keep the book by the chart so students can read it. Make a chart with five book titles posted along the top on square pieces of paper. Write students' names along the left side in a column. Draw vertical and horizontal lines for a grid. When students have read the book, they can color in the square. The object is to make a colorful chart, just as Elmer is outrageously colorful, to draw attention to reading. Students can make a giant head, ears, tail, and legs for Elmer as well.

## A BIG BIRD OF BOOKS

Create a large bird shape and have students add a feather for every book read. They can print the book title, author, illustrator, and their name on the feather. Have them use felt pens and additional paper if needed to create three-dimensional features (eyes, beak, legs, claws).

## MY READING LIST

For their classroom portfolio, have a reading guide sheet available for students so that they can keep track of their reading record. (See Reproducible Activity Pages.) They should list the title, author, illustrator (if different from the author), a brief description of the main idea of the book, and a rating of the book.

A rating system, such as one star (OK), two stars (good), and three stars (excellent), can be used. Students should be able to tell the rationale (why) for rating the book. What did they especially like? What seemed to be missing in the one-star review? Why did a book merit three stars? Were the descriptions of the setting particularly well done? In time, you can help students develop critical thinking and reflection, resulting in more complex and sophisticated reasons. It is a good idea for students to share their book opinions, backed up by information in the text, and for others to ask meaningful questions. This takes practice.

# FOCUS ON LANGUAGE ARTS

## INTRODUCTION

Briefly, the Language Arts component of the curriculum includes reading, writing, speaking, listening, visual arts, and dramatic arts. These are all elements of *communication*. Language Arts activities are interwoven throughout the curriculum, and we work with these elements every day. *They are enablers.* Some examples of the widespread use of the Language Arts are:

- Reading: We *read* a math problem, a letter, a thermometer, a story.
- Writing: We *write* a friendly letter, a report, a poem, a note, a list.
- Speaking: We *ask* a question, *tell* a story, *give* an oral report, *discuss*.
- Listening: We *listen* to directions, to a symphony, to a message on the intercom from the office.
- Visual Arts: We *illustrate* a story, *make* a puppet, *construct* a visual aid for a Social Studies project, *paint* a class mural.
- Dramatic Arts: We *act out* part of a story, we role-play, we put on a play using puppets to dramatize a news event.

The importance of Language Arts cannot be overlooked. However, we need to work with subject matter content as well, and students must learn important skills in Math, Social Studies, Science, and other curricular areas. *We do not focus upon one to the exclusion of the other.* There is a body of information that students need to learn and this takes practice, hard work, memorization, study, drill, and even homework in an effort to learn and retain information so that students can become literate. Learning, therefore, requires hard work on the part of the student and this concept needs to be instilled in them. Learning is not always "fun." Learning means achievement and building upon the skills we have already mastered. It is a never-ending process and requires focus.

Our aim is to have students become "literate." This means expanding the term *literacy* so that it includes the subject matter areas as well as the Language Arts. Students need to be literate in Math skills, Spelling, Geography skills, Science concepts, Social Studies, and so on. We need to help students become well-rounded, literate students in grade three.

# MORE READING OPPORTUNITIES

Some reading skills have been addressed in the previous section; however, many more reading opportunities will be available this month and every month throughout the year. Reading is intertwined with all subjects in the classroom, and it is difficult to separate it completely when working with the "process" of reading.

## INDEPENDENT READING

Have students read silently on a daily basis. Since reading is a skill, it needs to be practiced. Reading improves as students engage in reading. Children learn to read by (1) gaining a knowledge of letter/sound relationships (phonics), and (2) practicing by engaging in reading and reading-related activities. Even if they are leafing through a picture book, students are picking up words, visual images, and concepts. Keep your classroom library well stocked with library books. For independent reading, *it is important to select books that are below their instructional level;* otherwise, students will not be able to read smoothly and get the practice they need. Find out what the second-grade teacher is using, and get some of those books in your classroom library.

## INDEPENDENT READING QUESTIONS

When students finish a book, encourage them to make a list of at least three questions they have about the book, a character in the book, a city in the book, and so on. For example, if the text deals with giraffes, encourage them to determine what they would like to know about giraffes. Some questions might be: What do they eat? How big are they? Where can we find them in the wild? What different types are there? Why do they have such long necks? How fast can they run?

In other words, encourage students to become curious about matters that go beyond the text.

## THE "WHAT" AND "WHY" OF ENCOURAGING CURIOSITY AND CRITICAL THINKING

Select a short fable or fairy tale that most children are sure to know. Reread it aloud to the class for enjoyment. Then have students work with a partner to formulate two questions they would like to explore in order to gain additional information. Go on a hunt at the library for this information. Share the findings with the entire group so that everyone is enriched by the additional facts.

For example, select the popular story *The Three Billy Goats Gruff.* Read it aloud. Then tell students that you will go back over the story together with the idea of formulating questions that could be explored in their spare time. By modeling this with the group, students are learning how to engage in this process independently. Some possible questions for this particular tale may include:

- This tale takes place by a bridge. What does the word "bridge" mean?
- Is there a bridge in your city? If so, what is the name of it?
- What are bridges made of?
- Find out what the longest bridge is in the state or country.
- Why are goats called "Billy goats"?
- Do goats have fur or hide?
- What is the shape of their hoof? (split) Because of its design, what does it enable them to do? Could a dog or cat do this?

## LEARNING THROUGH GAMES

Extend learning for children through the use of games that involve movement of their body. For the students who learn kinesthetically and for those who display evidence of hyperactivity, this helps get out the wiggles. But movement games also provide an opportunity for students to learn "how much space their body takes up," of which some students aren't aware. That's one reason they bump into things or other students. These games also promote good listening and increase attention span. So, be sure to include games in your daily classroom activities. Try "Three Billy Goats and the Bridge" for a beginning.

### "THE THREE BILLY GOATS AND THE BRIDGE" Game*

*Materials Needed:* drum (or dowel sticks or rulers for tapping); 8 chairs, 4 on each side, placed in a straight line to represent the edge of the bridge; pole, or rope, to hang over the chairs to denote the overhead bridge; and table to crawl under at the edge of the bridge.

*Directions:* Set up this simple obstacle course. Put two poles up high and two down low by laying them across the backs of the chairs.

Once students are familiar with the story, the object of this activity is for students to get across the rickety bridge. They are to step over the low poles (or rope) and crawl under the high poles (or rope) and move to the end of the bridge by crawling under the table. Then they can go to the end of the line for another turn, if there is time. They are not to make a sound because the trolls are sleeping! When the drum can be heard (one student beats the drum or taps with rulers), it means the three trolls are snoring. When it is quiet, it means they are waking up, and students going over/under the bridge must freeze in place. Students can continue when the snoring can be heard again. IF students make noise during the game (falling over, moving a chair), one of the trolls wakes up and takes that player to a corner of the room where he or she must remain quiet for two minutes. Then the player can return quietly to the end of the line. Students move over and under the bridge when the snoring continues.

This game will not fail to grab students' attention. It increases listening skills (listening for the signal, freezing on signal), increases attention span, improves balance, and gives students an opportunity to become aware of spacial relationships. All of these skills contribute to learning in other areas.

## MORE STORIES FOR CREATIVE DRAMATICS

Using the previous activity as a starting point, encourage children to explore books they are reading independently in the classroom for appropriate movement games or creative dramatics experiences. This is another important way that children learn. They can act out the story, or create a dance, or dress up as a character and retell part of the story. They can also explore the topics further by formulating questions and then searching for the answers. Some suggested books are:

- *Song and Dance Man* by Karen Ackerman
  (action with tap dancing)
  (questions about grandfathers and their professions)
  (questions about tap dancing and show business)
- *Miss Nelson Is Missing* by Harry Allard
  (discussion about student behavior when there is a substitute teacher)

*Source: *Teacher's Handbook of Children's Games* by Marian Jenks Wirth (Parker Publishing Company, 1976).

- *Two Bad Ants* by Chris Van Allsburg
  (simulated movement of ant colonies)
  (questions about ant colonies, types of ants, the function of ants in our environment)

## MAKING BOOKMARKS

Students can make their own bookmarks from card stock and decorate them with borders and designs, using colorful marking pens. Cut in about an inch from the top and bottom edge to make a fringe. Some may wish to use the bookmark to record titles of books read this month. Be sure to have students make new bookmarks regularly.

Have a "Mystery Bookmark" contest. On one side, students can make a picture and write words that are directly from a story they've read. On the other side they can write the title. How many students can guess the title? How many students are "stumped"?

## MAY WE USE PICTURE BOOKS IN GRADE THREE?

Absolutely! Picture books are so sophisticated today in terms of the elegant artwork, styles, colors, and designs that many art teachers are using them at the high school and college levels. So, grade three certainly deserves the same opportunities and advantages.

Some students may feel they are beyond picture books, so it will be your job to bring them back to the joy of these books. You can go to the library and bring in an abundance of these books to share with students. One thing students need to know is that, for the most part, picture books are written at a third-grade reading level, so they are right on target in terms of text.

## WHAT? ALPHABET BOOKS IN GRADE THREE?

Yes! This genre becomes more challenging and sophisticated all the time and holds appeal not only for very young children, but for older children and adults as well. The charm and versatility of the letters and the ways in which they can be used to create a new twist make the ABC book journey a rewarding trip. Here are some that are highly recommended:

- *Alphabet Soup: A Feast of Letters* **by Scott Gustafson.** This book provides a good mix of humor and alliteration as the main animal character, Otter, prepares for an Open House. The first page contains a letter of invitation and the second page shows Otter mailing them, which shows the function of the alphabet letters—to communicate. Then we're off on a potluck adventure of alliteration with Cricket's Cracker Crane and Mole's Mushroom Mine, among others.
- *Wildflower ABC* **by Diana Pomeroy.** The charm of this book lies in the realistic portrayal of lovely wildflowers captured in intricately carved and appliqued potato prints. A glossary of plant names is included.
- *Alphabet City* **by Stephen Johnson.** This book has no printed letters or words on the page. The illustrations look like photographs and invite the reader to take a walk through a city and to stay visually alert for natural lines and shapes that suggest alphabet letters. Suddenly sidewalk cracks or angles of structures call out to us in terms of letters.

- *The Butterfly Alphabet* **by Kjell B. Sandved.** This book contains stunning photographs of magnified butterfly wings that reveal shapes resembling letters of the alphabet.
- *Tomorrow's Alphabet* **by George Shannon, illustrated by Donald Crews.** This challenging book provides a puzzle in two pages. The first page contains the hint; the second has the answer of the future. The letter B, for example, has a big green letter B on the left page with a nest of eggs and reads "B is for eggs . . ."; look to the right page and you see a nest of fledglings and read "tomorrow's BIRDS."

# WORD ORIGINS AND SAYINGS*

## GETTING HOOKED ON VOCABULARY AND SAYINGS

The English language is enriched with colorful speech patterns. Where did these terms and sayings come from? Where did they originate?

On the chalkboard, using colored chalk, write a colorful saying that can be left on the board all week. Students can copy it down in their notebook or journal. Talk about the saying. What could it possibly mean? How did it get into the language? How are sayings made up?

On one side of their notebook page, students can write on Monday what they know about the saying and what things they'd like to know. By Wednesday, explain the term if no one has found out. If a student claims to have found the meaning, he or she needs to document the source by giving a book title and page number OR by giving the name of the person they used as a reference. Then spend the rest of the week using the colorful phrase in speaking and writing.

Here are four phrases for September. Use one each week to generate interest in vocabulary and colorful sayings. Students will begin hunting them down.

1. **"He has something up his sleeve."** A different plan, an alternative, or even a surprise. This term can be traced back to the garments and costumes of the fifteenth century when the sleeves were made from a great deal of material and were draped from the elbow to the wrist. Items could be stuffed into them. Sleeves were used as "pockets."

2. **"to cry wolf"** If you cry for help but are only kidding, people won't come running when you cry out and really need their help. See Aesop's Fables, "The Boy Who Cried Wolf."

3. **"to pull up stakes"** To move from one place to another. It is thought that this figure of speech is from Colonial times when one drove stakes (iron or wood) into the ground to signify boundaries. If you were to pull up your stakes, it meant you were moving on. The land could then be claimed or "staked out" by someone else.

---

*Source for sayings is *Heavens to Betsy! And Other Curious Sayings* by Charles Earle Funk.

4. **"It's all wool and a yard wide."** It's genuine. It's the real thing! When wool was spun at home, you knew how much you had. But when a traveling salesman came through, you might not get what you paid for. So, in the New England states, people began to use this saying as a slogan to reassure people that they weren't getting cheated. It means you will get what you paid for. No surprises.

## BOOKS ABOUT LANGUAGE AND SAYINGS

Some books that will be helpful as you investigate word origins are: *It's Raining Cats and Dogs . . . and Other Beastly Expressions* by Christine Ammer, and *In a Pickle and Other Funny Idioms* and *Mad as a Wet Hen* by Marvin Terban.

# WRITING SKILLS

## SET UP A WRITING PORTFOLIO

Use a three-ring notebook or make a portfolio cover by folding in half a sheet of 12- by 18-inch colorful construction paper. Students can use felt pens or crayons to put their name on the cover, give it a title, and decorate it. Then all writing samples can be stored therein and cleared out every two weeks. Samples of the best work can be saved. Class portfolios can be stored in the individual student desks or stations, or in a large, attractive classroom box labeled "Our Fabulous Writing Portfolios."

## WHAT TO KEEP IN A WELL-GROOMED WRITING PORTFOLIO

- Keep a "name sheet" in this portfolio. On the first school day of each new month, students can write their name underneath their signature recorded the previous month. Each sample should be written carefully and slowly and should show improvement. This serves as a good progress record.
- Samples of creative writing, and poetry. These can also be illustrated.
- Samples of report writing for subject areas.
- Samples of practice writing, such as formation of letters.
- A "writer's notebook" page so that students can jot down ideas for future writing, or a phrase that comes to mind to use in a poem, or a word that holds appeal because of its rhythm.

## KEEPING A JOURNAL

This calls for another folder. Many students enjoy keeping a daily or weekly account of their learning progress. Some wish to write short stories or plays and keep them in this folder. Others draw diagrams or maps of content they are learning about.

Often students will be asked to select material from this source so that you can read it and provide feedback. Feedback can be in the form of a written note on a piece of paper (self-stick note) that is attached to the page. Some students enjoy this form of feedback and often set up a written dialogue with you that helps them with their writing.

## WORKING ON HANDWRITING AS A SKILL

If you do not have a formal writing program, you can set up your own. Many students are beginning to learn cursive writing in third grade. Some began in second grade, but by this time, the small muscles of the hand are developed to the point where many students become excellent at handwriting and take pride in good writing. Some who floundered in an earlier grade may suddenly be surprised at the control they have over a pencil. Let's take the time and opportunity to nurture this new-found ability.

Model the correct way to hold a pencil. Work on this throughout the month. Remember that some left-handed students write with an arched overhand hook. This movement is apparently controlled by the brain, so you may have two different types of left-handedness in your classroom when it comes to holding the pencil. Allow the left-handed student to determine what is comfortable and natural.

## PRACTICE THE UNDERSTROKES—BUT IT'S NOT A RACE

This is the stroke that begins on the bottom line and goes upward, as if following the curve of a bowl. Have students practice making this stroke in the air. Then they can practice making several rows of the understroke on their writing paper in the following way:

- Make one row starting at the bottom line and going up to the middle line (one space). Repeat for a second row.
- Make one row starting at the bottom line and going up to the top line (two spaces). Repeat for a second row.

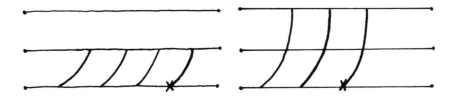

Circulate among the students while they are practicing. After your modeling, check to see that they are holding their pencils correctly; if not, then carefully adjust their fingers on their pencil. (Keep doing this throughout the month.) Check to see that their paper is at the correct angle. Remember, left-handed students should have their writing paper slanted to the right, whereas right-handed students should have their writing paper slanted to the left. Caution them to move the pencil slowly, as if driving a car up a steep hill. In the beginning, a slow pace is one of the secrets to good writing. This is not a race. At this point, give plenty of praise if it is deserved. Even hold up good writing samples so that the students will see what is expected of them.

Demonstrate the understroke lowercase letters one at a time on the chalkboard while students are observing. Have them put their pencils down, out of their hands, so that they attend to what you are saying and doing. The understroke lowercase letters to practice, one row at a time, are as follows. (See Reproducible Activity Pages.)

You can make these letters on the chalkboard and have students trace over them. It's good practice. Some students like to do this during free time and recess.

## ON TO THE OVERSTROKES—WATCH THE CURVES!

Demonstrate the overstroke motion in the air, facing away from the students, so that they get the idea. Next, demonstrate it on the chalkboard. Note that the overstroke for lowercase letters only takes up one space, even though the rest of the letter may go into the upper or lower spaces on the writing paper. The overstroke lowercase letters to practice, one row at a time, are:

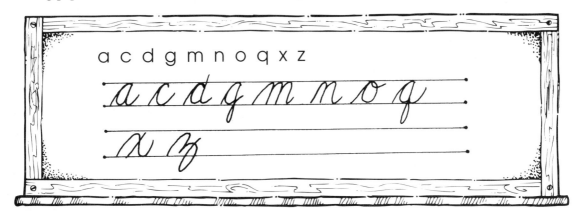

## DETERMINE THE RUBRIC FOR YOUR HEADINGS

What's a rubric (rōo′brick)? It is a set *procedure* to follow for a desired outcome. Introduce the word to the students and tell them they will be meeting it again throughout the year when it comes to writing final reports, letters, descriptions on 4- by 6-inch cards used as labels for projects, and so on. Right now, tell the class the rubric, or standard, uniform procedure to follow when putting a heading on their paper. This heading is for all written work such as Math, Spelling, Social Studies, or Science reports and so on.

A sample rubric is as follows:

Name                                            Date
Subject                                         Specific Title


                        (skip two spaces)



Begin writing

The reason for teaching this is important. It creates a structure and uniformity for all written work and builds organization skills. It tells students where to put their *name* on the paper (otherwise, many forget to put it on, or put it on at the last minute in the upper right or upper left or anywhere there is space on the page). It requires that the paper have a *date*. The content of the paper is easily identifiable. For example, *Subject:* Social Studies, *Specific Title:* Report on Polar Bears, OR *Subject:* Math, *Specific Title:* Column Addition.

# SPEAKING SKILLS

## THE ART OF PUBLIC SPEAKING

It is important to determine the purpose for speaking. This can be to inform, to persuade, to entertain. Explain the differences to students. These can be placed on a chart in the classroom. Examples:

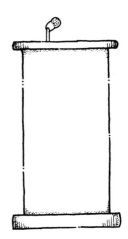

To inform:     • announcing an upcoming school event
               • telling what is on the lunch menu for the day
               • explaining the rules of the game

To persuade:   • urging students to attend a school program
               • coaxing students to vote for a class president
               • promising to carry out certain procedures if
                 elected to a class office

To entertain:  • role playing an event
               • putting on a puppet show
               • retelling an amusing story that was read

Students need to gain experience in each area. They can work independently or in small groups.


## WHAT IS YOUR BODY SAYING?

This is a good opportunity to discuss the importance of not only the tone, quality, and speed of the voice, but also of posture, eye contact, and gestures—known as nonverbal communication. Have students observe speakers on TV who they think are effective. Why do they consider them effective? What are they doing with their hands? Do they look friendly or is their brow furrowed and knitted? Are they mumbling? Can they be understood? Where are they looking?

Encourage students to practice speaking in front of the mirror or in front of a good friend so that they can present a self-confident demeanor to their audience. This will take time and much practice, but it will make many students into effective speakers at an early age.


## STAND UP—SPEAK UP—IT'S TALK TIME

It is important for students to be able to stand before a group and speak clearly and distinctly. They need to determine their purpose for speaking (to inform, entertain, and so on). If five students are members of a "speaking group" and two are speaking, what are the other three doing so that they do not detract from the speakers? (They can strike a pose, look over the heads of the audience, look toward the door, and so on.) Another consideration is the length of the talk. Keep it short.

If students work together in small groups, they can practice giving a speech, a report, a poem, an announcement, a news update, and so on to each other. Part of this can be done through choral speaking, which is effective for the shy student. Then they can make a presentation to the entire class. When an individual or individuals are speaking, there must be guidelines for audience behavior such as attentive listening, no put-downs, serious questioning that addresses the facts, and any other guidelines that the students themselves wish to put into effect.


## RETELLING A STORY—SHARE THE GOOD NEWS

When students read an especially good story, have them sign up to retell it before the class. They may use visual aids or props to help tell it effectively, but they need to use their own words. This develops vocabulary, helps with the sequence of ideas from beginning to end, improves memory span, and gives students practice speaking before an audience. These important skills can be developed and improved throughout the year as students continue the reading/retelling process.


## THE STROLLING STORYTELLERS

The book *Wilfred Gordon McDonald Partridge* by Mem Fox is an excellent picture book to use for retelling a story, for using props to help trigger the memory, and for gaining experience with reading, speaking, listening, and writing skills. It offers an opportunity to talk about the *main idea* of the story as well. Students can work independently with this project, or with a partner, or even in small groups. Once they have it perfected for their own classmates, they can go around (stroll) to younger classes to retell it and thus start the "Strolling Storytellers from Room _____."

In this book, Wilfred Gordon lives next door to a home for seniors and becomes great friends with them. His favorite person seems to have lost her memory, and he is determined to help her regain it. So, where better to start than to ask the seniors the question, "What is a memory?" They all have different opinions such as "something warm," or "something sad," or "something that makes you happy," and so on. So, Wilfred Gordon goes home and gets a basket and finds something warm, something that makes him happy, sad, and so on. When he takes the basket to his good friend, she wonders why he's bringing her such a strange collection, but then she fingers the items and they do bring back fond memories. This provides a good intergenerational reading experience.

Begin by asking students their definition of a memory. Listen to various responses. Then tell them that the story deals with that issue, and read it aloud. Discuss the story. What is the main idea? Do they have a better understanding of *memory*? Students may be better prepared to write about a favorite memory or a least favorite memory after this book. Urge them to make an illustration and to share their writing.

Students can obtain a large basket and put in items that they deem appropriate for retelling the story. They do not have to be the same items as those used in the story; they can be completely different. Seeing what props students bring in is interesting and fun for their classmates. OR, students can make the props from construction paper and scrap items in the classroom. Then, at designated times, take the story basket around to the younger grades and share the story. The props serve as a good device for helping the story-teller(s) convey the message. Be sure to have one person introduce the title, author, and illustrator of the story at the beginning and again at the end.

## MOOSE AND MUFFINS, AND PIGS AND PANCAKES, MAKE A GOOD STORY MAP

*If You Give a Moose a Muffin* and *If You Give a Pig a Pancake* are two favorite books in the series by Laura Joffe Numeroff with illustrations by Felicia Bond. For these books, students can create a circular story map that will help them with the retelling.

Using this type of book as a *story stem,* have students brainstorm to come up with unlikely combinations that would make a similar amusing story. Print on the chalkboard:

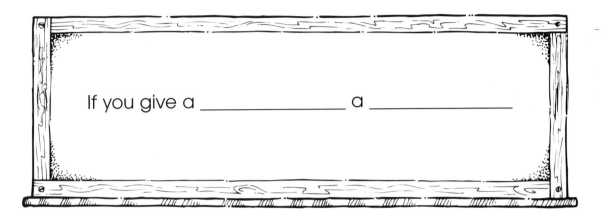

If you give a _____ a _____

Present some ideas such as "If You Give a Frog a Button," "If You Give a Fish a Hotdog," or "If You Give a Mole a Mulberry." Then write the ideas on the board that are suggested by the students. They're now off on their own round of storytelling!

## SHAKE UP A GOOD STORY

Cut up 25 red squares and 25 yellow squares. Distribute one of each color to the students. (Make more, if necessary.) Have them print the name of an animal or bird on the red square, and the name of some type of food on the yellow square. Collect them in a paper bag and give it a good shake. Have students reach inside and get one red and one yellow square. They now have the beginning of their "If You Give a _____ a _____" tale, and can use the same format as that mentioned in the previous activity.

Students are engaged in writing, speaking, and listening. They may want to make a story map as well.

## SPEAKING RULES FOR A CLASSROOM THAT PURRS RATHER THAN BARKS!

Determine in advance whether you prefer to have students raise their hands before speaking out loud when you are having a large group information session or small group sessions, OR whether students are allowed to speak out when they choose. Perhaps the rules differ for different activities. When having a guest speaker, for example, it would be preferable for students to take notes and then ask questions at the end for a question/answer period. Whatever you decide, make sure students know what is expected of them.

Also determine the volume of sound that is comfortable for everyone when students are working throughout the day. Have a signal for students to stop what they are doing when the sound has escalated. Examples: Ring a bell, flick the overhead lights, clap your hands rhythmically to get attention, ask students to "freeze" right where they are so that you can give instructions, and so on.

The tighter the rules in September, the better. You can always relax them as the year goes on, but it is exceedingly difficult to make the rules more stringent later.

# LISTENING SKILLS

## THE IMPORTANCE OF GOOD LISTENING SKILLS

We gain most of our information from listening, so it is an important skill to develop. In our culture, we are bombarded with auditory and visual stimuli, and many students have learned to tune out much information by grade three. However, in order to become a good learner and a successful student, good listening skills must be practiced.

## IT'S STORY TIME

Read aloud to students each day. This is a good time for attentive listening. Students can:

- Listen and retell what has happened.
- Listen and predict what will happen.
- Listen for specific words that describe a character or a setting.
- Listen for a word that is new.
- Listen for a musical word.
- Listen for the message (main idea) of the story.

At the end of the reading session, have students share what they learned or discovered during attentive listening. This is a skill that can be developed with practice.

## SHARED LISTENING AND ATTENTIVE LISTENING

Read a picture storybook aloud to the entire group, but have different subgroups listening for different things. Some of the specific things for which students are listening can be taken from the items mentioned above, such as words that describe a character, words that describe the setting, and so on. When the story is finished, go back and review the information from the different groups. This is called *shared listening.* It may help to write some of the information on the chalkboard or on a large sheet of chart paper.

Next, reread the story and this time students are more inclined to engage in *attentive listening,* which means actively listening to the story because now they know specifically what to listen for. (Notice that in this activity we are using the reading, speaking, and writing process in addition to listening, because the language arts are intertwined.)

## SHH! I'M AT THE LISTENING STATION

Have an audio area (with headsets, tape recorders, and tapes) set up in the classroom where students can go to quietly listen to books on tape, books that you or other students have read aloud, directions for a fire drill, directions for a tornado drill, rules for Learning Centers, classroom rules and regulations, and so on. Having a tape of directions is especially helpful for students who may have missed this information for one reason or another. Hearing the teacher's voice is also reassuring for the anxious child.

## WHICH OF THE "BIG TEN" CAN YOU IDENTIFY?

Have a sound box or basket into which you put a variety of sound items, such as a bell, music box, stapler, paper (for tearing), comb, key ring with keys, scissors, a small purse that snaps, and so on. Aim for ten items.

Have students take out a piece of scrap paper and, in a vertical column on the left, write the numerals 1–10.

Tell the students that you have ten items that each have a different sound. They are to close their eyes and try to determine what the item is. Then, keeping the items hidden from view, make the sounds one by one. After that, have students guess what they are and show them the item. This is an enjoyable listening experience. But there's more . . .

## WHAT *COULD* THE "BIG TEN" BE?

Tell the students that you will once again make the sounds in the same order, only this time you want them to close their eyes and think of what the sound could be in the city or in the country. (Have them write their response or call it out.) Do this for all ten items. Their imagination will be activated by this creative listening experience.

## LET'S JUMP RIGHT IN AND CREATE A "BIG TEN" SOUND STORY

As a total group, create a story in a country setting or a city setting, keeping the ten sounds in mind. When the story is written down on a chart, distribute the ten items and have students make the sound at the appropriate place in the story. Have students redistribute the ten items until each person has had a turn.

Students can work individually, or with a partner, to create a sound story using these items. A wide variety of stories will come from this common listening experience that will delight the students, and make the listening exercise enjoyable.

This experience makes for an increased awareness of background sounds in the environment, movies, television, and informational videos. It is also helpful for sound production when students are retelling a story, giving a report, or putting on a puppet show. Students will have a sharpened awareness of the physical world.

## LANGUAGE ARTS SUMMARY

This section on Language Arts is just the beginning. Throughout the month and the year, notice that in each area of the curriculum the students will be engaged in the process of reading, writing, speaking, listening, and creating products. These skills are intertwined. In a sense, they are the *glue* that holds the content together. We will work on improving and refining the glue, but without something to adhere to, the glue itself is not enough. Third graders are at a period in their development where they can handle more content.

# FOCUS ON SPELLING

If you have a specific spelling program with a teacher's edition, take advantage of all the opportunities for learning that have already been provided for you. Here are a few more ideas.

## THE WORD WALL

Many students are familiar with the word wall from previous grades and find it very helpful when they are writing. Use kraft paper and secure it to a large segment of the wall or a big bulletin board. Have felt marking pens available. Teachers use the wall in different ways. Some group the words by subjects, such as days of the week, or all animal words in one area, and all types of weather words in another. Some use red felt pens for words that are sight words and need to be memorized. Some use purple felt pens for lyrical or musical words found in poetry or verse. In the end, it is a wall of words that students will, hopefully, find useful as a resource for their writing as they work to master the spelling of the words. Sometimes students are asked to write the words on the word wall. *Remember:* If a wall word is a spelling word for the week, be sure to cover it up during test time.

## WORD WALL SPELLING TIME

Have students practice writing words from the word wall during a given week. Then, at the end of the week, select ten words from the word wall, cover them up, and give the students a spot quiz on the spelling of the words.

## FIVE STEPS TO GOOD SPELLING—SAY IT, SPELL IT, COVER IT, WRITE IT, CHECK IT

When students are studying their words, they can use the *say, spell aloud, cover, write, and check* method. This should become an automatic five-step procedure. It gives them a framework to use and helps build good study habits.

## COMMERCIAL SPELLING PROGRAM—IF IT WORKS, USE IT

For decades, the format used in spelling books for producing good spellers has been something like this:

MONDAY:
- Introduce the new spelling words for the week.
- Point out similarities, such as patterns and rimes (*ay, at, et,* and so on).
- Point out root words and endings.
- Have students write each word three times.

TUESDAY:
- Write each spelling word three times.
- Look up the meaning of the word in the dictionary.
- Write the meaning.

WEDNESDAY:    • Take a pretest on the words to see which ones require further study.

• Write each word in a sentence.

THURSDAY       • Write the words in alphabetical order.

• Work with a study buddy today.

FRIDAY:           • Study independently.

• Take test.

• Teacher can have students exchange papers and correct the work for immediate feedback.

So, if this works for your students, do it!

## SPELLING SCRAPBOOK

Make a spelling chart of words. Then have students search through old magazines and cut out a picture that goes with the spelling word. Pictures will vary, but it shows that words may have more than one meaning. For example, if the spelling word is *ring,* students may cut out a diamond ring, or a group of students playing in a ring, or a picture of a telephone with the word r-r-ring beside it. These are all useful associations and help to jog the memory.

## WHAT SHAPE IS THIS WORD IN?

Print the spelling words and put boxes around them. This provides a visual clue, and since spelling is primarily a visual task, it helps the brain to assemble the shape of the word. Print only the box shapes and have students fill in the correct spelling word.

Students also enjoy creating the spelling shape when writing the words in a sentence. Then students can exchange papers and fill in the correct letters. They have two clues with this activity— the visual shape and the context.

## I'M THINKING OF A WORD

Students take turns giving clues for a word. Other students listen and then raise their hand rather than call out the word. Clues can be something like this:

"I'm thinking of a word . . ."

. . . That rhymes with _____.

. . . That has "b" as the third letter.

. . . That means the same as _____.

. . . That sounds like it's growling.

. . . That is beautiful.

## A PLACE TO BEGIN—25 INSTANT WORDS

If you do not have a commercial spelling program, consider using the 25 Instant Words* for the monthly list of words to memorize. Use six or seven of these words each week, along with words that rhyme (i.e., bright, fright, night, sight) or word families or rimes (i.e., *ay*, *el*, *ill*, *or*, *am*). The words from 1–25, or most common words ranked in order of frequency of use, are listed below. A goal of ten spelling words to master each week is considered adequate.

| the | of | and | a | to |
| in | is | you | it | he |
| was | for | on | are | as |
| with | his | they | I | at |
| be | this | have | from | that |

## SUSTAINED SILENT SPELLING—THE GUMDROP CLUB

We've had Sustained Silent Reading, so now let's start up a Sustained Silent Spelling period several times during the week. Even five minutes would make a difference. Spelling takes time and it takes practice. Impress upon students that if people didn't know how to spell, they wouldn't be able to communicate. If you can't spell "twenty" dollars, and spell "thirty" dollars instead, you could be out ten dollars.

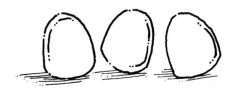

After this sustained period, students could be given gumdrops for a reward. See if it improves spelling scores in your classroom. We're looking for spelling champs. Let's go, Gumdrops!

# FOCUS ON MATH

## SET UP A MATH LEARNING CENTER

Determine when students can work here, and how many, and for how long. Have a sign-up sheet. Students can go to this attractive center to check their answers, check their understanding, and gain review and reinforcement experiences. Third-grade students still need manipulative experiences, so have these materials available, as well as activity cards that present problems to solve. This is a starter list to which items can be added:

$$3 + 7 = 10$$

---

*Source: *The Reading Teacher's Book of Lists, 4th edition* by Edward B. Fry, Jacqueline Kress, and Dona Lee Fountoukidis (Prentice Hall, 2000).

### Counting

commercial materials

paper clips

buttons

counting sticks

nuts

egg cartons

paper/pencils

counting chips

books on counting

number lines

several calculators

activity cards

### Measuring

sandbox sand or
    beans, lentils, peas

plastic measuring cups

measuring spoons

pots and pans

rulers of various types

yard stick

string

books on measurement

paper/pencils

trundle wheel

activity cards

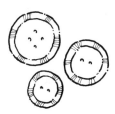

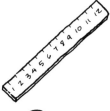

### Time/Temperature

various clocks (digital and analog)

thermometers

containers for water and ice

timers

paper/pencil

weather maps

newspaper weather maps

activity cards

### Geoboards

colored rubber bands

paper/pencil

activity cards

### Cuisenaire® Rods

activity cards

### Pattern Blocks

activity cards

## DAILY MATH DRILL

Use addition and subtraction math cards and do 5 minutes of math drill each morning. This can be done right after the morning exercises and before the other work of the day begins.

Flash the cards and all students can answer. Another day, flash the cards and call upon different students to answer. Another day, flash the cards and have students play "Around the World." In this game, one student stands next to the seat of another student and the first one to say the answer moves on to the next student. Ready? Flash the card and the first one to answer moves on to the next student, and the process is repeated. Some students stay in their seat and others keep moving.

The main thing is to focus upon the familiarization and memorization of these facts for instant recall. Students must know them by heart (rote memory). They need this information for the rest of their lives. Learn them now. (See Reproducible Activity Pages.)

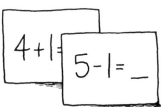

## DAILY LESSON PLANS IN MATH

Spend from 35 to 40 minutes each day with your math lesson and daily math concept. Find a Teacher's Edition of a current basal text series for grade-three level and check it for lessons and activities. Students need daily review and new challenges in math.

---

# Lesson Plan

1. **Purpose:** What students should learn from this lesson.

2. **Materials:** What is necessary to help teach and learn this lesson.

3. **Procedure:** Steps for the lesson:
   a. Review—Determine if it's helpful for this concept.
   b. Motivation—Try to "link" to real-life experience or previous learning.
   c. Orderly presentation of new material:
      (1)_____
      (2)_____
      (3)_____

4. **Check-up:** Are students with you? Are they on track? How can you determine this? Use one or two of the following methods:
   • verbal feedback—Ask them to talk about how they arrived at a particular answer, or how they solved a problem. Students do this in different ways and learn from one another.
   • check sheet—Show the work.
   • worksheet—Demonstrate that they know it.
   • Diagram their work.

5. **Reteaching:** What to do when several students don't understand:
   • Use a method different from the one you used.
   • Use manipulatives.
   • Pair student with someone else who has gained mastery and have students work together.
   • Pull out several students and work with them another time.

6. **Evaluation:** How do you know students understand?
   • They can verbalize the procedure.
   • They can complete a worksheet.
   • They can demonstrate it in some other way (diagram, draw, use concrete objects).
   • Test.

7. **Teacher Notations:** Make notes of who has grasped the concept, who is working toward mastery, and who is struggling and needs additional instruction and experience. Prepare to reteach.

8. **Math Center:** Determine how you can use a follow-up activity at your Math Center to give students additional experiences, and set it up after school for the next day.

9. **Teacher Evaluation After the Lesson:** Do I need to give students additional experiences tomorrow during the math lesson? Do I need to reteach this in a different way? Can we go on to build upon this concept?

## I'M A WALKING NUMBER

Students may not have thought of themselves as mathematically designed, but they are. Have them check their face for numbers (eyes, nose, mouth, ears). Count teeth. Count body parts. What's inside their body and how many? This calls for some library research. Read the book *The Magic School Bus Inside the Human Body* by Joanna Cole, with illustrations by Bruce Degen, for an exciting math/science adventure through the body. This is also available on video.

Get two large pieces of kraft paper and put them on the floor. On one sheet, a boy can lie down flat and two or three other boys can trace around him with a felt-tip pen. On the other sheet, one girl can lie down and two or three other girls can trace around her with a felt-tip pen. Boys can work on their project and the girls on theirs. The object is to fill in the features, inside and out, making math notations along the way in a "sidebar." (In some classrooms where modesty is an issue, some teachers have solved this by having students lay a piece of paper over the figure, outline, decorate, and cut out clothing, and then create a flip book that opens from the top [neck] or side). (See Reproducible Activity Pages.)

## REVIEWING PATTERNS

Review patterns such as AB/AB; ABC/ABC; and AABAB/AABAB.

This can be done with musical instruments or just by using clapping, snapping fingers, opening and closing hands, slapping thighs, etc. You need to be the leader, using a strong voice, and repeatedly saying, for example, "AB, AB, snap, clap, snap, clap, AB, AB, snap, clap, snap, clap, and stop."

- AB can be demonstrated by: snap fingers, clap hands. (Say "Snap, clap, AB.")
- ABC can be demonstrated by: snap fingers, clap hands, open hands wide to extend fingers. (Say "Snap, clap, open." Also use "ABC" and "1,2,3.")
- AABAB can be demonstrated by: clap, clap, snap, clap, snap. (Say "Clap, clap, snap, clap, snap." Also vary this by saying, "AABAB" and "1,1,2,1,2.")

The more complicated the pattern, the more practice students need doing this. They will also come up with their own patterns. Use body parts and have students touch their heel, touch their toe, touch their elbow, touch their nose, hands on hips, and so on.

## LOOK FOR PATTERNS IN CLOTHING

A plaid shirt could be an ABC/ABC pattern or a checkered blouse could be an AB/AB pattern. Clothing has stripes that are wide and narrow, and some patterns include bars and crosses.

Look for patterns on the soles of athletic shoes. Some of these are complicated. Have students step on a wet paper towel and then immediately step on a sheet of kraft paper and trace around the pattern. Compare the patterns.

A color can be identified by a letter, so if yellow = A, blue = B, and red = C, a clothing sample could represent an ABC pattern.

Have students bring in material swatches and determine their pattern. Also, get discarded wallpaper sample books at a wallpaper and paint store and look for repeat patterns. (See Reproducible Activity Pages.)

## PROBLEM SOLVING

This is a strand that will run through your Math program throughout the year. The problem may be one that is worked out through computation (addition and subtraction); through mental math (figuring out the answer or a solution in your head); through use of manipulatives (moving around concrete objects); and by actually solving a problem that crops up in the classroom (such as, not enough chairs at a center, someone is reading a book that someone else wants or needs, etc.). Students need to gain practice working toward solutions.

# FOCUS ON SOCIAL STUDIES

## A GOOD CITIZEN

What does it mean to be a "good citizen"? Essentially it means to be a team player, to follow the rules, and to be a good contributor. There are other characteristics of being a good citizen. Ask students what *they* are looking for in a "good neighbor" or a good teammate. Here are some suggestions to list on the chalkboard. Use students' own words when possible.

| | | |
|---|---|---|
| honesty | dependable | prompt |
| good humor | willing to listen | plays fair |
| open-minded | respect for others | accepts responsibility |
| cooperative | friendly | trustworthy |

# SEPTEMBER CITIZENSHIP FOCUS

Tell students that this month, in this classroom, these three traits will be of concern to all of us: *honesty, respect for authority,* and being *trustworthy.* Remember to praise students when you find them displaying these characteristics. Make sure they know the meaning of these terms, and that they are able to state each meaning in their own words.

For example, what does the term "respect for authority" mean to an eight-year-old? One student might say you need to obey the rules, another may say it means doing what those in charge tell you to do, and so on. When you can get it in their own words and the words of their classmates, there is apt to be more of a concrete understanding of the abstract term. At this age, students are team players and like to have rules that everyone can follow. It makes for a secure and safe environment.

## KEEP A CITIZENSHIP FOLDER

Students can take a piece of 18- by 24-inch construction paper and fold it in half. They can decorate the outside of it in an attractive manner with crayons or felt-tip pens. Then, inside have a separate sheet for each of the three traits referred to above.

After a class discussion, have students write a short paragraph that defines the trait. Then, on the remainder of the sheet, they can write notes when they have a personal encounter with someone displaying or not displaying this trait; when they read about it in a news article; when they read about it in a book; when they see it on a television news program or other program; and so on. Throughout the month, have students share their observations with others.

## THE FBI "MOST WANTED" POSTER

Explain that the FBI (Federal Bureau of Investigation) keeps a list of the "10 Most Wanted Criminals" in the country. Tell students to look for these photos the next time they go into a Post Office.

Today, however, in this classroom, the FBI is on the lookout for Good Citizens, and that means the students. You will need a large size piece of heavy poster paper and an ink pad. Print THE FBI MOST WANTED LIST—WANTED FOR GOOD CITIZENSHIP across the top. Then have students come up one by one to be fingerprinted. They can place their fingerprint anywhere on the posterboard that they choose. You can initial it in pencil and, later, when everyone has been fingerprinted (thumb or forefinger), students can carefully print their name under their fingerprint. Display this proudly in the classroom. They all start off the year as good citizens! (Some teachers display the beginning-of-the-year class photo along with this activity.)

## GOOD CITIZEN BADGES

Students can make a large construction paper badge and print "I Am a Good Citizen in Room ____" on it. Then they can place their fingerprint in the middle and proudly wear the badge. Three paper streamers, like ribbons, can be pasted onto the badge. The streamers can stand for honesty, respect for authority, and trustworthiness. Remind students to feel proud and stand tall when they walk in the hall today. Parents might be interested in having these fingerprints.

# PATRIOTISM

## FLAG SALUTE

For students who speak English as a second language, it will not take an exceptionally long time for them to be able to say the words, since they will hear this pledge daily. At first they will not know all of it, or what it means, but the repetition of the daily pledge will eventually make sense to them. Then you can work from there.

A mature, dependable student from a fifth grade would make a good teacher assistant for this task.

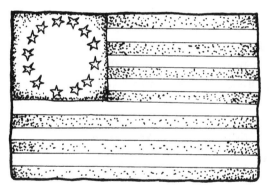

Remember to have students stand at attention, feet together, back straight, facing the flag, right hand over the heart. During this time there is no talking, no moving about, no shuffling feet—everyone is focused. It is one of our first lessons in citizenship.

Tell students that you are proud of the way they stand and speak out clearly. This reinforces the behavior, and the next day it will be even more commendable. Remember, you are the role model.

## FLAG FACTS

It was George Washington's idea to have a special flag to represent the colonies (later to become the United States). Three colors were selected: red for courage; white for liberty; and blue for loyalty. The thirteen stripes represent the original thirteen colonies, and there is one star for each state.

Students can become flag designers. Step back in time to 1777, and design a flag that represents courage, liberty, and loyalty in the thirteen colonies. After making a sketch, use felt-tip pens to create the flag on construction paper. (Use a sheet of $8\frac{1}{2}$- by 11-inch paper to represent the surface of the flag.) Submit the flags to a democratic classroom vote—secret ballot, with the winning design selected by the majority of votes. Display these red, white, and blue flag designs on the bulletin board, with the winner in the middle.

Since there were many craftspeople in the colonies, students may wish to submit their designs on wood, cardboard, or by stitching or drawing them onto fabric. Parents may be willing to donate some of this material to the classroom.

# AREA OF FOCUS: OUR CITY

Throughout the year, we will be studying the city in which we live, characteristics of a city, and other cities in the USA. We will also touch upon our country—the United States of America. But first, our very own city.

## MAKE A KWL CHART OF THE CITY

Have a large sheet of paper to work on. Put the name of your city at the top (or where the school is located). Then make three columns and label them K, W, L. This stands for What I *K*now, What I *W*ant to Know, and What I *L*earned.

Students can tell what they already know about their city and this information can be recorded on the chart. This may lead to what they want to know about their city. Work with these two columns. Later, the material can be organized into a web of the city. Finally, fill in the last column with what they learned.

## CITY SLEUTHS

Students may already know some of these interesting facts, and others will need to be researched. For starters, they can check at the library, the historical society, the chamber of commerce, and also ask parents or older members of the family or neighbors for information. These are some things to find out:

- How did the city get its name?
- How old is the city? When was it established? By whom?
- What is the layout of the city?
- What are the major street names? river names? lake names?
- Does it have a "nickname"? (Example: The Flower City, the Riverboat City, the City of Automobiles)
- What is the city best known for?

## 3-D CITY MAP-IN-A-BOX

Students can create a map of the four corners of their city or some well-known area in the city. This can be done in a shallow box, with colored construction paper used for roads (brown), rivers (blue), and grassy areas (green). Students can use cereal boxes, cylinders, and other food boxes to cover with paper and paint to make the familiar buildings. Clay can be used for statues. Students can bring in toy miniatures (cars, people) for the map, or these can be created from construction paper. Fasten a kraft stick to the back of the object with tape, then put it into a piece of clay as a holder. This can be as busy or as simple as the students desire. Be flexible with this project, since it will grow and develop as students become involved with it.

## CLAY TILE CITY CENTER

On a small, square slab of clay, students can create an area of the city of interest to them or they can recreate a mini-city center. Use toothpicks to draw lines in the clay for roads and the rippling river, and indentations for blades of grass. Then students can use modeling clay to mold buildings, traffic, people, trees, street signs, and so on. These can be glazed and fired in the kiln later in the month.

## GREEN CITIES

All around the country there is an effort being made to turn America green. Overgrown lots that house trash are being transformed into gardens. This area can lift your spirits, especially in a big city. So, find out what's going on in your city. A good reference book is *Greening the City Streets* by Barbara A. Huff, with photos by Peter Ziebel. (In Vienna, Austria, people are planting green gardens and plants on their high-rise balconies. One artist even kept goats. He said that city people get too far away from nature and need to return to it for their good health.)

# HOLIDAYS AND CELEBRATIONS

### LABOR DAY

This legal holiday is the first Monday in September and celebrates *work*. The holiday is usually on the last weekend before school starts and families have one last chance for a holiday before children settle down for another year of school.

Although our employment rate fluctuates, it is usually high in relation to other countries around the world. People need to work in order to earn money for their families. Discuss the work contributions made by family members in this classroom.

## CITIZENSHIP DAY

September 17 is the anniversary of the signing of the Constitution. Foreign-born citizens who have lived in the country for five years are eligible for citizenship. All who meet the requirements take an oath of allegiance on this day. Are there any students who have first-hand knowledge of this special event? All students should be proud to recite the Pledge of Allegiance on this very special day.

## GRANDPARENTS DAY

This is a day set aside to informally celebrate grandparents. Although not a federal holiday, many communities celebrate this day in different ways. It's an opportunity to make a special greeting card and send it to grandparents.

## ROSH HASHANAH (NEW YEAR) AND
## YOM KIPPUR (DAY OF ATONEMENT)

During a ten-day period, which may fall either in September or October, people of Jewish faith all over the globe examine their behavior over the past year and seek forgiveness for any wrongs they may have done. Jewish people worship in a synagogue. An excellent resource book is *Menorahs, Mezuzas, and Other Jewish Symbols* by Miriam Chaikin, with illustrations by Erika Weihs.

## KENNEDY CENTER OPEN HOUSE ARTS FESTIVAL (NATION'S CAPITAL)

This annual open house invites local performers and artists on all stages. There is much audience participation. The website is www.Kennedy-Center.org.

# FOCUS ON SCIENCE

### WHAT ARE THE THREE MAIN SCIENCE AREAS?

Make a chart of the Science areas to display in the classroom. Students can make an individual one for their Science Folder to be used as a checklist. When students read a newspaper report or a book on one of these topics, they can make a check mark next to it. Students like to look for books on Science experiments in the library, too. Bring these books back to the classroom for some possible investigation activities.

| *Earth Science* | *Life Science* | *Physical Science* |
|---|---|---|
| water | plants/seeds | energy |
| weather | animals | light |
| ecology | animal cycles | machines |
| earth | human body | magnets |
| space | health/nutrition | sound |
| | | electricity |

### SCIENCE CENTER—THE CURIOSITY SHOP

Set up a Science Center in the classroom with a wide variety of books and materials, such as a microscope, magnifying glass, binoculars, prism, eyedropper, sand timer, scales, thermometer, plastic see-through containers, pencils, plain paper, graph paper, sample graphs, pairs of garden gloves, spoons, and so on. This area will be flexible and the materials will change each month as we develop a new topic to explore.

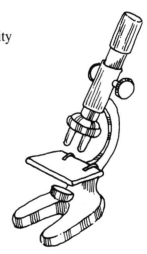

## IF I MAKE A GRAPH, AM I DOING MATH OR SCIENCE?

You could be doing both. Scientists collect a massive amount of data, or information. One way to deal with this information is to *organize* it. Often, after material is organized, a graph is made of the information, so that the person looking at the graph can get an "instant picture" of the subject matter instead of leafing through piles of papers and materials.

Encourage students to be on the alert for the working relationship between Math and Science. Here's a jingle that may help them to remember:

> *Without rock, can you have roll?*
> *If you have cereal, do you need a bowl?*
> *Without water, can you take a bath?*
> *Where you have Science, you also have Math!*

Students can make bar graphs this month of materials that they find in nature . . . rocks, leaves, weeds. Collect, organize, graph! (See Reproducible Activity Pages.)

## THE SEASONS COME, THE SEASONS GO

We are on the cusp of a new season—autumn, or fall. Daylight hours grow shorter and there is a longer period of night in many parts of the country. Three vocabulary words need to be introduced when we discuss a change of seasons: *rotate, revolve, axis.* The Earth rotates daily (every 24 hours), revolves around the Sun approximately once per year (every 365 days), and tilts on its axis away from the Sun in its journey around the Sun.

## WE CAN REVOLVE AND ROTATE

Students can physically demonstrate their knowledge of these three terms.

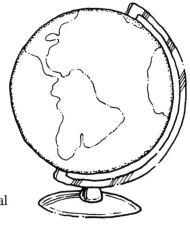

For *rotate,* they can physically turn around and around and around. One complete rotation represents one day, so students do not need to do this hurriedly, but, rather, in a deliberate manner.

For *revolve,* have a fixed point in the classroom representing the Sun, such as a basketball in the middle of the floor. Students can form a circle around it and move around it so that they end up at the same point. One revolution is equal to one year.

Also, have students revolve around the Sun (basketball) while rotating (twirling). Make one complete twirl for each day.

Next, divide the circle into four sections by placing different colored pieces of yarn on the large circle. Use orange for autumn, white for winter, yellow for spring, and green for summer. As students rotate and revolve around the sun, they are representing different seasons of the year.

For *axis,* students can tilt away from the Sun (basketball) during winter, and slowly begin to tilt toward the Sun in summer.

## DANCING TO THE SEASONS

To further grasp the concept of rotation and revolution, students can slowly move around the circle. For *winter,* they can fold their arms across their chest. For *spring,* they can unfold their arms and hold their hands up to their face. For *summer,* they can do a continual motion of reaching up and back, up and back with outstretched arms. For *autumn,* they can make a ripple motion with their fingers to simulate falling leaves.

Play music in the background that is slow and soothing. Have students be on the alert for music that represents the different seasons. What musical instrument could represent the sound of each season? What colors?

## RUSTLE AND CRACKLE—AUTUMN LEAVES

In autumn, the leaves turn colors and begin to dry out in many parts of the country. Have students collect a wide variety of leaves from the neighborhood and their home area. Have containers in the Science Center to store them. How can they be categorized? (size, shape, color, number of leaves)

Students can look at leaves under the microscope. They can draw the cells and shapes they see from the leaves (and stems) of different trees. (See Reproducible Activity Pages.)

## INVITE A NATURALIST TO SCHOOL

Many parks have programs for children. Arrangements can be made to have a park ranger or naturalist address the class visitors. Then, it may be possible for them to visit your classroom during another season as a follow-up. Find out what equipment they use in studying life forms in nature (bags, butterfly netting, shoe boxes for collections, a personal notebook for daily entries, etc.). Perhaps you can add some of these materials to your Science Center.

## WE ARE ALWAYS INTERESTED IN WEATHER

We'll be keeping track of weather throughout the year. This month, we can use the large classroom calendar to record the weather and the temperature for the day. Outline the symbols in black and use bright colors to fill in the symbols. Place a thermometer outside the window and one inside (if you don't have a combination indoor/outdoor thermometer).

The calendar weather symbol recordings can be as follows:

sun     rain     snow     wind     cloudy

# SEPTEMBER AUTHOR STUDY: MARGARET MAHY

This author, popular with third graders, was born in Whakatane, New Zealand. She began her career as a librarian and is a member of the New Zealand Library Association. She has received many awards for the over 100 books she has written, including the Boston Globe/Horn Book Award for *Memory*. The book *17 Kings and 42 Elephants* was selected as one of the ten best illustrated books in 1987 by the New York Times Book Review. She has won the Carnegie Medal twice, and in 1993, she was awarded The Order of New Zealand, her country's most prestigious honor. Margaret Mahy's hobbies are reading and gardening. She lives in New Zealand, where she is considered the most well-known writer of books for children.

Welcome Margaret Mahy, a delightful storyteller, into your September classroom.

## BOOKS AND SUGGESTED ACTIVITIES

### *MAKING FRIENDS* (ILLUSTRATED BY WENDY SMITH)

Mrs. deVere is a small, lonely woman who gets a large dog for her large house. Mr. Derry is a large, lonely man who gets a small dog for his small house by the sea. These two people pass each other while walking, but are too shy to speak. But that's before they each got a dog. The dogs barge around, and bounce around, and pounce around in such a tangle that Mrs. deVere and Mr. Derry can't help looking at one another. A new friendship is formed.

## ACTIVITIES TO ACCOMPANY *MAKING FRIENDS*

1. Read the book aloud so students can enjoy the story. Then have a discussion of ways that we can make friends when we don't have one. These people finally had something in common—dogs—to talk about. What else do people have in common that enable friendships to build? (cats, sports, bicycles, scooters, sport teams, hobbies, and so on) Pair students together, and give them five minutes to talk to see what they have in common.

2. *Dog Names.* One dog was named "Oberon"; the other, "Titania." Students will enjoy telling the names of their pets, whether they are dogs or cats or birds. Ask them how the pets got their names.

3. Reread the two pages aloud that describe the types of dogs—"shaggy dogs, baggy dogs, soppy dogs, floppy dogs, strong dogs, long dogs, harmonious dogs and dogs that sang out of tune." Notice the rhyming words. Perhaps students can write a descriptive sentence for a dog that uses different words, yet rhyme.

4. Focus on making friends this month. Encourage students to make new friends in the class-room. When it's time to choose partners, ask students to choose someone they haven't worked with before.

## *THE THREE-LEGGED CAT* (ILLUSTRATED BY JONATHAN ALLEN)

A delightful story that centers around an orange cat with a peg leg who longs to roam the world. But Tom the tabby is stuck indoors with a woman who is standoffish. She has a brother who roams the world, though, and when he comes for his yearly visit in his orange furry hat perched on top of his bald head, it makes her uncomfortable. What would the neighbors say about a drifter? When the brother leaves, his furry hat feels nice and warm. When he walks by the seaside, the hat begins to purr. "Horrakapotchkin!" The brother has carried off a happy tabby!

## ACTIVITIES TO ACCOMPANY *THE THREE-LEGGED CAT*

1. Locate New Zealand on a world map or globe so that students can see where their author-of-the-month is located. Is it far away? Is it large or small? What continent is it near? Some students may be interested in learning more about this area.

2. When reading the book aloud, the students are sure to enjoy it and will want to read it again. Talk with students about the fanciful, imaginative story. Explain that some stories are pure fantasy and are written for the enjoyment of the reader. They can begin to keep a list of stories that are just plain fun!

   Ask students to put themselves in the place of the cat character and imagine what something is like *before* the cat sees it and then *after* he sees it as it really is (like the sea that wasn't pink and fizzy after all). Students can draw before/after art pictures of the scenes, and use descriptive words just like the author.

3. *Danny the Drifter and Tom.* It looks like these two will become fast friends. Students can draw a diagram and keep a diary for a week of where they've been.

4.  Students can write a postcard from Tom to Mrs. Gimble. Draw a picture on one side of the postcard and write the message on the other side.

5.  Have students imagine what Mrs. Gimble will say when she finds out that the "cat" she's holding on her lap is really her brother's old hat. Right now she says "it's cheap to keep, and always asleep." (Point out to students that this author uses a great deal of internal rhyming in the text—i.e., cheap/keep/asleep; revolting, molting Russian hat).

6.  "Horrakapotchkin!" is an exclamatory expression. Urge students to be on the lookout for others in stories that they read.

## 17 KINGS AND 42 ELEPHANTS (ILLUSTRATED BY PATRICIA MACCARTHY)

The book has been called a delicious nonsense poem. The poem tells the story of the kings riding atop elephants, as they swing and sway and make their way through the jungle. We meet up with a number of different animals, such as the "proud and ponderous hippopotomums" and eventually other animals join in the sing-song romp. Sheer enjoyment for young readers!

## ACTIVITIES TO ACCOMPANY 17 KINGS AND 42 ELEPHANTS

1.  First read it aloud without the pictures so students can enjoy the rhythm and rhyme. Then read it again, and this time enjoy the delightful illustrations as well. This is a book that students will return to for the rhyme and for the detailed art work.

2.  The style of the art work is called *batik,* which is a hot wax, paint, and dip process. Students can be on the alert for other books done in this style and perhaps find an art book in the library on batik.

3.  Ask students to identify their favorite illustration. However, instead of saying, "I like the one of the lions," they will need to say the verse that accompanies the illustration, such as "My favorite is tigers at the riverside drinking lappily, knew the kings were happy as they marched along."

4.  The kings are in wonderfully fanciful, colorful costumes. Students can create their own kings at the easel or with construction paper. Notice that the rhythm of the text carries over into the illustrations which seem to swing and sway.

5.  *Play on words.* Point out to the students the play on words that this author uses. She takes liberty with words and invents new ones. She refers to "baggy ears like big umbrellaphants" and the tinkling tunesters, twangling trillicans, who "butterflied and fluttered by" the great green trees.

## THE GREAT WHITE MAN-EATING SHARK, A CAUTIONARY TALE (PICTURES BY JONATHAN ALLEN)

It's not easy being an out-of-work boy actor, such as Norvin. He's not exactly good looking, and, in fact, looks more like a shark. He loves to swim, but the water is so crowded. Aha! That's when Norvin concocts his fiendish plan. Soon Norvin has the water all to himself—or does he?

## ACTIVITIES TO ACCOMPANY *THE GREAT WHITE MAN-EATING SHARK, A CAUTIONARY TALE*

1. Draw attention to the subtitle, *A Cautionary Tale.* The word *cautionary* is derived from *caution,* which means to be careful. So right away, even before reading the story aloud, there are yellow lights flashing for the reader. We are going to learn a valuable lesson here.

2. Read the book aloud and enjoy it. Then go back over it and look for the second layer of meaning. Lead students to discover that Norvin has tricked people, so is it any wonder, then, that when he shot out of the water kicking and screaming with terror that people might have ignored him? How did Norvin put himself, and others, in danger?

3. Compare this book to the Aesop tale, *The Boy Who Cried Wolf.* Can students see any similarities? (Lie, be discovered, and people won't believe you.)

4. *Discussion.* Would students want Norvin for a friend? What qualities are we looking for when we make friends?

## *DOWN THE DRAGON'S TONGUE* (ILLUSTRATED BY PATRICIA MACCARTHY)

Mr. Prospero is a very tidy, important businessman with a clean white shirt, shiny shoes, and a hand-painted tie that looks like a fruit salad. "You can do it, You can do it" is the motto hanging in his office. All is well with Mr. Prospero until he goes home and his twins tug at him to go and play at the playground. He goes under protest, and ends up having the most fun of anyone else in spite of the puddles and his torn business suit.

## ACTIVITIES TO ACCOMPANY *DOWN THE DRAGON'S TONGUE*

1. Read the story aloud and enjoy it. Examine the faces of the story characters. What does Father's face reveal about him when he's at the top of the dragon's tongue slide?

2. Call attention to such words as *whoooosh! swiiish! wheee!* and *woooow!* that describe the noises as they go down the slide. Can students come up with any more descriptive words? Point out to students that the words are drawn out by using at least four vowels, and have them draw out the words with their voice.

3. If this were a story on TV, what might Mrs. Prospero, a songwriter, think the background music should be like? Where would it be slow, fast, faster? When would it be soft, loud, loudest?

4. Mr. Prospero has become like a kid again. He's having fun. Perhaps students can share a time when someone in their family "became like a kid again" and engaged in the joy of an activity or game with family members.

**Note:** Margaret Mahy has written over 100 books for children, so we have just scratched the surface. Her books are enjoyable, fun, and add a carefree aspect to the life of a young child that is so richly deserved. Have students be on the lookout for more of her books and read them, report on them, and—when possible—read them aloud during story time for all to enjoy!

# REPRODUCIBLE ACTIVITY PAGES
# FOR SEPTEMBER

## READING/LANGUAGE ARTS

Reading/Writing Checklist

My Bird Feather Reading Record

Practice Overstroke—Lowercase Letters

Practice Understroke—Lowercase/Two-Space Letters

A Listening Exercise

My Spelling Planner

Story Chain (Web)

## MATH

I'm a Walking Number

Finish the Pattern

Mini-Addition Flashcards

Mini-Subtraction Flashcards

## SOCIAL STUDIES

Good Citizen Badge

Good Citizen I.Q.

## SCIENCE

My Science Reading Record

Collect, Organize, Graph!

The Good Breakfast Match

## AUTHOR STUDY

Join Margaret Mahy on a Journey

**Student's Name** _____

# Reading/Writing Checklist

| Skill | Comments |
|---|---|
| 1. Phonics<br>• Knowledge of letters and sounds<br>• Can blend letters | |
| 2. Main Idea<br>• Grasps primary focus of story<br>• Predictions—makes reasonable statements of what comes next | |
| 3. Punctuation<br>• Understands function<br>• Uses correctly in reading and writing | |
| 4. Inference<br>• Makes assumptions based upon:<br>    text<br>    visual clues | |
| 5. Spelling<br>• Above average<br>• Good progress<br>• More practice needed | |
| 6. Handwriting: Letter formation<br>• Above average<br>• Good progress<br>• More practice needed | |
| 7. Letter Writing<br>• Shows understanding<br>• Uses correct form | |
| 8. Root Words<br>• Can identify | |
| 9. Compound Words<br>• Is able to construct using root words | |
| 10. Contractions<br>• Uses appropriately | |
| 11. Story Web<br>• Can construct<br>• Can follow information | |
| 12. Retelling<br>• Can retell story using own words | |
| 13. Journaling<br>• Shows interest<br>• More practice needed | |

# My Bird Feather Reading Record

Color in a feather when you read a book in the genre listed.

Your aim is to end up with a colorful bird.

# Practice Overstroke—Lowercase Letters

a   a   a

c   c   c

d   d   d

g   g   g

m   m   m

n   n   n

o   o   o

q   q   q

x   x   x

z   z   z

# Practice Understroke—Lowercase Letters

©2002 by The Center for Applied Research in Education

**Name** _____  **Date** _____

# A Listening Exercise

Marcus McRabbit is all dressed to listen. You can, too. Listen for the following and then share information with classmates.

1. Listen and re-tell what you heard.

2. Listen for a musical word.

3. Listen and predict what will happen.

4. Listen for a main idea. What is it?

5. Listen for a word that is brand new.

# My Spelling Planner

Use these helpful activities for this week's spelling words.  Color in the shape when you complete the work.  Do one each day.

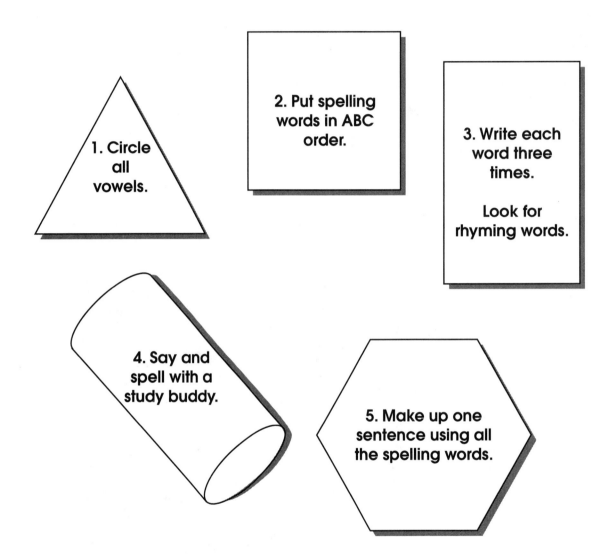

1. Circle all vowels.

2. Put spelling words in ABC order.

3. Write each word three times.

Look for rhyming words.

4. Say and spell with a study buddy.

5. Make up one sentence using all the spelling words.

Unscramble the 5 words for shapes on this page.

1. qasure    _____
2. rntigeal   _____
3. yldreicn   _____
4. eatrcegln  _____
5. egnhoax   _____

Name _____     Date _____

# Story Chain (Web)

Read a book and fill in the missing links with words and pictures.

**Major Character**          **Minor Character**

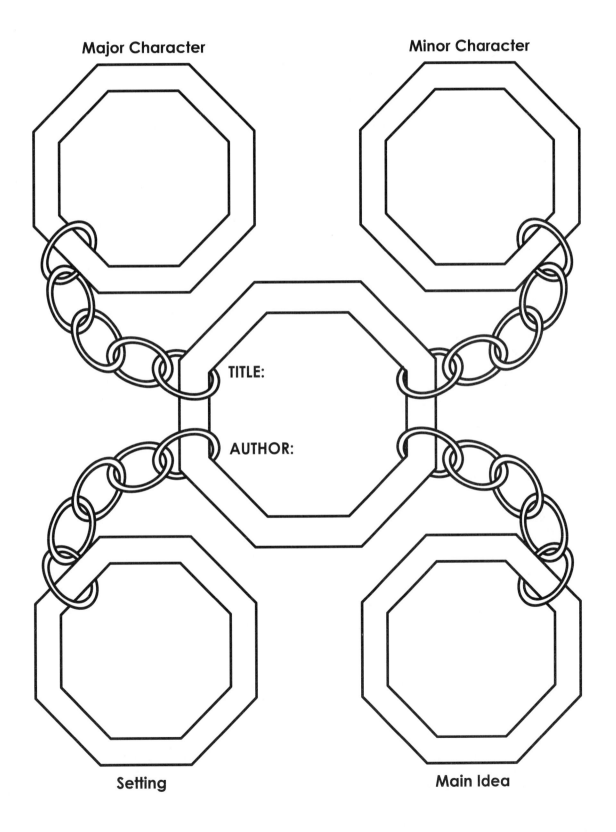

TITLE:

AUTHOR:

**Setting**                          **Main Idea**

# I'm a Walking Number

Think of your body in terms of numbers.

Start measuring.

Start counting!

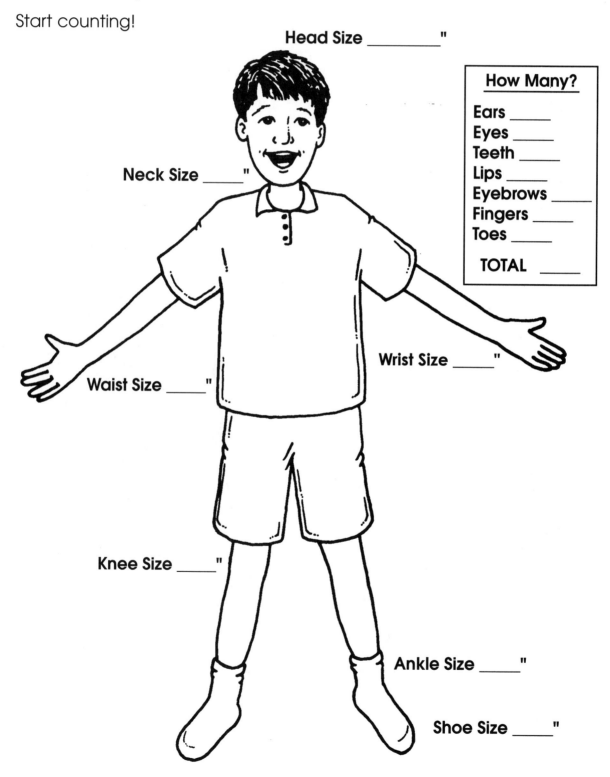

Head Size _____"

**How Many?**

Ears _____
Eyes _____
Teeth _____
Lips _____
Eyebrows _____
Fingers _____
Toes _____

**TOTAL** _____

Neck Size _____"

Wrist Size _____"

Waist Size _____"

Knee Size _____"

Ankle Size _____"

Shoe Size _____"

Name _____     Date _____

# Finish the Pattern

This tree has many patterns for P. McParrot, Esq., to finish.  Can you help?

**Make two patterns below:**

1.

2.

**What's your clothing pattern?**

# Mini-Addition Flashcards

Cut on the lines. Print answer on reverse side.

| | | |
|---|---|---|
| 5 + 4 | 8 + 6 | 4 + 7 |
| 7 + 4 | 9 + 2 | 3 + 7 |
| 5 + 3 | 4 + 5 | 6 + 4 |
| 4 + 8 | 7 + 7 | 6 + 8 |
| 6 + 9 | 2 + 9 | 7 + 5 |
| 5 + 7 | 3 + 5 | 4 + 6 |
| 7 + 3 | 8 + 4 | 9 + 6 |

# Mini-Subtraction Flashcards

Cut on the lines. Print answer on reverse side.

| ○○○○●● | ○○○○○ | ●●●● |
|---|---|---|
| 11 - 7 | 9 - 4 | 7 - 4 |
| ●●●●● | ●●●● | ○○○ |

| ○○○● | ○○○●●● | ○○○○○○ |
|---|---|---|
| 8 - 5 | 12 - 9 | 11 - 3 |
| ●●●● | ●●●●●● | ○○●●● |

| ○○○○○○○○ | ○○○○● | ○○● |
|---|---|---|
| 16 - 4 | 9 - 5 | 6 - 4 |
| ○○○○●●●● | ●●●● | ●●● |

| ○○○●● | ○○○○ | ○○●● |
|---|---|---|
| 9 - 6 | 7 - 3 | 8 - 6 |
| ●●●● | ●●● | ●●●● |

| ○○○○○○ | ○○○○○○ | ○○○○ |
|---|---|---|
| 12 - 5 | 11 - 2 | 7 - 2 |
| ○●●●●●● | ○○○●● | ○●● |

| ○○○○○ | ○○○○ | ○○○○● |
|---|---|---|
| 10 - 3 | 8 - 3 | 10 - 6 |
| ○○●●● | ○●●● | ●●●●● |

| ○○○○○○○○ | ○○○○○○ | ○○●●● |
|---|---|---|
| 15 - 6 | 12 - 4 | 10 - 8 |
| ○●●●●●●● | ○○●●●● | ●●●●● |

# Good Citizen Badge

Color. Cut out the badge. Wear it with pride.

_____

is a good citizen in ROOM ____

·honesty · dependable · friendly · prompt · cooperative · · trustworthy ·

In each eagle bubble, print a word that describes our good citizen.

# Good Citizen I.Q.

Select the best term from the ABC Citizen Bank and write it on the appropriate line. Then, rate yourself on this quality ( 😊😐☹️ ).

### ABC Citizen Bank

| **A** | **B** | **C** |
|---|---|---|
| • honesty | • dependable | • prompt |
| • good humor | • good listener | • fair-minded |
| • open-minded | • respects others | • trustworthy |
| • cooperative | • friendly | • accepts responsibility |

(B) 1.  Josh welcomes classmates with a smile.

       Quality: _____

(C) 2.  Lori listens to both sides before forming an opinion.

       Quality: _____

(C) 3.  Carlos is always on time.

       Quality: _____

(B) 4.  Give the job to Ashley and she'll do it!

       Quality: _____

(C) 5.  Mrs. Jones sent Jamal to the office with the lunch money.

       Quality: _____

(C) 6.  You can always count on Kalisha!

       Quality: _____

(B) 7.  Gage pays attention to what you say.

       Quality: _____

(A) 8.  Ask Tony if you want the real answer.

       Quality: _____

(A) 9.  B.J. is always in a good mood.

       Quality: _____

(A) 10. Jane will listen to both sides of the story.

       Quality: _____

(A) 11. You can count on Mark to pull his share of the load.

       Quality: _____

(B) 12. Tara has a right to her opinion and so do you.

       Quality: _____

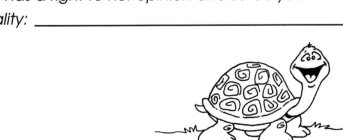

The letter A, B, or C in front of the number tells you which word bank list to use.

**Name** _____

# My Science Reading Record

Read a book in each area. Keep a checklist.

| EARTH SCIENCE | Book | Date |
|---|---|---|
| water | | |
| weather | | |
| ecology | | |
| earth | | |
| space | | |
| **LIFE SCIENCE** | **Book** | **Date** |
| plants/seeds | | |
| animals | | |
| animal cycles | | |
| human body | | |
| healthy/nutrition | | |
| **PHYSICAL SCIENCE** | **Book** | **Date** |
| energy | | |
| light | | |
| machines | | |
| sound | | |
| electricity | | |

Name _____    Date _____

# Collect, Organize, Graph!

Keep a visual record of each of these items that you have found in nature. Draw a picture of it in the square. Label it. Compare information with classmates.

| Total: _____ | Total: _____ | Total: _____ |
|---|---|---|
| | | |
| | | |
| | | |
| | | |
| | | |
| | | |
| leaves | rocks | weeds |

# The Good Breakfast Match

Color each picture below. Then cut the boxes apart on the lines.

TO PLAY THE GAME: Lay the cards face down on a grid. Turn over two cards. If the cards match, you may keep them. If the cards do not match, turn them back over. Then the next player takes a turn. Try to remember where each picture is located. The player with the most matching cards wins the game.

# Join Margaret Mahy on a Journey

The 3-legged cat and the owner's brother are world travelers, and your city is next on their list. Write a letter to them that will help them to see the highlights.

**Dear** _____,

# OCTOBER

# OCTOBER BOOKS

**Baer, Edith.** *This Is the Way We Go to School, A Book About Children Around the World.* **Illustrated by Steven Bjorkman (New York: Scholastic, 1990).** This book, told in rhyme, takes the reader on a journey to school by way of school bus, ferry boat, cable car, skis, train, bicycle, and even radio. At the end is a list of 22 students and a map that shows where they live.

**Brown, Ruth.** *Alphabet Times Four, An International ABC* **(New York: Dutton, 1991).** Underneath each lovely painting per page is a row of print containing a word in four different languages, representing something from the picture. The four languages are English, Spanish, French, and German.

**Cole, Alison.** *Perspective* **(New York: Dorling Kindersley, 1992).** This is one in a series of the DK books on a variety of topics that appeal to children. This book deals with perspective in art, artists, and is a good book for browsing time.

**Flournoy, Vanessa and Valerie.** *Celie and the Harvest Fiddler.* **Illustrated by James E. Ransome (New York: Morrow, 1995).** Set in the late 1800s, this story is about a girl who hopes to have the best Halloween costume and succeeds in a mysterious way. Large paintings in autumn hues.

**Lewin, Ted.** *Market!* **(New York: Lothrop, Lee & Shephard, 1996).** From the chilly Highlands of the Andes to the jungles of Africa, and from the souks of Morocco to the New York waterfront, people come to market. Join in this colorful visual adventure and see what markets look like all over the world.

**Morgan, Rowland (compiler).** *In the Next Three Seconds.* **Illustrated by Rod and Kira Josey (New York: Lodestar, 1997).** What will happen in the next three seconds, three minutes, three days and nights, three weeks, three months, three decades? A good book for the curious. In the next three minutes, for example, people will save 600 trees by recycling paper.

**Scieszka, Jon and Lane Smith.** *Math Curse* **(New York: Viking Penguin, 1995).** You can think of everything as a math problem. It can drive you zany. It turns up everywhere, and in every subject. You can't get away from it. This book is laughable and informative, and can be read again and again.

**Wildsmith, Brian.** *Brian Wildsmith's Amazing World of Words* **(Brookfield, CT: The Millbrook Press, 1997).** The author has taken fourteen themes (such as space, desert, ocean) and given each topic a double-page spread. For each one, there is a picture to examine, a border with illustrations, and word labels for many of the items shown in the picture.

**Williams, Linda.** *The Little Old Lady Who Was Not Afraid of Anything.* **Illustrated by Megan Lloyd (New York: Crowell, 1986).** A woman is returning to her cottage in the woods when she is followed by two shoes that go CLOMP, CLOMP, pants that go WIGGLE, WIGGLE, shirts that go SHAKE, SHAKE, and so on. Children enjoy acting out this story favorite with real props.

**(CHAPTER BOOK) White, E. B.** *The Trumpet of the Swan* **(New York: HarperCollins, 1970).** A good read-aloud book about a trumpeter swan, named Louis, who is handicapped. He can't trumpet. What's more, he's in love with a beautiful swan named Serena and wants to impress her. Louis is determined to overcome his handicap. In the process the entire classroom is charmed by this story. Throughout the year read Charlotte's Web and Stuart Little by this same author.

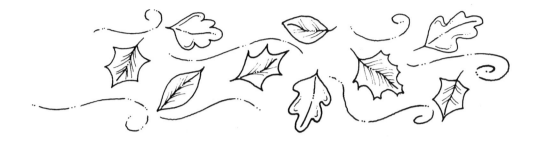

# OCTOBER

By this time, the classroom should be organized. Students should know the routine and what is expected of them. Are you, as the teacher, pleased with the way the students are behaving and working together? If not, then follow this procedure. STOP. Have a class meeting and present your concerns. Draw up a list of things that need to be worked on. If the morning does not go any better, then STOP. Even if you have to stop repeatedly during the day in order to get your message across regarding classroom management and behavior, it is best to do it now, early in the year. Don't wait. Use the STOP method for an entire week. If students become tired of it, they will begin to get the message that this won't change unless they do. Close down some of the Centers to reduce the amount of movement and confusion until the group gets used to working together in an amicable and cooperative manner. Be sure to praise them for good behavior so they understand the expectations. Point out to them when you don't have to stop at all for a whole morning or a whole day.

Classroom rules and consequences should be visible on large posterboard. Some teachers use a numbering system, placing a number before each rule. If a person is stepping out of bounds, the teacher can say, "Jimmy, number 3," or "Valerie, number 1." Point to the poster, so they can read the rule and know what your concern is.

This works. Since individuals are often focusing upon what *they're* doing and not upon the classroom as a whole, they may get too loud, or start to disturb others, or move about too rapidly in the classroom, or even, for example, chase after someone who has a blue marker they want to use. Sometimes they're not aware of their actions. Their behavior needs to be shaped so that it falls within acceptable boundaries. As the teacher, *your* focus is upon the entire group as well as the individuals within it, so you need to keep on top of classroom management *at all times*.

# FOCUS ON READING

## FICTION AND NONFICTION BOOKS—IDENTIFY THEM

Help students distinguish between these two types of books and stories. *Nonfiction* contains factual information. *Fiction* may contain some facts, but is also comprised of information that is fabricated, or made up, to make a good story. Together, list some of the elements of both on the chalkboard. Use the words that students supply when possible. Here are some suggestions to help you get started on the list:

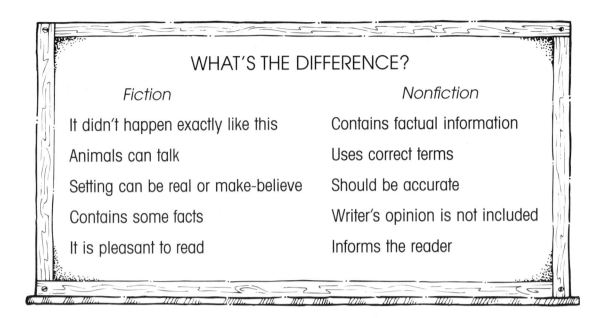

WHAT'S THE DIFFERENCE?

| Fiction | Nonfiction |
| --- | --- |
| It didn't happen exactly like this | Contains factual information |
| Animals can talk | Uses correct terms |
| Setting can be real or make-believe | Should be accurate |
| Contains some facts | Writer's opinion is not included |
| It is pleasant to read | Informs the reader |

Have students name books they have read that are works of fiction and books that are non-fiction. Be sure to have several examples of each type available to show to the students. This will help illustrate the points being made.

## FICTION AND NONFICTION—WHEN DO I USE EACH?

Make another list and this time you can determine with the students when it would be appropriate to use each type of printed material. Use their words when possible, and urge them to be specific. This activity can be done initially in a large group to get the ideas flowing. Then have students break into smaller groups, or work with a partner for more ideas. Share the lists. The following will help get you started:

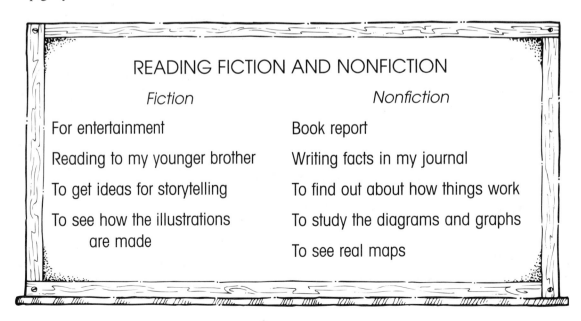

READING FICTION AND NONFICTION

| Fiction | Nonfiction |
| --- | --- |
| For entertainment | Book report |
| Reading to my younger brother | Writing facts in my journal |
| To get ideas for storytelling | To find out about how things work |
| To see how the illustrations are made | To study the diagrams and graphs |
| | To see real maps |

## ILLUSTRATIONS FOR FICTION AND NONFICTION BOOKS

Select two picture books on the same topic. One can be a storybook (fiction) and one can be an information book (nonfiction). Then examine the illustrations and make a chart describing the contrasts. Suppose "Squirrels" is the topic. You select the picture book *Squirrels* by Brian Wildsmith, and an information book on squirrels. Your chart might look something like this in the beginning:

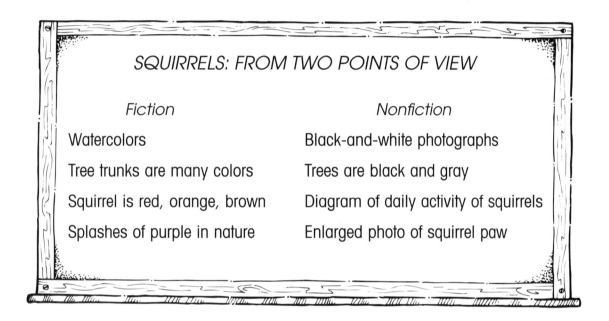

SQUIRRELS: FROM TWO POINTS OF VIEW

| Fiction | Nonfiction |
| --- | --- |
| Watercolors | Black-and-white photographs |
| Tree trunks are many colors | Trees are black and gray |
| Squirrel is red, orange, brown | Diagram of daily activity of squirrels |
| Splashes of purple in nature | Enlarged photo of squirrel paw |

Help students determine that with some fiction, the illustrations can be fanciful. With nonfiction, the illustrations (or diagrams, graphs, maps, sketches, etc.) are more accurate. In both cases, the visual and the verbal information work together, but in different ways. The illustrations in both types of books have merit. In the recent past, information books have relied more heavily upon color, borders, designs, and different artistic techniques to make the books more appealing. Students can pick up ideas for their own book reports in the content areas by examining nonfiction books (Social Studies, Science, Health, etc.).

## ILLUSTRATIONS FOR TWO DIFFERENT PICTURE BOOKS— SAME TOPIC (FICTION)

In order to convey the idea that artists communicate in different ways, select two picture books (fiction) on the same topic. We can use the book mentioned previously, *Squirrels* by Brian Wildsmith, and compare it with the picture book about squirrels entitled *Nuts to You* by Lois Ehlert. *Squirrels* is illustrated with bright watercolors, while *Nuts to You* is illustrated using bright colors with the technique of collage. Have students examine the two books carefully to note how each artist conveys information to the reader in terms of color, line, design, mood, etc. Use descriptive words that tell what the squirrels look like as seen through the eyes of two different illustrators.

Now for the bonus! At the end of *Nuts to You*, the author has a section entitled "Squirrel Talk," and it is here that we see the combination of fiction and nonfiction material in the same picture

book. This is an excellent example for third graders to study and learn from for their own book making. Fiction and nonfiction working together to provide a quality reading experience for students will motivate them to place greater value on the role of art and illustrations in communication as they produce their own books, posters, and factual reports. Now is the time to begin building awareness of the role of art in many types of books. Some students begin to work more carefully and take more time. Give them an opportunity to work with collage in art because many children experience success with this medium on the first try.

Visit this Binney & Smith website for drawing and painting experiences that include crayons, markers, paint, pencils, modeling clay, and others:

http://www.crayola.com/art_education/

## PARTS OF SPEECH—REVIEW RIBBONS

Make long, thin ribbons of different colored paper and label them with the four parts of speech (Noun, Adjective, Verb, Adverb). Begin to make a list, and students can add to it. Tack the paper ribbons to the word wall, but let students take them down for independent skill work, and then return them. Students can create their own parts-of-speech ribbons and roll them up and secure them with a paper clip or rubber band. Students can keep them in their individual 3- by 5-inch card file box along with word cards. This is a good resource for vocabulary review, writing, spelling, and reading.

## WHAT DO THE PARTS OF SPEECH DO? DO THEY WORK?

Yes. The different words have different jobs to do. The following might help explain the role of these important words.

| NOUN (person, place, or thing) | ADJECTIVE ("shows off" the noun) |
|---|---|
| house | charming house |
| boy | cute boy |
| garden | flowering garden |
| street | busy street |

| VERB (word of action) | ADVERB (tells about the action; usually ends in ly or ily) |
|---|---|
| slow | slowly |
| greedy | greedily |

Ask students to be on the alert for these four parts of speech as they read sentences in order to see how they work. Start with a simple sentence, and then expand it. This activity can be done with the entire group so that they get the instruction and see it modeled on the chalkboard. Then they can work independently, with a partner, or in groups of three. Here are some starter ideas:

The dog barked.

The shaggy dog barked.

The shaggy dog barked slowly.

The old shaggy dog barked slowly.

The maid called.

The kitchen maid called.

The kitchen maid called loudly.

The new kitchen maid called loudly.

The telephone rang.

The wall telephone rang.

The wall telephone rang repeatedly.

The blue wall telephone rang repeatedly.

Use color coding to underline nouns in red, adjectives in orange, verbs in green, and adverbs in blue. (See Reproducible Activity Pages.)

## PARTS-OF-SPEECH PICTURE BOOKS—RUTH HELLER

To help make the study of language painless, introduce your students to the stunning series of picture books that turns the spotlight on parts of speech in clever verse, with rich, colorful illustrations. The author/illustrator is Ruth Heller, and your students will repeatedly pour over these books. *Merry-Go-Round, A Book About Nouns* makes nouns come to life with pictures and verse such as: "Nouns name a person, place or thing . . . a damsel, a forest, a dragon, a king. These NOUNS are all COMMON, and they're very nice but PROPER NOUNS are more precise."

*Kites Sail High, A Book About Verbs* makes the reading, and the looking, enjoyable. The pages of this book *show* the verbs at work through the illustrations. There are only a few words per page, and together the visual/verbal union makes children laugh and enjoy the language. The book begins with, "A VERB is really the most superb of any word you've ever heard. . . . Verbs tell you something's being done. Roses BLOOM and people RUN, pelicans FLY, kites SAIL high, and rabbits quickly MULTIPLY." All this and we're on page ten already because of the double-page spreads. Students will definitely want to "paint verbs" after this book experience. There are ten books in this outstanding language/poetry/art series.

## PREFIX: SKILL BUILDING AT THE BEGINNING

A prefix is a group of letters added at the beginning of the root word. If students gain an understanding of the meaning of the prefix itself, it will be helpful when the prefix is encountered in independent reading.

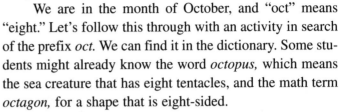

We are in the month of October, and "oct" means "eight." Let's follow this through with an activity in search of the prefix *oct*. We can find it in the dictionary. Some students might already know the word *octopus,* which means the sea creature that has eight tentacles, and the math term *octagon,* for a shape that is eight-sided.

Look for other prefixes we find at the beginning of a root word. Underline the root word. In what way does the prefix change the meaning? Here are some to get you started:

dis:     dis<u>agree</u>, dis<u>honest</u>          re:     re<u>write</u>, re<u>heat</u>

micro:   micro<u>wave</u>, micro<u>scope</u>        tele:   tele<u>phone</u>, tele<u>vision</u>

mis:     mis<u>fortune</u>, mis<u>count</u>         un:     un<u>certain</u>, un<u>happy</u>

Prefix meanings: dis—opposite, micro—small, mis—wrong, re—again, tele—far, un—not.

## FIND THE ROOT WORD, ADD A PREFIX, CHANGE A SENTENCE

Use the root word *agree* in a sentence. Then add the prefix *dis.* Now, use the word *disagree* in that sentence to change its meaning. For example:

I agree that it's time to feed the dog.

I disagree that it's time to feed the dog.

How many other words can be changed with the prefix *dis*? Students can work with a partner to make a list of at least three words.

Try other prefixes, such as *il* (not), *sub* (under), and *ex* (former).

That is a legal act.

That is an illegal act.

Br-r-r. It must be zero outside.

Br-r-r. It must be subzero outside.

Shanda is our president.

Shanda is our ex-president.

How many other words can be changed with the prefixes used above? Students can work with a different partner to make a list of at least three words. These exercises are excellent for building vocabulary.

## SUFFIX: SKILL BUILDING AT THE END

A suffix is a single letter or a group of letters we can add to the *end* of a root word. Perhaps the suffixes most familiar to students are *s, ed,* and *ing.* Take the opportunity to review these, to see how many can be added to the root word. Make a chart that has four columns. One is for the root word, and the other three are for the suffixes. Write the root word in the first column on the left, and see how many of the suffixes "make sense."

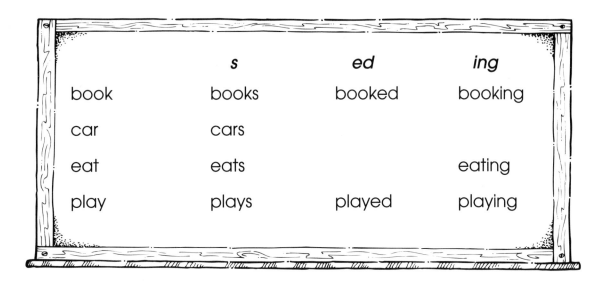

| | s | ed | ing |
|---|---|---|---|
| book | books | booked | booking |
| car | cars | | |
| eat | eats | | eating |
| play | plays | played | playing |

Students can do this on their own or with a study buddy. Start with a list of ten words. Keep on going as time permits. It is a good activity for discovering what works with certain words. It will help students not only in reading, but with writing, speaking, and spelling as well. Also, note that some words change form internally for past tense as in the word "eat." We do not say a person "eated" his dinner, but rather he "ate" his dinner. This is a good lesson in correct grammar.

## SUFFIX CATEGORIES FOR BEGINNERS

While suffixes can be categorized as those to use with the various parts of speech, that is not our intent in this book. We can do other activities throughout the month with various suffixes, or letter groups, that are good for beginners.

You will need two sets of small cards, one in yellow and one in blue (or the colors of your choice). Write the suffix letter groupings on one color set, and write various words on the other set. *Note:* The word set will contain more cards than the suffix set.

A student takes ten word cards and places them in a vertical row, just like a step ladder. Take one of the suffix cards, place it

| able | or | er | en | est |
|---|---|---|---|---|
| ette | ful | ish | less | ly |

to the right of each word individually, and sound it out to determine if it is a word that makes sense. Use the dictionary as a resource to verify a word. The following is a list of some suggested suffix cards and word cards:

- SUGGESTED SUFFIX CARDS (BLUE): able, or, er, en, est, ette, ful, ish, less, ly, ness
- SUGGESTED WORD CARDS (YELLOW): teach, act, major, comfort, fright, weak, father, mother, grandfather, grandmother, good, kind, full, care, thought

Have students list all of the words they can verify. Use them in a sentence. This activity is good for reading, skill building of vocabulary and spelling, and enriching student writing and speaking.

(From the word cards above, we can get the new words of teachable, actor, majorette, comfortable, comforter, frightful, weaker, weakest, weakly, and so on.)

## WHERE CAN WE LOCATE INFORMATION?

Build up your classroom resources. How many of the following resources do you have available in the classroom? How many are available in the school library? Perhaps several can be obtained from the public library for use in your classroom. Others, such as pamphlets, may be obtained by writing to local groups such as the Chamber of Commerce, Auto Club, a museum, an art gallery, the zoo, etc. Gradually introduce the resource terms and resources to students throughout the month and the year, and look for ways to integrate them into the Reading and Language Arts program, as well as the content areas. They can be used as resources to document information that students use in reports.

- *Dictionary:* Each classroom should have a large one that is accessible and centrally located. Encourage children to bring in a pocket dictionary, if they have one. This resource shows proper pronunciation, word histories, sentence usage, synonyms, etc.
- *Pictionary:* This provides both visual and verbal information. Students may be encouraged to make their own.
- *Glossary:* A list of terms, often found at the end of a book, that explains the meaning of certain terms or words in the book.
- *Thesaurus:* A book that contains a list of synonyms for well-known words.
- *Encyclopedia:* A volume of books from A–Z, containing information about a variety of subjects.
- *Handbook:* A manual of facts or instructions. (Also known as a guidebook.)
- *Directory:* A listing of names, terms, and words that pertain to a particular topic.
- *Telephone Book:* A list of names, addresses, and phone numbers of people in the community who have a telephone. Also, the Yellow Pages give valuable information, along with Government Pages, and Business Pages.

- *CD-Rom:* Offers dictionaries and subject matter information.
- *Video tape:* Visual/verbal medium for viewing and listening.
- *Cassette tape:* Verbal/audio medium for listening.
- *CD:* Listening (music, information).
- *Film:* Viewing (photographs, 35-mm slides, 16-mm motion picture films).

Students need to learn the names of these resources and their purposes. (See Reproducible Activity Pages.)

## LITTLE BROWN BAG OF RESOURCES

You will need the following: (1) a plain brown bag filled with tickets on which you have written questions, and (2) three specific resource books on display. These can be changed periodically.

Students reach inside the bag, read the question, and call upon another student to select the correct answer by holding up the specific resource material.

Place a dictionary, telephone directory (phone book), and thesaurus on a table. Review the purpose of each. Reach inside the bag, remove a ticket, and read the question you have written on it. Call upon a student to answer the question by going to the table, holding up the correct resource, and saying its name. Then that student may reach inside the brown bag and repeat the process.

For the dictionary, telephone directory, and thesaurus, here are some sample questions to write on the tickets:

- Where can I find out what the word "territory" means? (dictionary)
- Where can I find the name of a dentist near the school? (Yellow Pages, phone book)
- I need another word for "book." (thesaurus)
- Does the word *close* have a "z" or an "s" in it? (dictionary)
- What's the number of our local TV station? (phone book)

- "Hello," said Mary. "Hi," said Mike. "How are you?" said Mary. "I'm fine," said Mike. (Find another word for "said.") (thesaurus)

## LITTLE BROWN BAG, LITTLE NUMBER SIGNS

Play the same game as above; this time, however, label your resources. Attach a card with a large 1 on the dictionary, a large 2 on the phone book, and a large 3 on the thesaurus. Then distribute three tickets to each student. They can print large numerals 1, 2, and 3, one on each card. Now when you reach inside and read the question, students hold up the appropriate number sign to indicate which resource they would use. This way, you can get immediate feedback from all students.

## LITTLE BROWN BAG, LITTLE ANSWERS TO QUESTIONS

Play a variation of the same game as above. Have five or six individual students reach into the bag, one at a time, get a question ticket, and read it aloud. Then that day (or the next), they are responsible for finding the answer and reporting to the class.

*Variation:* The five or six individual students aren't the only ones who look for the answers. Other class members must do so as well, and the ones who reached into the bag can call upon a class member to give the answer, and prove it.

## MAKE A PICTIONARY OF RESOURCE BOOKS

Make a tiny book, about 4- by 4-inch, from construction paper. Draw and label the resources mentioned above. Give a written clue on the back of the page that helps the student figure out the purpose of the resource. Students can keep this in their Reading Portfolio for future reference when they are working independently.

A large chart may be made for the classroom. Students can print or write the name of the resource on the chart, and others can do the illustrations.

# FOCUS ON LANGUAGE ARTS

## <u>MORE READING OPPORTUNITIES</u>

This month, the Language Arts are in full swing in the classroom. The term *language arts* has been broadened to one of *communication arts*. Students are reading, writing, speaking, listening, and—by this time of year—are usually engaged in the visual arts with their project work. Visual arts and performing arts are two extremely important forms of communication in the classroom. They help to enrich the learning process.

## INDEPENDENT READING

Some specific reading skills have been addressed in the previous section. In addition, students should be reading independently and keeping track of their reading record. They can read in a variety of genres, such as adventure, biography, folktales, historical fiction, holiday books, number books, alphabet books, information books, and so on. If, for example, a student has read six books on airplanes thus far and is not interested in moving on, it is your job to have a conversation with that student to help her or him investigate other genres. Perhaps having the student explore picture books for older students may lead to the development of an ABC book of airplanes in which the student diagrams and labels the parts, or focuses upon different areas of the world and various destinations for

travel. When you make your routine visit to the public library, keep this student in mind as you make selections. Then just by saying to the child, "Dexter, I thought you might like to take a look at this book because . . ." might be all that Dexter needs to broaden his reading experiences.

On the other hand, since students are now able to read chapter books, they may read a book by an author and want to read another and another by that same person. This is a natural, normal reading pattern for third graders. For some assistance, keep checking in the beginning section of this book each month for suggested book selections and at the end of each month for the author study.

## AUTHOR BOOK CLUB

This may be the time to begin an Author Book Club in the classroom. Select three different authors, or have students select them, and have students read at least two of their books. Then they can join the Author Book Club and discuss the books. Some teachers have these book chat sessions during the lunch period, once a week in the classroom, with perhaps four or five students who are focused on this activity, while the rest of the class is at lunch. It's a rewarding time for the teacher and the students.

## AUTHOR STUDY OF PICTURE BOOKS

For students interested in the interplay of the visual and verbal connection, and how illustrations convey information, picture books offer a wonderful learning opportunity. Some writers create their own illustrations whereas others have different illustrators for each text. This is an opportunity for students to discuss the different challenges facing an author/illustrator as opposed to that of an author who must have someone else read the work and illustrate it. For students who are interested, this is an excellent time to work with a partner, or in teams, to develop a short book.

Here are some helpful picture book and chapter book suggestions for authors (A) or author/illustrators (A-I) who have completed a body of works. In this way, children may read and enjoy the same writer.

- Cynthia Rylant (A):
  *And the Relatives Came* (a warm, loving family reunion)
  *Mr. Griggs' Work* (a postman who loves his job)
  *Missing May* (loss of adult in the family)

- Eve Bunting (A):
  *The Wednesday Surprise* (an adult learns to read)
  *The Wall* (Vietnam wall visit)
  *Smoky Night* (a night of rioting in the big city brings some people together)

- Chris Van Allsburg (A-I):
  *The Widow's Broom* (a cleaning is in order)
  *The Garden of Abdul Gasazi* (a bit of magic)
  *Jumanji* (playing a board game that comes to life)

- Patricia Polacco (A-I):
  *Pink and Say* (Civil War, multiethnic boy story)
  *The Trees of the Dancing Goats* (Christmas/Hanukkah)
  *The Bee Tree* (sometimes sweet things require work)

Visit Patricia Polacco at her website: www.PatriciaPolacco.com. There you will visit her studio and farmhouse in Michigan, and see what new books she's working on.

## HORSEFEATHERS, HOGWASH, AND HORNSWAGGLED!

These three terms are used when it is apparent that something is false. If you don't believe a statement, you can say, "Horsefeathers!" or "Hogwash!" but if you fall for it, you've been "Hornswaggled!"

These terms are not so common today as they once were, but they are fun to use and still carry the same meaning.

Students can make up TRUE/FALSE statements, but instead of using the word "false" they can use "horsefeathers" or "hogwash." Did they get "hornswaggled"? (See the Word Origins Section below for the term *hoodwink*.) (See Reproducible Activity Pages.)

# WORD ORIGINS AND SAYINGS*

In September we worked with sayings. During October we will be working with five unusual words and the origin of these words in an effort to build vocabulary and motivate students to be inquisitive about word origins. Once again, write one word per week on the chalkboard. Introduce it on Monday, and have students find out as much about the word as possible. Then, on Wednesday or Thursday, give them this explanation. Many new vocabulary words may be presented to the class with the explanations.

1. **gargoyle.** This word stems from the French word for "throat" or *gargouille,* which led to the English translation of gargoyle. It is from the thirteenth century, when architects and masons had the task of providing a means whereby rainwater could be diverted away from the walls under the roof of a cathedral or other edifice. Expert workers carved them and must have been amused by the ornamental, grotesque gargoyles that spewed forth water gushing from their throat.

   Check to see if there are any gargoyles on public buildings or atop cathedrals in your city. Students can design a gargoyle this week and learn the origin of the word.

2. **hedgehog.** The second part of the word, *hog,* refers to the swinelike appearance of the snout, but the animal is not a member of the swine species. In England it makes its home among the rows of hedges that line the streets, hence its name. It is a member of the porcupine family, and its French name is *herisson,* or "bristler." The term "porcupine" can be traced to the Latin *porcus spinosus,* or "thorny pig."

---
*Source: *Horsefeathers and Other Curious Words* by Charles Earle Funk.

As a bonus, can students discover the children's literature author and illustrator who has adopted the hedgehog as her symbol? He appears in her picture books, sometimes hiding in the borders, and can be found on her website. (*Answer:* Jan Brett. Hedgie can be seen on her website at www.janbrett.com.) If you have not contacted her website, be sure to do so. She has many materials for students that can be downloaded and reproduced. Check for the ABC and Number flashcards. Make sure to have a Jan Brett festival of children's books along with the word this week. Some to include are *The Mitten, The First Dog, Trouble With Trolls, The Hat, Berlioz the Bear,* among others.

3. **loophole.** A loop was a window in the late Middle Ages. Literally translated, this word means a very narrow "window hole." This tiny slit of a window on the outside was widened considerably inside and an archer could take aim from a broader range. Today we refer to a loophole as a way out, or an escape hatch, or even something that needs to be tracked down and fixed.

4. **hoodwink.** In the sixteenth century, the word *wink* meant to have one's eyes closed. When hoods on coats or cloaks became fashionable, if the hood fell forward over the eyes, a person became *hoodwinked* or blinded.

    Purse snatchers and thieves took advantage of this and pulled their hoods tight to disguise their appearance, and thus *hoodwinked* their victims. In games, such as Blindman's Bluff, some refer to putting a cloth over the eye as *hoodwink.*

    For indoor or outdoor recess, play an old-fashioned game of Blindman's Bluff.

5. **portmanteau.** In sixteenth-century France, a *portemanteau* was the officer who carried the king's cloak in a soft, leather case. Eventually, *portmanteau* became the name in England for the travel case itself.

    Poet Lewis Carroll added another meaning by coining two words and referring to them as a *portmanteau word.* For example, the word "chortle" came from "chuckle" and "snort."

    Students can enjoy playing with the language by coining their own portmanteau words—combining two words to make a new one. Have them print the two original words on the back of a tiny card, and the new word on the opposite side. This is often a springboard to creative poetry and writing.

# WRITING SKILLS

## WHEN DO YOU WRITE A BUSINESS LETTER?

A business letter is the term used for a formal letter that is written when you want to get information or share information. It can be a letter written to a company, a business, a government official, and so on. It is usually written to someone you do not know personally. The first thing you have to do is to establish a *purpose* for writing, and to write clearly and legibly. A letter that is sent in the mail represents the sender. This needs to be impressed upon students. Make a list on the chalkboard of possible reasons for sending a business letter.

Try to write a letter and actually mail it to a government agency, or the fire department, or the police department, or to someone in a position to answer specific questions that are brought up by the Science, Health, or Social Studies sections this month. When students receive a reply, it is an incentive to write more letters.

## WHEN DO YOU WRITE A FRIENDLY LETTER?

Students might want to write a letter to a relative in another city so they can share some information. Write to a friend or former classmate. Write to someone who is sick, wishing him or her well. Thank someone for a present you received.

Write a general friendly letter about your classroom at school and what is going on there. Fold the letters and put them into a shoebox that is made to look like a letter box. Then deliver the letters within the classroom. Students can answer the letter they received.

## HOW DO I KNOW WHERE TO WRITE THE INFORMATION?

Here is the format and diagram for a letter.

- Heading (upper right corner)
- Inside address (for business letter only)
- Greeting (on left)
- Body of letter (indent first line)
- Closing (lower right, in line with heading)
- Signature (directly under closing)

```
                                          Your street address
                            (HEADING)     City, State ZIP Code
                                          Date

Name
Street Address          (INSIDE ADDRESS)
City, State ZIP Code

Greeting (GREETING)

    _____

_____

_____(BODY OF LETTER)_____

_____

                                          _____ (CLOSING)

                                          _____ (SIGNATURE)
```

You do not need an inside address for a friendly letter. The other five sections remain the same.

# BECOME A WRITING MECHANIC

Letter writing is an excellent way to teach, and to practice, the "mechanics" of writing. Here is a starter kit for a good writing mechanic. Learn the terms, and also know when and how to use them:

| *Here's the Tool* | | *It's Use* |
|---|---|---|
| • | period | at the end of a sentence<br>after abbreviations |
| , | comma | between day and year (date)<br>between a city and state<br>after the greeting (friendly letter)<br>after the closing<br>throughout the body of letter |
| ? | question mark | at end of sentence when asking<br>    about or for something |
| , | apostrophe | in friendly letter only for<br>    informal use (I'll, aren't) |
| " " | quotation mark | before and after the title of<br>    a magazine article, and<br>    radio and television programs<br>before and after direct dialogue |
| ! | exclamation mark | when you wish to express<br>    emotion (joy, surprise) |

There are other tools used in writing, but these are some of the major ones that students will need to master in order to write a good letter.


# LET'S WRITE A FRIENDLY LETTER RIGHT NOW!

First, get ready. Distribute a lined sheet of paper to each student. You should have students make sure their pencils are sharp, they are sitting in an upright writing position, their paper is slanted in the correct direction, and they are holding the pencil correctly.

Using lined chart paper, or lines on the chalkboard, you can model the correct writing procedure while students observe. *They are not writing along with you, but, rather, they are watching.* Write the first line of the return address slowly and carefully. Then students can pick up their pencil and put a tiny dot on the lined sheet where they think the return address should begin. You will need to go around quickly and check each student before he or she begins writing the first line. Make any necessary adjustments for them in terms of line or spacing. After students have written the first line, have them put down their pencil.

Now model the second line. Then students write it on their own writing sheet. Do this line by line so that students get the benefit of your modeling and immediate feedback while they are in the process of writing.

Repeat this procedure until the letter is finished. This exercise can be done throughout the month. Take your time. Students are just learning. (See Reproducible Activity Pages.)

## CHILDREN'S BOOKS THAT INCLUDE "WRITING"

These books may be helpful to students in that they show how writing is developed: *How a Book Is Made* by Aliki; *Deadline, From News to Newspaper* by Gail Gibbons; and *If You Were a Writer* by Joan Lowery Nixon and illustrated by Bruce Degen.

Books that have writing as an integral part of the story include *Stringbean's Trip from Sea to Shining Sea* by Vera B. and Jennifer Williams; *Letters from Felix* by Annette Langen and Constanza Droop; and *The Jolly Postman or Other People's Letters* by Janet and Allan Ahlberg.

Be sure to have books of this type in your Writing Center from time to time to encourage and enliven student writing.

# SPEAKING SKILLS

## WE CAN RETELL AND WE CAN RESTATE

Give students an opportunity to retell a story that has just been read in class. For some students, this is easy; for others, it is difficult. Give students ample opportunity to do this throughout the month.

Students can also restate an announcement from the office that was just made on the intercom. Give them an opportunity to restate a short message that you read from a memo pad. (Note that retelling and restating are directly related to active listening. This activity will strengthen listening skills, especially when the students know they will have to verbally communicate information they just heard, using their own words.) Practice this skill often.

## SLOPPY SAYS, "CORRECT THIS SPEECH"

Make a game of correcting poor speech patterns, or sloppy speech. Two hand puppets would add some joy to the game. (Imagine a floppy, sloppy dog puppet correcting a toothy alligator puppet, or two parrot puppets engaged in conversation.) You can say something incorrectly and students can raise their hands to signify they want to correct it. Then everyone says it correctly. Some suggestions are as follows:

| SLOPPY TALK | CORRECT SPEECH |
|---|---|
| Where ya goin'? | Where are you going? |
| I'm speakin' to ya | I'm speaking to you |
| Cancha tell? | Can't you tell? |
| A drinka milk | A drink of milk |
| Gimme that | Give me that |
| Putcher shoes on | Put your shoes on |
| I like ta sing | I like to sing |
| Put it rii cher | Put it right here |
| I ain't goin' | I am not going |
| SHTrike one! | Strike one! |

## LEARNING HOW TO TAKE NOTES FOR RETELLING

For retelling and restating, give students an opportunity to learn how to take notes. This can be done using a videotape that can be played over and over. First, play it for one minute. Stop the tape and talk about what is going on. Write down a word or two to help jog the memory. Then continue the tape for another minute or two (depending upon the group). Stop the tape and, again, talk about what is going on. What are some "key" words that can be written down about this segment of the tape? Have students write them down, or "note" them.

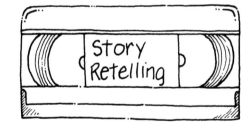

After a period of two more minutes, stop the tape. Give students an opportunity to write down a key word or two.

Next, ask students to retell what went on in the tape so far, using their own words. When they all concur, check the key words they have written down. Now, rewind and replay the tape for five minutes. Then stop it. Are they satisfied with their retelling or restating from the notes they took? Discuss this.

Continue with the tape and run it for two minutes. This is a long time when students are just learning to take notes. After the two minutes, turn off the videotape and discuss the words and the summary that students wrote down.

Encourage students to take notes when watching a TV program, when listening to someone read aloud, or when listening to the principal address the school over the intercom system. *This activity involves active listening, writing, speaking, and reading* of material written by the student. It points out, once again, the interrelationship of the Language Arts and how one cannot be easily separated from the other.

Focus upon this skill repeatedly during the months ahead. It will serve students well once they learn how to take notes. They are actually sifting information for the *main idea.*

## SIFTING FOR INFORMATION

Using the analogy of sifting through a great deal of information to get the main idea, do the following activity. Set up a box with sand and a hand sifter. Place tiny pebbles with words on them in the sand. Have students scoop up sand in the sifter and carefully shake it back into the box. They

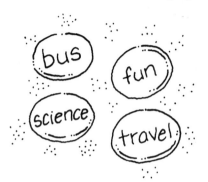

should have some pebbles left with words on them. What "message" can they get from these pebble words? Explain it in their own words. Then mix up the sand and pebbles and try again.

Explain to students that taking notes is like sifting. The grains of sand represent all of the words they heard. The pebbles represent the important words, the key words, the main idea. This kinesthetic activity may be most helpful for a number of students. It could enable them to understand the purpose for taking notes. Encourage students to contribute pebbles and words to the box.

## MORE SIFTING

Another activity that gets results is to put "miniatures" in the sand. These can be miniature trucks, cars, people, animals, fruits, and vegetables. Have students sift carefully. When they have several of these miniatures together, what can they tell about each one? Can they weave them together in a story?

If you have a map of the community, where would these miniature items be placed? This draws map skills into your storytelling and conversation.

## DRAW AND TELL

Make a cassette tape recording that gives descriptions or directions. It can be directions for procedure during a fire drill, proper behavior in the lunch room, procedure to follow on the playground, and so on. Then have students make a diagram or picture or map of the information they just heard. From this, have students verbally relay the information to the class, or to you, or to a study buddy. This activity will appeal to the aural learner and visual learner, and will strengthen those two modes of communication for everyone. Note that the speaking is preceded by listening and writing in this activity.

# LISTENING SKILLS

## SELECT A TITLE

Read a short paragraph or a short story to the class or a small group. Then read three possible titles for this work. Have students select the one they think goes best with the information. They will need to listen carefully to the information in order to make a wise selection.

This can also be done with a newspaper article. Read it aloud and have students write a short, clipped headline. They can read their headline aloud. Then show them the one that the newspaper reporter selected for the story.

## THE RODNEYVILLE PUMPKIN SHOW

Read this aloud to students and tell them that you will ask them questions about this story at the end.

"Every year in Rodneyville there is a pumpkin show and festival on the third weekend in October. One event that draws huge crowds is the weighing in of the pumpkins. The biggest pumpkin to date weighed 300 pounds. People come from miles around to buy and taste the pumpkin treats, such as pumpkin burgers, pumpkin pie, pumpkin cake, pumpkin cookies, pumpkin waffles, pumpkin pancakes, pumpkin ice cream, and pumpkin muffins. They have pumpkin-carving contests and every hour they give prizes for the funniest and the most beautiful pumpkins. They crown a Pumpkin Princess, but an orange buggy labeled The Pumpkin Coach wisks the princess away before the clock strikes the hour."

Ask these questions to see how well students could remember the facts, as they listened attentively:

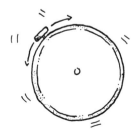

1. Where does the show and festival take place? (*Rodneyville*)
2. What month? (*October*)
3. Is there a specific date? (*the third weekend in October*)
4. Name three foods you can buy. (*see pumpkin treats above*)
5. Who is crowned? (*Pumpkin Princess*)
6. For what do they give prizes? (*carved pumpkins*)
7. What does "The Pumpkin Coach" look like? (*an orange buggy*)
8. How much did the biggest pumpkin weigh? (*300 pounds*)

Explain to students that sometimes we only hear a story once, so we need to train ourselves to listen attentively so that we can recall the facts. This often happens on a radio program. Then when we tell someone about what we heard, we need to have our facts straight. Also, newspaper reporters sometimes hear information only once and then have to report it. So, let's sharpen our listening skills.

## ATTENTIVE LISTENING

Many students need practice, and more practice, with this type of listening. Attentive listening means listening for specific information. Talk with students about sharpening this listening skill. Have a discussion about when they would be especially in need of this skill. Here are six ideas to help get you started:

- what the teacher says when giving fire drill instructions
- what parents say when they drop you off at a friend's house
- what parents say when you are going to a performance in a theater
- what the vet tells you to do for your sick pet
- what the doctor suggests you do to prevent a cold
- what the bus driver says when you ask for directions

After you finish reading this list, ask students to repeat as many of these six suggestions as they can remember. Then discuss these six ideas and have students share information about times when they did learn by attentive listening.

At least once per week do an attentive listening exercise with the class. They require this skill which takes practice.

## A SOUND STORY

Give students a sound to associate with each story character. Then when the story is read aloud, the students can listen for the *key word* and say the sound out loud briefly while the story is continued. This does train students to focus their attention.

The cast of characters and sounds can be written on a story chart. The entire class can say the sounds. Later, when they are more familiar with the story, assign four or five students to say the sound for each character. Rotate these assigned roles so that students will have to listen for another character before saying a sound. Then remove the story chart sounds and see if students can remember the sounds by heart without looking at the words. This gives the class a variety of listening exercises to do with this silly story, and they enjoy hearing the chorus of voices and sounds.

| *Characters* | *Sounds* |
| --- | --- |
| Queen Emmaline | Oh! Oh! |
| Prince Albertine | Hmmmmm |
| Princess Clairbert | Ay, yi, yi |
| Frog Winneborg | Poof! |
| Brass Bell | Clang! |
| Mosquito | Z-z-z-z |

### QUEEN EMMALINE AND FROG WINNEBORG

One sunny day, Queen Emmaline (**"Oh! Oh!"**) was gardening under the lilac trees, when Frog Winneborg (**"Poof!"**) appeared from out of the blue. "Get out of my garden," demanded Queen Emmaline (**"Oh! Oh!"**). "Oh, but Queen Emmaline (**"Oh! Oh!"**)," said Frog Winneborg (**"Poof!"**), "I, Frog Winneborg (**"Poof!"**) am a good friend of Prince Albertine (**"Hmmmm"**) and Princess Clairbert (**"Ay, yi, yi"**).

"You don't say!" said Queen Emmaline (**"Oh! Oh!"**). "I'll have you know that my dears, Prince Albertine (**"Hmmmm"**) and Princess Clairbert (**"Ay, yi, yi"**) would never play with a mere Frog Winneborg (**"Poof!"**). "Well," demanded Frog Winneborg (**"Poof!"**), "why don't you ask Prince Albertine (**"Hmmmm"**) and Princess Clairbert (**"Ay, yi, yi"**)." "I shall do that at once," sniffed Queen Emmaline (**"Oh! Oh!"**).

Then Queen Emmaline (**"Oh! Oh!"**) rang a brass bell (**"Clang!"**) and it sounded all over the garden and the kingdom. It was a signal to Prince Albertine (**"Hmmmm"**) and Princess Clairbert (**"Ay, yi, yi!"**) to come running, which they did.

Queen Emmaline (**"Oh! Oh!"**) demanded to know if they knew this critter, this muddy frog that called itself Frog Winneborg (**"Poof!"**). Before Princess Clairbert

("**Ay, yi, yi**") and Prince Albertine ("**Hmmmm**") could answer, Frog Winneborg ("**Poof!**") was stung by a giant mosquito ("**Z-z-z-z**") and jumped so high in the air that he landed on Queen Emmaline ("**Oh! Oh!**") and kissed her right on the lips! At that, Frog Winneborg ("**Poof!**") went poof and was changed into the long lost King Albertclaire of Winneborg, the husband of Queen Emmaline ("**Oh! Oh!**"), who had just fainted and landed in the mud. But, thanks to that mosquito ("**Z-z-z-z**"), they all lived happily ever after. THE END.

## SETTING A MOOD FOR LISTENING

During the last week of October, read holiday stories in the semi-darkness. Gather everyone in a circle. Draw the shades, turn off the lights, and use a great big flashlight to shine on the book page as you read aloud. Show the illustrations by flashlight, too. What a treat! It will get the attention of students and they'll be quiet listeners.

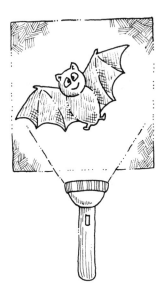

## STORYBOOK TREATS

When reading a book about apples, serve an apple treat. When reading a book about a particular food, see if you can incorporate that food into the experience as a treat for good listening. If, for example, you are reading a book about apples or Johnny Appleseed, serve apple slices. It won't be costly if students get mouse-size bites.

## LISTEN TO POETRY

Some poetry invites listening, and the book that you can count on for this is Shel Silverstein's *Where the Sidewalk Ends.* It is the one poetry book that teachers, librarians, parents, and students seem to know and yet never tire of. So, settle back with a good dose of poetry that students will sit still for and will listen to. By third grade, many of them will have their favorite poem in this book and will request it.

There are many other delightful poets such as Jack Prelutsky, Myra Cohn Livingstone, David McCord, and others too numerous to mention. During Poetry Month in our April Authors section, we will salute poet J. Patrick Lewis, among others. Meanwhile, a good anthology of children's poems is entitled *Sing a Song of Popcorn,* edited by Beatrice Schenk deRegniers and illustrated by many Caldecott Award-winning artists.

# FOCUS ON SPELLING

## ABC ORDER

Put the spelling words in alphabetical order. When two words begin with the same letter, instruct or remind students to go to the second letter for ABC order. Students can write each word three times.

## CREATING SPELLING SENTENCES

Make up a sentence using all of the spelling words. Try a sentence that makes sense; then one that is a silly sentence; and one that is a spooky Halloween sentence.

## ORANGE-AND-BLACK SPELLING

Write spelling words with black marking pen on orange paper in the shape of a pumpkin. At the Writing Center, students can cut out other Halloween shapes, such as a pointed hat, cat, witch, broom, and practice writing their words on these shapes. Make a Halloween Spelling Book for the week and learn to spell some holiday words also.

## SPELLING BUDDIES

Have students pair up this week with a spelling buddy to practice writing and saying the words. Spelling buddies can change from week to week.

## SPELLING BINGO

Give each student a Spelling Bingo blank grid. (See Reproducible Activity Pages.) They can write the spelling words of their choice, taken from the list for the month of October, in the spaces. Each card will be different. Cut out orange and black paper squares to cover up the words when they are called out. Play the game with the entire group for review. Small groups of students enjoy playing this game, too.

## HOT ON THE TRAIL OF BIGFOOT

Students can trace their two shoes on paper, cut them out, and write their spelling words on these shoe shapes. Then fasten these "footprints" to the upper part of their shoes using a paper clip, or a tiny wooden clothespin, or a rubber band. They can wear these on their feet for half a day and then remove them. Spellers who get all words correct on their final test on Friday can tack these shoe shapes onto a cutout of a "big foot" made for this purpose.

Why "Bigfoot"? See if students can "track down" information at the library about this real or imaginary creature of the wilds. This is the month of spooks, and goblins, so let's include a spelling Bigfoot.

# FOCUS ON MATH

## FLASHCARDS

Work with flashcards daily for rote memorization. Have students make their own sets and work with them independently or with a partner. Periodically make math computation headbands and students will see the computations throughout the day.

## USING THE MEMORIZED FACTS, WITH DISCUSSION

Memorizing the facts is not an end in itself. Students need to *use* the facts so that memorization is being done for a purpose.

Here is an example: Ask five students how many brothers and sisters they have. As these numbers are given to you, write them on the chalkboard. Suppose these are your numbers: 2, 1, 2, 3, 2. Write them vertically. Then have students add them up, on their own. Ask for the answer. (10).

Now for the discussion. Ask students how they added to get the answer. You will find a variety of methods here. These are some possibilities:

- "I added them in order."
- "I saw three 2's and said 6, then plus 1 is 7, and 7+3 is 10."
- "I saw 1+3 and that makes 4. Then I added by two's and said 6, 8, 10."
- "I see 2+1+3 and that makes 6. Two more 2's is 4, and 6 plus 4 is 10."

## DISCUSSING THE PROCESS

Talking through the procedure above is valuable to all students because they see that there are many ways to add the same five numbers. Some may have never thought of a different way before the discussion.

Put another five numbers on the chalkboard and ask students to add them up. Again, talk it over and see how many different ways students arrive at the same answer. Point out to them that they are using their addition facts.

Some students get hooked on this five-number procedure and like to see how many ways they can reach the same answer. Working with a partner is most helpful. Adding seven numbers makes another challenge. Some students like to work up to nine numbers in the column. (See Reproducible Activity Pages.)

Keep discussing "math solutions" throughout the year. When students are working in small groups, always ask them to report on how they arrived at their answer. At this time, everyone is instructed and expected to listen very carefully to the procedure being described.

## QUILT PATTERNS

One good way to work art into patterns is through quilt designs. Students can go through picture books checking for quilt patterns. Some excellent resource books are: *Eight Hands Round, A*

*Patchwork Alphabet* by Ann Whitford Paul, with illustrations by Jeanette Winter; *The Seasons Sewn, A Year in Patchwork* by Ann Whitford Paul, with illustrations by Michael McCurdy; *Patchwork Tales* by Susan L. Roth and Ruth Phang; and *Stitching Stars, The Story Quilts of Harriet Powers* by Mary E. Lyons.

## WORKING WITH GEOMETRIC SHAPES: MAKING QUILT PATTERNS

When creating quilt patterns, students can gain practice working with squares and triangles to make repeat designs. First, you will need to cut an abundance of 1- by 1-inch squares of various colored construction paper. When cut on the diagonal, this becomes a triangle. Give students squares of paper that are 3- by 3-inch. Then, just for practice, have them create a bird on one square, a tree on another square, and something of their own choosing on another square. Paste them down.

Students need to see the picture books mentioned above, or others on quilts, in order to be comfortable with triangular trees and birds. Other names for quilt designs in squares are: schoolhouse, flying geese, necktie, kite's tail, corn and beans, north star, and bear's paw. Have students think in terms of color and pattern.

When students have decided on a pattern and on the color, they can draw it on graph paper and then color it in as the first step.

Next, they can use the one-inch squares again to create their design on a sheet of paper. (See Reproducible Activity Pages.)

## PROBLEM SOLVING FOR THE QUILT FRAME

Take a sheet of 9- by 12-inch paper. Pretend this is the blank quilt. Now we have to section off the squares. Students can use their rulers to mark off every third inch along the top and bottom (3", 6") and draw a connecting line. How many lines will be drawn vertically? (2) How many from side to side? (4, connecting at 3", 6", 9") How many squares will there be all together? (12)

Some students may need help with this in order to have an exact measurement, so make sure you are circulating around the room to offer assistance. Depending upon the group, you may want to do this with small groups of students to get started.

Once students have their square shapes on the page, they can use their sketched design to help make the pattern. They can print lightly on each square exactly what is going to go there, or use an "A,B" notation.

Direct students not to paste anything down in a square until they are sure it belongs there. If a student should paste something down in the wrong square, it can be covered with a clean white square.

When quilts are finished, have students name them. Frame them with construction paper and display them in the classroom. They make a lovely quilt bulletin board.

## PUMPKIN MATH

During this month and next, work with pumpkins in the classroom in both Math and Science. Use a cloth measuring tape and measure the circumference of the pumpkins. Are they alike or different? Will the small ones have as many seeds as the larger ones?

Only you must handle the knife to cut the circular top (or hat). You will need newspapers on the floor and containers to hold the seeds. Students can take turns scooping out the seeds with their hands or with a long-handled spoon. Keep the seeds from each pumpkin in a separate container and wash off the excess pulp. Then spread them out to dry. Next, place them back in their clean containers.

**Estimation:** Make estimation sheets and have each student sign up. After examining the seeds and sifting through them with their hands, decide *how many* there are and write that number on the sheet. When all have done their estimations, it's time for the next step.

**Counting:** Count the number of seeds in each pumpkin. Students can count them by 1, 2, 5, and 10. Anyone close? How many overestimated? Underestimated?

**Books:** Make books in the shape of an orange circular pumpkin to show the growth of a pumpkin from seed to pumpkin. The final surprise page can show a pumpkin dessert (pie, cake, cookies, ice cream). (See Reproducible Activity Pages.)

## MORE WORK WITH ESTIMATION

Throughout the year have students estimate numbers from things available in the environment (buttons, paper clips, rubber bands, and so on). Some students consistently overestimate, while others consistently underestimate. They need to keep a record of the "under" and "over" categories so they can work on improving their skills in this area. This is where working in groups is helpful when students are talking through the process. The thought processes of the student who is closer to the target needs to be "heard" by the others.

## LET'S USE MATH TO BAKE MARY J.'S PUMPKIN CAKE

When there is a chance to cook in the classroom, it provides an excellent opportunity for math learning. This is a recipe for baking a pumpkin cake.* Many students have not been involved with the process of baking a cake "from scratch." In the home, they may either use box cake mixes or buy a cake at the grocery store.

Where does the math come in? People who bake and cook need to be *accurate* with math. They use dry and liquid measures, count, and handle measuring tools. They preheat the oven and the reading of the temperature is measured in degrees. The cake is baked for a prescribed period of time, so the baker has to have one eye on the clock or use a dependable timer. The cake has to cool for a pre-

---

*Be aware of any food allergies students may have.

scribed period of time before icing can be added, or the icing will melt (so we need to be patient). Also, the baker needs to make the icing, and this calls for more liquid and dry measurement.

**MARY J.'S PUMPKIN CAKE**

You will need:

| | |
|---|---|
| 2 cups sugar | 4 eggs |
| 1½ cups salad oil | 2 cups flour |
| 1 can pumpkin (2 cups) | 1 teaspoon salt |
| 2 teaspoons baking soda | 1 cup walnuts or pecans |
| 3 teaspoons cinnamon | an oblong cake pan (9 by 12) |

Combine all of the above ingredients and mix well! (You can add them in the order listed.) Bake in a 350-degree oven for one hour. Remove from oven. Let cool before icing.

**ICING**

1 pound powdered sugar

1 stick butter or margarine

1 cream cheese, 6- or 8-oz. package

1 teaspoon vanilla

chopped walnuts or pecans (optional)

Mix well. Spread over cool cake. Spread chopped nuts over the top of the icing. Enjoy this delicious cake!

## MORE MATH WITH MARY J.

The cake is ready to eat. The paper plates and napkins have been counted and set aside. Plastic forks have been placed on the plates. Now, how many students are there? How many pieces of cake will we cut? Don't forget the teacher! Do we want to include the principal or the custodian? It depends on how large we make the slices, doesn't it? This is a good "problem solving" situation.

Once the decision is made (and this can be worked out on a diagram or a grid), you handle the knife. Cake is served. *We do not begin to eat until everyone is served, seated, and ready.* This is an etiquette rule that can be taught along with the serving of the cake. It applies to all situations, especially when we are invited to someone else's home to eat and when being served in a restaurant. Now, *bon appétit* (French). Ummm! *Delicioso* (Spanish).

# FOCUS ON SOCIAL STUDIES

## OCTOBER CITIZENSHIP FOCUS

This month, in this classroom, the trait that concerns all of us is *dependability*. Be sure students understand the meaning of the term. Do you keep your word? Do you do what you say you will do? Do you "follow through"? Can we count on you?

## THESAURUS CHALLENGE

This month we have an opportunity to use one of the resources referred to in the September Reading section, the thesaurus. Using copies of different thesaurus books, see how many synonyms students can find for *dependability*. Be sure to give them time to list them on their pages in their Citizenship Folder.

## ROLE-PLAY

Students at this age like to be engaged in role-play, and many groups learn in this way as an alternative to sitting and listening. Set the ground rules so that students will take this seriously. You need good listeners and a spirit of cooperation to engage in this activity. First, use the concepts that the class worked on in September. Then go on to the October good citizen trait of dependability.

Situation One: (*You tell what the action will be, set the scene as narrator, oversee the action, and make judgments. Thus, you are very much a part of the role-playing situation and not merely a facilitator.*)

One designated student acts as teacher and one acts as the student. The rest of the class is attentively and quietly watching and listening, but they do not leave their seats. They do not make any comments at this time.

The student portraying the teacher is getting ready to accompany the class to the lunchroom. (This person pretends to line up the class and "exits" to a corner with them.) Then the designated student returns because he/she forgot his/her lunch box, and goes directly to the lunch box area and takes one. Then the student looks around and heads toward the teacher's desk, opens a drawer, and takes toy money from the drawer that is kept in a box there for those students who need to borrow lunch money. The student hurries out to join the group.

**Discussion:** Make sure students come to the conclusion that this is not an *honest* act. The money does not belong to that student and it is wrong to take it. It may not be missed now, but it could deprive someone of borrowing lunch money. It is an act of *disrespect,* and this person is not *trustworthy.* (Concepts we worked on last month.) This is not a *dependable* person. (Do not leave students with the idea that it is "cool" to get away with something like this.) Keep reinforcing the students who are voicing objections to the behavior of the student who is out of line.

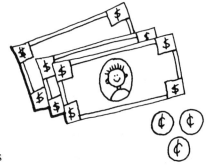

**How does a person change?** In order to give students some ideas for options to atone for this behavior, it is wise to talk about what the students can do to ease their conscience, to make amends, and to try to make the situation right again.

Situation Two: It is time for gym. Two boys were not prompt about getting ready, and are still straightening their area and putting on gym shoes. The teacher says she will take the class to gym

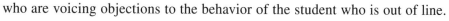

and be right back. She asks if she can *depend* on them. They say that she can. When left alone, they begin to play rough indoors. In an attempt to be funny, one boy picks up an eraser and throws it at the other boy and knocks over the fishbowl. It comes crashing to the floor. What should the boys do now? What is the *honest* thing to do?

**Discussion:** What can the boys do to show they are *honest? trustworthy? dependable?* Discuss these issues:

- Should they admit the problem right away?
- Can they be expected to replace the fish bowl?
- Should parents be notified? (yes)

Can we teach them to be dependable? Would it help to:

- Have them replace the fish? (Will this work?)
- Put them in charge of feeding the new fish? (Will this work?)
- Put them in charge of cleaning the fishbowl? (Will this work?)
- Put them in charge of burial for Chester and Perky, the two fish who expired? (Will this work?)

What can they do to show *respect* for the classroom?

- Offer to help do extra things that they initiate.
- Take on extra responsibilities for a week.
- Apologize to the class—a verbal or written statement.

For these situations, have the students discuss them, work out solutions, and then role-play the solutions. Students can come up with more discussion situations for the month of October.

You must take an active role in this experience and serve as the voice of experience and the role model. Never let students think that aberrant (*turning away from what is right*) behavior is "cute." Squelch that notion. Remember, students follow the strongest leader, and if it isn't the teacher, then it is the student(s) who is acting out. Left unchecked, the class as a whole will begin to show disrespect. Tread carefully but purposefully. Students respect a strong teacher leader.

# PATRIOTISM

## WHAT ARE OUR GIFTS OF NATURE?

Some areas of our country have waterfalls that generate power for electricity, such as Niagara Falls, New York. But other cities have waterfalls, too. Where is the nearest one in your city? Other gifts of nature include coal, iron ore, clay, shale, fields of rich soil for growing food, forests, woodlands, quarries, ponds, lakes, and so on.

Perhaps students haven't thought about these natural wonders as "gifts of nature" and just take them for granted. It's time to begin to have some lessons in appreciation of our wonderful country and its riches. Along with this, teach students the song "America, the Beautiful":

*Oh, beautiful for spacious skies,*
*For amber waves of grain,*
*For purple mountain magesties*
*Above the fruited plain.*
*America! America!*
*God shed His grace on thee,*
*And crown thy good with brotherhood*
*From sea to shining sea.*

## NATURAL WONDERS

Our national parks are national treasures, and students need to know that if they live near one, they are indeed fortunate. We can always find out more information about areas even if they are right in our own backyard. Contact the National Park Service for brochures that contain pictures and factual information.

Some impressive natural wonders are listed below. Have students locate these on the map. Which one do they live closest to? Check to see if students have visited any of these sites. Add more to the list.

| | |
|---|---|
| Grand Canyon (AZ) | Howe Caverns (NY) |
| Carlsbad Caverns (NM) | Niagara Falls (NY) |
| Everglades (FL) | Cape Cod (MA) |
| Glaciers (AK) | Painted Desert (NM) |
| Great Rocky Mountains (west) | Yosemite Falls (CA) |
| Appalachian Mountains (east) | The Palisades (NJ) |

Obtain copies of maps of your area. How close are you to the nearest natural wonder; perhaps right in your own backyard?

# AREA OF FOCUS: OUR CITY

## CONTINUE THE CITY STUDY—CULTURE

There are more opportunities for your city study. For example, what is the cultural climate of your city in terms of the following:

- museums
- science center
- zoo

- art gallery
- planetarium
- college

- theaters
- conservatory
- symphony or band

For small towns, find out where the closest cultural centers are in relation to the topics listed above. Find out if a field trip is feasible.

## TRANSPORTATION IN THE CITY

How do people get around? Is there a taxi service, busses, streetcars, subway system, rail system? How far away is the nearest airport? What is its name? How do students get around? What transportation system have they had experience with? This is a good opportunity to make a Transportation Graph.

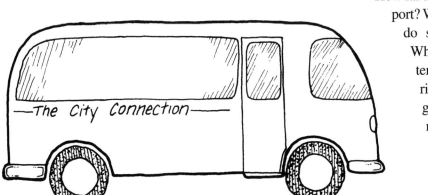

## SIRENS AND BELLS

What are these for? Where are they located in our city? Is there a warning system in place if there is a weather alert? How can we find out the answers to some of these questions? (Write a letter to the meteorologist at the local news station. Write a letter to the city council or the mayor's office.)

## TOURIST ATTRACTIONS

If visitors were coming to your city, where would you want to be sure to take them? Students can make Travel Posters for their fair city.

## SPOT TOURIST ANNOUNCEMENT

Students can engage in some role-play. They can pretend to be a public relations person and do a one-minute spot announcement on TV to try to entice people to visit the city.

## TRAVEL BROCHURE

Collect travel brochures so that students know what they look like. (Many hotels and motels have them in their office. They are also available at rest stops along thruways, and often through the local Chamber of Commerce.) Have students make some for their city. Collaborate or work together in groups of three for this interesting project.

# HOLIDAYS AND CELEBRATIONS

## HOLIDAY WINDSOCKS

Students can work in groups to make windsocks for the holidays this month. Hang them from the ceiling in a corner of the room, or decorate the door with them.

## COLUMBUS DAY

This federal holiday is usually the second Monday in October. Christopher Columbus sailed for the government of Spain under the rulership of King Ferdinand and Queen Isabella in 1492. There were many Native Americans—people Columbus called Indians—here at the time he landed. So the question of "discovering" America is being debated, but Columbus certainly did open the way for trade and immigration from Europe to the Americas.

In Latin America this day is called Dia de la Raza (Day of the Race). Young children climb into decorated cardboard boxes that represent the Niña, Piñta, and Santa Maria, and shuffle from one side of the room to another in a reenactment of the voyage.

This provides an opportunity for students to make large boat boxes for a race, or just to sit in one for a quiet reading opportunity.

## UNITED NATIONS DAY

This organization, established in 1945, has its headquarters in New York City. The organization works toward world peace, and has many projects to help nations in need. On October 24, many students collect money for UNICEF (United Nations International Children's Emergency Fund).

The UN flag is light blue with the Earth, in white, as viewed from the North Pole centered in the middle. Students can locate the flag in magazines this month, and become familiar with it and its purpose.

## HALLOWEEN

The early settlers did not celebrate this holiday. It is believed that the Irish and Scots (Celts) brought the "trick or treat" custom to the USA and Canada. In ancient days, it was believed that spirits roamed the Earth on Halloween, October 31, and people had to disguise themselves so as not to be recognized. In France, children went begging for flowers to decorate the graves of relatives and friends. Mexico has a national celebration at this time, and families set out food on the doorstep for dead relatives who come back to visit in spirit form.

Jack-o'-lanterns were first made in Ireland. They were carved from turnips, gourds, or beets and used to light the way at night. Eventually it became the custom to carve the faces in pumpkins at

Halloween because of the abundance of these orange, gourd-like fruits with many seeds at this time of year. (Pumpkins eventually rot, wither, and die, whereas gourds can be dried and painted and used as decorations. They can be cut in half and used as drinking cups or for dipping water. In days of old, gourds became candle holders for night lights and were used well into the winter months.)

Today children and many families see this as a festive time for dressing up in costumes and going door to door for "trick or treats." Parties include such games as bobbing for apples that are floating in a big tub of water. Also, a three-legged race is fun. Two children stand side by side and stick out the leg closer to their partner. Then a clothesline is used to tie their legs together, so two legs become one. Then at a signal they race across a field. The winning team is the one who is the fastest.

Dolls can be made from corn husks, and ornaments from wheat. This is the time for making dried apple doll heads. Peel the skin, carve the features, and let the apple dry and wrinkle. Then, using sticks as a frame, dress the boy or girl doll and make a hat, too.

## CHILDREN'S MAGAZINE MONTH

Check out the website  www.edpress.org. Also, encourage students to check out magazines at the local library and to share the information with the class. Find *Crinkles, Girl's Life, Boy's Life, Odyssey,* and *Spider.*

## WHITE HOUSE FALL GARDEN TOURS (NATION'S CAPITAL)

Check the website for the White House for information regarding this annual event: www.whitehouse.gov.

# FOCUS ON SCIENCE

### SET UP A WEATHER STATION

Create an area in the classroom specifically designed for weather news. Books on all types of weather, graphs and graph paper, and newspapers that have maps and graphs showing the weather across the state in which you live are valuable tools.

Also, begin to track weather in other parts of the world. Use newspapers, such as *USA Today,* that have full pages devoted to weather. Select three cities in three different areas of the country, and keep track of the temperatures for the month. Record the high's and low's. Continue to work with weather news and information throughout the year.

In some areas, TV weather reporters will come to your classroom and talk about weather and leave equipment for your use. Then they'll check back with you periodically for weather readings in your area. Call the local TV station to see if such a program is available in your city.

## WEATHER AFFECTS PEOPLE

As the days grow cooler and shorter in many parts of the country, there are changes in the clothing that people wear and in the amount of time they spend outdoors. Ask students to determine the amount of time spent outdoors in summer activities and in autumn activities. We may see the need to shift to some daily indoor exercise.

Have a stair-step in the classroom so that students can step up and down a certain number of times daily. Keep a checklist. If possible, have an exercise bicycle in the classroom. The cycle can be used as a reward for good work in a curricular area, or a good test score, or for a display of good citizenship, or as a reward for a student who is making an extra effort to study and learn. Students can earn 2 minutes, 3 minutes, 4 minutes, or 5 minutes on the cycle. The cycle needs to be carefully monitored and managed by you. It is a "hands off" item.

## SEEDS ARE "GOING TO THE DOGS"

Many plants produce seeds, and in autumn there is an abundance of seeds. Many seeds need a get-away spot so they can become embedded in the ground. Some seeds have burrs and can hitch a ride on a dog's furry tail or leg, and some hitch a ride on people's clothing as they tramp in the woods or along trails.

Maple leaves produce a winged seed that is propelled along by the wind. Some people call these seeds "nature's helicopters." When these wings begin to appear, students can locate the ones that have been propelled farthest from the tree. Use a ruler to measure the distance. Some land as far away as over a hundred feet. The farther away they get, the better chance they have to take root. Otherwise, if they fall under the tree and stay there, they will not get enough sun and nourishment.

Students can bring in maple helicopter seeds and during outdoor recess devise ways to see how far they can make them twirl and travel.

## THE TUMBLING TUMBLEWEED

This whole plant travels along in the wind. It's a self-contained traveling plant and carries its seeds with it. In the autumn when the seeds mature, the mother plant scatters them to the winds. Each plant produces over a million seeds.

An excellent resource for the study of seeds is *The Reason for a Flower* by Ruth Heller. It is a picture science book, told in rhyme, with colorful illustrations. In this lovely book the reader learns that "the reason for a FLOWER is to manufacture . . . seeds."

## COLLECT SEEDS FOR PROJECTS

Students can collect seeds from nature. Have containers available so students can categorize them by color, shape, size. If you have enough, you can make seed pictures, or a collage of seeds, or even seed designs. First, draw a rough sketch of a design. Then draw the design on a sheet of 9- by 12-inch construction paper. Use thin glue and spread it on a section at a time. Carefully place the seeds on top of the glued area and press down. Lay flat to dry. (**Tip:** Using a colored paper plate as a background makes a nice frame for a seed collage, and encourages students to work in a circular design.)

## MUSICAL INSTRUMENTS WITH SEEDS

*You will need:* heavy-duty small paper plates, a variety of seeds (rice, nuts, peas, beans, lentils), glue, and markers.

*Procedure:* Place several seeds on different paper plates. Then turn a clean paper plate upside down on each plate that has seeds. Glue the edges together and allow to dry thoroughly. When dry, staple the edges and use colored markers to decorate the plates with colorful autumn designs. Students can shake the seed instruments in time to a variety of tunes. Listen for the different sounds they make.

## SEEDS ARE STORED FOOD

Rather than plant seeds in the ground, we can eat seeds. For example, bread, muffins, and cakes are made from wheat and corn that have been ground or mashed to make flour or meal. Let students experience grinding or mashing seeds.

Ask parents to send in favorite recipes using seeds (rice, corn, wheat, and so on). Compile the recipes and make a class "Seed Recipe Book." We can expand the seed menu to include things like rice pudding, corn relish, and cereal dishes.

## AUTUMN HARVEST AND MARKETS

Harvest celebrations take place all over the world. This is a rich month for bringing in a "farmer's market" to your Science table.

A good book to help you with the study of markets in general is *Market!* by Ted Lewin. In this diverse book, we see markets all over the globe. We travel to the outdoor markets of Ecuador, Nepal, Ireland (horse market), U.S.A. (fish market in New York City), and Moroccan markets with donkey parking lots. It's a grand adventure!

Send a note home to parents explaining that you are having a country market table for science investigation. Perhaps they would be willing to send in something for it, such as a huge cabbage head, or gourds with unusual bumps and designs, or a large stalk with brussel sprouts growing off the sides so that students can see how these vegetables actually grow, and how they appear in their natural state.

This calls for weighing; classifying by size, shape, color; and cooking and tasting some of the vegetables.

What does a rich purple eggplant taste like? What does a waxy rutabaga taste like? Let's cook them and find out. (A little nutmeg or allspice lightly sprinkled on any cooked, fresh vegetable does wonders for the taste.)

## SPEAKING OF TASTING

Have a large mirror in class and encourage students to take a good look at their tongue. (Discourage the use of hands for this activity.) Or, work with small groups and students can use hand mirrors. They can stick out their tongue and see the bumpy "taste buds." In the very back of the tongue, the buds can detect bitter and sour tastes. Sweet taste bud detectives are along each side and toward the middle, and the whole tongue is used for discovering salty tastes and cheesy tastes.

Plan to have small morsels of food that represent the five types of taste, and let students put their taste buds to work.

| | | |
|---|---|---|
| Salty—pretzels | Sweet—cookie | Cheesy—cheese slice |
| Sour—pickles | Bitter—lemon drop | |

(See Reproducible Activity Pages.)

## PROBLEM SOLVING WITH SCARECROWS

For centuries farmers have tried ways to scare birds, especially crows, away from their crops so that they would have enough to harvest for their family or to take to market. The scarecrow, a figure flopping in the breeze, has evolved from culture to culture. The sudden movement scares away birds. A good resource is *The Scarecrow Book* by James Giblin and Dale Ferguson.

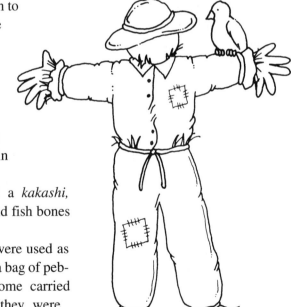

In Ancient Greece, wooden figures were put in the fields with cloths draped around them that blew in the breeze.

In Japan, farmers made a scarecrow called a *kakashi,* which means a bad smell. They hung rags, meat, and fish bones from a stick and placed it in the field.

In Germany, young boys of peasant families were used as "bird scarers." They roamed through the fields with a bag of pebbles and stones that they threw at the birds. Some carried wooden clappers to scare off the birds. Later, they were replaced with scarecrows, more like the ones we know today.

Native American Indians hung dead crows from long poles to scare off crows.

Early settlers from Europe who came to America made scarecrows from old clothing, and hung bones from them to rattle in the wind. The Dutch used the term *bootzamon,* or boogeyman, for their scarecrows. (See Reproducible Activity Pages.)

Students can make their own version of a scarecrow and name it. They can bring in old clothes which can be stuffed with either straw or newspaper that has been crinkled up. Use old gloves and shoes and a straw hat. What will be used for the head? A real pumpkin? A paper bag with a face painted on it? The scarecrow can be propped up or made to sit on the floor in a cozy reading area. The class can decide on a name for their scarecrow and read stories to it.

## SOMETIMES SOLVING ONE PROBLEM CREATES ANOTHER

When crows became scarce in number, creepy crawly bugs began to eat away at crops. These were bugs that the crows ate. Were farmers any further ahead? Discuss the concept of solving one problem and creating another.

The scarecrow was eventually replaced with chemicals like DDT. These chemicals were sprayed on seeds before they were planted, and the crops were dusted with them. Birds ate the seeds, got sick, and died. But what about people? Was the chemical harmful to them? Yes. So, now what? Time for some more problem solving by the class. Also discuss the concept again of solving one problem only to create another.

Students can go to the library to find out what is being used today to protect crops. Is it still a problem? What is "genetically altered" farming all about?

## HAVE A SCARECROW CONTEST IN YOUR SCHOOL

In some schools, each class creates its own scarecrow and places it outside the door. The scarecrow must look scary, and it must have items hanging from it that rattle in the wind (spoons, tin cans, and so on).

Other schools have a more modern version of the scarecrow contest. Scarecrows are made in the likeness of characters from books or from everyday life. Perhaps a scarecrow contest is possible for your school. It calls for team spirit, cooperation, and problem solving.

# OCTOBER AUTHOR STUDY: ROBERT D. SANSOUCI

Robert D. SanSouci (San-soó-see) is a master storyteller. He lives in the San Francisco, California, area and likes to travel. He finds interesting stories in his travels which he then *rewrites* for children of all ages. He is particularly skillful at adapting folklore for children.

Mr. SanSouci likes to collect old children's books. He has worked in and managed bookstores, and is a consultant for Walt Disney Feature Animation, in Burbank, California. He is a lecturer for elementary schools, middle schools, and higher education.

His books have received many distinguished awards. He has made a contribution to children's literature by adapting a diversity of stories from many lands, for today's readers.

Please welcome Mr. SanSouci into your classroom.

## BOOKS AND SUGGESTED ACTIVITIES

### THE TALKING EGGS, A FOLKTALE FROM THE AMERICAN SOUTH (ILLUSTRATED BY JERRY PINKNEY)

This book is a Caldecott Honor Book and recipient of the Coretta Scott King Award for illustrations. It is a spellbinding tale of two sisters. Rosie is spoiled and lazy but she's her mother's favorite. Blanche is sweet and is the one who does all the chores and hard work for her mother and sister. One day, Blanche does a kindness for an old witch-woman and this catapults her into a miraculous world where cows have two heads and bray like mules, and rabbits in fancy dress dance the Virginia reel. Blanche, being an honest girl, can be trusted and carries out the woman's wishes and arrives home with new finery and riches. The jealous mother and sister scheme to have Rosie meet the witch-woman, and that's where the turn-about tale begins. The old woman knows evil when she sees it, and the greedy sister and her mother get what they deserve in the end.

## ACTIVITIES TO ACCOMPANY *THE TALKING EGGS*

1. Reread the story and enjoy the pictures, especially the chickens of every color, and the cow with two heads and horns like corkscrews. Encourage students to draw their own versions of the colorful chickens. Also, paint the beautiful eggs that cry out "Take me."

2. Have students reenact this turn-about tale. What props will be needed? Who will play the old woman who removes her head and how will that be done?

3. In this story, good is rewarded and evil is punished. Have students think of other folktales they have read where this is also true and make a list of them. What are the lessons to be learned?

4. Encourage students to put themselves in the place of the girls. Which one would they be more likely to act like—Rosie or Blanche? Can we learn a lesson from this tale?

## *THE RED HEELS* (ILLUSTRATED BY GARY KELLEY)

The setting is New England, and Jonathan Dowse is a shoemaker who travels the country with his tool kit to find families in need of shoes or shoe repair. He stays with the family until the job is done, and then moves on. One night he has to pass through a woods and remembers a warning that strange things happen there. Hopelessly lost, he stumbles upon a tidy cottage and is welcomed by the mistress. In return for lodging, he offers to fix her shoes. But when he sees the red heels he becomes alarmed, for red shoes are supposed to be the sign of a witch.

But Jonathan Dowse is already smitten, and when he sees the fair maiden put on the shoes and whisk up the chimney, he follows her and they dance between the moon and the clouds. They do this for a time, until one day Jonathan says he must be on his way, and that she must stay where she is happy. He works hard and soon owns a shop, but the maiden, Rebecca, is on his mind.

One day, Rebecca comes to his shop, ready to turn in her red-heeled shoes for a pair of sturdy, plain work shoes that a good wife would wear. Speechless, Jonathan asks her to return the next day. Then he sets about his task in a way that makes them both happy in the end. This is an enchanting New England love story that draws upon the folklore of that area.

## ACTIVITIES TO ACCOMPANY *THE RED HEELS*

1. This story has an element of magic. Have students identify the places in the story where magic is present. Are there any special words to be said and any special items?

2. Get an old pair of women's shoes and paint the heels red. Girls can dance in them. What music will they choose that would go with the dreamy setting in the pictures? An old pair of men's shoes with the heels painted red will complete the picture for a dancing couple.

3. Students can draw a picture of what the couple saw in their night dancing travels. Use the book illustrations to get an idea for an aerial view.

4. *Still life with fruit and vegetables.* This could be the title of a painting or drawing by students. In the fourth full-page drawing in the story, Gary Kelley shows the still life along with pottery jars and the red-heeled shoes. Students can use this as a springboard for a drawing lesson. (Remember, when you draw from art, you are learning about light and shadow, size, and shapes. Many student artists learn by sitting in art museums copying the work of masters before them. It's difficult and takes practice.)

5. Use some of the pumpkins and gourds that have been brought in this month for the classroom harvest table, and make a still-life arrangement that students can sketch with pencil or chalk. They can also paint still life with vegetables at the easel.

## THE BOY AND THE GHOST (ILLUSTRATED BY BRIAN PINKNEY)

This story combines the winning elements of a ghost, a hidden treasure, and an appealing young character, Thomas, who sets out to make his fortune. He has the type of innocence that succeeds in folk literature. Because he shows kindness to a stranger, Thomas is led to a big southern plantation in which a treasure is hidden but guarded by a fearsome ghost. When Thomas meets the ghost, bit by bit, he manages to keep his wits about him and in the end receives a handsome reward.

## ACTIVITIES TO ACCOMPANY *THE BOY AND THE GHOST*

1. Go through the book and locate the words that Mr. SanSouci uses that represent sounds in the haunted house. There are words like "Scriiitch" and "Whoomp" and "Thunk!" Students can gain an awareness of how sounds are represented by letters to enrich their own story writing. The term for this is *onomatopaeia.*

   Create such sounds as dropping a book on the floor, scraping a desk along the floor, opening a cupboard door, and so on, and have students write representative letters for these sounds.

2. The boy meets the giant "bit by bit." This introduction of the giant uses the formula of "three times" that is often associated with magic in folklore—three sillies, three wishes, and so on. Encourage students to be on the alert for "three" in folktales and fairy tales, and report on their findings to the class.

3. *Dramatic storytelling.* This story lends itself to a dramatic telling. What props can be gathered to make it exciting? How will the three pieces of the giant be represented? Will students use a flannel board? Clay?

4. At the end of this book, the author has a full-page message for the reader about this tale. The plot came from two brief "negro ghost stories"—one from Alabama and one from Virginia. Ghosts turning up in pieces are found in folk literature in Spain, England, and Germany.

   When people traveled they took their folktales with them, and perhaps the setting of a castle in Germany eventually becomes a farm in the south. Go through a variety of folktales, old ones and updated tales, for the purpose of locating the setting. Is it in a specific country? Is it deliberately vague?

5. *Discuss rewards.* What do students think about Thomas who shares his reward with others? What would they do with a reward? If the person receiving the reward is greedy, what might happen?

## *THE FAITHFUL FRIEND* (ILLUSTRATED BY BRIAN PINKNEY)

This is a Caldecott Honor Book and a Coretta Scott King award winner as well. The setting is the island of Martinique in the Caribbean. This folktale draws upon African, European, and South American traditions and imagery. It is a story of romance, courage, and true friendship between two boys who become as close as brothers. The willingness of one friend to sacrifice his life for his friend gives an old man the power to break a spell that had been cast upon them.

## ACTIVITIES TO ACCOMPANY *THE FAITHFUL FRIEND*

1. Locate the Caribbean Sea and the island of Martinique on a map or globe. Perhaps some students have visited there, or an island nearby. This is the setting for the story.

2. *Make scratchboard art.* The art work in this story is a scratchboard technique. On a 9- by 12-inch piece of manila paper, students can fill in the paper with crayon. Make patches of color all over the page, leave nothing blank. Press heavily on the crayons. Next, cover this with black tempera paint or black India ink, and allow to dry. Plan the picture on another sheet of paper and then, using the edge of a sharp instrument (toothpick, scissors, tiny screwdriver), *slowly and carefully* "draw" the picture on the black surface so the black will be scratched away and the bright colors will appear as if by magic. Study the flowing lines in this picture book and the very thin lines and thick lines.

3. *Problem solving.* Each time that Hippolyte saw the zombies in the forest and heard their warnings, he thought of a way around the problem. Hippolyte is an excellent problem solver. Ask students for other ways they might solve the same dilemmas that he faced.

4. *Friendship.* Have a discussion of what makes a good friend. Remember the old adage that to have a friend, one must be a friend. What qualities are we looking for in a good friend? List them. Then let's practice them.

5. "One good deed deserves another" is an old adage. How does this apply in this story, when the stranger steps forth in the end and turns the evil one into stone? Who is he? Why is he doing this good deed?

    Have a frank discussion with students about the concept of doing good for others without expecting anything in return. A kind heart and a good attitude will bring riches to them during their life. Ask students to name a kind thing they have done for someone else and how it made them feel. Tell them that it will, indeed, make them feel good inside to do good things for others. Where can we begin?

## *CINDERELLA SKELETON* (ILLUSTRATED BY DAVID CATROW)

This freshly created tale of Cinderella takes place in a graveyard where all of the characters are skeletons. But even Cinderella Skeleton is mistreated by her stepmother and stepsisters. In this retold tale (year 2000), Cinderella has to do all of the work, such as:

*She hung up cobwebs everyplace,*
*Arranged dead flowers in a vase,*
*Littered the floor with dust and leaves*
*Fed the bats beneath the eaves;*
*She had no time for rest or fun.*

When she goes to the frightfully famous Halloween Ball, she flees before daylight but not before the Prince grabs her red shoe and cracks off her leg bone at the ankle. Then the Prince goes out in search of the maiden with the missing leg bone that fits the craggy one he has with the shoe attached.

This tale leaves children shivering, gasping, and howling for joy at the same time.

## ACTIVITIES TO ACCOMPANY *CINDERELLA SKELETON*

1. This tale is just right for an October festival of Halloween stories. Decorate a corner of the room as Cinderella Skeleton might have done.

2. *Rhyming.* The book is told in rhyme. Have students try their hand at working with rhyming words to tell a good story.

3. *Illustrations.* After reading the book aloud, go back through it and study the illustrations. Notice that the colors are of bright blues, electrifying yellows, scorching reds, and so on. It is not the typical orange, black, and white that we associate with Halloween. Perhaps students can choose to illustrate a section in the more traditional Halloween colors, for this untraditional yet familiar tale.

4. *Setting.* Discuss the setting of this tale. Compare it with another version of the Cinderella story. Does the switch from a castle setting to a cemetery setting make it a more ghostly tale? Can we think of another story where the setting could be changed, or updated, and yet remain the same? An old country setting in a city setting perhaps?

5. Halloween is a time for ghosts and skeletons, and so the author has taken poetic license to change this Cinderella tale to a holiday setting. How can we change this tale for another well-known holiday, such as Christmas or Easter? How would the characters dress and what would the setting look like? Students can draw a scene from this story.

**Note:** Robert SanSouci, prolific writer, teller of tales, and award winner, can feed our imagination and enrich our studies. Students are sure to find more books by him in the library. In his book *N. C. Wyeth's Pilgrims,* he uses the paintings of this renowned artist to help tell the tale of the first Thanksgiving. Also, be on the lookout for *The Six Swans; The Legend of Scarface; The Song of Sedna; The Enchanted Tapestry; Sukey and the Mermaid; A Weave of Words: An Armenian Tale; The Tsar's Promise: A Russian Tale; The Samurai's Daughter: A Japanese Legend;* and many others.

# REPRODUCIBLE ACTIVITY PAGES
# FOR OCTOBER

## READING/LANGUAGE ARTS

The Fiction vs. Nonfiction Witch

Parts of Speech for Lunch

My Mini Book of Resources (3 pages)

Letter-Writing Form

Spello

Story Vine (Web)

## MATH

Column Addition

Pumpkin Math

Make a Quilt Pattern

The Masked Money Bandit

Who Can Buy Pizza Today?

## SOCIAL STUDIES

Travel Poster—My Home Town

Gifts of Nature Memory Game

Join the Firefighters!

## SCIENCE

Our Sense of Taste

Make a Scary Scarecrow

## AUTHOR STUDY

Ingredients for a Fairy Tale/Folktale

# The Fiction vs. Nonfiction Witch

This witch likes books and is boiling up some good stories. Put **F** in the square for the make-believe sentences (fiction). Put **NF** for the real facts.

Nonfiction contains facts.

Fiction can contain some facts, and also made-up material.

Color the witch for a fiction book.

☐ Yellow + blue makes green.

☐ President Lincoln is on the nickel.

☐ Water is good for you.

☐ 10 + 12 + 6 = 37

☐ Railroads were built after jet planes.

☐ May is the 6th month of the year.

☐ Washington, D.C. is the nation's capital.

☐ A squirrel has small hoofs.

☐ President Adams is on the dime.

☐ Rabbits lose heat through their ears.

# Parts of Speech for Lunch

This ogre is hungry for parts of speech. You can help prepare lunch. Use your crayons to underline the parts of speech.

red—nouns
orange—adjectives
green—verbs
blue—adverbs

**Nouns**
**Verbs**
**Adverbs**
**Adjectives**

1. The dog barked.

2. The shaggy dog barked.

3. The shaggy dog barked slowly.

4. The old shaggy dog barked slowly.

1. The maid called.

2. The kitchen maid called.

3. The kitchen maid called loudly.

*you can make dessert!*

1. The phone rang.
2. The wall phone rang.
3. The wall phone rang repeatedly.

1.
2.
3.

©2002 by The Center for Applied Research in Education

# My Mini Book of Resources

Name: _____

**Directions:**

1. Color and cut out the 7 pages.
2. Cut the strips and paste on the bottom of the appropriate page.
3. Staple the book.
4. Use as a resource.

Dictionary

Words and Meanings

paste strip here

A List of Terms at End of Book

G L O S S A R Y

paste strip here

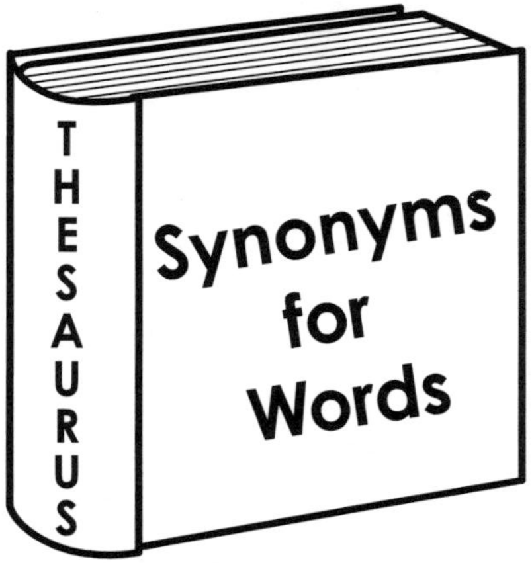

PHONE BOOK

Name
Address
Phone
Number

paste strip here

---

Volume of
Books from
A-Z on
Many
Topics

ENCYCLOPEDIA

paste strip here

---

Synonyms
for
Words

THESAURUS

paste strip here

---

HANDBOOK

Book
of
Instructions

paste strip here

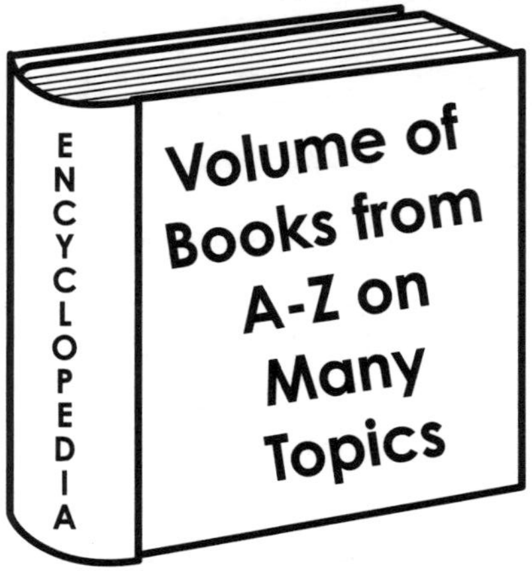

# Strips for Mini-Book

What does the word "territory" mean?

I need another word for "street."

What is the number of the local T.V. station?

Where can I find a list of all the rocks in this book?

How does this machine work?

I need information about food, clothing, and shelter.

Cut out these strips. Paste them on the correct page in your mini-book.

# Letter-Writing Form

You will need:
return address, date, greeting, body of letter, closing, signature

# SPELLO

Use your spelling words, word wall words, and other words to make a gameboard. Each board will be different.

| | | | | | |
|---|---|---|---|---|---|
| on | the | this | | | |
| | | | | | |
| | | | | | |
| | school | | | | |
| | | | | | |
| | | | | | |
| | | | | | |

Use a word list to call out words.

The winner has a cover on all words in a row.

# Story Vine (Web)

Use this diagram to map out a story you read or write.

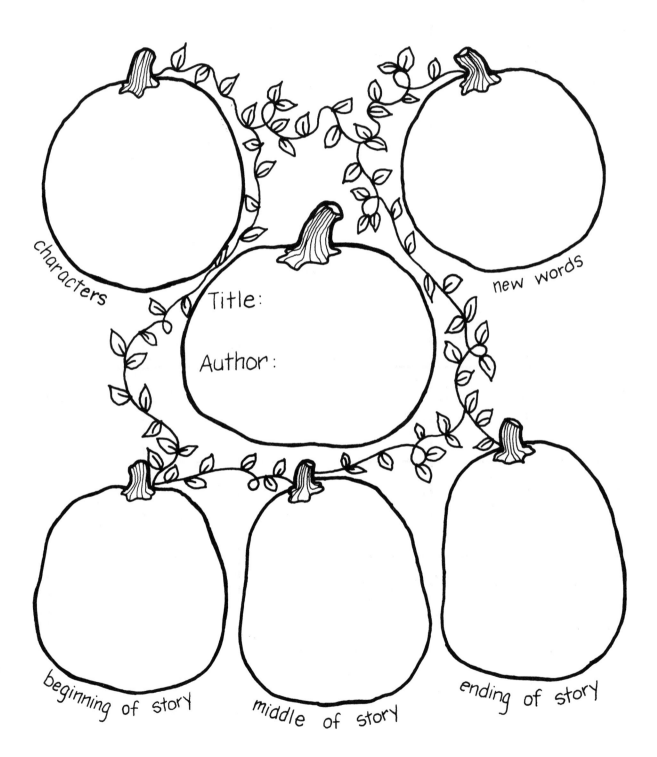

characters

new words

Title:

Author:

beginning of story

middle of story

ending of story

# Column Addition

How did you arrive at the answer?  Show your steps in the spaces provided. Then share your page with a partner to see how many different ways you can get the answer.

2
1
2
3
2
___
10

| A. | 2 + 2 + 2 = 6 |
|----|----------------|
| B. | 1 + 3 = 4 |
|    | 6 + 4 = 10 |

6
3
4
1
5
___
19

| A. | 6 + 4 = 10 |
|----|-------------|
| B. | 3 + 1 + 5 = 9 |
|    | 10 + 9 = 19 |

4
6
2
5
1
___

| A. | |
|----|--|
| B. | |
|    | |

8
1
2
7
6
___

| A. | |
|----|--|
| B. | |
|    | |

6
9
3
5
2
___

| A. | |
|----|--|
| B. | |
|    | |

4
5
2
6
7
___

| A. | |
|----|--|
| B. | |
|    | |

6
4
4
6
3
___

| A. | |
|----|--|
| B. | |
|    | |

9
3
8
2
2
___

| A. | |
|----|--|
| B. | |
|    | |

4
3
2
8
6
___

| A. | |
|----|--|
| B. | |
|    | |

7
5
2
1
6
___

| A. | |
|----|--|
| B. | |
|    | |

Name _____    Date _____

# Pumpkin Math

Look at the seeds. Estimate the total number. Then count them.
How did you do?

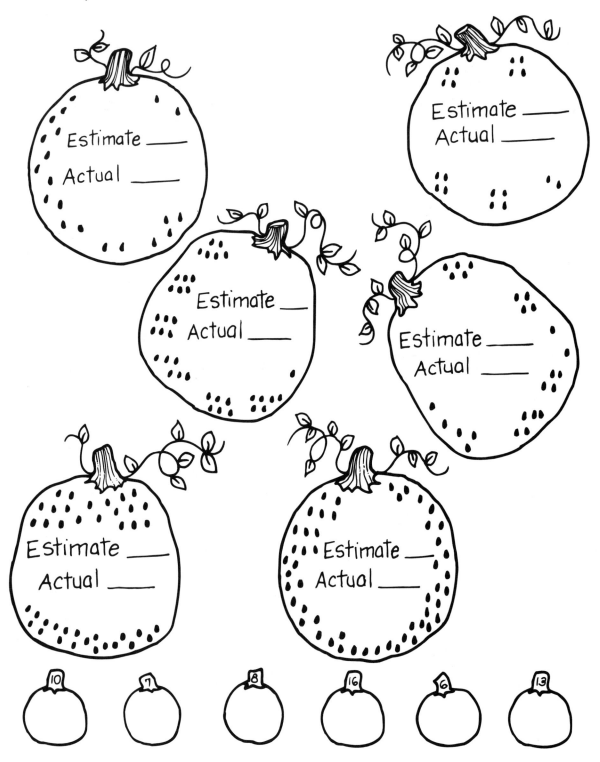

Decorate the little pumpkins with the number of seeds shown on the stem.

# Make a Quilt Pattern

Use these spaces to make your pattern. You can use geometric shapes to make designs ( ▢ ◯ ◇ ▭ ).

|  |  |  |  |  |  |
|---|---|---|---|---|---|
|  |  |  |  |  |  |
|  |  |  |  |  |  |
|  |  |  |  |  |  |
|  |  |  |  |  |  |
|  |  |  |  |  |  |
|  |  |  |  |  |  |
|  |  |  |  |  |  |
|  |  |  |  |  |  |

# The Masked Money Bandit

Ronnie Raccoon just found a kettle filled with pennies and nickles. He does not know very much about money and wants your help. Examine a real <u>penny</u> and a real <u>nickel</u>, and see if you can answer his money questions.

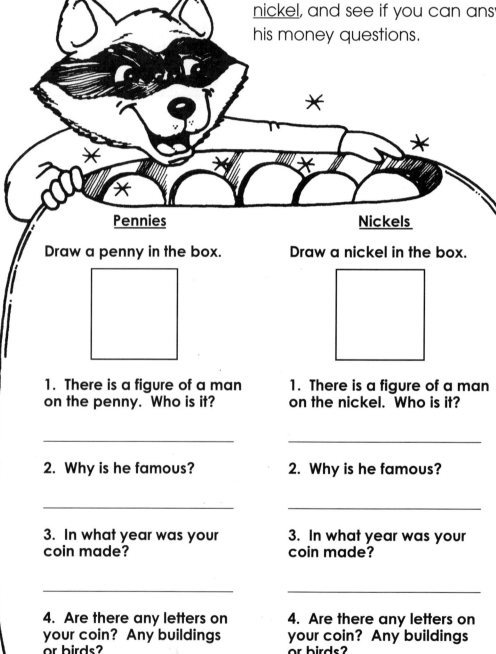

**Pennies**

Draw a penny in the box.

**Nickels**

Draw a nickel in the box.

1. There is a figure of a man on the penny. Who is it?

_____

2. Why is he famous?

_____

3. In what year was your coin made?

_____

4. Are there any letters on your coin? Any buildings or birds?

1. There is a figure of a man on the nickel. Who is it?

_____

2. Why is he famous?

_____

3. In what year was your coin made?

_____

4. Are there any letters on your coin? Any buildings or birds?

Make a crayon rubbing of each coin on the back of this page. Write your money facts on the back, too. Ronnie Raccoon says, "Thank you!"

# Who Can Buy Pizza Today?

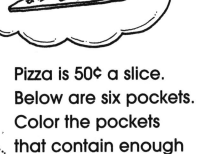
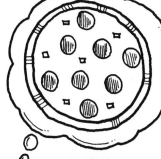

Pizza is 50¢ a slice.
Below are six pockets.
Color the pockets
that contain enough
money to buy
pizza today.

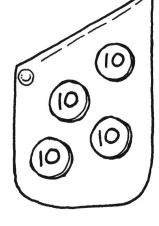

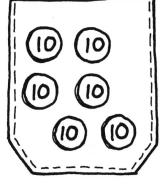

# Travel Poster—My Home Town

You have been selected to make a travel poster for your city. Think of four points of interest that you want to advertise. Make your poster colorful.

# Gifts of Nature Memory Game

Color each picture below. Then cut the boxes apart on the lines.

TO PLAY THE GAME: Lay the cards face down on a grid. Turn over two cards. If the cards match, you may keep them. If the cards do not match, turn them back over. Then the next player takes a turn. Try to remember where each picture is located. The player with the most matching cards wins the game.

# Join the Firefighters!

Fire Prevention Week is in October. Winfield Bear has an important message:

"Plan a fire drill at home.
Be prepared."

Use your crayons
to show Winfield's
bright new firefighter's
uniform.

Name _____     Date _____

# Our Sense of Taste

The tongue is lined with cells that sense <u>five</u> different flavors. They are: salty, sweet, sour, bitter, and cheesy (sometimes called "umami"). Any taste bud can detect any flavor.

    Make a tongue collage. Cut out ten colorful pictures of food—two from each group—and paste them on the tongue spaces. This will help you to recall the five different tastes.

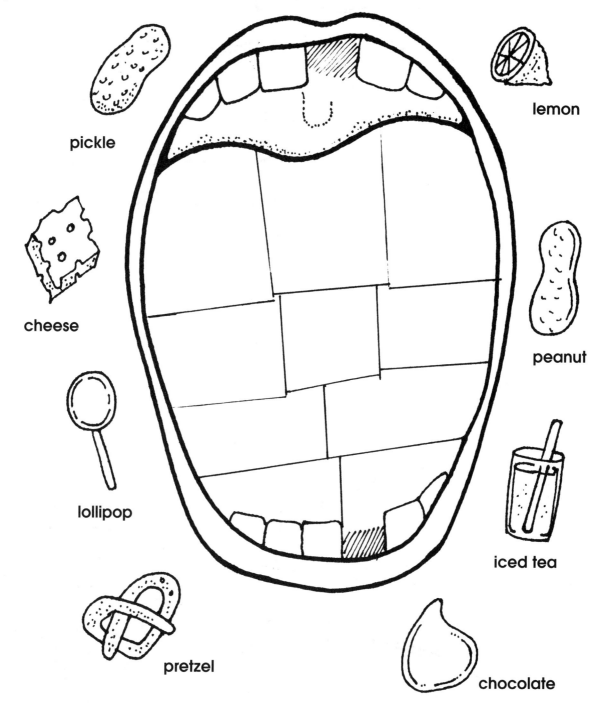

pickle

lemon

cheese

peanut

lollipop

iced tea

pretzel

chocolate

# Make a Scary Scarecrow

Scarecrows have been used by farmers for a long, long time.  In Japan, farmers hung rags, meat, and fish bones on their sticks. Indians hung dead crows.  Make a colorful, scary scarecrow that will do the job!

The Dutch called theirs "bootzamon" for boogeyman.

# Ingredients for a Fairy Tale/Folktale

Robert SanSouci is a good storyteller. Use some of these ingredients and cook up a good tale.

Color the seven ingredients that could be used in a fairy tale.

Fairy Tale

Magic

colorful words

1 2 3 Things happen in threes

"once upon a time"

Animals that talk

true facts

Good and bad characters

Happy endings

# NOVEMBER

# NOVEMBER BOOKS

**Bruchac, Joseph.** *The Circle of Thanks: Native American Poems and Songs of Thanksgiving.* **Illustrations by Murv Jacob (New York: Bridgewater, 1996).** A collection of poems retold by Abenaki writer Bruchac, and illustrated by Cherokee painter Jacob. There is also additional information about the poems and the culture from which it originated.

**Brumbeau, Jeff and Gail deMarcken.** *The Quiltmaker's Gift.* **(Duluth, MN: Pfeifer-Hamilton Publishers, 2000).** A generous quiltmaker sews the most beautiful quilts and gives them away to people in need. The king wants one to make him happy, but the quiltmaker has a different plan for him. A charming fable that celebrates the joy of giving.

**Cohen, Caron Lee.** *The Mud Pony.* **Illustrated by Shonto Begay (New York: Scholastic Inc., 1988).** A poor little Indian boy wants a pony so much that he molds one out of clay, and it takes on a life of its own. This real pony sees the boy through a number of trials, and soon people begin to see him as a special brave boy.

**Cowley, Joy.** *Gracias, The Thanksgiving Turkey.* **Illustrated by Joe Cepeda (New York: Scholastic, 1996).** A humorous story, set in New York, about a loving Latino family. Miguel has a special attachment to Gracias, a turkey that makes it to the Thanksgiving table—but not as the main course.

**Hamilton, Virginia.** *When Birds Could Talk and Bats Could Sing.* **Illustrations by Barry Moser (New York: Blue Sky Press, 1996).** Bird and bat tales are imaginative and include verse or song and end with a moral for children to live by. These tales were rewritten for children to make them smile as well as learn. Striking illustrations.

**Hoyt-Goldsmith, Diane.** *Day of the Dead, A Mexican-American Celebration.* **Photographs by Lawrence Migdale (New York: Holiday House, 1994).** Every year, on November 1 and 2, families in Mexico and also Mexican-Americans in Sacramento, California, celebrate this holiday that honors relatives who have died. This informative book shows people in the process of preparation and the actual celebrations.

**Isaacs, Anne.** *Swamp Angel.* **Illustrated by Paul O. Zelinsky (New York: Dutton, 1994).** With flamboyant vigor and good humor, this exaggerated tall tale gives the reader an adventure along with Angelica Longrider, who is to become the greatest woodswoman in Tennessee. Even Thundering Tarnation, the bear she wrestles, can't keep this swamp angel down for long.

**Mott, Evelyn Clark.** *Dancing Rainbows: A Pueblo Boy's Story* **(New York: Dutton, 1996).** Young Curt is proud to be Tewa and participate in feast-day rituals and dances. Text is informative and lovely photographs explore the purposes behind tribal dancing.

**Pilkey, Dav.** *'Twas the Night Before Thanksgiving* **(New York: Orchard Books, 1990).** Children enjoy the rhythm and the rhyme of this story which uses the same formula as *The Night Before Christmas.* It inspires some students to try out their own rhyming skills.

**(CHAPTER BOOK) Fox, Paula.** *One-Eyed Cat* **(New York: Dell, 1986).** A boy takes aim with a sling shot, and his own life becomes changed as it hits a small cat. He tries to care for the cat and to leave it food. Eventually his burden is too big to bear alone, and he shares it with his mother, who helps him to live with his shame and guilt and to move on.

# NOVEMBER

Your classroom should be humming along by November at a comfortable speed, with a noise level that is satisfying for all students—and for you, too.

Children who are just learning need to be praised often and genuinely for their efforts. Make a point of praising students with your words, a smile, a knowing look, raised eyebrows, and a gentle pat on the shoulder. Your comments on their papers should be positive. Of course they'll make mistakes, because they're just learning. So create an atmosphere where students feel free to make errors; otherwise, some might stop trying—and that would be a very big mistake.

If the class has a good attitude toward learning, toward classmates, and toward you, it might be they are holding up a mirror to your modeling and reflecting the actions of a sincere person who cares about them. If things are not going so well as you'd like, there's still time to fix them. Call a class meeting and express your expectations. Call parents and have a meeting. Let's all adjust our attitudes—including yours. Find something special to like about each student in your care.

# FOCUS ON READING

## WHAT IS A COMPOUND WORD?

First, write the term "compound" on the chalkboard. Explain to students that "compound" means to mix, or unite. When we speak of a compound word, we are uniting two words to make a different word. Here are some examples to use:

| | | | | |
|---|---|---|---|---|
| day | + | light | = | daylight |
| school | + | yard | = | schoolyard |
| school | + | bus | = | schoolbus |
| air | + | plane | = | airplane |
| dump | + | truck | = | dumptruck |

131

## A PICTIONARY OF COMPOUND WORDS

Have students be on the alert for compound words for an entire week while they are reading. They can locate compound words in their reading books, magazines, newspapers, and especially dictionaries. They can keep a list of the many compound words they find. Then create a Pictionary of Compound Words. If the word they find is a noun (name of picture, place, or thing), it will be easy to illustrate. If not, it will be a challenge for students to find a way to visually express the word. Accept all visual expressions that the student can explain. If they're having difficulty thinking of an illustration, talk about shapes, colors, and lines that might be useful.

## COMPOUND WORDS—FIND YOUR OTHER HALF

Make a list of compound words on a sheet of paper. Cut them into strips. Then cut the strips in half so that the compound word has been cut in two. Put the strips into a container and shake it. Then have students reach into the container, one at a time, and draw out a half strip. When everyone has a half strip, the job is for students to locate the other half of their word, or its partner. When they do, they can sit down and print their word. Encourage students to do this in a quiet manner so as not to "tip off" other students who are searching for their other half.

When all students have located their word partner, have them collaborate on a sentence that uses the compound word. (See Reproducible Activity Pages.)

## COMPOUND WORDS—FILL IN THE HUMMING BLANKS

Make a list of five compound words on the chalkboard. Have students take out a scrap piece of paper and print the numerals 1 through 5 down the left-hand side.

Next, slowly read a sentence aloud that contains one of the five compound words, but when the compound word is reached, make a humming sound instead. Give students time to select one of the words from the chalkboard and write it on their paper. Then read another sentence making sure to hum instead of saying the compound word. When all five sentences are finished, read each sentence aloud, this time having the students say the missing word in unison.

Keep trying this with more compound words throughout the month so that students begin to recognize the idea that two words are joined to make another word.

## A FRESH APPROACH TO COMPOUNDING WORDS AND IDEAS

The book *Koko's Kitten* by Francine Patterson, with photographs by Ronald H. Cohen, is about a captive gorilla named Koko who learned to communicate by using sign language. Koko acted lovingly toward a little kitten that she referred to as "All Ball." To her, the kitten may have resembled a soft ball that was rolled up. Koko was shown a half-mask of the type that could be used at Halloween, and when asked what it was she signed "eye hat."

While these are not exactly compound words, the idea is the same: putting two words together to describe something. For example, as in "eye hat," the mask is worn over the eye or worn on the face to cover it, much as a hat is worn on the head to cover it.

Some students might be interested in reading this book, or it can be read aloud. The book is available from the public library. Also, many of the students would enjoy coming up with new words for items in the classroom, as seen through Koko's eyes. This gives students a fresh approach to the language and a new interest in vocabulary and the meaning of words. (Some examples could be: earmuffs [hearing lids], wool mitten [hand house], felt pen [soft stick].)

A favorite children's literature book to read aloud, and one that could accompany this playful language activity, is *A House Is a House for Me* by Mary Anne Hoberman, with illustrations by Betty Fraser. Told in rhyme, this delightful book contains many verses, such as "Barrels are houses for pickles, And bottles are houses for jam. A pot is a spot for potatoes. A sandwich is home for some ham." This is an opportunity to enrich student vocabulary and to perceive things in a different way.

## SIGN LANGUAGE

Students may become interested in sign language from the information they learn about Koko, the gorilla who learned how to sign. A good picture book that will prove helpful is *The Handmade Alphabet* by Laura Rankin. Invite a knowledgeable adult or older student into the classroom to give a lesson on signing.

## WORKING WITH CONTRACTIONS (*HAVE*)

Contractions will be a review lesson for many students and it may be new material for others.

Explain the definition of "contraction," which, in this case, is to omit (leave out) letters to shorten a word.

Here are some sample contractions that can be printed on the chalkboard. Group them together to make it easier.

Print the word "have" on the chalkboard and explain that you are going to shorten this word by leaving out the letters "h" and "a" and using an apostrophe mark in their place ('ve). Then print the words "I have" and right under it print "I've" so that students can see the first part of the word "have" or "ha" is missing. Make up two simple sentences, one without the contraction and one with it. For example, say: "I have received a letter." Then, "I've received a letter." Do this for each word in the "have" group. Work with one group each day.

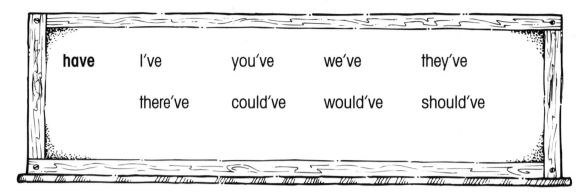

| have | I've | you've | we've | they've |
|------|------|--------|-------|---------|
|      | there've | could've | would've | should've |

## WORKING WITH CONTRACTIONS (*NOT*)

Explain to students that the word "not" is often shortened in informal speech and writing to "n't." Only one letter is missing or left out in this case. Write the words as follows on a large sheet of chart paper, on the chalkboard, or on the word wall. Print the two words at the left and the contraction on the same line:

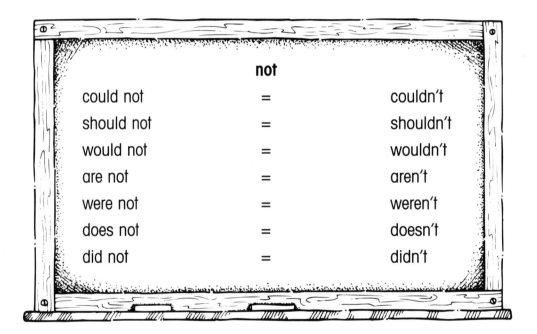

**not**

| could not | = | couldn't |
|-----------|---|----------|
| should not | = | shouldn't |
| would not | = | wouldn't |
| are not | = | aren't |
| were not | = | weren't |
| does not | = | doesn't |
| did not | = | didn't |

## CHESTER COULDN'T, SHOULDN'T, WOULDN'T, AND DIDN'T

Contractions are used in informal speech and not used in formal speech, so this is an ideal lesson for working with two puppets that represent opposites. Using paper bags, make one puppet look serious and the other look informal (or make a cat and a dog, an owl and a robin, a pirate and a ship captain).

Have the two engage in a question-and-answer dialogue. The puppets can be used along with a stuffed animal or another handmade puppet that can be referred to as Chester. This helps to make the lesson more lively and interesting.

SERIOUS PUPPET: Could not Chester climb the stairs?

INFORMAL PUPPET: No, Chester couldn't.

SERIOUS PUPPET: Should not Chester be outdoors?

INFORMAL PUPPET: No, Chester shouldn't.

SERIOUS PUPPET: Would not Chester eat his ham?

INFORMAL PUPPET: No, Chester wouldn't.

SERIOUS PUPPET: Did not Chester just yawn?

INFORMAL PUPPET: No, Chester didn't.

ALL: No! Chester couldn't, shouldn't, wouldn't, and didn't!

Select two different students to hold the puppets and repeat the above as a chant. Students will easily learn it, and some may want to play with the puppets during indoor recess. They are actually playing and working with contractions at the same time. Because of the musical nature of the chant, some students will begin to sway rhythmically to the words.

A variation is to repeat the questions, as follows:

SERIOUS PUPPET: Could not Chester climb the stairs?

INFORMAL PUPPET: Couldn't Chester climb the stairs?

SERIOUS PUPPET: Should not Chester be outdoors?

INFORMAL PUPPET: Shouldn't Chester . . .

SERIOUS PUPPET: Would not Chester eat his ham?

INFORMAL PUPPET: Wouldn't Chester . . .

SERIOUS PUPPET: Did not Chester just yawn?

INFORMAL PUPPET: Didn't Chester . . .

ALL: No, Chester couldn't, shouldn't, wouldn't, and didn't!

Students can think up their own questions. Also, the formal puppet can ask the question and all students can answer for the informal one. They enjoy this type of activity, and are learning from the repetition. (See Reproducible Activity Pages for puppets.)

## MORE CONTRACTION GROUPS

| **will** | | | **are** | | |
|---|---|---|---|---|---|
| I will | = | I'll | you are | = | you're |
| it will | = | it'll | they are | = | they're |
| we will | = | we'll | who are | = | who're |
| who will | = | who'll | we are | = | we're |
| they will | = | they'll | | | |
| that will | = | that'll | | | |
| there will | = | there'll | | | |
| what will | = | what'll | | | |

## CONTRACTIONS IN SENTENCES

Have students read simple sentences that are written on the chalkboard or on a chart. Leave a blank space in the sentence and print the contraction, as well as the two words that it stands for, underneath the blank. Have students read the sentence and then decide which one sounds better, or which one is the correct form in terms of the informal or more formal context. Here are some sample sentences.

---

1.  Mary said, "_____ go to the store."
                     I'll       I will

2.  "_____ soon be time to meet the public, Your Majesty."
       It'll      It will

3.  "_____ the winner!"
         You're          you are

---

(See Reproducible Activity Pages for a contraction activity.)

## I'M A MAJOR LEAGUE "CONTRACTION SPORT"

Newspaper and magazine writers abbreviate written language in order to gain space for more information. This written material provides a good resource for students to find contractions. Have several sports magazines available, as well as a number of sports sections from the Sunday and weekly newspapers. Limit the activity to just the subject of sports. See how many contractions students can find and circle in the headlines and in an article. This may be surprising!

Ask students to listen to about ten minutes of a baseball or football game being broadcast on television, and write down the contractions. (*Note:* You might want to videotape a segment of a game and bring in the tape to replay in the classroom.) Newscasters talk rapidly and use contractions, so listen carefully!

Also, make a five-minute cassette-tape recording of a team game in progress that is being broadcast, so that students can play it repeatedly to listen for contractions or collapsed speech patterns. The game moves fast, and contractions speed up speech. How many can students hear?

## MAKING INFERENCES

As you read picture books aloud to the class, give students opportunities to make inferences—thinking beyond the text. If a character speaks harshly, for example, what kind of a mood might the person be in? If a car is pulling into a driveway and children run to greet the occupants, what can be inferred? If a family is camping in the woods and a bear is seen creeping up to the campsite, what can be inferred? If the chickens run and scatter when the wolf is coming to call, what can be inferred?

Look more closely at the illustrations in the picture book. What inferences can be made? Often the illustrations give us much more information than the text. For example, if a shadowy form can be seen following a person home, what do we infer from this? If a pot is boiling over and no one is tending it, what can we infer? If the dog is pulling and tugging at a tablecloth and a pot of flowers is teetering close to the edge, what can we infer?

## INFERRING—BEFORE STORY TIME

Hold up several picture books, one at a time, that have colorful covers. Ask students to make an inference, based on just the picture, of what the book might be about. Most students will have success with this.

Select one book and go through it together, examining the illustrations and discussing them. Make connections to what students know. What can they infer about this book? Then read the book aloud. At the end, students most likely will have gained more insight into characters and events, and will have strengthened their powers of inference, by going beyond the actual story itself.

## INFERRING—AFTER STORY TIME

When we make an inference, we draw a conclusion based on information that is in the written text or illustrations. After reading a story, have a discussion about how students think a particular character is feeling. Did the character learn a lesson? How do students think a character will behave the next time? Did someone get his or her *comeuppance*? (new vocabulary word) If so, how did that person feel?

By the responses of the class members, you can tell who is in tune with the message and who still needs more work on the subject of making inferences. If a student is not able to make inferences, check to see if he or she is getting the story message, or the main idea. If not, then more work is needed on the main idea of the story. Students won't be so successful working with story inference unless they get the basic message.

## VOCABULARY BUILDING THROUGH READING

Vocabulary building can be done by reading aloud daily to students and discussing some of the new words you come across.

Authors use descriptive words in their writing that students usually do not hear in everyday speech, so it is important for you to be on the alert for these new words. Write them on the chalkboard so students can see what they look like. Pronounce them and have students repeat the words so they can learn to articulate the correct pronunciations. Select a word and put it to work. Students can earn points for using the word in some way, either spoken or written.

Each day, or each week, have students write a new word in their journal that appealed to them. It could be the sound of it, or just the fact that a certain character said the word—it doesn't matter, as long as it is a word that is "new" to the student.

## VOCABULARY BUILDING—GUIDED READING

If students are reading from a basal reader or structured text, the new words for each story are often listed in the teacher's guide. Before reading, write the words in a list on the chalkboard. Describe a word, or break it down into parts. For example, the word *Mississippi* starts with the letter M, has four s's, four i's, and two p's—Mississippi. Spell it rhythmically, accenting each letter i as it is said aloud:

# Mi·ssi·ssi·ppi

Other rhythmical patterns for this word are: "Mi, double s, i, double s, i, double p, i" and "Miss-iss-ippi."

Look for any words that may have rhyming patterns, and have students circle the letters that are alike.

Look for double consonants in the words and have students draw a circle around them.

Look for words that end in *ing,* signifying that there is a root word in there. Let the students find it.

## WORDS ARE MAGNETIC

Use magnetic letters that adhere to the chalkboard, or cloth letters that adhere to the flannel board. Either way, you can construct words and focus on vocabulary building. Students get to handle the letters and to note the shapes of them, which will help them in their writing as well. Print simple activities on cards and have students work together during independent work time. Two students can construct the words and a third student can copy them. Then the two students can copy them from the third student's notes. Here are some sample activity card ideas:

- Construct two words that end in silent "e."
- Construct two words that begin and end with the same letter.
- Construct two words that have a rhyming pattern.
- Construct two words that look different but sound alike.
- Construct a root word, then put different endings on it.
- Construct three words—a one-syllable word, a two-syllable word, and a three-syllable word.

## BEGINNING WORD SORTS

Students can sort the flashcards from reading lessons into categories that they formulate. This causes them to study the words closely and to gain practice working on letter associations. Encourage two students to do this together.

The challenge becomes for two additional students to think of a different way to categorize the words (by meaning, sound, beginning letters, and so on).

After reviewing the first sort, and sharing the second word sort, ask students if they can think of another way to sort these into categories that are different. Have them do it.

## "OUT OF SORTS"

When we say someone is "out of sorts," we mean the person isn't in a very good mood, or isn't acting like he or she usually does.

When we do word sorts with a set number of flashcards, some of the words that don't fit the categories defined can be declared as "out of sorts."

The challenge becomes for the class to see if they can make some semblance of a category or categories for these "out of sort" words. Keep trying. It's amazing what students can see in these words. They may end up with twelve more categories, but they're applying the rules and learning.

Take the words that have been categorized as "out of sorts" and have students use those words as a basis for listing similar words. For example, if the word that is out of sorts is "rough," students can use that as a category to find words that have the same meaning. This is a good time to use the thesaurus. Use library books, newspapers, and magazines for this challenge.

## COMPARE AND CONTRAST

Comparing and contrasting are two activities that can be used in Reading, Language Arts, Math, and Science. Looking for similarities and differences is an excellent skill to practice. It is extremely helpful in learning new material and working with material that we already know.

In this case, give students a list of characteristics that describe two story characters, A and B. Then present them with a situation. How do they imagine the two different characters will react? Compare and contrast these two characters. Do this exercise as a total group so that you can model the procedure.

When this is done, break into groups of two or three to compare and contrast a different set of characteristics. Through the smaller groups, students will be more inclined to participate and voice their opinions.

| *Character A* | *Character B* |
|---|---|
| elderly | elderly |
| not strong | not strong |
| mean | kind |
| harsh | calm |

*Situation*

A boy falls on the sidewalk and is in pain.

What will Character A do?

What will Character B do?

Discuss this. (Character A may well ignore the situation, whereas Character B may call out for help. OR they might both try to get help.) Remind students that sometimes other characteristics come into play as well as those we see or know, and in this case both characters could act in the same way. They will learn that it is often difficult to predict how a character or person may behave, and that is a valuable lesson. (It is also an opportunity for you to remind students that *reading books is exciting* because we never know how a character may react or behave.) We might have a fairly good idea, but we never really know. It is possible for characters to change.

## COMPARE AND CONTRAST—DIFFERENCES

Students can make contrasts and comparisons in writing and also in art form. Take a sheet of 9- by 12-inch paper and fold it in half the long way (vertically). Print "apartment" on one half and "suburbs" on the other half. After students have engaged in brainstorming and have printed some words or phrases under each heading that help describe the *differences* in housing, they can draw a picture of each at the bottom of the paper.

| Apartment in high rise | House in suburbs |
|---|---|
| elevator | garage door |
| revolving door | screen door/storm door |
| inside mailbox with key | mailbox on outside |

Additional subjects to use for comparisons are: dogs/cats; jungle/zoo; day/night; corner store/mall; bus/taxi; skates/scooter; winter/summer; autumn/spring; January/June; hands/feet.

## COMPARE AND CONTRAST ACTUAL ITEMS (REALIA)

First compare and contrast actual items for similarities and differences. Then have students write about them and share their writing. We're engaging in critical observation, writing, reading, listening, and speaking.

Set up a basket, or table display, with some items to compare and contrast. Let students handle them, hold them, weigh them, and then write about them, diagram them, and draw them. Remember, *you will need two of each item and they must be different, yet similar.* Here are some items to get you started:

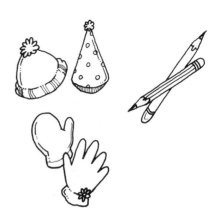

| | | |
|---|---|---|
| scissors | pencils | pens |
| balls | photo frames | rulers |
| hats | bags | gloves/mittens |

# FOCUS ON LANGUAGE ARTS

## MORE READING OPPORTUNITIES

Some reading skills have been addressed in the previous section; however, many more reading opportunities will be available this month and every month throughout the year. Reading is intertwined with all subjects in the classroom, so it is difficult to separate it completely when working with the "process" of reading.

### INDEPENDENT READING—BOOKS ON TAPE

Record keeping is necessary so that it can be determined if students are reading on their own. By this time, some students will have read numerous books, while others may have only read a few. For those who have only read a few, set up a Reading Station with books on tape so that students can look at the book and the words (visual) and hear them being read at the same time (verbal).

When doing record keeping, count this as one of their books for independent reading. Use an asterisk (*) to denote that the book was recorded on tape. Students will still need to list the main characters, the setting, the main idea of the story, and the ending. They can also write a brief summary and their evaluation.

This may be an incentive for the more reluctant readers. If you can't get these books on cassettes from the local library, then have older students make the tapes. This is a good way to get fifth and sixth graders involved.

## INFERRING THROUGH PICTURE BOOKS:
## *THE MOONBOW OF MR. B. BONES\**

Read a picture book aloud to the class. Have students write a short paragraph about a character, a setting, or the plot (story line) that shows an understanding of the term *inference.*

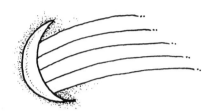

An enjoyable book to read aloud, and one that is filled with underlying inferences, is *The Moonbow of Mr. B. Bones* by J. Patrick Lewis, with illustrations by Dirk Zimmer. One of the main characters, a boy named Tommy Morgan, is a good one to keep an eye on throughout the story. This new boy in town says he's "seen everything worth seein'." When he buys a jar of Moonbows from Mr. B. Bones, he does something no one has ever done before: He opens it! (*What can we infer from this boy's behavior about the type of person he might be?*)

How does Mr. B. Bones handle Tommy's reaction? (*He gives the boy his money back. How would Mr. Bones be feeling right now? Does the author tell us, or can we make an inference?*)

How does this boy's attitude affect others? (*They ignore Mr. B. Bones, as Tommy takes away their hopes and dreams. Does the author tell us their dreams are dashed, or can the reader just sense it, or infer it?*)

Later that same night, a character named Polly steps outdoors in the chill and cries out in joy! It's the *moonbow.* (The jar that Tommy bought.) The townspeople run outdoors in the moonlight to see the magnificent moonbow. It's awesome—like a rainbow, only it's in the night sky. (*The book characters don't see Tommy's reaction, but the reader does. What inference can we make from his reaction to the moonbow?*)

Mr. B. Bones never returns, but on certain nights ever after, people come from miles around to see what some refer to as the Moonbow of Mr. B. Bones. People ask what causes it, and "one boy tells the story best." (*Why do you think the author says one boy [Tommy] tells this story best? In his explanation, what is Tommy inferring when he says the sky must be as clear as a glass jar? In terms of our treatment of others and our own experience, what inferences can we make when we read this story? Discuss other inferences that students make reference to.*)

Mr. B. Bones sold jars of Sundrops, Snowrays, Rainflakes, and Whistling Wind along with other mysterious labels. Perhaps some students will be inspired by this story to write their own.

## COMPARE AND CONTRAST WITH FAIRY-TALE CHARACTERS

It is easy to teach the concepts of "compare and contrast" when using characters from fairy tales because in this genre the character is usually one-dimensional, fairly predictable, and regularly acts in an "either/or" manner. Let's try the same format used this month in the Reading section, only this time with a fairy-tale character:

---

\*Permission to use this book in a lesson was granted by the author, J. Patrick Lewis.

| *Princess A* | *Princess B* |
|---|---|
| young | young |
| pretty | pretty |
| selfish | caring |
| quiet | loud |

Princess A          Princess B

### *Situation*

Each princess is told she may have two pieces of candy.

Princess B watches as Princess A takes three pieces. What do you think she will do? Why?

Princess A sees Princess B take one piece of candy. What do you think she will do? Why?

(Since we are dealing with stereotypes and fairly predictable behavior with fairy-tale characters, chances are that Princess B will snitch on Princess A, and that Princess A will find a way to get that second piece of candy.) Your students can compare the princesses' behavior, as well as contrast it as you discuss the situation.

## COMPARE AND CONTRAST WITH A VENN DIAGRAM

When using characters from storybooks, including fairy tales, you can engage in this exercise repeatedly. Select two characters to compare and contrast. These can be chosen from a book you are reading aloud to students, or from books with which students are familiar.

Using a Venn diagram, a concept widely used in mathematics, is very helpful when comparing and contrasting characters, and students seem to readily catch on to the procedure. Draw two circles that intersect. Label each one with the name of a character from a book. Print characteristics of one character in one circle, and characteristics of the other character in the other circle. If the two characters have a characteristic in common, that should be written in the middle where the two circles intersect.

A Venn diagram gives the student a visual picture of information, and the comparison is obtained quickly by studying the diagram. Students can also put features (hair, eyes, nose) on the two circles to represent the characters. It is an excellent way to compare and contrast one character with another in the same book or in different books. (See Reproducible Activity Pages.)

## "READ ALL ABOUT IT!" "NEWSPAPERS HERE!"

Newspapers can be examined in the classroom for the different sections. Sections help to organize the news stories. Secure a copy of *USA Today,* which has four separate sections, and use them in the classroom. Once students become familiar with newspapers and the type of writing that is in each section, they will be ready to try creating their own news page or a complete newspaper.

## NEWSPAPER HISTORY—*THE CHEROKEE PHOENIX*

During this month, when we focus upon Native American contributors, we need to remember one great leader, Sequoyah (1760?–1843), who became the only person to invent a practical alphabet all by himself. Thousands of Cherokees learned to read within months after his alphabet was introduced. He founded a newspaper, *The Cherokee Phoenix,* that was printed in both English and in Cherokee. A statue of Sequoyah stands in Washington, D.C.

## PICTURE BOOK—*PAPERBOY*

"Extra! Extra! Read all about it! Two cents a copy! Read the Cincinnati Times-Star."

That's the beginning paragraph of the picture book *Paperboy* by Mary Kay Kroeger and Louise Borden, and beautifully illustrated with colorful, realistic paintings by Ted Lewin. The year is 1927, and we are invited to take a step back in time when Willie Brinkman's friends played "red ball, red ball" in the alley, but Willie had a job to do, and his job was selling newspapers. The pictures depict a bygone era of radios and trolley cars. This story—not only about Willie, but about a great era in boxing—packs a punch!

# WORD ORIGINS AND SAYINGS

We will continue to work with word origins during November. Once again, write one word per week on the chalkboard. Introduce it on Monday and have students find out as much as they can about the word. Then give them the explanation on Wednesday. Many new vocabulary words may be presented to the class in this way. Encourage students to use "the word of the week" in their journal writing and in speaking.

1. **diamond.** This is a Greek word for the hardest known substance in nature. A Latin word also used for this quality was *adamus.* Later, adamus was turned into Old French *adamant* or unyielding, unshakeable. The word *adamant* was also used to describe diamonds. In Latin, the form *diamas* began to be used to distinguish diamonds from all other items referred to as adamus, or unyielding.

2. **junket.** This is derived from *juncus,* the Latin word for a marsh plant whose stems and leaves were woven into baskets. A type of sweet cheese made in these containers was called "junket." Later, it applied to a variety of sweets such as custards and pastries. From this sense, the word came to be used for outdoor picnics that involved food carried (often taken in baskets) for eating. This term eventually came to mean any outing or trip that involved pleasure or eating.

3. **denim.** A type of cloth named for the place in which it was made. In this case, the city is Nimes, France, where textiles are an important industry (de Nimes). Also, the term **jeans**, a durable, twilled cotton, takes its name from the Italian city of Genoa (Middle English *Gene* or *Jene*) where it was made and shipped abroad.

4. **biscuit.** Preservation of food presented a problem in earlier times, especially on long journeys. One way to get around this was with flat cakes of bread that were baked twice in order to dry them out. This word means, literally, "twice-cooked bread." Today it means any hard or crisp, dry, baked product.

5. **miniature.** Before the art of printing in Europe, books were handwritten. Often titles and headings were written in red to contrast with the dark ink. The Latin word for the red coloring is *minium.* Later, other colors were used and illustrations were drawn. The term for this process was *miniare* (Italian). Since most of these areas for illustrating were small, the Italian term *miniatura,* was used for them. The English borrowed the term and, eventually, *miniature* came to mean not only a small illustration or portrait, but anything very small.

# WRITING SKILLS

## PUNCTUATION DETECTIVES

Students need regular practice with punctuation, so this type of activity could be done weekly. Students can copy a paragraph from the chalkboard, and practice their penmanship at the same time. Or, you can prepare an activity sheet so that each student has an individual sheet.

The idea is to leave out critical punctuation marks and have the students add them to the copy. They will need to know in advance *how many* marks are missing.

Give them ample time to complete this type of exercise, and then correct them as a group so that the marks can be named and their purposes discussed. This is one way students can learn to attend to punctuation marks. Students do improve over a period of time, but they need practice.

## MASTER PUNCTUATION DETECTIVES

Students can generate their own paragraph or two with missing punctuation marks. How? Have them carefully copy the material from a reading text, reading book, or news article, but leave out all of the punctuation marks.

The student who prepares the paragraphs with the missing punctuation marks is the one in charge of the case. His or her name is put on the paper, along with the number of missing clues (punctuation marks). All of these papers are collected and shuffled and redistributed to the class. The students then become the street detectives. They have to read the copy and add the necessary missing clues, along with their signature. They're on the case.

When the students are finished, the copy can be handed in to you. The work can then be corrected by the master detective at a later time. This enables the students who wrote the copy to not be rushed through their own detective work. The person who wrote the copy can correct the work and *show the proof* by producing the book or newspaper from which the material was copied.

## DETECTIVE BADGES AND HATS

To get into the spirit of the punctuation detective activity, which most students really enjoy doing, have them make badges from shiny gold paper to wear while working on the case. The badges can also be made in the shape of a magnifying glass or in the shape of one of the punctuation marks. Some students like to make headbands or wear a certain hat while doing this activity.

## STAYING ON THE TOPIC WHEN WRITING

Have a "Question of the Day" or a "Question of the Week" that is written on the chalkboard. Students can use their writing journal for this exercise. What they are challenged to do here is to write a response that sticks to the point. This requires clearly stated ideas and use of pertinent information. This type of writing is often necessary in Social Studies and Science reporting.

Students can write and rewrite their responses and use the journal as a workbook. Then they can share their responses.

## LEARN THE ART OF CRITIQUING WRITTEN WORK

Students can learn the art of critiquing their own written work after they have all written a piece about the same topic or in answer to the same question. You are the key here, and can tell the students exactly what information is necessary in their response. In this way, students can review their work, put an X in the margin where the information appears, and see if anything is missing. They can make a note and then add it later. In that spirit, they have become a *critic*.

It is best if students learn to critique their own work before trying to critique that of others. Notice, this is an "art" and they will take their cue from you—the way questions are asked, the way suggestions are made, and so on. At no time do you become a critic of the student; rather, you are a critic of the *information* that has been gathered. This is an important distinction. To become a writing critic in grade three is to judge things according to a certain standard, *not* to engage in finding fault. Students do not automatically know this. It is learned. You become a very important model here.

## LOCATE RELATED IDEAS

Give students a sampling of six to eight sentences. These can be written on the chalkboard or on the overhead projector. The task of the student is to find the sentences that relate to the same topic.

First, read all of the sentences. Next, go through them again and put a red X in front of the ones that relate to one topic. Put a blue X in front of those that relate to another topic. Put a green X in front of those that relate to yet another topic. Here are some sample sentences to use at the beginning, and then you can make up your own.

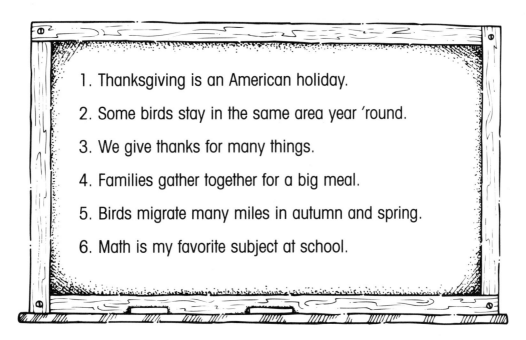

1. Thanksgiving is an American holiday.

2. Some birds stay in the same area year 'round.

3. We give thanks for many things.

4. Families gather together for a big meal.

5. Birds migrate many miles in autumn and spring.

6. Math is my favorite subject at school.

*Note:* Sentence categories are: (A) 1, 3, 4; (B) 2, 5; (C) 6.

## A CHART FOR RELATED IDEAS

Give each student a sheet of 8½- by 11-inch copy paper, and have them fold it in thirds the long way (vertically). Each space will be approximately three inches wide. This is a beginning exercise.

Have students print a different subject key word at the top of each column. For example, "Animals," "Government," and "Food." Next, tell them you will say a word. They will have to determine in which category it belongs and write the word in that column. They can be checked later.

For example, you can use the following words with the categories listed above:

lettuce, zebra, cat, president, pizza, senator

The students' columns should look like this:

| *Animals* | *Government* | *Food* |
|-----------|--------------|--------|
| zebra     | president    | lettuce |
| cat       | senator      | pizza  |

Students look upon this as a challenging game, and will ask if the class can "play" the "Category" game. Encourage students to think of different categories and words to use and submit them.

The purpose of this activity is to give students an opportunity to learn to categorize related ideas. Eventually, you can refer to this exercise when students are writing on a certain topic. Ask students to think of "related ideas" to enrich their writing.

Items in each column can also be further broken down into a web. Ideas can be generated and added to that. Then what? Hopefully, some varied writing on a single topic.

# LISTENING SKILLS

## OBSERVE A STORY VIDEOTAPE—NO SOUND

Observe a portion of a story video with the sound turned off for a period of 3 minutes. Have students predict what is being said by the person(s) doing the talking. Listen to the ideas suggested by the students, and then go back and replay the same story video. Students will now be doubly engaged in active listening. Compare the actual speech with the students' predictions.

## OBSERVE AN INSTRUCTIVE VIDEOTAPE—NO SOUND

Follow the same procedure as in the previous activity, only this time get an instructive tape from the

video collection at the library. An instruction for an art project is especially interesting and holds students' attention. After students have (1) listened to each other in terms of what they think the narrative is, then (2) attentively listened to the tape again, have them (3) actually do the art project.

Some students who especially like to write might be motivated to write out the narration for the directions.

## LETTER/SOUND LISTENING PRACTICE

Say a word. Ask students to raise their hand if they know the beginning sound.

Get at least five ABC books from the library and use these to get some interesting words. Again students are to listen for beginning sounds. They can say it or write the letter on a scrap piece of paper.

Use ABC books with large, oversized pictures. Show the pictures to the class, making sure to cover up the letter. Have students say the beginning letter or write it. Then check their answers so students have immediate feedback.

## LISTEN FOR LETTER CHANGEOVERS

A word often changes meaning when a letter changes. This requires careful listening. In this activity, tell students that you will say two words. The last letter of the first word has been changed to create a new word. Then have students say the words and tell which two letters have been involved in the changeover. This can be a written exercise or an oral exercise. Here are some words to get you started. Then encourage students to make up their own "letter changeovers."

| has | had | (s, d) |
| car | cat | (r, t) |
| from | frog | (m, g) |
| fur | fun | (r, n) |
| bat | bad | (t, d) |
| pen | pet | (n, t) |

## WHAT ARE YOUR CLASS REQUIREMENTS FOR LISTENING TO STORIES?

As the teacher, you have undoubtedly set up listening rules for story time or for that time when you are reading aloud to students or when presenting a class lesson. These rules are often posted on a chart in the room under the heading of Good Listening Behaviors. They include: No talking, no poking other students, keeping feet to yourself, and looking directly at the speaker. These work well, if practiced, when sitting in a circle.

However, third graders often prefer to sit at their desk while listening to a story. For this you will need to determine whether or not you will allow them to continue working on something else. It is highly recommended that in the beginning, until good listening habits are established, the rule is that *everything is off the desk* and students are simply engaged in the process of listening to the story. They need to master this skill. Some students like to put their head down on their desk or on their arm as they listen. Some like to sprawl out and get comfortable. Determine what your expectations are, voice them to students, and be consistent in carrying them out.

## GOOD LISTENERS' READING CHANT

Teach this chant to students in class, and eventually they will learn it and join in. When you're ready to begin to read from a storybook, strike up the chant. Students can say it with you as they put away their desk supplies, or clean off a table, or throw away scrap paper, and get themselves ready to settle down to a good story treat. They should be in their seats and ready when the last word is said. *Then* say the chant again so that students get a quick workout as a group, which will help set the stage for individual and group listening:

> *Whether we sit up straight and tall or*
> *Whether we do the "reading sprawl,"*
> *Whether our head is held up high or*
> *Whether we look you in the eye,*
> *Whether we give ourselves a rest*
> *and lay our head upon the desk,*
> *There's one thing that won't be missin',*
> *We are ready to learn and listen!*

# SPEAKING SKILLS

## BECOME A TOUR GUIDE

We have used various types of videotape suggestions this month in Language Arts, and for our speaking emphasis we can turn to travelog videotapes. Play them with the sound turned off for the usual 3 minutes. Then play the same part again with the sound still off. Have students describe what they are seeing. Help them to determine that they are "selling" the viewer on the location and need to use descriptive language. Those aren't just mountains in the background. They are "majestic, snow-covered mountains." That isn't just a field. It's a "field of golden grain laughing in the sun."

Have students become narrators as the film is played again and again in the background. When everyone has had a turn (students work with partners), play the videotape one last time with the sound and listen to that narration. Some students will like their own better. If they do, have them determine reasons why.

## BECOME A TOUR GUIDE FOR YOUR CLASSROOM

Encourage students to become a tour guide for the classroom. If visitors come to class, what would the guides want them to see? Have a discussion and make a list. Then have students work with a partner and take turns taking classmates on a classroom tour.

Arrange to have someone come in from another class for a brief classroom tour. Or arrange for a teacher from an upper class to send students to be taken on a tour of the classroom. Invite the principal to drop by for a tour.

When parents or visitors come to the classroom, arrange to have them taken on a tour of the classroom by the student guides. Give everyone a chance—take turns. You might want to team some chatty students with others who are extremely quiet, and hope that the quiet ones will eventually become able tour guides, too.

## BECOME A TOUR GUIDE FOR YOUR SCHOOL

If you have access to a video recorder, make a videotape of the school and include the outside of the building, the office, the special rooms (music, library, gym, cafeteria, nurse's office, etc.). Be sure to include special displays. Parents are often willing to assist with this type of project.

A portion of this special video can be used to show the classroom. Select two guides to narrate this segment as the viewer is taken on the tour, since this will have been practiced many times.

When the videotape is available to the class, play it, observe it, and talk about what the narration should be. Have students make a cassette recording to play in the background. This way everyone in the class will have an opportunity to say (or read aloud) something of interest.

This promotes student pride in your school and in your classroom. It promotes good speaking skills.

## CREATE A DYNAMIC MOVIE BOX

If you don't have access to the technology listed in this section, there are other ways to make productions that students enjoy.

*Materials:* You need a big box, paint or paper to cover it, brushes and paint or paste, two cardboard paper towel rolls or two wooden dowels, sheets of drawing paper or "frames," and masking tape.

*Procedure:* Count the number of students in the classroom. That is the number of drawings (frames) needed. If you decide to make this a movie about the school, use the same procedure mentioned earlier for videotaping.

Cover the box with paint or paper. Cut a big square out of one end for the screen and two holes on each side for the dowels. Students can provide the artistic drawings of the building, the office, the special rooms, the classroom, and so on. (Since this is a movie to be treasured, remind students that they will need to work slowly with their art—no scribbling in the background. Only solid colors will do for the background.)

Determine who will create the frame needed for the title page. The next page can show a dedication to the school, signed by all the students in the class.

Each student will work on his or her own drawing. The drawings will be put in order and carefully taped together on the back with masking tape. Tape the top of the first frame to one dowel or paper roll and the last frame to the second dowel. Time to roll the cameras (in this case the dowel rods or towel tubes). This will take two students—one on each side of the box.

Students can go through this frame-by-frame procedure and write the narration. Each student can speak into a cassette recording for his or her frame. Decide if there will be music playing in the background while students are speaking.

Many students will thoroughly enjoy working on this project and others, hopefully, will get swept up by the tasks as they begin to actually see it take shape. They can work on it during indoor recess time as the weather turns colder. It is guaranteed to create many speaking opportunities.

Each student will be very proud of the movie box when it is completed and when others are invited to see it. They can take it around and put on the presentation for the younger children in their classes. There will be a buzz of excitement and energy!

Hopefully, you will videotape this cardboard movie box presentation. It will be priceless. You can show it to parents during Open House, many of whom will want a copy.

# FOCUS ON SPELLING

## SPELLING FLASHCARDS

Make flashcards of the spelling words for the week. Use this procedure while students work with partners. Then the partners switch roles:

- Partner A *shows* the word; Partner B *spells* it.
- Partner A *covers and says* the word; Partner B *spells* it.
- Use this procedure (show/spell/cover/spell) for three words.
- Partner A *calls out* the words one by one (out of order); Partner B spells each one.

## COLOR-CODED FLASHCARDS

Make two sets of spelling flashcards in different colors. Distribute them, face down, to the students. Then call upon all students holding the same color card to come to the front (or to a designated spot in the classroom). Each student takes a turn saying the word on the flashcard and spelling it aloud.

Then return to the first student. This person will say, "Where is my partner?" The person who has the identical word stands, says the word, spells it, and comes to stand beside his or her partner.

When finished, the students at their seats put their heads down. The spelling partners quietly go around the room and put their spelling card, face down, on a student's desk. Then the game is repeated.

## WRITING SPELLING WORDS

Call upon five students to go to the chalkboard. You say a spelling word. All five students write the same word and put down their chalk. Then, one by one, each student says the word and spells it. At that time, someone from the audience can challenge the spelling of a student. If it is incorrect, the challenger must correct it in writing.

## SPELLING SCRAMBLE

Prepare the spelling words on the chalkboard, or on a chart, in advance for the entire group. Scramble the spelling of each word. Students must write the unscrambled version, or the correct word, without looking at their spelling list. This list can also be prepared by you and photocopied so that each student has an individual worksheet.

Students enjoy creating their own spelling scrambles and deciphering other students' scrambled versions. Spelling scrambles are very helpful for students because they determine the correct order of the letters in the word.

```
1. etre
2. ratts
3. owsh
4. undos
```

## ALL HEADS UP—SPELLING GAME

Ask students to close their eyes. Write a list of spelling words on the chalkboard and deliberately misspell one word. When finished, call out, "All heads up." Students have to find the misspelled word. When they do, they raise their hand. Then the student who is called upon goes to the board, corrects it, and spells it out loud. Then the game leader (can be you or a student) says, "All heads down." Students must cover their eyes. The person who corrected the word now must erase a letter in a correct word and replace it with a different letter, so that the word is incorrect. Then, that person sits down. The game leader says, "All heads up." The game continues.

## THREE COLORS

Help students learn where letters are placed on the lines and spaces of paper. Have students visualize a house (or condominium) with a main floor, a basement, and an upstairs.

Where do the letters live?

- Lowercase letters are on the main floor: a, c, e, i, m, n, o, r, s, u, v, w, x, z.
- Letters that go from the main floor to the basement: g, j, p, q, y.
- Letters that go from the main floor to the upstairs: b, d, f, h, k, l, t.

Print the spelling words for the week with three different colors (using felt-tip pens, colored pencils, or crayons). Use the following formula: main floor—*blue;* basement—*orange;* upstairs—*green.* This is guaranteed to make colorful spelling papers.

**Four Colors:** To add another visual dimension to the configuration, have students make all vowels *red.* This makes students pause and reflect while writing or printing the words, and does call attention to the vowels, (a, e, i, o, u), giving students another clue that could prove quite helpful in the spelling of the word.

# FOCUS ON MATH

## MULTIPLICATION IS REPEATED ADDITION

Multiplication is *repeated addition* of the same addend. In other words, $3 \times 6$ is the sum of 6 plus 6 plus 6 (or the sum of 6 and 6, and then 6 more).

So, $3 \times 6$ is an indication that 6 has been used three times as an addend: $3 \times 6 = 6 + 6 + 6$.

Well, if multiplication is repeated addition, why don't we just keep on adding? Because the numbers get too large and it would take us forever to figure out an answer to a problem. So, multiplication is a shortcut once we have memorized the times tables.

**Hint:** If you are using a standard text, check to see if memorization of the times tables goes beyond nine. Some only go up through nine.

## MULTIPLICATION IS QUICKER

Suppose we say that a baker needs four dozen eggs today, and we know there are twelve eggs in a dozen. How many eggs is that? If Student A has memorized $4 \times 12 = 48$, then Student A knows the answer in an instant. If Student B has not memorized times tables through twelve, then that student would add the number 12, four times, or $12 + 12 + 12 + 12 = 48$.

Make up other grocery orders using multiplication examples, such as "times 6" or "times 7." Have students respond with the answer. Suppose they are working in a store and have to know the answer immediately? Suppose getting the order depends upon a quick response? Students can role-play examples while working toward memorization of the times tables. (See Reproducible Activity Pages.)

## MEMORIZING THE TIMES TABLES THROUGH TIMES THREE

Start with the ones, because they're easy. Any number times one is the number itself. So right away, everyone can score a big hit with "times one." But include it in your daily practice with flashcards.

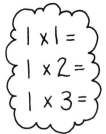

Next, "times two." Students like this and find it easy. These are the numbers they use when counting by two's, beginning with two. Times two means "double." Include it in your daily practice with flashcards.

Then "times three." Here's where the memorization becomes more difficult for some children. Tie it in with "skip counting" such as 3, 6, 9, 12, 15, 18, 21, 24, 27. (That's if you are memorizing through "times nine.")

Tie in the skip counting with body movement and have students stretch or strike a pose for each number. The analogy of a clock can be used for the first four numbers. Here are some examples:

Say "three": students pretend to be a clock and extend one arm straight up, and one arm straight out to the right side

Say "six": raise one arm straight up, one arm straight down at side

Say "nine": raise one arm straight up, and one arm straight out to the left side

Say "twelve": raise both arms straight up

Say "fifteen": hands on hips, twist to the right

Say "eighteen": hands on hips, twist to the left

Say "twenty-one": touch thumbs together

Say "twenty-four": touch thumbs and fingers together

Say "twenty-seven": fold hands and squeeze

Next, hold up the flashcards in order and have students go through this process again. Hold up $1 \times 3$, $2 \times 3$, $3 \times 3$, and so on. Students are "acting out" the answers.

When students have mastered the threes, mix up the flashcards so that they are out of order and have students "act out" the answers with body movements. This works well for the "times three" tables.

## MEMORIZING THE TIMES TABLES—FOUR THROUGH NINE

This is a process that requires repeated work on a daily basis. Use flashcards daily. Start with "times four" and have students memorize them before they go on to the next level.

Students need to know what these facts mean so that if they haven't memorized a fact, they can go back and construct it. Have counters available.

For $3 \times 4$, for example, lay out a group of four and four and four. That's three groups of four. Count them and get "twelve." The student rebuilds the information with this process. This is done until it is remembered and memorized. It's a tool you can give to the students to help them.

Another way to help is to move to the semiconcrete examples, and have students make groups with dots, or circles, or X's.

Periodically, give students a multiplication worksheet and have them show their work (using dots). In other words, what does it mean? What does it look like? (See Reproducible Activity Pages.)

# BUILD A MULTIPLICATION PIZZA BULLETIN BOARD RECORD

This is a good way to keep a class record of student progress. The aim is to find out how the class is doing at a glance. It serves as a motivation for students to work toward memorizing the facts. Perhaps those who have memorized the facts can be paired as "master chefs" with the "apprentices" who are just learning. This gives them both a reason to succeed.

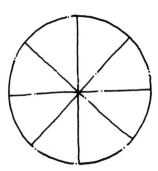

- Each student gets a white paper plate. This represents "times zero" (blank, nothing). It's the pizza crust.

- Each student gets a sheet of red construction paper. This represents "times one" (which everyone will master). Cut a circle out of the red paper (red sauce) to place on top of the white crust that is showing around the edges.

- Divide the circle into eight triangles (Draw line down the middle vertically, horizontally, and then in an X). Do this carefully so each section will be even.

Now, the unfinished pizzas can go up on the TIMES NINE PIZZA WALL with the student name underneath. It's time to go to work to build the pizzas.

- The first triangle to the right represents "times two." When students master this, they can place two white construction paper circles on that spot (onion rings).

- The second triangle represents "times three." When students master this, they can place three black circles on the triangle (black olives).

- The next triangle on the right represents "times four." When students master this, they can place four brown circles on the triangle (pepperoni).

- The next triangle on the right represents "times five." When students master this, they can place five green strips of paper on the triangle (green pepper).

Our pizza is halfway toward completion. Time to have a mini-pizza treat with English muffins, sauce, pepperoni, cheese. Place in toaster oven and enjoy!

- Now to the next half, where the bottom left triangle represents "times six." When students master this, they can place six yellow strips of paper on this area (cheese).

- Bottom left and up one, this triangle represents "times seven." When students master this, they can place seven more brown circles for more pepperoni. They earned it!

- One quarter left. This triangle represents "times eight." When students master this, they can place eight yellow circles on this area (pineapple).

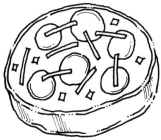

- This last triangle represents "times nine." When students master this, they can place nine tan strips on this area (sausage).

## AN EASY "SHORTCUT" TO MEMORIZING THE TIMES TABLES

Once students memorize the "times five" tables, they're relatively home free. Why? Because of the commutative property of the algorithms. That is, if you reverse the numbers, then the *product* of 3 × 4 is the same as 4 × 3, and 2 × 5 is the same as 5 × 2.

- Times Six: When you get this far, you've already memorized everything up to six, so you only have to learn 6 × 6, 6 × 7, 6 × 8, and 6 × 9. The other facts can all be reversed.

- Times Seven: When you get this far, you've already memorized everything up to seven, so you only have to learn 7 × 7, 7 × 8, and 7 × 9. The other facts can all be reversed.

- Times Eight: When you get this far, you've already memorized everything up to eight, so you only have to learn 8 × 8 and 8 × 9. The other facts can all be reversed.

- Times Nine: When you get this far, you've already memorized everything up to nine, so you only have to learn 9 × 9. The other facts can all be reversed.

## THE COMMUTATIVE MODEL

Make this configuration with concrete items or with X's on the chalkboard:

- Horizontally: It is three rows of seven, or 3 × 7.
- Vertically: It is seven rows of threes, or 7 × 3.
- The answer is the same: 21.

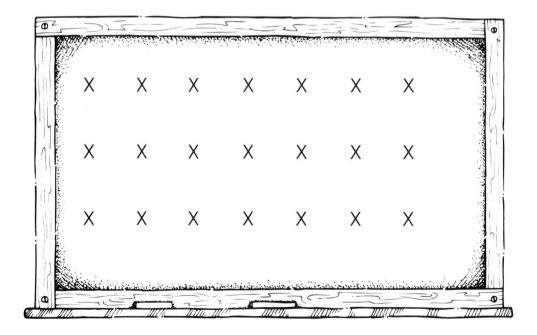

Have students make these "X" models with other multiplication facts, so they can understand them.

## HURRAY! WE MADE IT!

When everyone has succeeded, or when you determine that it is close enough because those remaining are struggling, have a pizza party for the class. This calls for a celebration! Ask for parent help with funding, or check with the Parent-Teacher Association and/or principal to see if money is available in petty cash for this project.

## MINI-PIZZA INFORMATION

Students can make their own mini-pizzas to keep a record of their progress. They will need a small-size white paper plate, and then build their pizza from there. Students may decide to be more adventuresome in where they place their pizza parts, even creating designs. For the big board though, we need a standardized pizza. (See Reproducible Activity Pages.)

## ANOTHER TYPE OF GRAPH

Throughout this process, which will take awhile, the record will be varied but we can still see at a glance how the class is progressing. For students who are interested in working on a large circle graph using this information, they can divide a circle in the same manner and place the appropriate number of items on the graph to represent the number of people in class who have succeeded in memorizing that particular times table. This pizza will look different, and will give us different information. It's a compilation of all the other information.

Have students compose three questions that can be answered by gaining information from this graph.

# FOCUS ON SOCIAL STUDIES

## NOVEMBER CITIZENSHIP FOCUS

This month we are stressing the good citizenship quality of *promptness*. Make a point this month of being on time and of getting work in on time. It's better to be early than late. Don't keep others waiting; it's not polite. (At this age, promptness may be related to the ability to tell time accurately and to judge the passing of time in an appropriate manner.)

## KEEPING TIME

Keep a silent sand-timer on the desks of students who can use additional help by focusing upon the passing of time and the need to accomplish something by the time the grains of sand all slide through the opening. This concrete example of time passing is quite helpful for some students who are off-ask and don't realize that time is moving along.

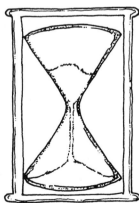

## BEING PROMPT ABOUT ASSIGNMENTS

Getting things in on time may be difficult for some students who have not mastered the concept of planning ahead and of delegating a certain amount of time each day to a task. (Often students who take music lessons, dance lessons, or other types of lessons learn the concept of spending a certain amount of time each day on assignments. They are often told in advance that a half hour or an hour a day is required, and the instructor can tell if the student is not doing this.) Have students keep a timesheet for work done on projects and certain subjects. Then compare student timesheets. Eventually students need to be led to the conclusion that the more time spent on task, the better the results. Encourage them to spend less time watching television and more on school work or boardgames or reading.

## ORGANIZING FOR SUCCESS

If an assignment is due in a week, or in two weeks, the students may benefit from having an organizer that "spells out" for them where they should be in relation to their long-term goal. Reminders written on the chalkboard are also helpful. Some students have simply not learned how to manage a chunk of time, so they need assistance. This is a learned skill.

# PATRIOTISM

## PATRIOTIC SYMBOLS

A "logo" is a symbol that stands for some place or some thing. The United States of America has many symbols, such as the flag, the Liberty Bell, stars and stripes, Uncle Sam, the Statue of Liberty, and others. Students can make cutouts of these this month and use them for cards, for posters, and for an abstract art design on 12- by 18-inch paper. These designs make an effective patriotic bulletin board. Stay with the patriotic colors of red, white, and blue.

Students can go on a Symbol Hunt through magazines and newspapers. Many symbols can be found in the advertising section. Cut out the symbols and begin to make a large photo montage for the classroom.

Some symbols this month include:

- *Bald Eagle*—This is our national mascot. It is three feet tall and has a wing span of up to twelve feet. Imagine an impressive papier-mâché bald eagle project for the classroom. It would generate much interest and enthusiasm for symbols. (Our national bird came close to being the wild turkey, which was Benjamin Franklin's choice.)

- *Liberty Bell*—This is housed in Philadelphia, PA. The first bell actually cracked the first time it was rung. The replacement (1835) also cracked. So, the Liberty Bell is quite famous for its cracked surface.

- *Statue of Liberty*—This beautiful symbol is located on Liberty Island in New York City's harbor. The statue was given to the United States by the government of France, and there is a smaller version in Paris, France. This statue is so immense that you can walk up a staircase to the crown and overlook the harbor.

To give students some idea of the dimensions of this great lady, use a trundle wheel (in the hallway or on the playground) to measure these body parts:

Length of hand  =  16 ft. 5 in.

Length of finger  =  8 ft. 5 in.

Length of nose  =  4 ft. 6 in.

Width of mouth  =  3 ft.

Width of eye  =  2 ft. 6 in.

A challenge would be to make the large face of Miss Liberty in chalk outdoors on the playground just by knowing the dimensions of the eyes, nose, and mouth.

## VETERAN'S DAY (ARMED FORCES)

The U.S. sets aside a day during November (the 11th) to pay tribute to the veterans of the armed forces who fought for their country. Many veterans died in wars. Students need to be made aware that they owe these men and women a debt of gratitude.

List the various armed forces and have students see what they can find out about them during library hour. Each one has its own song and symbols. From the public library, you can obtain a CD of service songs and play them so that students can begin to recognize them. Play them at first for listening and distinguishing one from another. Later, play them when engaged in certain types of activities. For example, when students hear a particular song, they know that it means to get ready to line up at the door soon, or get ready for music class, art class, gym class, and so on.

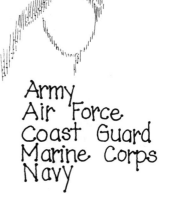

Army
Air Force
Coast Guard
Marine Corps
Navy

Students can write to a local recruiting office to find out information about the armed forces. Perhaps a guest speaker will be able to address the class on the various branches of the service:

| | | |
|---|---|---|
| Army | Marines | Air Force |
| Coast Guard | Merchant Marines | Navy |

In addition, many nurses served in the wars. The American Red Cross is an invaluable organization that still helps people in times of peace when disaster strikes all over the world. So, too, do the armed forces help when disaster strikes.

## VETERAN'S DAY GREETINGS

For Veteran's Day, make greeting cards and mail them to a nearby Veteran's Hospital. Be sure these lovely cards are done in patriotic colors (red/white/blue), with patriotic symbols, and that they say "Thank You." Find out if someone has relative(s) in one of these facilities, and send the cards and notes to them.

# AREA OF FOCUS: OUR CITY

## WEBSITE: GEOCITIES

You can enter the street address, city, state, and ZIP Code of any location in the United States, and this site will generate a map. You can sign up for a free personal home page or a free e-mail account through this site. It is http://www.geocities.com/BHI/geoviewer.html.

## WORK OPPORTUNITIES

Where do most people work in your city? Or do they commute to another city? If they commute, is there a special place nearby in an adjacent city where many of the people go to work?

Some cities have steel mills or coal mines or research centers or industries or entertainment centers. What's in your city?

A little town named Dresden, Ohio is known for its basket-making factory. Even its office building is in the shape of an immense basket, several stories high. Berea, Kentucky has a large college with a focus on crafts that are sold in the town. Hershey, Pennsylvania has a chocolate factory and a theme park. Orlando, Florida is home to Walt Disney World. Gloucester, Massachusetts has a fishing industry. Gettysburg, Pennsylvania has a famous battlefield. San Diego, California has a world-class zoo. What is the closest major attraction to your city? Is this a year-round attraction or is it seasonal?

## DO YOU HAVE A SISTER CITY?

A "sister city" could be a city that shares the same name as your city. Usually it is a city in another country, far away. If you have a sister city, how did this come about? Who visits back and forth between these cities? Let's find out. Check with the Chamber of Commerce or the mayor's office.

## HOW DIVERSE IS OUR CITY POPULATION?

Some cities have large populations of people who are recent arrivals in this country. Is your city one of them? If so, what are these cultural groups called? What are their language and native dress? Turn to the globe in the classroom and find out where their land is in relation to the USA.

## WHAT SPORTS ARE AVAILABLE IN OUR CITY?

Some sports are spectator sports, and some are for participation. First, find out if our city has any major sports teams (baseball, hockey, basketball, football) that compete with other teams in cities around the country.

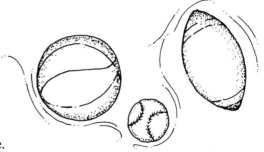

Do we have a city team? Bowling leagues? Skating competitions? Swim meets? Let's find out what people are interested in doing in their spare time.

## WHERE ARE OUR PARKS AND THE LIBRARY?

Most city areas have land set aside for people's enjoyment and pleasure. Where are these located in your city? Let's locate them on a city map. Can people go there to picnic, to swim, and to play ball? Are there swing sets available for very young children? Are there hiking trails and bike paths? Let's look into our own city parks as a source of free or very inexpensive entertainment. Some park naturalists offer classes in bird watching, hiking, and cross country skiing, and will come to school to talk about their programs and to show pictures. Some local parks have flower festivals during certain times of the year.

Students can make posters advertising their very own park and the nearest library. Does the library have special programs? Encourage students to obtain a library card. Draw a map showing how to get there. Be sure to include this information in your newsletter to parents. A good children's book with questions and answers about the city is *Do Skyscrapers Touch the Sky?* (a Time–Life Book for Children, 1994).

# HOLIDAYS AND CELEBRATIONS

## DIA DE MUERTOS

This Mexican-American celebration (pronounced DEE-ah dey MWER-tos) means Day of the Dead, and is celebrated on November 1 and 2. This celebration, revived in 1974 in Sacramento, CA, has its roots in ancient Mexico. At this time the family remembers and celebrates deceased relatives.

An altar or offering, *ofrenda* (oh FREN dah) is set up in each family living room. Boxes containing items made in previous years are brought out to decorate the altar. A sugar skull or *calavera* is in the center. On this special day, each child in Mexico is given a little sugar skull with his or her name written across the forehead in frosting. Bread is baked in the shape of people and called *pan de muertos* (PAHN day MWER-tos) or "bread of the dead." Special foods are made and people buy or make new clothes for this festival.

A procession is held, which ends at the cemetery where marigolds are placed in remembrance of deceased relatives. The marigold, or *cempasuchil* (sem-pah-SOO-chil), is called the "flower of the dead" in Mexico.

An excellent resource book is *Day of the Dead, A Mexican-American Celebration* by Diane Hoyt-Goldsmith, with photographs by Lawrence Migdale.

## GENERAL ELECTION DAY

This is the first Tuesday after the first Monday, and is observed usually during presidential or general elections. If this is a national election year, students can report weekly on newspaper articles. Also, it is a good time to hold classroom elections.

## VETERAN'S DAY

This holiday on November 11 was originally celebrated in honor of the armistice (peace) that ended World War I. Peace was declared on the 11th month, the 11th day, at the 11th hour (11/11 at 11:00). This special day is celebrated in all the states, District of Columbia, and Puerto Rico. On this day we honor all the soldiers who fought for this country or served their country. On this patriotic day, encourage students to dress in red, white, or blue.

## AMERICAN EDUCATION WEEK

This week, set aside in November, focuses on school. Many schools across the country have "Open House" when parents can visit the classrooms and meet the teacher. Parents are greeted by the teacher and see examples of their children's work on display.

What special activities will your school have this week?

## THANKSGIVING DAY

The fourth Thursday in the month, Thanksgiving is celebrated in all the states, District of Columbia, and Puerto Rico. This day is set aside as a day to give thanks for the blessings in our lives, and for families to get together. The traditional Macy's Day Parade in New York City is televised nationwide: Floats, huge balloons, and marching bands from all over the country perform in the parade.

Encourage students to count their blessings—not just material blessings, but blessings that include their family, health, school, and community.

Print the letters for "Thanksgiving" in vertical fashion on the chalkboard and have students think of two words that begin with that letter for which they are thankful. Perhaps an *ABC Book of Thanksgiving* would be an interesting and informative project for the entire class.

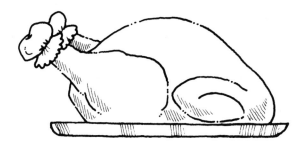

## CHILDREN'S BOOK WEEK

An entire week in November is devoted to celebrating children's books and reading. Over 5,000 children's books are printed yearly in the United States. This gives our children a tremendous opportunity to be exposed to a wide range of written material and excellent art at a young age.

Read aloud to your class daily. Give them an opportunity to read, and invite parents into your classroom to read.

# FOCUS ON SCIENCE

## AMAZING WATER!

Water is present on planet Earth in three different forms: liquid, solid (ice), and gas (water vapor or steam).

Check your map and globe in the classroom and see how much of the Earth is covered with water (more than 70%). *Most* of the Earth is water, and this often surprises students when they spin a globe. Students can check maps and globes to determine in what areas we find water in our country, in our state, and in our city. Make a list. Here are some names given to bodies of water. Are there any in your area? What is the difference of the water found in them?

| oceans | lakes | rivers | streams |
|--------|-------|--------|---------|
| ponds | brooks | falls | swamps |

## THE SALTY SEA MAMMALS

The oceans and seas are alive with fish, snakes, huge turtles, and sea mammals such as whales, dolphins, seals, and walrus. Mammals differ from fish in that they give birth to their young, instead of laying eggs. Also, mammals have lungs and must surface for air. They are warm-blooded as opposed to fish, which are referred to as cold-blooded.

- **The Baleen Whale.** This is one of two types of whales. Although the baleen whale does not have teeth, it does have fringes, just like long stiff strings, that hang from the gums of the upper jaw. This substance is called "baleen" and consists mainly of keratin, which is much like our fingernails.

    To reinforce the concept of the baleen, have the students examine their fingernails closely. Notice that although they are hard, they are pliable or flexible. How is the fingernail similar to a tool? (It can be used as a scraper and to help pick up items.)

- **The Toothed Whale.** These whales can measure in length from 5-foot dolphins to 54-foot great sperm whales. Use the trundle wheel to measure an "imaginary playground whale." The toothed whale uses its teeth as a tool to catch squid and fish, but it does not chew them. Rather, it swallows them whole. (Help students to conclude that with people, it's just the opposite. Teeth are used to chew food, not to catch it.)

- **The Killer Whale.** This is a real "sea wolf." Killer whales hunt in packs of 30 or 40, much like land wolf packs. They can travel up to 25 miles per hour as they speed through the water. Secure a goldfish bowl and fish, if you don't already have a classroom aquarium. How fast does a goldfish travel in one minute? How far? How can we measure this?

Bring in picture books by Eric Carle for the purpose of examining the sea creatures found in his books. Students can gain inspiration from these to create their own sea creatures.

## KEEP UP YOUR WATER LEVEL

Another amazing thing about water is that people are about 65% water. Our body uses water to keep our skin smooth, to help digest food, to chew food (saliva), to keep eye sockets moist, to keep joints working smoothly—and in other ways. Students can look for information in picture books on health to learn how the human body works and how it uses water. Let's keep healthy and drink plenty of good, clean water each day for refreshment.

We also get water into our system (body) via the food we eat and the air we breathe. Fresh fruits contain water or moisture. Watermelon even has *water* in its name, and is filled with water as well as juicy reddish pink fruit. Apples are mostly water, as are tomatoes. What about crunchy celery? Is that juicy? What about grapes? Cantelope? Students can begin to determine which foods hold moisture and which are dry. (See Reproducible Activity Pages.)

Ask students if their mouth ever feels dry. If so, it's a signal that they are thirsty and need some water. Encourage students to be aware of what signals they are getting from their body.

Name three food items, and have students raise their hands when they can determine "the wet one":

| A | B | C |
|---|---|---|
| cracker | pretzel | peach |
| chips | orange | corn flakes |
| apricot | peanuts | toast |

## FLOATING AND SINKING (VENN DIAGRAM)

Some things float along on top of the water, and some things sink to the bottom. Set up a "Sink/Float" station in the classroom. Have plenty of newspapers to help absorb the splashes, although students should be encouraged to work carefully.

You will need:

- a container for water
- various items to test
- a container for items
- paper and pencil

Collect objects that are made from different kinds of materials. Wood, rubber, plastic, and metal items are helpful.

Draw a Venn diagram (two overlapping circles) and label one "Sink" and the other one "Float." Set the items into the water one at a time to determine if they sink or float. Students can record this information by drawing the items in the appropriate space, or by writing in the name and drawing it later. (See Reproducible Activity Pages.)

## DO SOME ITEMS EVENTUALLY SINK? (VENN DIAGRAM)

This is where the overlapping part of the Venn diagram comes in. Some items are "Delayed Sinkers." For example, what happens to a floating sponge that eventually fills up with water? It sinks. What happens when a plastic bottle floating along on top gets tipped and fills up with water? It sinks. These items are recorded in the part of the Venn diagram that overlaps. Students can try other items that might fit into this category. Remember, it takes time, so patience is required for this activity.

## MAKING BOATS

Students can make a variety of boats that float. Boats can be made by folding aluminum foil into squares or rectangles. You can also make a boat from clay or balsa wood, or plastic bottles that float.

Do a boat experiment with them. Make tiny clay balls and see how many a boat can hold before it sinks. Be sure to have a scale handy to weigh and record the information.

A helpful book for making simple boats is *Projects With Water* by John Williams. Also look for *Water Projects* from the Design and Create series by John Williams.

## MAKING BUBBLES

*You will need:* one cup diswashing soap, five cups of warm water, bowl/cups, and drinking straws.

*Procedure:* Make four slits about $1/2$ inch long in the end of a straw to make a bubble pipe. Fold back the flaps. Scoop up some of the bubble mixture in a cup. Dip the bubble pipe into the liquid surface and blow gently.

This is best done out on the playground on a sunny day. The bubbles act as prisms, and the colors of a rainbow are reflected in them.

# NOVEMBER AUTHOR/ ILLUSTRATOR STUDY: JON SCIESZKA AND LANE SMITH

Jon Scieszka and Lane Smith collaborate as a team, but they also have done work individually. Jon Scieszka is the writer and Lane Smith is the illustrator.

*Jon Scieszka's* last name rhymes with "fresca." He has been an elementary teacher, a fine arts painter, a lifeguard, a magazine writer, and is now a full-time writer. He also delights students on author visits to schools and libraries. This author turns fairy tales upside down and brings a sense of the absurd and silliness to the familiar tales. His books have an appeal to all ages.

Students seem to enjoy *Lane Smith's* unconventional drawings, which are a departure from the usual type of illustrations for children's books. Many of his drawings have been termed as dark, or silly, but yet they hold appeal for many. While in college, he worked at Disneyland and enjoyed the artistic images there, especially at night when it was dark and he was alone. He moved to New York City from his native Oklahoma and became an illustrator.

These two talented men have made their mark by changing the face of children's books. Read them and enjoy them, and learn the lessons they are trying to teach through them.

# BOOKS AND SUGGESTED ACTIVITIES

## *SQUIDS WILL BE SQUIDS*

This book of fables gives the reader a fresh look at the morals and values that are being conveyed with brief use of text. Many are one or two pages in length. It's an amusing collection and an excellent teaching tool. Credit is given in the book to Aesop, who was famous for his short stories with a moral.

## ACTIVITIES TO ACCOMPANY *SQUIDS WILL BE SQUIDS*

1. This is a book to be savored. Read one or two fables per day. Enjoy them and discuss the meaning of the "moral" that appears at the end. What is the lesson to be learned? Children can share their experiences, and also learn from the lesson by improving or changing their own beliefs and attitudes.

2. Enjoy the art work that enriches the fables. Students can paint or draw a colorful character to go along with a fable written by the class.

3. *Format.* Point out the different size print fonts and the amount of white spaces on the pages. Students can use the computer or use a felt pen to write a one-page fable, taking note of space on the page and print size.

4. Read stories from the original *Aesop's Fables,* available in a school or public library. Many of these old tales are not illustrated, so this would be a splendid opportunity for students to create some colorful animal characters, just as illustrator Lane Smith has done.

5. The authors suggest that students might write their own fables, using animals as characters, rather than people. This book serves as a creative motivation and a good starting point.

## THE TRUE STORY OF THE 3 LITTLE PIGS

This book was an instant hit! It's the classic tale of *The Three Little Pigs* turned upside down. This falls into the genre of "Retold Tales" and is told from the point of view of the wolf. The wolf presents himself as a sympathetic, "poor me" character who just happened to knock on a couple of rickety doors trying to borrow a cup of sugar to make a birthday cake for his grannie. It's a side-splitting tale for all ages.

## ACTIVITIES TO ACCOMPANY *THE TRUE STORY OF THE 3 LITTLE PIGS*

1. Have the standard version of *The Three Little Pigs* available so that students can reread it and compare the situations. Review the original tale before reading this one aloud.

2. *Point-of-view.* This is an excellent vehicle for teaching this concept. Students will be eager to retell this one aloud from the point of view of the wolf.

3. Have a jury trial, with the wolf telling his version and the remaining pig telling his version. The class can vote on whether or not the wolf is guilty.

4. Review other classic fairy tales (*Cinderella, Hansel and Gretel, Jack and the Beanstalk,* etc.). Select tales that most children know by heart and have them tell the original version. Search for these books in the library and read them. Then turn them upside down just as this author/illustrator team did. Perhaps the class can begin by doing one together as a total group, and you can print it on large paper to hang in the classrooms. Illustrators can make drawings for it. Then students can copy this story and illustrate their own version.

5. Encourage students to rewrite their own tale from the point of view of the character who has been portrayed as wicked (witch, ogre, stepmother, giant, and so on). It stimulates writing, language development, and story illustration.

6. Compare illustrations in this retold tale with ones in a standard book of *Little Red Riding Hood.*

## THE STINKY CHEESE MAN AND OTHER FAIRLY STUPID TALES

Zany! That's the only word to describe this book that was an instant hit! The tales don't make sense, but have a shred of a familiar ring to them. There are ten tales in all, such as *The Really Ugly*

*Duckling* (who grows up to be ugly), *The Tortoise and the Hair, Cinderumpelstilskin,* and many more. The stories are constantly interrupted by the Little Red Hen who is frantic to tell her story, but everything is out of order, and the Table of Contents collapses. It's one delicious disaster after another.

## ACTIVITIES TO ACCOMPANY *THE STINKY CHEESE MAN AND OTHER FAIRLY STUPID TALES*

1. The more familiar students are with the real tales, the more they will get out of this book. But begin reading the tales so they will go on a hunt in the library for them. Perhaps a contest can be waged for the team that can find the most tales.

2. *Order of a book.* There is a definite order to putting a book together, and this one is totally out of order. By calling attention to that, it gets the attention of students who then are intent on learning the true order of a book. It's a wonderful teaching tool for this skill! Put it to work for you in the classroom.

3. *The Little Red Hen.* This character holds the book together, or otherwise it would be a collection of single tales. She keeps popping up unexpectedly, much to the delight of the reader. Be sure to point out that she is still ranting on the back cover of the book. Have students skip around and try to read just her story.

4. *"Who is this ISBN guy?"* It's on the back cover that the hen asks the magic question, and students are intrigued to find out what these marks, bars, and numbers stand for. Get a book at the library on this code, and students are off on another adventure with books.

5. *Illustrations.* Have students note the format of the book, including the zany illustrations as well as the print that is squeezed down by the giant's foot in "Jack's Bean Problem," and other print that is black, big, and loud! Note the variety of print on the page containing the "Giant Story," or non-story. Students may be able to make sentences with different print cut from magazines and newspapers and junk mail. They can take a cue from the illustrator and make a Cubist collage of the giant that appears in "Giant Story."

## *THE FROG PRINCE . . . CONTINUED*

As it says in the book, "You may think you know the story of the Frog Prince but you'll have to read on to find out the shocking truth about life happily ever after." In this retold tale, the Princess kisses the frog and he turns into a handsome Prince. But he's miserable! What now?

## ACTIVITIES TO ACCOMPANY *THE FROG PRINCE . . . CONTINUED*

1. There are many lovely versions of *The Frog Prince.* Find one or two at the library and read them aloud before reading this one. Then have students make comparisons of the stories and the illustrations. Which do they prefer? It's not a contest, but sometimes an enjoyable, stable fairy tale is reassuring, while the other type is refreshing. Students may find there's room for both.

2. *Discuss "wishes."* The message here is that if you get your wish, it doesn't come with a guarantee of happiness. This is a lesson to be learned—usually the hard way. Students can discuss

and list their three fondest wishes. Then write about one of the wishes that comes true but backfires, just like it did for the frog.

3. Take an illustration walk through this book. Get some ideas for how to portray the people and the brick walk.

4. Are students satisfied with the ending? Is there another solution? Can we be something that we're not? This is another good lesson to discuss.

## MATH CURSE

On Monday the teacher says, "You know, you can think of everything as a Math problem," and the next day we're off and running from one math problem to the next. We're working with many math concepts in this book (Mr. Scieszka used to teach math)—from telling time, to counting, to true/false, and questioning, estimating, working with money—and by the end of the day, we're math zombies. With the aid of the unusual, colorful illustrations, we find math interesting.

## ACTIVITIES TO ACCOMPANY *MATH CURSE*

1. Read the book aloud to the class, and enjoy the breathlessness and breadth of math from cover to cover.

2. Work math into other areas of the curriculum, just as this concept is presented in the book. How many ways can we work it in, once we have this book to use as a helpful guide?

3. *Different ways of counting.* Mrs. Fibonacci says there are different ways of counting and that she counts "1, 1, 2, 3, 5, 8, 13 . . ." Figure out her pattern. (Answer: 1+1=2, 2+1=3, 3+2=5, 5+3=8 and so on). Visit the planet Tetra and the planet Binary and figure out the patterns.

4. *Money and U.S. presidents.* Can we really figure out which multiple-choice answer is correct? Does "1 Lincoln equal 20 Washingtons"?

5. Students can use the Sports pages of the local newspaper to create math problems. Make sure they solve them and have the answer for those who attempt to solve them.

6. What part do the illustrations and graphics play in the attractiveness and appeal of this book? Discuss the shapes and use of color with students. Point out the milk carton and the numbers on a spongy background. Challenge students to make an attractive math illustration of their very favorite number.

**Note:** This author/illustrator team is bound to brighten up your month with many opportunities for learning. Students can keep hunting down the books by this creative team in the library. Look for *Knights of the Kitchen Table; The Good, The Bad and the Goofy; Summer Reading Is Killing Me; The Not-So-Jolly Roger;* and others. In addition, students will find books by Lane Smith that he did on his own, such as *The Big Pets* and a wordless picture book called *Flying Jake.* Jon Scieszka has teamed with illustrator Daniel Adel for *The Book That Jack Wrote.*

# REPRODUCIBLE ACTIVITY PAGES
# FOR NOVEMBER

## READING/LANGUAGE ARTS

The Contraction Cats

Find Your Other Half

Sentence Contractions

Related Story Ideas in a Bucket

I'm a Classroom Tour Guide

Storytelling Puppet (Boy)

Storytelling Puppet (Girl)

## MATH

Multiplication Mastery

Pizza Wheel Multiplication

Jimbo's Division Balloons

## SOCIAL STUDIES

Project Organizer Contract

Patriotic Symbols Concentration Game

## SCIENCE

Some Food Contains Water

Sink/Float Venn Diagram

## AUTHOR STUDY

The Stinky Cheese Man Mixed Up the Red Hen

# The Contraction Cats

Color the puppets. Cut them out and staple them back to back. One says something in formal speech. One repeats it, using contractions.

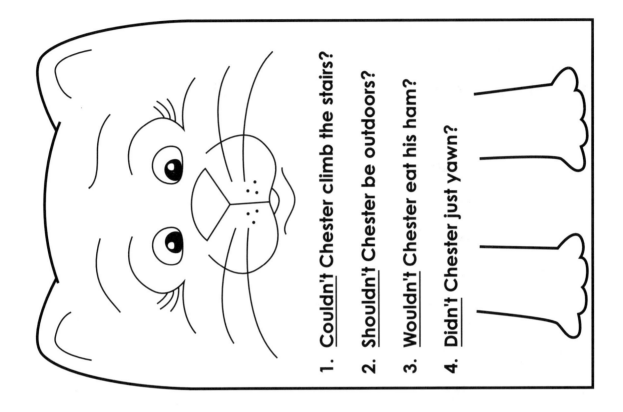

1. <u>Couldn't</u> Chester climb the stairs?
2. <u>Shouldn't</u> Chester be outdoors?
3. <u>Wouldn't</u> Chester eat his ham?
4. <u>Didn't</u> Chester just yawn?

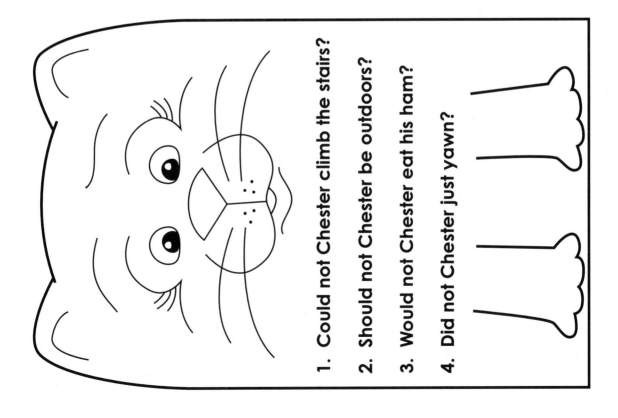

1. Could not Chester climb the stairs?
2. Should not Chester be outdoors?
3. Would not Chester eat his ham?
4. Did not Chester just yawn?

# Find Your Other Half

Cut these compound words in half. Put them into a bag and shake it. Play with a partner. Take turns pulling out a strip. The one with more compound words wins.

| ● | day | light | ★ |
| ● | school | yard | ★ |
| ● | air | plane | ★ |
| ● | dump | truck | ★ |
| ● | to | day | ★ |
| ● | stair | way | ★ |
| ● | tree | house | ★ |
| ● | run | way | ★ |
| ● | play | ground | ★ |
| ● | home | town | ★ |

# Sentence Contractions

Chatterbox Squirrel is trying to find the correct contraction for each sentence below. You can help. Circle the one that fits. Compare them with your classmates.

1. _____ be there in a minute.
   We've      I'll

2. Let me know if _____ going to the game.
   you're    they'll

3. When did you say _____ be there?
   they're    it'll

4. You _____ cross on a red light.
   this'll    shouldn't

5. _____ help with the clean up?
   Who'll    We're

6. I _____ know Carly was absent.
   wasn't    didn't

7. You can use it if _____ put it back.
   you'll    they're

8. Why _____ you say you're a good pitcher?
   hasn't    didn't

9. Mom and Dad _____ going to the show.
   isn't      aren't

10. I think _____ love the cookies!
    you'll    me'll

©2002 by The Center for Applied Research in Education

Make your own set of flashcards.

# Related Story Ideas in a Bucket

When you read a story, notice that it deals with the same topic. Each sentence relates to the main idea. Below are three story buckets about three different topics.

**A**
Story about
BIRDS

**B**
Story about
FOOD

**C**
Story about
WEATHER

Here are sentences that go in these story buckets. Place the appropriate letter on the line in front of the sentence. The first one is done for you to get you started.

**A** 1. "Looks like it's time for nest building," said Grandpa.

____ 2. It looks like it's going to rain.

____ 3. The store has a special on celery this week.

____ 4. I could use that for the salad I'm making.

____ 5. If it does rain, will we still have the picnic?

____ 6. The robins are busy making nests with mud and grass.

____ 7. The bluejays are flying in and out of the evergreens.

____ 8. We can always have a cookout and eat indoors.

____ 9. "Yep! The sky looks cloudy!"

____ 10. Bright red apples always make my mouth water.

____ 11. They have good-looking fruit in this store.

____ 12. Do the robins migrate here?

____ 13. "Oh, look! There's a patch of blue in the sky!"

____ 14. "Did I imagine it, or was that thunder?"

____ 15. When it rains, I like to read a good mystery book.

____ 16. "Did you notice the bright sky in that stormy painting?"

____ 17. Birds make nice music when they're all singing.

____ 18. "I'd like cheese and pepperoni on mine, please."

*Write a story using all the "A" sentences...*

*...or the "B" sentences...*

*...or the "C" sentences...*

**Name** _____    **Date** _____

# I'm a Classroom Tour Guide

You need to do two things to be a good tour guide. First, decide what you would point out to a visitor. Second, practice your guide talk.
   Use this page for planning your guide talk.

1. Where will you go?

   First _____

   Second _____

   Third _____

2. What will you say about books in the classroom?

3. What will you point out about the bulletin boards?

4. What will you say about Math?

5. What will you say about Science?

6. What special spot in the classroom will you be sure to mention?

# Storytelling Puppet

Color, cut out, and use as a storyteller mask or puppet.

# Storytelling Puppet

Color, cut out, and use as a storyteller mask or puppet.

# Multiplication Mastery

Fill in the missing answers.  Work carefully.  Check all the work.

A.
$$\begin{array}{r} 6 \\ \times 4 \\ \hline \end{array} \qquad \begin{array}{r} 5 \\ \times 5 \\ \hline \end{array} \qquad \begin{array}{r} 3 \\ \times 2 \\ \hline \end{array} \qquad \begin{array}{r} 4 \\ \times 3 \\ \hline \end{array} \qquad \begin{array}{r} 8 \\ \times 9 \\ \hline \end{array} \qquad \begin{array}{r} 7 \\ \times 6 \\ \hline \end{array}$$

B.
$$\begin{array}{r} 7 \\ \times 5 \\ \hline \end{array} \qquad \begin{array}{r} 8 \\ \times 6 \\ \hline \end{array} \qquad \begin{array}{r} 2 \\ \times 9 \\ \hline \end{array} \qquad \begin{array}{r} 7 \\ \times 7 \\ \hline \end{array} \qquad \begin{array}{r} 1 \\ \times 9 \\ \hline \end{array} \qquad \begin{array}{r} 4 \\ \times 6 \\ \hline \end{array}$$

C.
$$\begin{array}{r} 8 \\ \times 9 \\ \hline \end{array} \qquad \begin{array}{r} 6 \\ \times 3 \\ \hline \end{array} \qquad \begin{array}{r} 9 \\ \times 5 \\ \hline \end{array} \qquad \begin{array}{r} 3 \\ \times 9 \\ \hline \end{array} \qquad \begin{array}{r} 5 \\ \times 5 \\ \hline \end{array} \qquad \begin{array}{r} 4 \\ \times 5 \\ \hline \end{array}$$

D.
$$\begin{array}{r} 9 \\ \times 4 \\ \hline \end{array} \qquad \begin{array}{r} 9 \\ \times 9 \\ \hline \end{array} \qquad \begin{array}{r} 7 \\ \times 8 \\ \hline \end{array} \qquad \begin{array}{r} 6 \\ \times 5 \\ \hline \end{array} \qquad \begin{array}{r} 4 \\ \times 9 \\ \hline \end{array} \qquad \begin{array}{r} 9 \\ \times 8 \\ \hline \end{array}$$

E.
$$\begin{array}{r} 6 \\ \times 6 \\ \hline \end{array} \qquad \begin{array}{r} 5 \\ \times 7 \\ \hline \end{array} \qquad \begin{array}{r} 8 \\ \times 8 \\ \hline \end{array} \qquad \begin{array}{r} 9 \\ \times 2 \\ \hline \end{array} \qquad \begin{array}{r} 5 \\ \times 9 \\ \hline \end{array} \qquad \begin{array}{r} 6 \\ \times 7 \\ \hline \end{array}$$

F.
$$\begin{array}{r} 9 \\ \times 1 \\ \hline \end{array} \qquad \begin{array}{r} 5 \\ \times 4 \\ \hline \end{array} \qquad \begin{array}{r} 6 \\ \times 8 \\ \hline \end{array} \qquad \begin{array}{r} 5 \\ \times 6 \\ \hline \end{array} \qquad \begin{array}{r} 8 \\ \times 7 \\ \hline \end{array} \qquad \begin{array}{r} 9 \\ \times 3 \\ \hline \end{array}$$

Fill in the missing number.

$$\begin{array}{r} 6 \\ \times \square \\ \hline 42 \end{array} \qquad \begin{array}{r} 8 \\ \times \square \\ \hline 64 \end{array} \qquad \begin{array}{r} 3 \\ \times \square \\ \hline 27 \end{array} \qquad \begin{array}{r} \square \\ \times 5 \\ \hline 30 \end{array} \qquad \begin{array}{r} \square \\ \times 6 \\ \hline 36 \end{array} \qquad \begin{array}{r} 7 \\ \times \square \\ \hline 56 \end{array}$$

Name _____     Date _____

# Pizza Wheel Multiplication

Each pizza contains eight multiplication facts.  Write your answer on the outside.  Check with a partner.

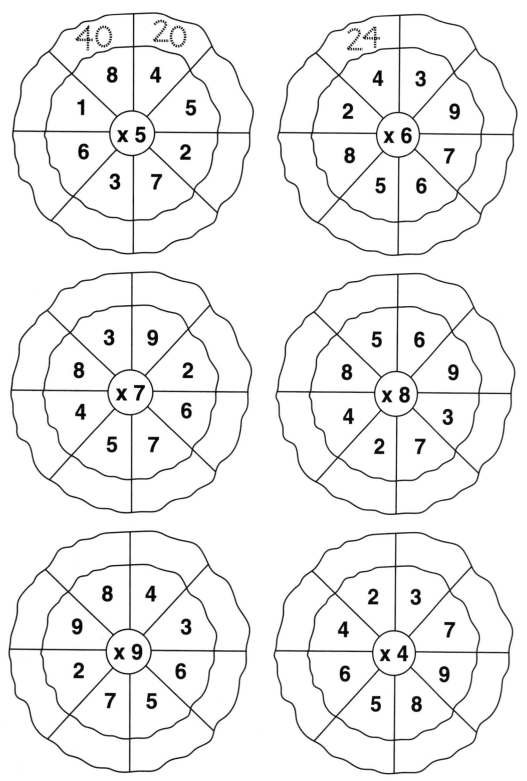

# Jimbo's Division Balloons

Each balloon contains eight division facts. Write your answer on the outside to help Jimbo keep the balloons in the air. Check your answers.

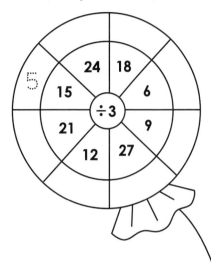

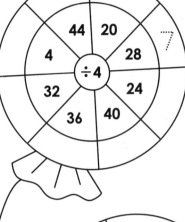

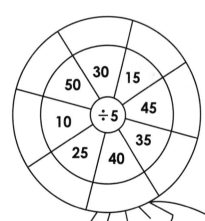

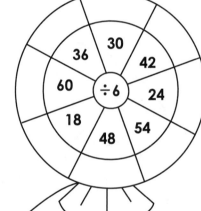

**Jimbo says:**
On the back, make two more balloons. Have a classmate fill in the answers. You can correct them.

Name _____    Date _____

# Project Organizer Contract

1. Name of project: _____

2. Materials list: _____

   _____

3. What I need to do each day:

| Monday | Tuesday | Wednesday | Thursday | Friday | Saturday |
|--------|---------|-----------|----------|--------|----------|
|        |         |           |          |        |          |

4. Where I can look for help:

5. Who I can ask for help:

6. Countdown to Due Date:

| 2 Days Before | Day Before | Due Date |
|---------------|------------|----------|
| I need to:    | I need to: | I'm ready: |

# Patriotic Symbols Concentration Game

Color each picture below. Then cut the boxes apart on the lines. TO PLAY THE GAME: Lay the cards face down on a grid. Turn over two cards. If the cards match, you may keep them. If the cards do not match, turn them back over. Then the next player takes a turn. Try to remember where each picture is located. The player with the most matching cards wins.

Name _____    Date _____

# Some Food Contains Water

People need to drink water daily. We also need fruits and vegetables.
Circle and color all of the foods that contain moisture. How many do
you eat? _____

grapes

apple

toast

watermelon

orange

nuts

pretzel

cucumber

plum

cracker

Name _____    Date _____

# Sink/Float Venn Diagram

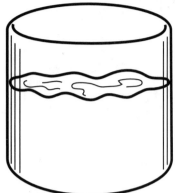

**You will need:** A container for water, a container for items, a variety of items.

**Procedure:** Place each item into the water. In the Venn diagram record the items that sink or float, and those that can do both.

# The Stinky Cheese Man
# Mixed Up the Red Hen

The Red Hen from *The Stinky Cheese Man and Other Fairly Stupid Tales* is confused about the order of the contents of a book. This is how she put them in order. Please make a new list and correct them. Thank you!

### HER LIST

1. The End
2. Title Page
3. Chapter Two
4. Dedication
5. Glossary
6. Table of Contents
7. Chapter One

### YOUR LIST

1. _____
2. _____
3. _____
4. _____
5. _____
6. _____
7. _____

# DECEMBER

# DECEMBER BOOKS

Books to Read!

**Andersen, Hans Christian, and retold by Tor Seidler.** *The Steadfast Tin Soldier.* **Illustrated by Fred Marcellino (New York: HarperCollins, 1992).** This is the timeless tale of the beloved one-legged toy soldier and the paper ballerina that he admires from afar. She would be the perfect wife for him, he dreams. At night when the people go to bed and all the toys come to life, the ballerina and the tin soldier are locked into each other's gaze. What will become of them? The illustrator brings new life to this charming tale.

**Base, Graeme.** *Animalia* **(New York: Harry N. Abrams, Inc., 1986).** A stunning visual treat! The book is filled with exotic and familiar creatures. It is a journel from A through Z, with a wealth of hidden objects and a treasury of alliteration.

**Guback, Georgia.** *The Carolers* **(New York: Greenwillow, 1992).** It's a winter evening, and five carolers travel through the town singing Christmas carols. As they stop outside each house, we see the Christmas preparations in progress inside. Each family joins the carolers and soon there is a colorful, singing troupe. The words and music of eleven carols are included. Delightful illustrations.

**Hague, Michael.** *The Perfect Present* **(New York: Morrow Junior Books, 1996).** A tender story about a rabbit who goes to a toy store to buy his sweetheart a special present. He buys a kangaroo, but the playful kangaroo bounces out of the door before it can be wrapped, and the merry chase is on. Double gatefolds open into winter panoramas with gorgeous illustrations.

**Melmed, Laura Krauss.** *Moishe's Miracle, A Hanukkah Story.* **Illustrated by David Slonim (New York: HarperCollins, 2000).** Classic story about holiday time in the home of a generous, poor man and a nagging wife. Moishe is given a magic pan for making latkes with the warning that only he must use it. But this is too good to be true for his greedy wife. So, when she tries out the pan—find out what happens.

**O'Neill, Mary.** *Hailstones and Halibut Bones.* **Illustrated by Leonard Weisgard (New York: Doubleday, 1961).** The book has been newly illustrated and published again, but this is the original. It's a treat for any month of the year—a poetry book about colors that appeals to the senses. Clear and fresh, and quiet and loud, and sensitive and magical. Each color is discovered in a unique way. It will become a favorite!

**Penn, Malka.** *The Miracle of the Potato Latkes.* **Illustrated by Giora Carmi (New York: Holiday House, 1994).** Tante Golda makes the most delicious potato latkes in all of Russia, but this year she's down to one potato. She has a saying, "God will provide!" as she shares her last potato with a beggar who tells her that one miracle leads to another. It will take a miracle to have a holiday latke party this year.

**Pinkney, Andrea Davis.** *Seven Candles for Kwanzaa.* **Illustrated by Brian Pinkney (New York: Dial, 1993).** A bright, colorful book that is helpful to students concerning the purpose and intent of this special holiday for African-Americans. The book has a warm feeling.

**Sabuda, Robert.** *The 12 Days of Christmas, A Pop-Up Celebration Book* **(New York: Simon & Schuster, 1996).** The timeless song of the 12 days of Christmas comes to life through pop-up engineering that the artist has designed to twist and turn the 3-D structures. A lavish treat!

**(CHAPTER BOOK) Fox, Paula.** *The Little Swineherd and other Tales.* **Illustrated by Robert Byrd (New York: Dutton Children's Book, 1996).** For a change of pace during this busy season, this little volume contains six classic fables that continue to delight young children and feed their imagination in a world of talking animals. They entertain and provide good lessons in values.

# DECEMBER

December is a busy month. It provides a lot of enjoyment for young children as they prepare for the holidays and for winter.

This festive time of year will enrich your Art and Music programs. Students can paint holiday pictures at the easel, and sing the songs of the season as well as listen to songs and instrumental music. It also provides an opportunity for parents to become involved in school by sharing customs from different cultures. Contact parents to see if they can bring in specific items that are used during the holidays. Some parents will come dressed in their native garb. Some will come with a sampling of food. Some will bring holiday photographs or 35mm slides of their native country. Some will show photographs and slides of this country as well.

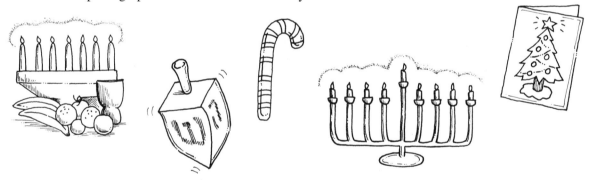

Tap into this rich resource to enrich the classroom environment. You can do this throughout the year in your Social Studies program. Also encourage parents to come to the classroom to read with students.

# FOCUS ON READING

## THE MAIN IDEA

What is the main idea? It is the *most important* information, the message, what you need to know. The main idea refers to the primary information given in a sentence, a paragraph, or a story. It's what the author is trying to say.

First, work with a simple sentence to determine the main idea or message given. Print the following sentences on a large chart, on the chalkboard, on the overhead projector, or have them printed in advance on copy paper so that each student can have one. Here are three sentences to get you started:

"Please throw out the trash," said Mrs. Gray.

Read the sentence aloud. Point to the quotation marks and remind students that someone is speaking. What is this person saying? The main idea should be quite clear in this simply stated message. (If the class has been doing work with newspaper headlines, which help determine the main idea, they can shorten the main idea using the words: *Throw out trash.*)

The gray squirrels are busy gathering nuts in autumn.

Read the sentence aloud. What is the noun? (*squirrels*) What are they doing? (*gathering nuts*) There's your main idea. Does it matter that they are gray squirrels? (*no*) Although the sentence tells when they are gathering nuts, is that the main idea? (*no*)

Carl got a sleek new silver scooter.

Read the sentence aloud. Locate a noun. (*Carl*) Locate another noun. (*scooter*) Nouns are often clues to the main idea. In this case these two words (*Carl, scooter*) help us with the main idea, which is that Carl got one. When dealing with the main idea, does it matter that it's sleek? (*no*) Does it matter that it's silver? (*no*) It may make a more interesting sentence than "Carl got a scooter," but it just adds information to the main idea.

## FINDING THE MAIN IDEA IN PRINT—MULTIPLE CHOICE

Write a list of simple sentences on the chalkboard or on a chart. Underneath each sentence, write a list of possible main idea selections. Explain that these are choices and there are more than one or two. We call this a multiple-choice exercise. Have students become familiar with the term *multiple choice.*

Read aloud the first sentence and the possible choices. Work with the students to select the best choice for the main idea. Then they can underline that choice. Do the second sentence in the same way. Then have students work independently. During this time, you can walk around the room to answer questions and check to see if students are able to complete the exercise. (Another time, have the students circle the letter in front of their choice; and still another time, have students print the letter of their choice on a blank line.) Here are some sentences to help get you started. The answers are: b, c, c.

1. The Red Delicious apples were on sale at the store.

    a. The apples are delicious.

    b. The apples were on sale.

    c. The apples were at the store.

2. The cat and the dog had a fight on the sidewalk.

    a. The cat and the dog were on the sidewalk.

    b. The cat and the dog got outside.

    c. The cat and the dog had a fight.

3. Tonight we are having a birthday party that will be fun.

    a. We will have fun tonight.

    b. Birthday parties are fun.

    c. Tonight we will have a party.

(See Reproducible Activity Pages.)

## FINDING THE MAIN IDEA IN MORE COMPLEX SENTENCES

Remember, we need to look for the essence, or the message, when we read the sentence. Suppose you could only say the message in two or three words. What would they be? That may help students when they are trying to select the main idea. Here are more sample sentences. The answers are: b, c, b.

1. "This is going to be a busy day, so please throw out the trash," said Mother.

    What is the most important information?

    a. It's a busy day.

    b. Throw out the trash.

    c. Mother is talking.

2. It was a sunny, windy, autumn day and the squirrels were busy burying acorns, as they do every year.

   What is the most important information?

   a. The day is sunny.

   b. It's autumn.

   c. Squirrels are burying acorns.

3. Carl got his wish! He unwrapped the huge box and in it was a brand new scooter.

   What is the most important information?

   a. Carl got his wish.

   b. Carl got a scooter.

   c. Carl unwrapped a box.

## FINDING THE MAIN IDEA IN A PARAGRAPH

A paragraph contains a lot of information about the *same idea.* Refer to the main idea as the head-line in the newspaper, or the *sound byte* that conveys the information in just a few words. Read a paragraph aloud. Then have students tell, in a sound byte, the main idea before they even look at the choices. When everyone is pretty much in agreement about the main idea, look for it in the printed choices that you have covered up. Here is a sample paragraph. The answer is the second choice.

> Claire and Emily rode the same schoolbus. Today they were busy talking about the Science project they were working on. The bus stopped at their stop, but they did not get off. The bus driver called out to them and they quickly gathered up their books and headed for the door. It's a good thing the bus driver was paying attention.
>
> What is the main idea, or the most important information?

- Claire and Emily rode the same bus.

- Claire and Emily almost missed their bus stop.

- Claire and Emily were working on a science project.

A sound byte on the nightly news might sound something like this: "Girls almost miss bus stop." Have students continue to read paragraphs and make sound bytes of the main idea. This will help them to focus upon what is important in the written text.

## READING PORTFOLIO

By now it is time for you and the students to do some work on streamlining their reading portfo-lios. Eliminate some of the old material, and add newer material. If some of the material is too important or precious to part with, remove it and have students bring in a 3-ring looseleaf. They can use a 3-hole punch and place the material in this looseleaf. Have students think up a catchy title for their reading portolio overflow materials.

The portfolio is usually maintained by you, although students have input. Remember, *the purpose is to give a profile of the child as a reader.* This portfolio is helpful for conferences with parents, the student, and the special-needs counselor.

## IT'S NEVER TOO LATE TO START A PORTFOLIO

The reading portfolio can be started at any time of the year. Students transferring from another school, another city, or another classroom within the building may not have one. So, just begin right now.

By way of review, here are some materials to include:

**Assessment.** Make one monthly about the student's progress. This can be in the form of a written statement or a checklist. These ideas can help get you started:

- listens attentively to stories
- is building a reading vocabulary
- is making letter/sound relationships
- shows an interest in reading books
- listens attentively when stories are read aloud
- excells in _____
- needs work in _____

**Samples** of work, such as reading tests and scores, and stories.

**Vocabulary checklist.** Periodically check the child's progress. Use the "First 100 Words List" (Fry et al.) as a place to begin.

**Alphabet and phonetic progress.** Can the student sound out new words? Does the student have a good grasp of letter/sound relationships?

**Reading list.** What books has the student read? (The student can keep this record.)

**Student as producer of information.** Keep samples of stories the student has written, books made, drawings about stories, journal entries, book summaries, and so on.

**Cover sheet.** Specific and general comments by you are placed here. Date this. Have occasional conferences with the student regarding progress.

**Discussions with students.** When you meet with students to talk about work in the portfolio, make it a friendly, nonthreatening experience. Enjoy the child's attempts. Make positive comments. When students are placing materials in their portfolios on their own, compliment them on this and tell them you are glad to see them taking an interest. Be curious about what they are placing there. This informal way of commenting and praising will soon bring other students to their portfolios, like bees to a honey jar, and they will begin to take more of an interest.

## LOCATING INFORMATION

This is a necessary skill in reading. A student needs to be able to find the exact spot where a certain bit of information is conveyed to the reader in order to be able to document the information. Encourage students to ask other students questions such as, "Where did you find that information?" "On what page did you read that?" "Was that on the first part or last part of the page?"

## GO BACK AND FIND IT

Have students read a page of print from a basal reader, an activity page, or a weekly newsletter. They all need to have the same printed material in front of them. Discuss the page of information after it is read silently and then aloud.

Have students find the exact sentence or place on the page where they find out a specific bit of information. When they find it, they can place their finger on the first word in the sentence and wait for others to locate the information. Then you can call upon someone to read it aloud. Is there agreement?

## LOCATING INFORMATION—READ AND STOP

All students have the same page of print. Ask them to read the page silently until they come to the part that tells "_____." Then they put their marker under that sentence and raise their hand. Students always seem to enjoy this activity. They are delighted when they find the information.

## LOCATING INFORMATION—THE FIVE W'S

Have students read short news articles from their weekly paper. Use five different colored crayons or colored pens to underline information they locate:

Who = red
What = green
When = blue
Where = orange
Why = yellow

If one or two of the five W's does not apply, have students leave the material blank.

## WHO IS TELLING THE STORY?

Students need to look for the voice behind the narration when they read a story. Sometimes a story is in the first person, and students will become familiar with the use of "I," as in:

- "I said no, I wouldn't do it."
- Who in the world does she think she is, I thought.
- Sometimes I wonder if Heather likes me.

With the use of the word "I," students still need to determine who is doing the talking.

## WHAT IS A NARRATOR?

When a story is being narrated (explain the meaning of this term to students as the voice in the background), be sure to talk with the students about who the narrator is. Who is doing the talking? Who is telling the story? Students need to be taught to be on the lookout for the person behind the voice. Sometimes the voice (narrator) is the author, and sometimes it is a character from the story.

If, for example, a book starts out in the following way, who is talking? Read it aloud to students and ask them. Discuss it. There are no quotation marks around speech, there is no "I," and there is no "said."

> In a village far away, there lived a wonderful wife who had a very good husband, but they kept pesky cows and goats who kept getting out and ruining the cabbage patch in the next field. One day, the farmer who owned the cabbage patch snatched up a goat and kept it. He wondered if anyone would miss it.
>
> That night, the good husband looked over his flock of sheep and shook his head. It seemed to him that one might be missing, and so he set out on foot to find it.

This information is coming from the author, the writer of the information, the narrator. The author is setting the scene for the reader. Point out that students often do this in their own writing. When they do, they become a narrator, too.

## HOW CAN WE TEACH NARRATION?

One of the best ways is by putting on a puppet show. The narrator sets the scene and the puppets have their lines to say. The narrator may have something to say part way through the puppet show that may help show the passage of time (such as, "The days and nights quickly passed and soon it was spring") or other information that the writers want the audience to know. Then, at the end as a summary of a tale, the narrator can step in again and sum it up. Students quickly catch on to the concept when they are involved in this type of activity.

## PUPPET-SHOW BEHAVIOR

Set rules for listening during puppet shows. Students need to learn to be attentive and polite to the performers. Take care of all personal needs before the show. Students may not get up to get a drink

of water during the show. They may not go to another area of the room to play and they may not talk.

Sit back, enjoy the puppet show, and learn to become a good audience member. (This teaching may carry over into a student's personal life when attending a movie or a live performance.) Be sure to let parents know in your monthly or semi-monthly newsletter that you are working on this skill.

# FOCUS ON LANGUAGE ARTS

## MORE READING OPPORTUNITIES

Some reading skills have been addressed in the previous section. However, many more reading opportunities will be available this month in the area of Language Arts and in other sections of the book as we go through the month and through the year. Always look for reading links to other subjects.

### HOLIDAY STORIES AND POEMS

December is a good month to read aloud to students, since they are usually keyed up over the upcoming holiday season and need to have some quiet time. One resource that should not be overlooked is that of magazines for students. Check your school library and local library. You can find many short holiday stories in the December issues. Ask the librarian for back issues as well. Be sure to look for these magazines for young children: *Cricket, Ranger Rick, Highlights for Children, National Geographic World, Cobblestone,* and so on.

### BELLS JINGLE, RING, AND DING-A-LING

Some words sound very much like the sound they are trying to convey. In this merry season, bells jingle, bells ring, bells go ding-a-ling.

Have students be on the lookout for words that resemble real sounds. These words are often used in children's poetry, children's books, comic strips, and even news headlines. Here are some to help get you started. In the beginning, be sure to emphasize the sound by drawing it out (exaggerating it), so that students understand that the word is making a representative sound.

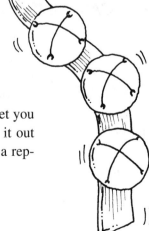

| dogs *bark* | cows *moo-o* | cats *me-ow* |
| ducks *quack* | geese *hiss-s* | owls *scre-e-ch* |

## FIND THE ONOMATOPOEIC WORD

Explain to students that when words sound like the word they are trying to convey, it is pronounced "On-Uh-Maat-Uh PEA' Uh."

Read the following sentences aloud. If students can *hear* this special word, have them raise their hand. Then call on someone to say it. (The words are underlined for your convenience.)

1. "Oink, oink," cried the little pink pig.

2. Carmen put his handkerchief up to catch his kerchoo!

3. The dishes clattered to the floor.

4. The big, husky growl came from the throat of the first dog in the race.

5. The engine sputtered and then stopped.

6. The water came out of the hose with a swish.

7. "Oh, here comes the choo choo," said Mother.

8. A howl came from the chilly night air.

9. The surface of the table was smooth.

10. All the children squealed with delight when they saw the fireworks.

## WORDS WITH ZEST

Pick the word from the group that *does not* belong because it does not have enough zest, or ping, and doesn't sing! (The words are underlined for your convenience.)

| | | | |
|---|---|---|---|
| bang | bark | boom | believe |
| chirp | clank | cousin | clatter |
| ticktock | whack | hi | slurp |
| fizz | ill | howl | squeak |

Once the students have the zesty words, they can make up a story using these words. It can be a zany story, a tall tale, or one that is realistic. This gets students working with vocabulary and creates an interest in the sounds of words. Then students can work on words that are quiet, too.

## IN TWENTY WORDS OR JUST TWO LESS

Summarize a story using twenty words or just two less. Remember, students need to tell something about the setting, the problem, and the solution. Can students also mention the main character? This is a challenge, but a worthwhile one. It helps students to select the most meaningful words. Complete sentences may not be important here—phrases and single words are okay.

## CREATING BOOK JACKETS

Examine book jackets on a variety of books in the classroom. Note the written information that is given in addition to the title and the author. Examine the illustrations. Then have students select a book and create a new book jacket for that particular book. Use it in the classroom.

Students can create an original book jacket and then create (write) a story that might be found inside. Students who enjoy the process of making the book jackets may be encouraged to make several for the Writing Center, and those who like to write stories (text) can create a story that goes with the cover page. Keep these books with the circulating books in the classroom.

## A TIMELINE OF EVENTS

A timeline is an excellent way to emphasize the beginning, middle, and ending of a story, with significant events that happen along the way. Is there more action before the middle or after the middle? Does this vary from book to book? Make comparisons. Students can use chart paper that has been cut into strips to record the events. They can also make illustrations.

For books that deal with flashbacks in time, use the technique of the cartoon bubbles for printed text, and place them on the timeline where they occur in the book, not when they actually happened.

Depending upon the book and the significance of the flashback, use the bubble technique for text and print a symbol in the bubble as well. Then place that symbol along the line so the reading audience can see when the event occurred and when the reader learned about it.

## BOOK POSTERS

Motivate students to create a poster-sized advertisement for a favorite book they have read up to this point in third grade. The students may examine ads in magazines and newspapers to determine what information could appear in the ad. Display the ads. Give students "one minute" to try to convince other students to read this book.

## READING FOR THE HOLIDAYS

Encourage students to keep up their reading effort over the holiday period. Convey the message that reading is enjoyable and can be done independently and quietly. A student can "get lost" in a good book when he or she feels there's nothing to do, or can't go outdoors to play. Challenge students to remember that holiday message.

In your newsletter to parents this month, encourage the giving of books as holiday gifts to their children.

## BOOK BAGGIE KITS

Make up at least four or five of these "Book Baggie Kits." In a large-size, self-locking plastic bag, place three felt-tip pens of different colors, safety scissors, glue stick, small squares of different

colored construction paper, and large sheets of paper (folded or rolled to fit into the baggie). Have students sign them out of the classroom to take home over the weekend (or for two nights in a row) so that they can work on a book-related project that has been discussed in class (such as a book jacket, book advertisement, or even bookmarks). When they return the materials, have the "Book Baggie Librarians" check the bags for contents and make a note of anything missing, except for the paper. Notify the student if something is missing,. The student should replace it so that the kit can be recirculated. However, have other kits available and ready to go so that the process is not interrupted while waiting for the return of an item or two.

When these kits go home, they may give some parents ideas for holiday gifts for students, such as colored pens and pencils, glue sticks, sticky note pads, scissors, etc., that will help students with their class projects. A general note tucked inside explaining the purpose of the kit would prove helpful to parents, too.

# WORD ORIGINS AND SAYINGS*

Once again we will work with words and their origins in an effort to build vocabulary and motivate students to be inquisitive about word origins. *This month the words are more familiar.* Write one word per week on the chalkboard. Introduce it on Monday, and have students explore the word in the resources available to them. On Wednesday or Thursday, give them an explanation of the origin of the word. Encourage use of it in their writing and speaking.

1. **rival.** This word is from the Latin word *rivalis* which means "of a brook or a stream." As a noun, the word *rivalis* refers to those who drink from the same stream. Just as two people want the same source of water, the word has come to mean two people competing for the same thing—or rivals.

2. **test.** This word was used in the Middle Ages for a shallow, porous cup. When impure gold or silver was heated in it, the impurities were absorbed in the porous cup (cupel), leaving the pure piece of silver or gold at the bottom of the cup. By the late sixteenth century, *to put something to the test* meant to determine its quality. Now it refers to any examination or evaluation.

3. **fur.** At one time animals were not referred to as having fur; they had *pelts*. The term *fur* was only used after the pelt had been removed from the animal and made into something to adorn a piece of clothing, such as a fur lining of a coat or a fur collar. The term was eventually broadened to include the short hairs of living animals.

---

*The Merriam-Webster Book of Word Histories, edited by the staff of G. and C. Merriam Co.

4. **surgery.** A doctor who is a surgeon works exclusively with his hands. The terms *surgeon* and *surgery* are both derived from the Greek *cheirourgos,* which means "working with the hand." Breaking the word down still further, *cheir* refers to hand and *ergon* refers to work.

5. **glamour.** This word is derived from the Greek and Latin words *grammar* and *grammatica.* Most people in the Middle Ages were unschooled, and there was a certain aura and even suspicion toward those who could read and write. Eventually there was a connection made in many languages between grammar (those who knew things) and magic. In eighteenth-century Scotland, grammar was altered to *glamer* or *glamour,* which meant a magic spell or enchantment. Today the word has been generalized to mean an alluring or fascinating personal attractiveness. Any reference to learning has been lost.

# WRITING SKILLS

## MORE WORK WITH RELATED IDEAS

Write a story on an overhead projector transparency and read it aloud all the way through. Have students determine what it is about (subject). Then reread it and circle or draw a line through the sentences that do not belong. Use a water-based pen for this part of the activity so that students can erase the areas that are eliminated, and do it again.

Students need repeated work on paragraphs with related ideas. We have worked on this in Reading, and can revisit it in Writing. At the Writing Center, have a stack of these transparencies available for students.

## THE WRITING CENTER

By this time of year, the Writing Center is a hub in the classroom. If you don't have this Center, it's not too late to set one up. It should be equipped with a variety of types of plain paper and lined paper, colored paper, construction paper, lead pencils, colored pencils, assorted felt-tipped pens with thin and thick nibs, erasers, scissors, glue, envelopes, and so on.

In your newsletter to parents, if you have not already done so, now is the time to call for old unused envelopes, note cards, postcards, and fancy writing paper. Many students are motivated to write lists of words on paper that is elongated.

Call for discarded typewriters as well. Many students like to practice their spelling words on old typewriters where they press down one key at a time.

Have several outdated telephones in this area so that students, as editors, newspaper people, and shop owners, can take pretend calls during a busy day (role-playing). They can write "breaking news" stories about zoo animals or a pet that got loose in the middle of traffic. Those who are running a restaurant can take orders for their pizza and sandwich specials. Use hats in this Center, too. Many students really enjoy role-playing while wearing a special hat. Third graders are still very much into role-playing activities, so capitalize on it for learning.

## CALLING ALL HATS

Ask parents to be on the alert for hats that they can send into the classroom for the Writing Center. When students wear these hats, they must write a story about something related to the hats. Football helmets help boys produce fantastic sport stories. An old-fashioned hat with flowers suddenly makes a lady of the wearer who will certainly need to pen an invitation to tea with a purple felt-tip pen. A baseball cap, surgeon's paper hat, firefighter's helmet, police officer's hat, a fast-food worker's hat, and so on, are all valuable motivational tools for inspiring and enriching writing in the classroom. Give it a try!

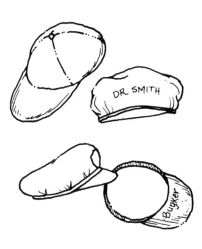

## WRITE THANK-YOU NOTES AT HOLIDAY TIME

Make a list of all the people in the community who have done work to make the neighborhood a better place to live. Include people in the school building (cafeteria workers, teachers of special subjects, office workers, nurse, custodian, principal, etc.) and in the immediate community (the crossing guard, the bus driver), and the general community (the mayor, fire chief, police chief, newspaper editor, nursing home activities directors, nurses, doctors, dentists, and so on).

Each student can write an individual note of thanks for the class. Talk about what the general message should be. *Review the procedure for writing a letter.*

Make drawings around the edge and a colorful border for the letter. Address the envelope and make a design on it. Don't forget the return address.

Postage for this project may come from a number of sources: petty cash, PTA, private donations. Be sure to include this request in your newsletter to parents.

## TAKING PHONE MESSAGES

Teach students how to record information that is heard by telephone. Cut up 8½- by 11-inch sheets of paper so that students can write on them. They can listen to recorded messages on a cassette recording made by you or by upper-class students who are helping in the classroom.

Students need to listen carefully and write quickly; they can always rewrite. The idea is to get the message down. The recordings can go something like this:

This message is for _____. It's now _____o'clock.
I want to let you know that _____

_____

_____.

My number is _____.                    Thanks, _____

                                                                                              (name)

This is a skill that, hopefully, will carry over into the home. Students need to learn the proper etiquette for answering the phone. (Some parents will instruct their children to not answer the phone when they are home alone, but rather to listen to a recording. If it is the parent calling, he or she may have a code word that the child can recognize and will then say "pick up.")

# SPEAKING SKILLS

## CELL PHONES IN THE CLASSROOM

Some parents have given *cell phones* to their youngsters, but with the understanding that they are used only when necessary.

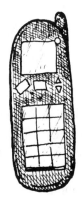

It would be a good idea to write this up in a newsletter to parents, among other messages, to get their feedback on how telephone answering, and the use of cell phones, is handled in the home.

All teachers should have a cell phone in the classroom with emergency numbers posted. Show students how to use it and when it would be appropriate to do so. (*Reminder:* Take it on all field trips and onto the playground. Some teachers wear a sleeveless vest over their regular clothing, with many pockets for supplies, and onc of the pockets houses the cell phone.)

It is very distracting to have individual cell phones of students ringing throughout the lessons and throughout the day, so check to see if there is a school policy on this issue. *Parents can always call the office to have a message sent to the classroom for their child,* which is how many schools handle this situation.

## THE PURPOSES FOR GIVING A TALK OR SPEECH

There are three main purposes for giving a talk: to inform, to persuade, and to entertain. Distribute a half sheet of paper to each student upon which is written one word: either *inform, persuade,* or *entertain.* Review these three meanings and their definitions. Then write a topic on the chalkboard, such as "Winter Sports," "A Good Diet," or a topic from something being studied this month in Social Studies, Health, or Science.

Have students work together in groups of three to generate ideas, with each person taking notes on the different purpose of his or her talk. How many ideas, for example, can they generate, as a group, for talking about "A Good Diet" to *inform* the listening audience about its importance, to *persuade* the listening audience to keep track of what they eat or to make healthy choices, and finally to *entertain* the audience with an amusing food story (real or fantasy)? This may require more than one "talking session" but students will have a better understanding of reasons for speaking to a group.

## CHORAL SPEAKING

Select a Christmas carol or holiday song and print it for all to see on the overhead projector. Use large print. Instead of singing the carol, say it together. First, you model two lines, then the students say those two lines together. Next, you say the next two lines and the students say those two lines together. Do this until you are halfway through the song, and say the part that you have practiced together. Do it again, making sure words are distinct and endings are not dropped. (We want to hear the final sounds of words.) Then complete the rest of the verse.

Do this again. Next, have half of the class speak while the other half listens. Then reverse the listening and speaking roles. The students should get better and better each time.

Next, divide the class into groups of five. Have each group select and practice a well-known song they plan to present to the group via choral speaking. This is an excellent vehicle for the shy child because each individual voice is blended into the group and no one is singled out.

# LISTENING SKILLS

## LISTEN FOR A SINGLE WORD CHOICE

Students are to listen carefully to the sentence with a missing word. They need to "fill in the blank" and say their first word choice. This helps strengthen vocabulary. It also gives you feedback regarding how well the student is attending to context clues.

The sentences can be stated or read aloud from the chalkboard, prepared in advance by you. Accept all answers that communicate meaningfully. Here are sample sentences:

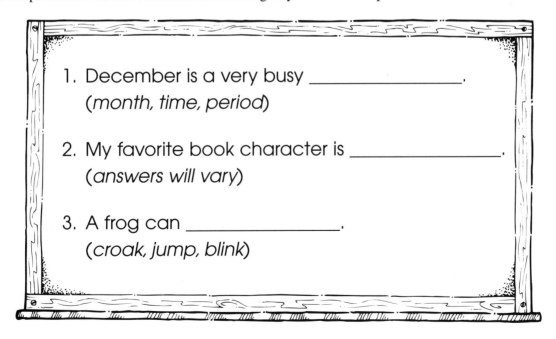

1. December is a very busy _____.
   (*month, time, period*)

2. My favorite book character is _____.
   (*answers will vary*)

3. A frog can _____.
   (*croak, jump, blink*)

## EXTENDING SINGLE CHOICES TO INCLUDE MORE INFORMATION

In this follow-up activity, students are instructed to build onto the sentence they already have by adding more information. Give them an opportunity to think about it because this is not a "single answer" fill-in-the-blank listening exercise as was the previous one. Have the students take it slowly and listen carefully. Your new sentences may look something like these:

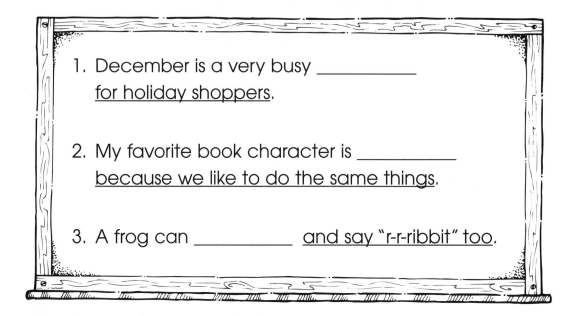

1. December is a very busy _____ for holiday shoppers.

2. My favorite book character is _____ because we like to do the same things.

3. A frog can _____ and say "r-r-ribbit" too.

## LISTEN FOR FESTIVE HOLIDAY SOUNDS

As students prepare for holidays that are most meaningful and important to them at this point in their lives, have them work together to make a list of festive sounds, or the sounds from their holiday. When the lists are completed, have them practice making the sounds, or simulating the actions for the special activity which would make a sound (such as pretend to ring bell, unwrap a gift, flip potato latkes, and so on). Each group should be encouraged to share its information while the class listens. (See Holidays in the Social Studies section for special holidays.)

## "THE TWELVE DAYS OF CHRISTMAS" (LISTENING)

This traditional English carol can be used as an interactive listening and speaking activity. Since there are twelve days in this carol, compare it with the twelve months of the year. Review the months as follows:

first—January               seventh—July
second—February           eighth—August
third—March                ninth—September
fourth—April               tenth—October
fifth—May                  eleventh—November
sixth—June                 twelfth—December

Next, determine when students have their birthday month. Ask all January's to stand and sit, then all February's can stand and sit, and so on through December.

Now, you say the carol, rather than sing it, and when the word *first* is said, all those who were born in January stand and remain standing until that verse is ended. Then the *second* verse is said aloud and all students who were born in February stand, and so on. Also, every time their number is said (when the verse is being recited backwards to numeral one), the students stand when the number is called. Throughout this exercise, students will be standing and sitting, up and down, many times. Eventually you will need to work on precision. Students must listen carefully. January really gets a workout.

Here is the song that you will read. *Students stand when they hear their number* (word underlined).

- On the <u>first</u> day of Christmas my true love gave to me:
    a partridge in a pear tree. (*All January people should stand at the word* "first" *and sit at the end of the verse.*)
- On the <u>second</u> day of Christmas my true love gave to me:
    two turtledoves (*All February people are standing.*)
    and a partridge in a pear tree. (*January people stand, then January and February sit.*)
- On the <u>third</u> day of Christmas my true love gave to me:
    three French hens, (*All March people stand.*)
    two turtledoves, (*All February's stand.*)
    and a partridge in a pear tree. (*All January's stand, then all sit.*)
- On the <u>fourth</u> day of Christmas my true love gave to me:
    four calling birds, (*All April people stand.*)
    three French hens, (*March's stand.*)
    two turtledoves, (*February's stand.*)
    and a partridge in a pear tree. (*January's stands, all sit.*)
- On the <u>fifth</u> day of Christmas my true love gave to me:
    five golden rings, (*All May people stand.*)
    four calling birds, (*April's stand.*)
    three French hens, (*March's stand.*)
    two turtledoves, (*February's stand.*)
    and a partridge in a pear tree. (*January's stand, all sit.*)
- On the <u>sixth</u> day of Christmas my true love gave to me:
    six geese a-laying, (*All June people stand.*)
    five golden rings, (*May's stand.*)
    four calling birds, (*April's stand.*)
    three French hens, (*March's stand.*)
    two turtledoves, (*February's stand.*)
    and a partridge in a pear tree. (*January's stand, all sit.*)

- On the <u>seventh</u> day of Christmas my true love gave to me:
    seven swans a-swimming, (*All July's stand.*)
    six geese a-laying, (*June*)
    five golden rings, (*May*)
    four calling birds, (*April*)
    three French hens, (*March*)
    two turtledoves, (*February*)
    and a partridge in a pear tree. (*January, all sit.*)
- On the <u>eighth</u> day of Christmas my true love gave to me:
    eight maids a-milking, (*All August's stand.*)
    *Repeat chorus.*
- On the <u>ninth</u> day of Christmas my true love gave to me:
    nine ladies dancing, (*All September's stand.*)
    *Repeat chorus.*
- On the <u>tenth</u> day of Christmas my true love gave to me:
    ten lords a-leaping, (*All October's stand.*)
    *Repeat chorus.*
- On the <u>eleventh</u> day of Christmas my true love gave to me:
    eleven pipers piping, (*All November's stand.*)
    *Repeat chorus.*
- On the <u>twelfth</u> day of Christmas my true love gave to me:
    twelve drummers drumming, (*All December's stand.*)
    *Repeat chorus.*
- AT THE END, EVERYONE IS STANDING, THEN ALL SIT TOGETHER.

**Variation One:** Students of the month speak the parts and stand/sit.

**Variation Two:** Students wave flags (4- by 6-inch pieces of colored material attached to a dowel rod; colored ribbons; or yarn) when their month is called. Standing and sitting is optional depending upon the group. Use these colors: January (white), February (green), March (blue), April (red), May (yellow), June (orange), July (violet), August (aqua), September (crimson), October (red-orange), November (brown), December (gray).

**Variation Three:** Play the musical recording and perform while listening. Then learn the song and sing along.

## BOOKS OF "THE TWELVE DAYS OF CHRISTMAS"

A variety of picture books have been made of this lovely verse. These include: *The Twelve Days of Christmas* illustrated by Claire Counihan with gingerbread characters; *The Twelve Days of*

*Christmas* illustrated by Jan Brett; *A Partridge in a Pear Tree* illustrated by Ben Shahn; and *The Twelve Days of Christmas,* a pop-up celebration by Robert Sabuda.

# FOCUS ON SPELLING

## TWO-TEAM SPELL DOWN

Go around the room and have students call out "1,2,1,2" until all have a number. Then all the one's will make a line along one side of the room and all the two's can line up along the other side. You call out a spelling word to Line 1, Student 1. The student repeats the word, spells it, repeats it. If correct, that student scores a plus point for the team. If incorrect, the team scores a minus point.

**Challenge:** If a player from Team 2 challenges the spelling and spells the word correctly, that student scores a plus point for his or her team. If a challenger spells a word incorrectly, a minus point is scored for his or her team. The object of the game is for a team to score more plus points.

## DECORATIVE FLASHCARDS

Students can create their own sets of Hanukkah, Christmas, and Kwanzaa shapes, and write their spelling words on them. Then match the shapes and words.

## DECORATIVE CHART STORY

Using the shapes that students have created for their holiday flashcards, construct and write a story on large chart paper. This makes a colorful spelling review sheet.

## CHALLENGING ORDER OF WORDS

If you have eight or ten spelling words for the week, have students write a sentence using each word. This is the challenging formula to follow:

Sentence one—spelling word is first; Sentence two—spelling word is second; Sentence three—spelling word is third, and so on.

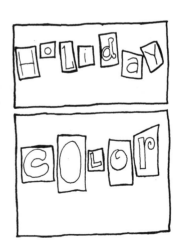

## CUT AND PASTE TO MAKE COLORFUL WORDS

Have students search through used magazines, newspapers, and junk mail for individual letters to construct the spelling words of the week. All of the letters can be different sizes, colors, and fonts. Students can cut a square around the letter rather than trying to cut out the letter itself. Construct each spelling word on a colorful sheet of paper—not necessarily in a row, but in an all-over array or design. This is an excellent activity for kinesthetic learners.

# FOCUS ON MATH

## ASSESSMENT

Time to work on records and student progress. Assess the computation ability of the students (addition, subtraction, multiplication, division). Mark items with M (mastery), P (progressing toward mastery), D (still developing).

- Does student show an interest in math?
- Does student try to participate during math lessons?
- Does student finish work?
- Does student go to the Math Center?
- Does student understand basic math terms?
- Can student work out number story problems?
- Does student have difficulty determining the problem?
- Can student determine most parts of a problem?
- Can student solve problems?
- Has student mastered addition facts?
- Has student mastered subtraction facts?
- Has student mastered multiplication facts?
- Has student mastered division facts?
- Does student show interest in graphing?
- Can student figure out problems using manipulatives?
- Does student show interest in using calculator?
- Can student measure with a ruler?
- Does student work well in small groups?
- Does student show interest in math picture books?
- Does student participate in math role-playing?
- Other

## A MULTIPLICATION JINGLE

Students can make up their own hand motions and body motions for this rhyme. It's also good to say in sing-song fashion when bouncing a ball or jumping rope. (Remember, students can learn and remember this easily, much the same way as they remember commercial jingles on television.)

*1 times 1 is one,*
*The mice are on the run.*

*2 times 2 is four,*
*The cat sneaked through the door.*

*3 times 3 is nine,*
*See the cat's eyes shine.*

*4 times 4 is sixteen,*
*That orange cat is looking mean.*

*5 times 5 is twenty-five,*
*The cat just ate that mouse alive.*

*6 times 6 is thirty-six,*
*The cat is leaping, doing tricks.*

*7 times 7 is forty-nine,*
*Catch a mouse and it is mine.*

*8 times 8 is sixty-four,*
*Mice are sneaking out the door.*

*9 times 9 is eighty-one,*
*Now the mice are on the run.*

*10 times 10 is one hundred,*
*Party's over, cat's in bed.*

## MAKE A MULTIPLICATION BOOK

Use the above rhyme to make a mini book. On the left side of the page, print the algorithm (for example, $7 \times 7 = 49$). On the right side of the page, illustrate the saying about the cats and mice. Make a title page and staple it together at the side. Students can leaf through this and say their rhyme, and also learn the multiplication fact by seeing it and hearing it.

Make up a set of flashcards for this catchy jingle, and have students say the answers by memorization. First, do them in order. Then, later, mix them up. (See Reproducible Activity Pages.)

## PROBLEM-SOLVING FORMULA

This works well for all problems, not just math. Follow these steps to assist in working toward a solution:

1. What is the problem? (Define it.)
2. Devise a plan for solving it. Think in terms of outcomes and/or consequences.
3. Carry out the plan.
4. Analysis: Did it work? What did/didn't work? Do you need to repeat steps 1, 2, 3?
5. What did you learn? Can another problem be solved in this way? How did this procedure help?

(See Reproducible Activity Pages.)

## PROBLEM SOLVING WITH PICTURE BOOKS (MORE ON QUILTS)

Perhaps the class has already completed their math quilts (October). Even if they have not, a good book that deals with problem solving is *The Quilt Maker's Gift* by Jeff Brumbeau and Gail deMarcken. In this book, an old woman makes beautiful quilts and gives them to the poor. The greedy King collects gifts from his subjects, but does not have one of these quilts. So he sets off to meet the woman, but she will not give him a quilt until he gives everything away that he owns. He refuses and dreams up numerous ways to solve the problem of obtaining a quilt. Look for a heart-warming compromise.

At the back of this book is information for visiting the King online at www.QuiltmakersGift.com. Here you will find puzzles and games for the book, and also stories of generosity from around the globe. There is quilt block lore and quilting activities for all ages, and contests and prizes, along with conversations with the author and artist.

## HOW MANY BEANS IN THE POT? (ESTIMATION)

Estimate the number of something in a set volume, such as beans in a pot, marbles in a jar, a jug of pennies, peanuts in a bag, peas in a cup, etc.

How do we estimate? We can just plain guess. But if you want a better approximation of the answer, you need to teach the skills of estimation.

**Teaching the Skill:** Set up a big jar of beans. Then you can take a smaller container and fill it with beans and actually count the number in that small container. Write it down. Then, if you know about how many of the small containers would be found in the large container, you can get

an approximation by multiplying the number of beans in the small container by the number of small containers found in the large container. It's better than a wild guess.

Suppose you have 2 cups of dried peas. Take a ¼ cup measurer and fill it with dried peas. Count the peas. Multiply by 8 (which is the number of quarter cups in two cups). That will give students an approximate number.

## CLOSER THAN A "PURE GUESS" (ESTIMATION SKILLS)

Take a clear container, cylindrical in shape, and fill it with dried beans. Count the number of beans *in a column* from top to bottom. Multiply that number times the number of items believed to be in one layer (the beans you can see on top represent a layer).

So, suppose you have 10 in a column (or ten layers) and about 24 in a layer (counting the ones seen on top). Multiply the two, $10 \times 24 = 240$, for an approximate estimate of the beans in the cylinder.

These are the skills of estimation that need to be taught. Students enjoy dreaming up their own problems and engaging friends in estimating.

They need repeated practice with this, so in your Math Center have dried beans, peas, corn, or nuts; measuring cups; measuring spoons; and large see-through containers of various shapes. (See Reproducible Activity Pages.)

## ESTIMATING LENGTH BY THE INCH

Each student will need a ruler. Have students stare at an inch. Put up their two forefingers to enclose one inch on the ruler. Tell them to get the feel or get the sense of an inch in their mind. With this mindset of an inch firmly in place, ask students to estimate some items in the classroom. Hold up these items one by one:

- a pencil
- a lunchbox (estimate from side to side, from top to bottom)
- a shoe
- a glove
- a small box
- their finger length

Have at the Math Center a basket of small items that students can use for estimation. Encourage them to bring in items, and keep changing the items in the container. They need repeated experience with this skill. (See Reproducible Activity Pages.)

## WORK ON MATH PORTFOLIOS

This month, if you have not begun, you can set up and begin to work on math portfolios. List the skills you are teaching and have a checklist to show whether the student has reached mastery, is approaching mastery with some understanding, or is not able to grasp the concepts. If you have already started multiplication and then division, record information about student progress by making notations as well. This format can be used to help with record keeping:

M = They have mastered the skill.

W = They are working toward mastery.

D = They are still developing the skill.

# FOCUS ON SOCIAL STUDIES

## DECEMBER CITIZENSHIP FOCUS

This month, because of the holidays, is an excellent opportunity to focus upon the ability to share and take turns. Our trait this month is *sharing*.

Students at this level generally understand the concept of sharing a toy or an item for a time, because they have learned that it will be returned or that their time will come again. Younger or more immature students haven't mastered the concept of sharing. They think they are giving something away that they want for themselves. It takes time to learn this fine trait, and even when students have learned it, they still need to work at it. Those who have mastered this trait and readily share need to be genuinely and lavishly praised by you.

## PROBLEM SOLVING

Here are some situations for students to discuss. Less mature students often learn new ways of thinking from the more mature group members during these discussions. It often leads to a subtle shift in behavior.

- Franco got a brand new toy for the holidays and his cousin wants to play with it even before it's unwrapped.
- DJ passed out the cookies, but he looked and there were three cookies left on the plate and four students waiting.
- Last week Kendall's neighbor played with his toys and broke one. He wants to play again. What could Kendall do?
- Tamra got a book from the public library, and Jemma wants to borrow it and take it home. What should Tamra do?

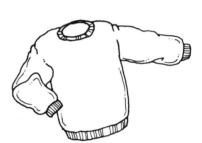

- Josh wants to borrow Mike's new sweater to wear at recess.
- Allyson wants to wear Anna's hat at recess.
- The principal has a new rule. *No borrowing clothes at school*. Will this solve a lot of potential problems?

## CITIZEN'S ARREST—SHARING

This month we need some tickets (or badges) in a central location in the classroom. On a given day, all classmates are able to approach a fellow citizen (classmate) and write him or her a ticket (or a badge) because that student was caught in the commendable act of sharing! Good luck with the hunt.

# PATRIOTISM

## THE NATIONAL ANTHEM

"The Star-Spangled Banner" is another name for our nation's flag, just as it is often called "The Stars and Stripes" and "Old Glory."

The verse, which later became the song "The Star-Spangled Banner," was written in 1814 by a young lawyer named Francis Scott Key, who also wrote poetry. The poem was called "The Defense of Ft. McHenry." Someone suggested that it went well with the rhythm of an old tune and eventually it got the name of "The Star-Spangled Banner." In the year 1931, some 116 years after it was written, it was proclaimed the national anthem.

In the United States, the flag is permitted to be flown 24 hours a day in only a few locations, and the birthplace of Francis Scott Key is one of them.

Teach the song to the students:

*Oh, say can you see by the dawn's early light*

*What so proudly we hailed at the twilight's last gleaming?*

*Whose broad stripes and bright stars through the perilous fight,*

*O'er the ramparts we watched were so gallantly streaming?*

*And the rocket's red glare, the bombs bursting in air,*

*Gave proof through the night that our flag was still there.*

*Oh, say does that star-spangled banner yet wave*

*O'er the land of the free and the home of the brave?*

## READ ALL ABOUT IT

The book *The Star Spangled Banner,* illustrated by Peter Spier, is a "must have" for the school, so call it to the attention of the librarian. In this book, the artist illustrates the first and second verses of the song. At the back of the book, verses three and four are written, so the potential for learning all four verses is there for any student who is interested or so inclined.

Also, the story of how the song came about is told at the end of the book. In addition, a copy of the song written in the hand of Francis Scott Key is included. The endpapers are a remarkable rendition by Mr. Spier of the flags of the American Revolution, and those of the United States of America, government, and its armed forces. This is a priceless study in itself.

## MORE SYMBOLS

To our growing list of national symbols, we can add these this month.

- *Uncle Sam.* Although there is debate about the origin of this figure, there's no mistaking this tall man, dressed in the colors of the flag, and with stars and stripes on his clothing. He wears a high top hat. Uncle Sam has the initials "U.S." just like the United States ("U.S."). Political cartoons began to spring up around 1813 that depicted this figure of "Uncle Sam" and soon everything owned by the U.S. government was said to belong to Uncle Sam. Probably the most famous picture became those used on military recruiting posters. (Some students have even included Uncle Sam in diagrams of their family tree.)

- *Betsy Ross.* Although no one knows for sure who made the first flag for our country, there are many versions of stories that George Washington asked Betsy Ross, a seamstress, to sew the flag. The story grew to be so popular that today when we see a white-haired woman figure sewing the first flag, the name of Betsy Ross springs to mind.

- *The Great Seal of the United States.* This is called the "coat of arms." It is the official symbol of our country. There is an eagle (the bald eagle is our national bird) with wings spread, clutching arrows (war) in one set of claws and an olive branch (peace) in the other. In its beak there is a banner upon which these words are printed in Latin: *E pluribus unum,* which means "one nation made up of many different people." A shield on the breast of the eagle represents the thirteen original states. Thirteen stars are above the head of this powerful bird, enclosed in a circle of white.

Describe this to students and have them draw it from the description. Then have them check their drawing alongside a photograph of the real symbol.

# AREA OF FOCUS: THIS IS MY COUNTRY, THE USA

## FIFTY STATES

The United States of America is made up of fifty states. States have some laws of their own, but all fifty states are loyal to the federal government.

Display a map of the United States. Students can begin to learn some of the state names and abbreviations. They need to learn the location of their state in relation to the rest of the country.

Also, is the state in the northern or southern part of the country? Eastern or western?

## I'M PROUD OF MY STATE

Students need to learn the following:

- the name of their state
- state flag
- state motto
- state capital

- how to spell their state's name
- state flower
- state bird
- size of the state

They can make state folders and keep all of the information together in one place.

## HELLO, NEIGHBORS

Students can check the location of their state on a map and learn the names of the states that border them to the north, south, east, and west. Some states are bordered by water.

**State Facts:** It will be interesting to have students hunt on a map for the two states that are surrounded by eight other states. (These states are Missouri and Tennessee.) Also, there is a place where you can stand in all four states at once. Can they find it? (The "Four Corners" of Utah, Colorado, New Mexico, and Arizona.)

Students can draw their state, put a star in the place where the state capital is, and label it. Then put a dot where their city is located and label it. Next, decorate the state with the state bird, flower, flag, etc. Also, sketch in the surrounding states and label them too. Study and learn this information. It is important to know the state name and its abbreviation.

## WHERE'S YOUR LOCATION?

Students need to know where they are in the United States. Are they, as a group, classified as:

|                |             |                 |
|----------------|-------------|-----------------|
| Northerners    | Southerners | New Englanders  |
| Midwesterners  | Westerners  | Easterners      |

Find out if students were born where they are currently living, or if they were in a different "category" before moving to their current state of residence. This may take some homework. Always let parents know when you will be needing this type of information for the class. It's simply an exercise. They may participate or not.

## STATE FACTS WORKING WITH MAPS

Obtain copies of the newspaper *USA Today*. On the back sheet of the front section there is a large map of the USA that should help familiarize students with their country. Make "Fact Cards" and use the map as a gameboard. Here are some ideas for cards:

- Find the Great Lakes. (How many can you name?)
- Find the "Finger Lakes." (How many can you name?)
- Which states have "North" as part of their name? Locate them. (North Carolina, North Dakota)
- Which states have "South" as part of their name? Locate them. (South Carolina, South Dakota)
- Name the state that begins with the letter "P." Where is it? (Pennsylvania)
- How many states begin with the letter "N"? (Eight) How many can you name? (North Carolina, North Dakota, New Hampshire, New Mexico, New Jersey, New York, Nebraska, Nevada)
- There are four states that begin with "New." Name them. (New Hampshire, New Jersey, New Mexico, New York)

- What country borders the USA on the north? (Canada)
- What country borders the USA on the south? (Mexico)
- What state is almost a perfect rectangle? (Colorado)
- What states or body of water border your state?

Students will enjoy making up their own map fact game cards.

There are also commercial jigsaw puzzles of the United States, which are helpful for students. If you can't purchase one, make one from the map on the back page of the *USA Today* newspaper. Glue the newspaper to poster paper. Allow it to dry, then carefully cut the shapes. When you get to New England, cut groups of states. Then scramble them up and piece them together into the USA map.

# HOLIDAYS AND CELEBRATIONS

## CHRISTMAS

Christmas in America is a mix of traditions and customs, mainly from Europe. The day of Christmas itself is celebrated on December 25, but many people celebrate on Christmas Eve, and throughout the season until the new year. It is a time for family gatherings and gift exchanges, singing carols, and doing good deeds for those less fortunate. Some symbols* of Christmas include:

- *Saint Nicholas.* This day is celebrated in Europe on December 6. We know jolly old St. Nick as a large elf in a red suit with a variety of presents in his giant backpack. In England he is called Father Christmas; in Germany he is known as Weihnachtsmann, and in France he is Pere Noël. Kris Kringle, or Sinterclaas, was brought to the United States by the Dutch immigrants.

- *Christmas Tree.* This symbolizes the green of spring that will return after winter. In European homes (German) they were lit only once, on Christmas Eve, with tiny candles (and were a fire hazard). Eventually in the United States, electric lights reduced the fire risk. Trees are decorated with flashy ornaments that are collected from year to year. Some classrooms decorate a tree for the birds with popcorn and peanut butter treats.

    A national Christmas tree is lit each year in Washington, D.C. Rockefeller Center in New York City is the scene of a huge, decorated tree each Christmas season.

- *Poinsettias.* This is a popular red Christmas flower from Mexico.

- *Mistletoe.* In early times the plant was called "all heal." Get caught under the mistletoe hung from the ceiling and you just might get a big kiss!

- *Christmas cards.* A German immigrant (Louis Prang) is the father of the American Christmas card. People send them to relatives and friends as a friendly greeting. Students make them in schools and give them to family members, community workers, and children in hospitals.

---

*Resource: *Christmas* by Jane Duden.

## CHRISTMAS CELEBRATIONS

In Canada, this holiday has a special flavor all its own because of the various ethnic groups in the country. Christmas Eve is January 6, and a candle is lit and placed in the window of Ukranian homes. Hay or straw is placed under the tablecloth when the table is set as a reminder of the humble beginnings of Christ. A variety of dishes are served, but they are all meatless and have no milk.

In addition to European celebrations, this holiday is celebrated in Mexico, Central America, South America, and many other areas of the world.

## HANUKKAH

This Jewish holiday held in early December is also called The Festival of Lights. Each day for a period of eight days, the family lights a candle in the *menorah* (candleholder) until all eight candles are lit. The middle candle is the one from which all others are lit. That candle is called the *shammash.* In some families, children receive a little gift each evening at dinner time. On the first night children receive money, which they call Hanukkah *gelt.*

- *Spin-the-Dreidel Game.* There are special games to play with the dreidel. Children take turns spinning the dreidel while a timer is running. The dreidel that spins the longest wins. Then the children start over again. There are other variations of games with the dreidel plus traditional games using the letters on the dreidel.

- *Spelling Variations.* Note that Hanukkah can also be spelled as Hanukah, Hanukka, Chanukah, or Chanukkah. Write the word vertically on the chalkboard, and students can fill in the space after each letter with a word that signifies the spirit of this season.

- *"Shalom!"* is the traditional greeting, which means *peace.*

- *Storytelling.* Being able to tell a good story is an important part of Jewish tradition. Students can locate folktale selections from the library and tell them in small groups, with a partner, or individually. Have an Isaac Bashevis Singer Festival and start it off with his book *When Shlemiel Went to Warsaw and Other Stories.*

Don't forget to read aloud *The Chanukah Guest* by Eric Kimmel. Children enjoy it every year.

## KWANZAA

This African-American holiday, developed in California in the 1960s, is a special time of celebration for a period of seven days. "Kwanzaa" comes from the Swahili word meaning the "first fruits" of the harvest.

Each day, for a period of seven days, the family lights a candle from a holder called a *kinara* (kee-NAR-ah). The middle candle in the center is black, and the green and red candles on either side are lit from the central candle.

*Zawadi* (za-wah-DEE) is the name given to gifts that children receive for hard work done during the year. (In Africa, children are not allowed to ask for gifts, nor to expect gifts.)

Family activities are held for each of the seven days. Many of these would be appropriate for classroom celebrations at this festive time of year:

1. Learn family traditions and traditions of ancestors.
2. Time to do something in the family, such as fix up or clean.
3. Ask the questions: "What is my strength?" "What can I contribute?" "What can I develop in myself?"
4. Create rhymes, songs, rhythms.
5. Enjoy a good harvest meal that includes corn, apples, and nuts.

## NATIONAL CHRISTMAS TREE LIGHTING (NATION'S CAPITAL)

Each year an evergreen tree is selected from one of the fifty states in the union, and it is situated in Washington, D.C. The lighting of the tree is an event that is often televised, so ask students to be on the alert for information about this in the newspaper and on the TV news.

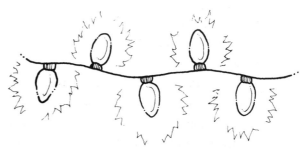

The tree in the White House has ornaments sent from people all over the country. Many artists are contacted and invited to contribute a handmade item for the tree. This is an honor for the artist.

## WHITE HOUSE CHRISTMAS CANDLELIGHT TOURS (NATION'S CAPITAL)

Many people visit the White House during this festive season. It is beautifully decorated and enjoyed by the visitors.

# FOCUS ON SCIENCE

## IRON MAGNETS

*Magnetite* is a natural magnet. Magnetite is the name given to natural rocks that have been in the ground, or earth, for thousands of years. The Earth itself is considered one great big magnet.

## LET'S EXPLORE MAGNETS

Magnets come in several shapes. There are long rectangular shapes (bar magnets), circular shapes, horseshoe shapes, and other shapes. When you put two bar magnets end to end, you can quickly find out whether they *attract* (join together) or *repel* (pull apart).

Have magnets available for students to experiment with.

## LET'S EXPLORE WITH MAGNETS

Set up a shoe box with a variety of items that students can try to pick up with a magnet. Make sure different types of materials are represented, such as rubber (rubber bands), cloth (string), paper (tissue), various coins, twigs, paper clips, nails, keys, safety pins, needles, and so on.

Students can make their own list of items that were attracted by the magnet and those that were not. What can they speculate about these two groups of items? Listen for all responses. What is the common element? Have students determine this.

## CHECK THE KITCHEN

How are magnets used in the kitchen in your home? Give students this assignment and then have them return with the information and compile it. Give them a couple of days or a weekend for the completion of the assignment. Perhaps you can make parents aware of this in your newsletter.

Students are often surprised to learn that a can opener can have a magnet that keeps the lid of the can in suspension once it is opened. Also, some refrigerator doors are magnetized as are cupboard doors. Have students keep searching. Many students will have magnets of different colors, sizes, and shapes all over their refrigerator door. These magnets fasten notes and photographs and pictures, and make a giant bulletin board and information center of the refrigerator. (See Reproducible Activity Pages.)

## MAKING REFRIGERATOR MAGNETS

*You will need:* jar of water, paintbrush, modeling stick, plate for mixing paint, clear all-purpose glue, self-hardening clay, small flat magnets, and poster paint.
  *Procedure:*

1. Make any shape of animal, bird, fish, dinosaur, etc.
2. Harden the shape by following package instructions.
3. Paint the clay; allow to dry.
4. Glue a magnet to the back of each shape. Dry.
5. When dry, the magnet will stick to the fridge because it is made of steel. What else will it stick to?

## MAGNETIC FIELDS

*You will need:* clear plastic or glass containers, iron filings, and various magnets (bar, horseshoe, ring).
  *Procedure:*

1. Sprinkle the iron filings in the container.
2. Move the magnet around *under* the container. The filings will move toward the ends of a bar magnet, because the ends are strongest. One end is a north-seeking pole and the other end is a south-seeking pole.

3. Use different magnets to make a variety of designs.

4. Experiment with the magnets and filings. If you put a piece of paper under the container, will the magnet still attract the filings? Suppose you put cardboard under the container, then what? Will it work with a thin piece of wood under the container?

5. Let's become scientific about this investigation and record our findings.

## THE SCIENTIFIC METHOD

Scientists are inquisitive people. They want to know what works and why it works. There is a scientific method for conducting experiments that will be useful to third graders:

1. Ask the question.

2. Determine how to go about finding the answer.

3. Investigate (experiment, collect, read, ask, and so on).

4. Form a hypothesis (a "good guess").

5. Test the hypothesis.

6. Conclusion (Were you right? partially right? wrong? what's the next step?). *Remember: Always keep a notebook.*

## MAKE AN ELECTROMAGNET

*You will need:* a dry cell or battery, insulated or bell wire, and a large iron nail.
   *Procedure:*

1. Peel the insulation (plastic cover) off of both ends of the wire, in about 2 inches (wire can be 16 inches in length or 24 inches in length).

2. Leave a space of about 6 inches on the wire, and begin winding it slowly and carefully around the nail. Leave 6 inches on that end, too.

3. Now wind each of the two exposed wires at the ends to the battery terminals.

4. The current in the battery is now flowing through the wire. This is an electromagnet.

5. Now is the time for experimentation: What can you pick up? How many items? Will the magnetism go through one item and pick up another? How many items can be picked up?

6. Suppose we use more wire. Will it make a stronger magnet and pick up heavier items? (*Yes*)

7. This time, use an iron screwdriver and repeatedly wind wire around it to make an electromagnet. Investigate. See what can be picked up. Use the scientific method for posing questions, carrying out the hypothesis, and drawing a conclusion. Record all findings in a science notebook like a real scientist does.

8. Investigate electromagnets in the environment. Find some interesting books at the library. Two helpful books are *My First Batteries and Magnets Book* by Jack Challoner (DK series); and *What Makes a Magnet?* by Franklyn M. Branley, with illustrations by True Kelley. (See Reproducible Activity Pages.)

## HEALTH TIP

December is a month for candies and goodies, but urge students to limit their intake. Make this "Healthy Snack Month" and encourage students to bring in an apple, banana, carrot sticks, and/or celery sticks for snack time.

## HOW DO HUMAN BODY SYSTEMS WORK TOGETHER?

Examine a hand rotary beater or a bicycle, and see how they work. The parts are interdependent. When one part moves, it makes another part move.

Make a comparison with the human body. Our body parts are interdependent, too. Bend down and pick something up from the floor. How did the hand depend on the wrist and arm? How did the arm depend on the elbow and shoulders? How did the shoulders interrelate with the back? How did the back relate to the legs and feet? Were the eyes involved?

This body interrelatedness will be new information for many students, and is an intriguing finding.

Have them go on the alert for "connections" in themselves and in their environment. Make three lists and label them: Body Connections, Nature Connections (soil and plants, day/night, seasons), and People-made Connections (traffic lights/traffic movement, various machines, roller-coaster rides, amusement park rides), and so on.

# DECEMBER AUTHOR STUDY: CHRIS VAN ALLSBURG

This author/illustrator has always been at the top of the list for children. The all-time, seasonal favorite *The Polar Express,* a Caldecott Award Winner, established Van Allsburg as a premier creator of picture books for children's literature. As a writer, it's difficult to fit him into a category. He comes closest to surrealistic fantasy. What seems impossible becomes real, and his books leave the reader with a question mark. "Did I miss something?" one may wonder, and pour back over the book again only to be left with a delightful story and something to think about.

His childhood was spent in Grand Rapids, Michigan. As a youngster, he loved to draw and eventually majored in Fine Arts in college and went on to earn an advanced degree in sculpture from The Rhode Island School of Design. His wife saw his potential for creating picture books and she, and an author friend, encouraged him to send his drawings to an editor—and the rest is history. His trusty dog appears in all of his books, and children like to look for him.

Log on to www.chrisvanallsburg.com to visit this author's world, and to read his Caldecott acceptance speeches, and a summary of his books, as well as other interesting information. As you peruse this site, click onto the picture of the trusty dog to go back "home."

# BOOKS AND SUGGESTED ACTIVITIES

This month we will work in a different way with the author study. *First,* we will have an annotated list of some of Mr. Van Allsburg's books. *Second,* there will be a suggested list of ways this body of works can be studied in the classroom.

## THE POLAR EXPRESS

Read and thoroughly enjoy the wonder and magic of this book. It's an other-worldly holiday classic. Late on Christmas Eve, a young boy boards a train bound for the North Pole. When it arrives, Santa offers him any gift he desires. The modest boy asks for a bell from the reindeer harness. On the way home the bell is lost, but on Christmas morning, there it is under the tree. When the boy gives it a shake, the bell makes a most beautiful sound—but only true believers can hear it. (Caldecott Medal Winner)

## JUMANJI

Peter and Judy are bored and restless. The game under the tree looks like any other box game to them, but they thought they'd give it a try anyway. The directions that someone wrote on the bottom of the box should have been a tip off. It reads: "Free game, fun for some but not for all. P.S. Read instructions carefully." The children take off the cover and unfold the gameboard. Before long, the jungle game takes on a life of its own and the neat house is upset by a lion on top of the piano and a dozen monkeys tearing the kitchen apart . . . and that's just the beginning!

## THE WIDOW'S BROOM

Minna Shaw, a lonely widow, helps out a witch who has fallen from the sky on a broom that is losing its full power. The witch regains her health, leaves in the middle of the night, and—to Minna's surprise—leaves the broom behind. The broom begins to do helpful household chores inside and outside. But the neighbors say it's "wicked." One day two boys get a well-deserved thrashing from the broom. For the neighbors this is the final straw and it spells doom for the companion broom, but does it? A clever ending.

## THE SWEETEST FIG

Monsieur Bibot, a cold-hearted dentist, is given two ordinary looking figs in payment for some dental work that he administered to an old woman. She says they're very special and can make his dreams come true. Angry that she will not be able to pay, he does not give her pain medicine for her aching jaw. Certainly Monsieur Bibot does not believe in such nonsense and yet when he eats the fig after dinner, he must admit it is the sweetest he's ever tasted. The next day, he realizes that his dream from the evening before is coming true. Determined to make better use of the second fig, Bibot learns to control his dreams. Ah, but can he control Marcel, his dog? There's the twist.

## THE Z WAS ZAPPED

This is referred to as "A Play in Twenty-Six Acts" performed by The Caslon Players, and presented by The Alphabet Theatre. You could refer to it as a guessing game between illustrations and text. Oddly enough, there are 26 players, just as there are 26 letters of the alphabet. Could it be a clever ABC book in disguise?

## BAD DAY AT RIVERBEND

No one came and no one left this town. Then one day a mysterious substance appeared on both coach and horses that wouldn't come off. It was greasy. Soon it was everywhere. Something had to be done about it and Sheriff Ned aimed to do it. This is another surrealistic journey into the imagination.

## THE WRETCHED STONE

Something has gone amiss with the crew of the ship *Rita Anne*. They were perfectly all right when the ship set sail, but there has been a dreadful and dangerous change. The crew no longer communicates. Could it have anything to do with the huge, glowing rock that was found the week before? Perhaps it should not have been brought aboard the ship. What wretched powers does this rock hold? How will the captain be able to save himself and his feverish crew? Beautiful visual scenes and a provocative question.

## ADDITIONAL BOOKS

Other works by this author/illustrator include *The Garden of Abdul Gasazi; Ben's Dream; The Wreck of the Zephyr; The Mysteries of Harris Burdick;* and others.

# SUGGESTED ACTIVITIES TO ACCOMPANY
# THIS COLLECTION OF WORKS

By grade three, many of the students will be familiar with some of the works of this author/illustrator. However, he is worth a second, third, and fourth look. Even adults enjoy reading the books again after not having seen them for a time.

These books are to be read, enjoyed, and discussed. Students are intrigued with them. Some of them leave students puzzled and they want to read them again to see if they've missed something. Students often discuss the books with a partner or in groups of three to check on what the other students are thinking.

Students need to know that the books contain an element of other-world fantasy. Here are a few suggested ideas, but students will come up with more possibilities to explore.

## CREATIVE WRITING

Van Allsburg says that he takes what he calls a "what if . . . what then . . ." approach to his books. So, students can begin their own writing by using this approach. As a class, they can make a list and develop the ideas on their own or in small groups.

- Use the "what if . . . what then" approach at the end of these books. They often leave the reader up in the air, so it's possible to write a continuation or even a sequel.

- Go back through the book to determine the main character, the setting, and the passing of time. Which one of these factors does the author change?

## READING

Read the book aloud without showing any pictures. Then find out what students want to see, and show the actual pictures and discuss them. Students can create the drawings that the illustrator did not draw.

- The books invite further reading and integration into other subject areas. The book *Jumanji*, for example, can be a springboard for a study of geography and a location of the animals. Also, a study of the animals themselves is a possibility. Where can we find these animals? Are they all wild?

- *The Sweetest Fig* calls for a character study. What was this character like? Did he get his just due? Also in this book, introduce students to The Eiffel Tower and have them find a library book that shows them what this really looks like. Perhaps this can fit in with a study of Paris.

- *The Widow's Broom* is one book students will want to talk about. Which broom was burned? Find the page where the author tells us that the widow already has a broom. Did the neighbors grab the wrong broom? It would seem so. (Some students may need to be directly led to this conclusion during discussion time.)

- *The Wretched Stone* turned men into monkeys, or lower animals. What could possibly shine in men's faces and cause them to sit glued before it, and laugh and not talk to each other? Could it be something students are watching a bit too much of? The author doesn't say.

## ART

Students are extremely fortunate to be exposed to this high quality of art work. Many of the drawings invite a study of perspective.

- Students can draw while sitting on the floor and looking up at an object.
- They can sit under their desk and draw what they see from that perspective.
- Items can be arranged on a desk and students can sit so that they are looking at the items at eye level and draw from that point of view.
- *Two Bad Ants* is a good book to use for a study of perspective. How would we see things if we were the ant? "What if . . ." we were a bird or a giraffe?
- Go through a book and study the light and shadow in an illustration. If the light is coming from one direction, how does the illustrator show this? Select one or two items to draw from the book and focus upon light and shadow. *The Z Was Zapped* is a good book for this activity.
- At this age students are capable of "contour drawing." They can get their paper and pencil ready, and then draw an object or a person with one continuous line, never looking at the paper and never taking their eyes off the object. When the line of the subject goes up, the pencil goes up. When the line of the shoulder slants down, the pencil makes a slanting line downward. No erasing. Keep repeating this exercise so students will "draw what they see"—*not* what they think they see.

## MUSIC

Several of these books have been made into a videotape or a cassette tape. They can be secured at the library. What music can be heard in the background, if any? What types of music do students think would go along with the book *The Garden of Abdul Gasazi* or *Jumanji* or *The Stranger*? Which instruments can send shivers up our spine? Which instruments can shout?

- The bell in *The Polar Express* can lead to the use of tinkling bells or clanging bells in the classroom this month. Use different sounding bells for different signals. Shake a bell but hold the clanger still, and ask students to tell what they hear "in their head."

**Note:** Chris Van Allsburg, prolific artist and writer, can feed our imagination and enrich our studies. Since he is a sculptor, students can be encouraged to work with clay to make a character or object from one of the books. Once they make it, "what if . . ." and "what then?"

A class ABC book is a natural activity after reading *The Z Was Zapped*. The students can create their own interplay of the visual and verbal using this book as a model and a springboard. Other books by the author/illustrator include *The Stranger; Just a Dream; Ben's Dream; The Mysteries of Harris Burdick;* and others.

Enjoy the reading, the story twists, and the artistic pages. Treat students to a month of book adventures that they will always remember. This is children's literature at its finest.

# REPRODUCIBLE ACTIVITY PAGES
# FOR DECEMBER

## READING/LANGUAGE ARTS

What's the Main Idea?

Pesky Cows and Goats (Story Starter)

Jingle, Ring, and Ding-a-Ling Words (Onomatopoeia)

My Holiday Reading Record

Paco Parrot's Spelling Sentence Formula

The Folktale Problem-Solving Recipe

## MATH

Estimation by the Inch

Bean Pot Estimation

Class Birthday Graph

Multiplication Pineapple Rings

## SOCIAL STUDIES

Hello, Neighbors!

I'm Proud of My State

## SCIENCE

Refrigerator Magnets

Magnets Attract and Repel

Make an Electromagnet

## AUTHOR STUDY

Jump Aboard the Polar Express!

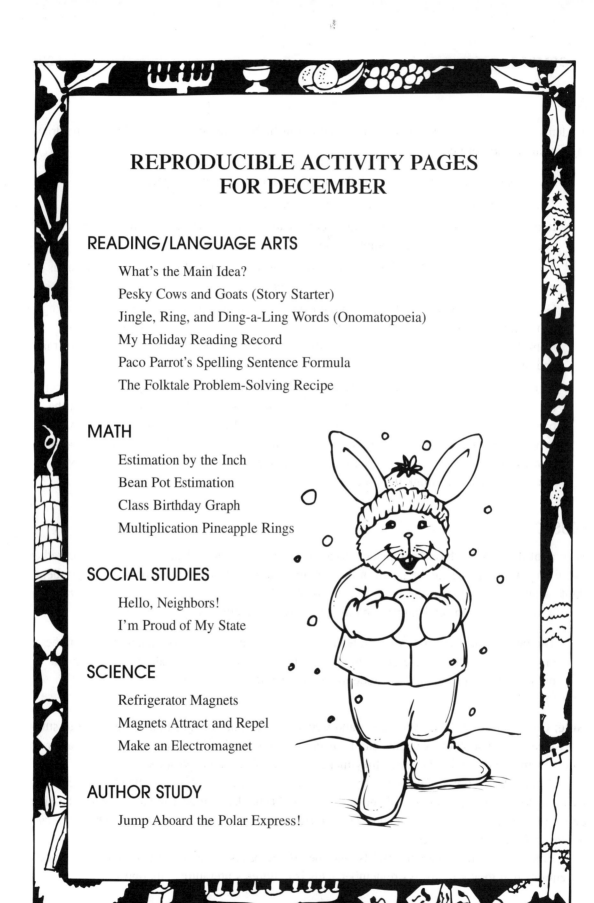

# What's the Main Idea?

Read each sentence carefully. What is the main idea? Below each sentence are three choices, or *multiple choices*. Select one. Circle it. Proofread your work.

1. The Red Delicious apples were on sale at the store.
   a. The apples are delicious.
   b. The apples were on sale.
   c. The apples were at the store.

2. The cat and dog had a fight on the sidewalk.
   a. The cat and dog were on the sidewalk.
   b. The cat and dog got outside.
   c. The cat and dog had a fight.

3. Tonight we are having a birthday party that will be fun.
   a. We will have fun tonight.
   b. Birthday parties are fun.
   c. Tonight we have a party.

4. "This is going to be a busy day, so please throw out the trash" said mother.
   a. It's a busy day.
   b. Throw out the trash.
   c. Mother is talking.

5. It was a sunny, windy, autumn day and the squirrels were busy burying acorns, as they do every year.
   a. The day was sunny.
   b. It's autumn.
   c. Squirrels are burying acorns.

6. Carl got his wish! He unwrapped the huge box and in it was a brand new scooter.
   a. Carl got his wish.
   b. Carl got a scooter.
   c. Carl unwrapped a box.

# Pesky Cows and Goats (Story Starter)

Below is the beginning of a story, but it has no middle and no ending.
That's where you come in. You can become an author and write the story
and help solve the problem. Share your story with classmates.

**TITLE:** _____

*In a village far away, there lived a wonderful wife who had a very good husband, but they kept pesky cows and goats who kept getting out and ruining the cabbage patch in the next field. One day, the farmer who owned the cabbage patch snatched up a goat and kept it. He wondered if anyone would miss it.*

*That night, the good husband looked over his flock of sheep and shook his head. It seemed to him that one might be missing, and so he set out on foot to find it.*

_____

_____

_____

_____

_____

_____

_____

_____

_____

**Continue on the back if you need more space.**

Name _____  Date _____

# Jingle, Ring, and Ding-a-Ling Words (Onomatopoeia)

Some words have a sound to them, like geese that hiss-s-s and owls that screech! When words sound like they are making a noise, that is known as "onomatopoeia." It sounds like this: "on-uh-maat-uh-PEA' uh."

In the sentences below, find the special "sound" word or words. Underline these words. Then write them on the back of the page. *Can you hear them?* Look for 5 more in books and write them, too.

1.  "Oink, oink," cried the little pig.

2.  Carmen put his handkerchief up to catch his kerchoo!

3.  The dishes clattered to the floor.

4.  The big, husky growl came from the throat of the first dog in the race.

5.  The engine sputtered, and then stopped.

6.  The water came out of the hose with a swish.

7.  "Oh, here comes the choo choo," said Mother.

8.  A howl came from the chilly night air.

9.  The surface of the table was scratchy.

10. All the children squealed with delight when they saw the fireworks.

# My Holiday Reading Record

Keep track of the holiday picture books you read. Enjoy the sights, the sounds, and the art work. Do you hear any music in the background? Record your impressions below.

| BOOK TITLE | AUTHOR/ ILLUSTRATOR | TYPE OF ART | MY COMMENTS |
|---|---|---|---|
|  |  |  |  |
|  |  |  |  |
|  |  |  |  |
|  |  |  |  |

Name _____   Date _____

# Paco Parrot's Spelling Sentence Formula

If you have 8 or 10 spelling words for the week, write a sentence using each word. This is the formula to use:

Sentence 1:  Put spelling word first.

Sentence 2:  Put spelling word second.

Sentence 3:  Put spelling word third.

Got the idea? Ready? Enjoy!

1. _____

2. _____

3. _____

4. _____

5. _____

6. _____

7. _____

8. _____

9. _____

10. _____

Name _____

Date _____

# The Folktale Problem-Solving Recipe

As you read many folktales, you will notice that there is a "formula," or a recipe for them. The recipe consists of three things: (1) Setting, (2) Characters, (3) Problem. The problem is always solved and the tale ends on a happy note. Below are some samples of the three necessary ingredients.

### Setting

In the land of the setting sun
In a place where it never rained
At the edge of the world
Halfway between north and south
In a land far, far away

### Characters

king and queen
wicked stepmother
farmer and his wife
three sisters or three brothers
a fool (who wins in the end)

### Problem

the hens stopped laying eggs
the princess would not laugh
the prince was turned into a rock
the trees refused to grow apples
the crops would not grow tall

## Once

there lived a _____
(Setting)

who _____ and a _____
(character(s))                              (character(s))

Now, one day _____
(problem)

_____

_____

(Use the back of this sheet if you need more space to write.)

What is your title? _____

# Estimation by the Inch

The line below is one inch in length. Study it. Stare at it. Then check these <u>real</u> items in the classroom. Estimate their length in inches. Then use a ruler to get the actual measurement.

————     1"

| **Width of Door** | **Length of Table** |
|---|---|
| Estimate _____" <br> Actual _____" | Estimate _____" <br> Actual _____" |
| **Width of Window** | **Length of New Crayon** |
| Estimate _____" <br> Actual _____" | Estimate _____" <br> Actual _____" |
| **Length of Scissors** | **Length from Doorknob to Floor** |
| Estimate _____" <br> Actual _____" | Estimate _____" <br> Actual _____" |

Name _____  Date _____

# Bean Pot Estimation

How many beans?  First estimate.  Then count and record.  Compare answers with classmates.

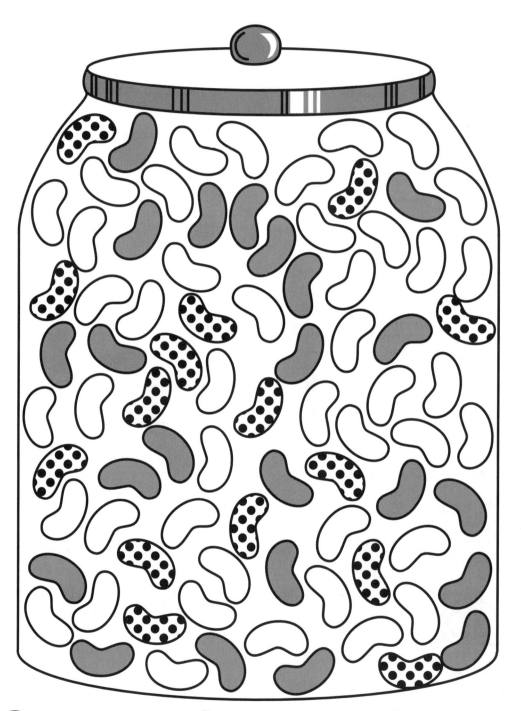

 **Estimate** _____
**Actual** _____

**Estimate** _____
**Actual** _____

 **Estimate** _____
**Actual** _____

# Class Birthday Graph

Let's take a good look at our class. List the months on the chalkboard, and make a tally mark to represent each student born during that month. Or put their names on the board. How many are there for January? Color that many squares. Do the same for each month. Select different colors for each month to make your graph colorful. You can put names in the squares.

| How Many ↑ / Month → | Jan. | Feb. | Mar. | Apr. | May | June | July | Aug. | Sept. | Oct. | Nov. | Dec. |
|---|---|---|---|---|---|---|---|---|---|---|---|---|
| 7 | | | | | | | | | | | | |
| 6 | | | | | | | | | | | | |
| 5 | | | | | | | | | | | | |
| 4 | | | | | | | | | | | | |
| 3 | | | | | | | | | | | | |
| 2 | | | | | | | | | | | | |
| 1 | | | | | | | | | | | | |

# Multiplication Pineapple Rings

Use the pineapple rings below to help you with your multiplication facts. The ring in the middle has been left blank. Decide which numeral you will place in the middle of each ring. Place the answer on the outside of the ring.

With real pineapple, you can conduct a science experiment. Cut off the top and place it in water. Watch the green top grow into a big plant. Measure its growth.

Name _____  Date _____

# Hello, Neighbors!

Pretend you are in a helicopter flying over your state.
Draw its shape in the middle. Now, fly to the
North, South, East, and West. Show us your
neighboring states. Label carefully.

What are
the state
capitals?

# I'm Proud of My State

Look up the information needed and draw it in the space provided. Work slowly and carefully. Then work with a study partner to learn the information.

| | |
|---|---|
| state flag | state bird |
| state motto | state quarter rubbings |
| map of state (shape) | state capital |
| "Natural Wonder" in my state | states that border mine |

Name _____    Date _____

# Refrigerator Magnets

You have just been hired by a design company to create 3 refrigerator magnets. They can also hold the art that you made, and you can show that, too.

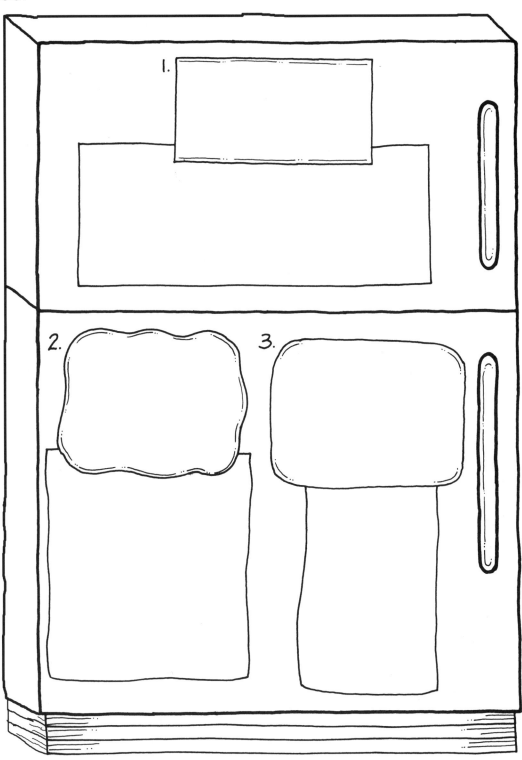

Name _____  Date _____

# Magnets Attract and Repel

Magnets come in different shapes and sizes. They attract some things and repel others. Use the horseshoe magnet below to record your findings.

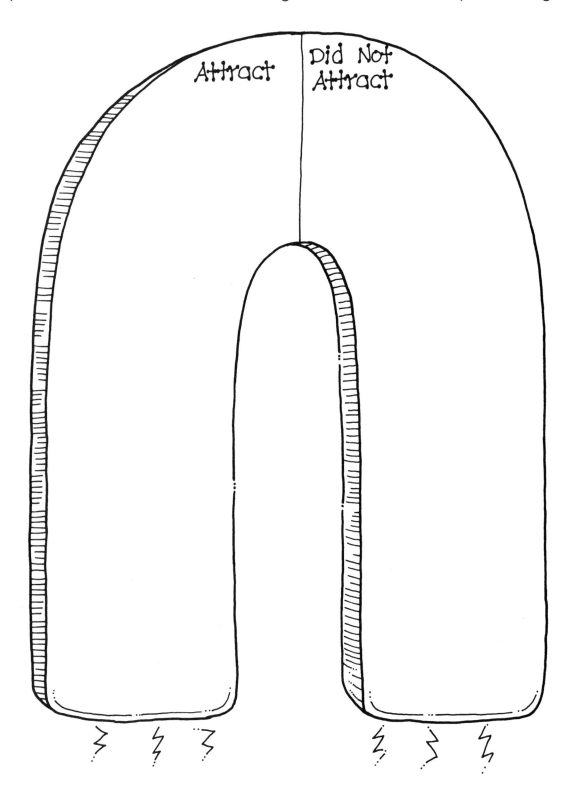

Name _____    Date _____

# Make an Electromagnet

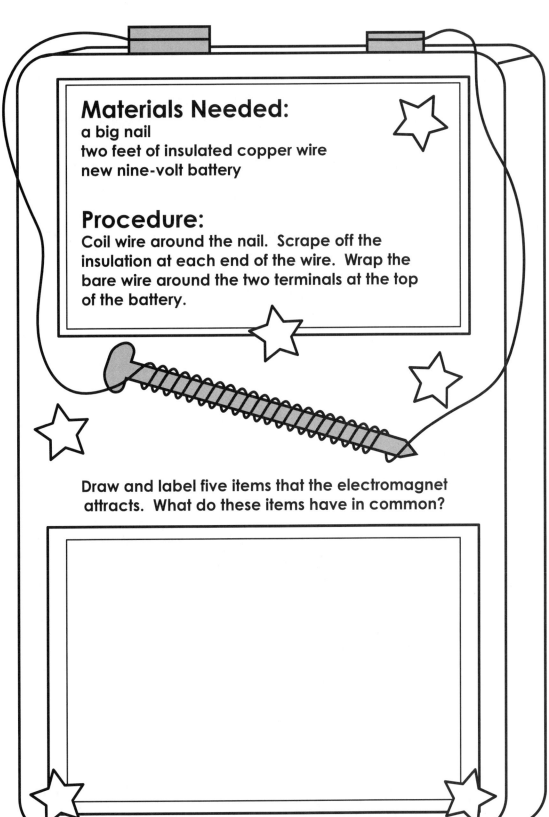

## Materials Needed:
a big nail
two feet of insulated copper wire
new nine-volt battery

## Procedure:
Coil wire around the nail.  Scrape off the insulation at each end of the wire.  Wrap the bare wire around the two terminals at the top of the battery.

Draw and label five items that the electromagnet attracts.  What do these items have in common?

# Jump Aboard the Polar Express!

This train is making an imaginary journey! When author/illustrator Chris Van Allsburg writes a story, he starts with "WHAT IF ..." and goes to "WHAT THEN?" Let's jump aboard with some story ideas. Print directly on the train cars.

Then choose one of your ideas. Develop your story on another page and illustrate it just like an award winner. What media will you choose?

# JANUARY

# JANUARY BOOKS

**Agard, John.** *The Calypso Alphabet.* **Illustrated by Jennifer Brent (New York: Holt, Rinehart, and Winston, 1989).** This book introduces the cultures and customs of the peoples of the Caribbean. It is a poetic journey, and the scratchboard illustrations with vibrant colors give the book a rhythm of its own.

**Bartone, Elisa.** *Peppe the Lamplighter.* **Illustrated by Ted Lewin (New York: Lothrop, Lee & Shephard, 1993).** In a tenement on Mulberry Street in Little Italy, New York, Peppe and his poor family are without food. His papa is sick so Peppe gets the only job he can find—lighting the lamps at night. Will his papa ever be proud of him? The illustrations glow from the page showing the reader what life was like before electricity.

**Chinery, Michael.** *All About Baby Animals.* **Illustrated by Ian Jackson (New York: Doubleday, 1990).** An excellent information book about caring for animals, baby talk, keeping clean, and growing up. Excellent pictures of animals in their natural habitat. Also included are baby names. For example, cats have *kittens* and so do rabbits.

**Dunrea, Oliver.** *Deep Down Underground* **(New York: Macmillan, 1989).** In this book a "moudiewort" (Scottish word for mole) digs down underground and keeps burrowing as animals scamper and scrunch to get out of the way. Illustrations give the reader an X-ray view of the action. Many opportunities for counting and learning animal names.

**Howard, Elizabeth Fitzgerald.** *The Train to Lulu's.* **Illustrated by Robert Casilla (New York: Bradbury, 1988).** Two sisters enjoy their independence as they take the train from Boston to Baltimore by themselves in the 1930s. Radiant paintings depict the sights seen from the train.

**Jackson, Ellen.** *CinderEdna.* **Illustrated by Kevin O'Malley (New York: Lothrop, Lee & Shephard, 1994).** The traditional Cinderella lives next door to the modern CinderEdna. Both go to the ball and both get their man. But CinderEdna goes for the younger brother, Rupert, who runs a recycling plant and a home for orphaned kittens.

**Millman, Isaac.** *Moses Goes to a Concert* **(New York: Farrar Straus Giroux, 1998).** Moses is deaf, as are his classmates, but that doesn't stop them from attending a concert. They hold balloons in their lap to feel the vibrations. The percussionist, also deaf, meets with the children and allows them to try out all of her instruments. A joyful book.

**Pinkney, Andrea Davis.** *Alvin Ailey.* **Illustrated by Brian Pinkney (New York: Hyperion, 1993).** Young Alvin knew he wanted to be a dancer after seeing Katherine Dunham and her dance troupe. He studied dance in Los Angeles and New York and founded his own dance company.

**Variale, Jim.** *Kids Dance: The Students of Ballet Tech* **(New York: Dutton, 1999).** Thousands of New York City children have learned to dance at this first public school for ballet. This exuberant picture book will convey the excitement and vibrancy of ballet to a young audience.

**(CHAPTER BOOK) Wilder, Laura Ingalls.** *Little House in the Big Woods* **(New York: HarperCollins, 1961).** This is one in a series of Little House books, and in this one we experience the delight of a visit to a general store in pioneer days. There are barrels of candy, kegs of nails, shoes, dishes and just about anything you'd need. (Many classroom activities can flow from this book and from the series to enrich the curriculum.)

# JANUARY

Happy New Year! It's time for a fresh beginning in our classroom. It's also a time for review.

When students return to school after a long period of time off, they are generally quiet the first day or two. This is an excellent time for reviewing classroom-management expectations, in addition to reviewing in general, and for writing new rules and consequences if this would be helpful for classroom management.

Make sure the classroom looks fresh, with no remaining signs of the December holiday seasons. This new beginning offers a time for making resolutions, for setting goals, and for creating some new areas of interest in the classroom. It's time to take stock of the Learning Centers. Are there enough? Are they attractive? Do they need to be freshened up in terms of their backdrops and printed materials if they're to be kept in place throughout this month? Do new bulletin boards need to be made? Check to see if students need to make fresh nametags for their desks.

Welcome the students and get down to business right away.

A good way to start the day is by calling the roll and having students respond. This brings the class together and quiets them. Then have the salute to the flag and sing a patriotic song. Each week a different student can be selected as the class "standard bearer"—the one who gets the flag from the holder, and holds it during the pledge and the song. The "morning ceremony assistant" leads the Pledge of Allegiance and the song. Follow this routine daily. It provides stability for the class as a team and is something students never forget.

Later in the day, interesting information about holiday experiences can be shared. Your motto for this and every month is: Be firm but fair, be consistent, and be well prepared for instruction.

# FOCUS ON READING

## REASSESSMENT

This is the time to reassess students and to change study groups if necessary or feasible. If the class is working with a basal reader text, use the assessment materials located there. For other assessments be sure to include material that has been taught since September. Check the assessment skills section, located in September's Focus on Reading, in an effort to check some of the basic skills.

Some areas and skills to check in the beginning of January are:

- *phonics* and the students' knowledge of letter/sound relationships
- *main idea:* Can students grasp the primary focus of a story?
- *predictions:* Can students make reasonable statements about what may come next in a story?
- *punctuation:* Can students use this correctly in their work?
- *independent reading:* Are students keeping an up-to-date list?
- *inference:* Are students able to make assumptions based upon the text and upon visual information conveyed in illustrations?
- *spelling:* Is this a skill that needs more attention, more study, more practice?

- *letter formation*: Is handwriting becoming more and more legible?
- *letter writing:* Do students know the correct letter form to use and can they then write a letter using this form?
- *multiple-choice test-taking:* Are students able to select the correct answer from among several?
- *compound words:* Do students recognize the root words and can they construct a compound word?
- *contractions:* Do students recognize contractions and the words they stand for?

## ADDITIONAL REASSESSMENT

As anyone can readily see from the material listed above, there are many skills to address on the student's road to literacy. These skills will be revisited in this book throughout the year because we must remember that, even though it has been *taught* once or twice, it does not mean it has been *learned* by the student. Skills must be revisited in a variety of ways.

Here are some additional assessments to make this month that are more general in nature:

- *information resources:* Are students using these and are they able to determine where to locate information?
- *reading portfolio:* Is this up to date and ready for the new year?
- *word wall:* Is more space needed or can a new sheet be placed over the old one if space is at a premium?
- *journal:* For students who have been having difficulty writing in journals for one reason or another (lack of interest in writing, poor penmanship, incorrect knowledge of punctuation, and so on), this may be the time to begin with a fresh journal, so that students don't have to be greeted daily or weekly with prior problems in writing. (Some teachers prefer a fresh journal at the beginning of each month.)
- *story web:* Can students create a web using story information, such as main characters, author/illustrator, setting of story, conflict or problem to be resolved, resolution?
- *story map:* Can students do a circular map of the story?
- *retelling:* Are students able to retell a story using their own words?

## READING AND SPELLING HELP

The following Instant Words* First Hundred are essential words for students to learn to recognize instantly and to spell correctly.

The first one hundred words make up about half of all written materials—that's 50 percent, so students *must* learn these words by heart.

| Words 1–25 | 26–50 | 51–75 | 76–100 |
|---|---|---|---|
| the | or | will | number |
| of | one | up | no |
| and | had | other | way |
| a | by | about | could |
| to | word | out | people |
| in | but | many | my |
| is | not | then | than |
| you | what | them | first |
| that | all | these | water |
| it | were | so | been |
| he | we | some | call |
| was | when | her | who |
| for | your | would | oil |
| on | can | make | its |
| are | said | like | now |
| as | there | him | find |
| with | use | into | long |
| his | an | time | down |
| they | each | has | day |
| I | which | look | did |
| at | she | two | get |
| be | do | more | come |
| this | how | write | made |
| have | their | go | may |
| from | if | see | part |

*Source: *The Reading Teacher's Book of Lists,* 4th edition, by Edward B. Fry, Jacqueline E. Kress, and Dona L. Fountoukidis (Paramus, NJ: Prentice Hall, 2000).

## CONSONANT BLENDS

By now, students should know that consonants are all of the ABC letters, minus the vowels. There are twenty-one of them. There are many sounds in the language that are made by blending two consonants together. These can occur at the beginning, middle, or ending of a word. Some examples of the consonants "br" at the *beginning* of a word are listed here:

| | | |
|---|---|---|
| brush | bread | brisk |
| brand | brain | breakfast |
| brace | bran | breeze |

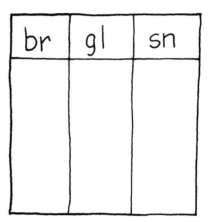

Have students repeat the sound of "br" after it is modeled by you. Then have students use this blend with each of the *long* vowels, as follows:

br–a    br–e    br–i    br–o    br–u

As students say these blends with the vowels, have them repeat them until a word comes to mind. List all of these words on the chalkboard.

## THE BLEND CHANT

Repetition of br–a, br–a, br–a (use long a) may bring forth the word br–ave (brave), br–ake (brake), br–ain (brain). So have students rev up their phonics motors, say the blend with a vowel three times, and on the fourth sound, try to come up with a word. When several words have been said, write them on the chalkboard and say them with an emphasis on the blend. As the class does this together, it resembles a chant:

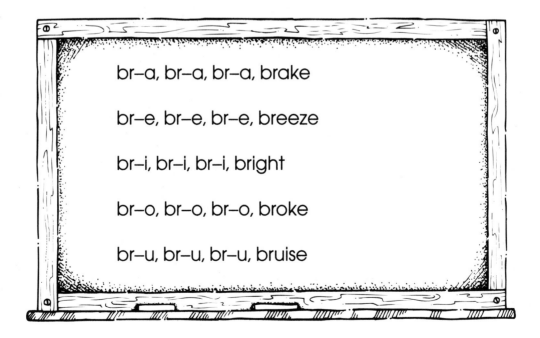

br–a, br–a, br–a, brake

br–e, br–e, br–e, breeze

br–i, br–i, br–i, bright

br–o, br–o, br–o, broke

br–u, br–u, br–u, bruise

**Other blends to use for chants.**  Other blends to work with and to construct words with are:

| bl | cr | cl | dr | fl |
|----|----|----|----|----|
| fr | gl | gr | pl | pr |
| sc | sk | sl | sm | sn |
| sp | st | sw | tr | tw |

## BLENDS IN THE MIDDLE

Consonant blends don't always appear at the beginning of the word. Sometimes blends are in the middle of words. Working with the "br" blend, we can see that this occurs in the middle of these words:

| umbrella | zebra | vibrate |
|----------|-------|---------|
| celebrate | library | cobra |

Display these words on a wall chart or the chalkboard.

## SILLY CONSONANT BLEND SENTENCES

Using the six words above, have students construct a silly or fanciful sentence that doesn't have to make sense. It's the type of sentence that could appear in a make-believe story. Here's one to get you started:

> We went to the <u>library</u> to <u>celebrate</u> reading. The <u>zebra</u> carried a striped <u>umbrella</u>, and the <u>cobra</u> began to <u>vibrate</u>.

Students are gaining an awareness of consonant blends when they engage in this type of activity. Also, in writing the fanciful sentences they are setting the foundation that will produce more descriptive phrases in their own writing. It's an enjoyable activity, as well as being a *phonics* activity. Some students will begin to do this in their spare time because they enjoy the idea that there are no strict rules to follow in their fanciful sentences. They're still learning.

## GO ON A CONSONANT BLEND SEARCH

Use junk mail, newspaper ads, magazine ads, and other sources of print to find consonant blends. Circle them. How many did students find on one page, on two pages? These can be written on a chart. Some words will appear more than once so keep track of the words. Are some of the words used more frequently in ads than other words? This could be an interesting adventure. (See Reproducible Activity Pages.)

## REVIEW FICTION ELEMENTS

There are usually the following in stories: main character, a problem or challenge, and a conclusion. Quite a bit of activity or action occurs between the stated problem and the conclusion. Have students keep track, in writing, of these story elements in an imaginative way. (See Reproducible Activity Pages.)

## SET A PURPOSE FOR READING—GUIDED READING

Set a *purpose* for reading before students begin reading the same story. Have students read to find out specific information. List questions on the chalkboard for which they are to write the answers. Later, students can compare answers.

If the questions are general enough, the same questions can be used if students are reading different books. Some general questions are:

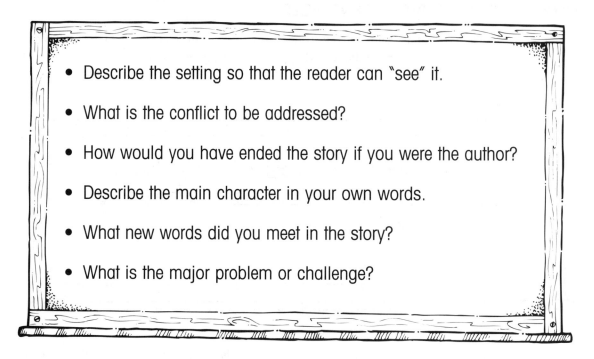

- Describe the setting so that the reader can "see" it.

- What is the conflict to be addressed?

- How would you have ended the story if you were the author?

- Describe the main character in your own words.

- What new words did you meet in the story?

- What is the major problem or challenge?

## MAKING VOCABULARY PREDICTIONS PRIOR TO READING

Before reading a picture book aloud to students, first show them the cover and tell them what the story is about and where it takes place. You may even want to include some of the characters and a story event. This motivates the students to want to hear the story. Then have students predict some vocabulary words they could meet in this particular story. Write them on the chalkboard or on chart paper. Then read the story aloud. Did students meet any of the predicted words listed?

After this, have students rewrite their version of an event in the story, or a description of a character, or the setting, and include words from the predicted words list.

It's also possible to have students use the actual text and copy a paragraph or two. Then substitute their words for ones that the author used. This way, students are working with synonyms in addition to using their predicted words list.

## MORE WORK WITH PREDICTION

Give students the title of the story prior to reading. Introduce the new or unfamiliar vocabulary words. From this bit of information, the students need to become story detectives and try to predict what the story could be about. Then read it. Check their predictions.

# FOCUS ON LANGUAGE ARTS

## MORE READING OPPORTUNITIES

Many more reading opportunities are available this month and every month throughout the year. Reading is intertwined with all subjects in the classroom, and it is difficult to separate it completely when working with the "process" of reading.

## STORY "WEBS" AND WEAVINGS

How did the word "web" get started as a synonym for the "flow chart" that was used for many years in the business world, or for the "concept map" used in science? Maybe students can come up with some ideas, since by this time they have been introduced to origins of words and sayings.

If students are familiar with spider webs and the orbs, encourage them to see in the spider's web an intricate pattern, a connectedness between one part and another in much the same manner as one part of a story is connected to the other.

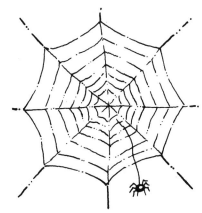

Introduce students to the concept of "weaving" so they will know that the weaver interlaces many threads or yarns to form a fabric. Encourage students to think of the threads and yarns as characters, setting, details, incidents, and events in the story. The end result, or interlacing of these threads, becomes the story itself once it has been told.

The main thing—whether calling it a web, a weaving, a map, or something else—is for students to know that each term is used to denote a *diagram* of a story.

## STORY CLOTHS

Traditionally, the Hmong embroidery tells a story. A book that explains this is entitled *Nine-in-One Grr! A Folktale from the Hmong People of Laos* by Xiong Blia. Along with the explanation is a story cloth that tells the tale of the land that is in danger of being overrun with tigers. Can the land be saved? Have the students find this book at the library and read it to find out.

## ANANSI THE SPIDER FINDS A WEB

Familiarize students with Anansi the Spider, the trickster from African folktales. They can "weave a yarn" or "weave a story" of their own making about a storyteller who was "spinning a yarn" while weaving on a warm, sunny afternoon, and fell asleep in the process. Anansi would be just the one to take the fabric and the credit for the weaving and call it a "web" that he created, now wouldn't he?

For inspiration, and for a reintroduction to Anansi the Spider, have some picture books of these stories in the classroom and also read one or two of them aloud. It's always enjoyable for children to listen to familiar beloved tales. (Also have them use their dictionary as a resource for checking such words as *weave, web, orb,* and *spider.*) Two good Anansi tales to help us get started are *Anansi the Spider* by Gerald McDermott and *Anansi Finds a Fool, an Ashanti Tale* as retold by Verna Aardema.

Look in February's Focus on Language Arts for more trickster tale titles.

## THE WEBBING PROCESS

Usually there is a core idea or title at the center of the web design. Then strands or lines are drawn from the center to points outside along the edge. These are often labeled and relate to the core idea. Information can be listed under the labels. The process of making a web is called "webbing" and there are many varieties. A typical beginning story web might look something like this:

Encourage students to be inventive and create their own story webs, making artistic designs and drawings.

## A CHARACTER WEB

After reading a story, have students select a character and think of the qualities that character has. How do we, as readers, know that this character has a particular quality? Using those bits of information we can make the following character web:

1. Place the character's name in the center of the page (and draw the person's shape around it).

2. Draw straight lines out from the character (top, bottom, sides) and write a quality that the character possesses (honest, timid, brave, angry).

3. Draw the straight line to a shape or a "cartoon bubble." In that shape print the information to support the claim that this person has that characteristic.

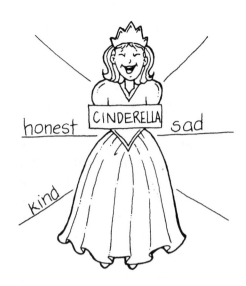

## A CIRCULAR STORY WEB

For this particular type of web or map: (1) Select a book title and write that in the center of the page. Underneath it, write the author and illustrator. (2) On a separate sheet of paper, list the beginning, middle, and ending of the story. Then list events that happened in between that are important to the story. Be sure to count them. (3) On the sheet with the title and author, sketch a circle around the edge. Then sketch the number of necessary shapes or cartoon bubbles around the circle. In these spaces, either draw an item or print words that will help retell the story. When finished, some of these story webs are miniature works of art.

An excellent teacher resource book is *Webbing with Literature, Creating Story Maps with Children's Books* by Karen D'Angelo Bromley.

## USE WEBBING IN ALL SUBJECTS

Make colorful, imaginatively designed, and creative webs this month for a topic being studied in each content area, such as Social Studies, Science/Health, Math, and so on. Creating a web helps to outline and synthesize information. Students can think up their own headings, and the titles can be interesting, such as "Bake a Story Cake," "The Story Tree," or "All Aboard! Railroads in the USA" (with a diagram in the shape of a train). (See Reproducible Activity Pages.)

# WORD ORIGINS AND SAYINGS*

This month offers additional sayings to introduce on Monday. Write one per week on the chalkboard. Have students speculate about the saying and look up some of the words in the dictionary in an effort to help solve the riddle of how this saying came into our language.

*Source is *A Hog on Ice and Other Curious Expressions* by Charles Earle Funk.

1. **a song and dance.** Taken from American vaudeville, this phrase refers to performers who come on stage and open the act with a song and a dance. The phrase has acquired two other meanings: (a) "to give a song and dance" when telling something, or especially offering an excuse, and (b) because the song and dance man had to come in exactly on cue, one is said to "go into one's song and dance" when giving a carefully rehearsed story or statement or speech or even conversation. It's all been done before.

2. **a round robin.** This phrase is associated with British sailors who were signing a petition to protest something aboard ship. The captain was the ultimate authority, so to instigate a petition or to be the first to sign it would be a punishable act. Consequently, a ship's crew wrote their signatures in a circle, as though the signatures were spokes coming from a hub. You couldn't determine who signed it first, and you couldn't punish the entire crew. It is thought that the name comes from the French *rond ruban,* but it is not certain.

3. **That's the ticket!** An expression of approval that comes from a mispronunciation of the French word *etiquette.* Put the accent on the second syllable and it will sound like *eh-TICK-ett.* Around the 1800s "that's etiquette" (the correct thing) slid into "that's uh-TICK-ut," to "that's the ticket." So, it still means the right thing or the right way.

4. **baker's dozen (13).** In this case, a dozen means thirteen. In thirteenth-century England, a law was enacted regulating the price of bread by weight because some professional bakers prepared their bread so that it had many holes in it (like swiss cheese) and you didn't get what you paid for. Bakers were viewed with suspicion. Because scales were not reliable, and because bakers did not want to be fined, many of them distributed thirteen loaves of bread when twelve were ordered. Then when a customer ordered a loaf of bread, he got it *plus* a slice from the thirteenth loaf, thus assuring that the customer was getting full weight.

5. **left holding the bag.** Perhaps this originally meant buying something live in a bag with a hole in it. The cat (chicken, turkey) gets out, and one is left holding the bag. The saying now means being left in the lurch, and having to bear the responsibility for something that was not one's fault.

# WRITING SKILLS

## CLASSROOM SLOGAN

Have students write and submit a slogan for your classroom. This slogan should be a positive message, and should show that the class is working on good manners and good citizenship. Some classrooms have chosen a slogan similar to the following:

| | |
|---|---|
| This Class Has Class | Our Class Pulls Together |
| We're #1 and Like It | Good Manners Jets |
| www.Great.Class | TOPS, and Still Climbing |

When students have submitted their slogans and all have been read aloud, it's time to vote. The top three (with the most votes) are voted on for a second time. This time, the one with the most votes wins as the slogan.

## A SLOGAN DESIGN

Now that the class has decided on a slogan, the students need to print it or write it, as on a bumper sticker, and then make a design around it. Again, students can vote on the design OR you can ask for volunteers to create the design, OR the creator of the slogan that won can select a design. Make copies of the final designed slogan on the copy machine so that each student has one. Put one on the outside of your classroom door or over the door.

## RENEWED HANDWRITING EFFORT

Students need to continue to practice the formation of the letters. (Refer to September for the letter strokes.) See Reproducible Activity Pages for upper- and lowercase alphabet styles. Reproduce this material so that each student has a copy.

## LETTER TRACING

Write alphabet letters on an overhead transparency with permanent ink and place this model in the Writing Center. Students can place a blank transparency sheet over the top of this copy and secure it with a paper clip. They can then use a water-based pen to slowly and carefully trace over the top for practice. When they are finished, the water-based pen marks should wipe off with the help of a little water.

## PRACTICE WRITING A FRIENDLY LETTER

Using the same technique as above, carefully write a brief friendly letter on a lined sheet of paper. This time, run off copies so that each student has one. Then students are to slowly and carefully trace the text, concentrating on the letter formations.

Next, have each student take a blank sheet of lined paper and copy the brief letter as carefully as possible. Do this regularly for help with fine-motor control that is necessary for good penmanship.

You should do a "penmanship pencil" grasp check regularly to see if students are holding pencils correctly.

## WRITE A DRAGON STORY

January is the month of the Chinese New Year, and dragons are associated with Asia. In folklore, the dragons of the East breathe a fine mist and the dragons of the West breathe fire. In their quest for power, do they cancel out one another? This sounds like a good subject for an action-packed folktale. Students can write their final copy on dragon shapes.

The dragon is sometimes described as a combination beast called a hippogriff. It sometimes has the head of a camel, horns of an elk, eyes of a rabbit, ears of a cow, neck of a snake, belly of a frog, scales of a carp, claws of a hawk, and feet of a lion. This should make for some very colorful dragons! Write on!

## REVIEW THIS WRITING FORMULA

If you are not using this formula for creative writing, now is a good opportunity to begin. These are the five major elements addressed in creative writing:

1. PRE-WRITE       (Time to think, make notes.)
2. WRITE              (Get the words down on paper.)
3. EDIT                (Make changes here and there.)
4. PROOFREAD      (Check spelling and punctuation.)
5. REWRITE          (Prepare clean copy.)

This formula can be written out and displayed in the Writing Center, or in an area in the classroom (perhaps on the word wall).

# SPEAKING SKILLS

## SHARED EXPERIENCES

Have students share information about their favorite holidays. This can be done in groups of three so that everyone gets a chance to talk and to listen as well. If there is something the whole group should know, let each individual group decide what it will be.

## SALUTE TO THE FLAG

The beginning of the new year is another opportunity to review the Pledge of Allegiance, to learn the words by heart, and to discuss the proper citizenship behavior with the flag.

Be sure the flag is prominently displayed in the classroom. You should show the appropriate behavior for the pledge by standing at attention. Have students stand. Point out to them that their backs are straight, shoulders are back, feet are together, and their right hands are over their hearts in a gesture of loyalty and respect.

Say the stanza, one line at a time, and then have students repeat it. Be sure to speak distinctly.

*I pledge allegiance to the flag*
*of the United States of America*
*And to the republic*
*For which it stands,*
*One nation under God, indivisible,*
*with liberty and justice for all.*

By way of review, each morning should be started with this pledge and then with a patriotic song ("My Country 'Tis of Thee"). Select a new standard bearer weekly to hold the flag for the pledge, and a new assistant who stands beside the standard bearer and says, "All stand" (all students stand at attention), "Ready" (students put hand on heart), "Begin" (student leads the pledge). Your strong voice must also be heard. This is not the time to be talking, rummaging through a desk drawer, or reading a bulletin. Everyone should be saying the pledge and singing.

When the song is completed, the standard bearer returns the flag to the holder; the assistant says, "You may be seated"; and all students sit down in their seats. You then thank the two assistants and greet the students with announcements for the day.

This is done each day for several reasons. One is to instill in students a sense of patriotism and loyalty to the country in which they live. Soldiers fought and died for the right of students to say this pledge and to sing the song, so that should be honored.

Also, where else will children learn to do this? It is the responsibility of the school to teach the pledge and the song so that when these students go out into the world, they will be able to engage in this activity and not just mouth the words. It is something they will do, hopefully, for the rest of the lives, so they need to learn it now. We see this practice at sports events and on other occasions, so have students be on the lookout for it.

## SPEAKER FEEDBACK

After a student has given a report, presented a new game, or described how a game is played, have the speaker ask if there are any questions. Was the message clear? What additional information was needed? By engaging in this activity, the speaker will learn how to become a more effective communicator.

The students asking the questions need to learn to stick strictly to the facts that were presented. They do not express "feelings" about the presentation, such as "I don't think I'd like that game" or "I don't like sports." This is not the time for *them;* it is the time to give feedback to the speaker on the effectiveness of communication.

## FOCUS ON "NOT SPEAKING"

There needs to be a sender and a receiver when communicating. If a student is not engaged in a give-and-take conversation, or has not been asked to address the class, then why speak? Why call out? Why disturb others with speech? Some students are used to expressing themselves at all times because they have not been taught that it is inappropriate. There is a time to talk and a time to be still. As the new year begins, it would be an appropriate time to make a resolution to be vigilant about "not speaking."

# LISTENING SKILLS

## CAN ALL STUDENTS HEAR WELL?

This is a good time to make some changes in seating arrangements so that if you have a student or students who have hearing impairments, they may sit closer to the "action." Be sure to look directly at students who are hearing impaired when giving directions, or repeat directions while looking their way. Anything you say while facing the other direction may well be lost on these students.

Check with the office to see if hearing tests are scheduled this term for all students. If a child is not hearing well, it is often the case that the child cannot articulate words correctly and has speech problems. Alert the speech teacher and ask for an evaluation. Be sure to call this to the attention of parents during conference time. Also make a note on permanent records regarding any special evaluations and measures taken to correct the problem.

## LISTEN FOR QUIET SOUNDS AND WORDS

The students had listened in December for sounds with zest, like *bim! bam! boom!*

Now, let's listen for sounds that are quiet, such as "hush," the soft "coo" of a dove, and the "mew" of a newborn kitten.

Say these words and have students tell whether they sound loud or soft:

| | | |
|---|---|---|
| humming | crowing | barking |
| growling | cooing | watching |

Label several lists in the classroom and have students fill them in. These could be: Quiet Sounds in School; Quiet Sounds at Home; Quiet Sounds at Night.

Also have a large sheet of kraft paper available so that students can search through newspapers and magazines for quiet words. These can be cut out and pasted on the quiet chart.

*Note:* A focus on "quiet sounds" will often have the effect of quieting down the classroom. So, you may want to keep this in mind and revisit this activity in May when the end of the school year is approaching.

## DO COLORS TALK? DO THEY SHOUT? DO THEY SPEAK SOFTLY?

Work with color words and encourage students to bring in swatches of material or actual items with colors that are "gentle" and swatches of colors that are "loud."

For example, a bright, shiny, red button is LOUD; a soft, baby-blue hat is QUIET; a red-and-green checkered cloth can be LOUD; a violet-and-white checkered cloth can be QUIET.

Have students print their quiet words with quiet-colored crayons on pale-colored paper. Have them print their loud words on bold-colored paper with loud-colored crayons.

To learn more about colors in our environment, be sure to include the all-time favorite *Hailstones and Hailibut Bones* by Mary O'Neill. The author explores each color in rhyme. The poems are entitled "What Is Red?" "What Is Orange?" "What Is White?" and on through all of the colors in terms of what sounds they make, how they smell, how they make us feel, and how they are to the touch and taste. The book appeals to the five senses and is an excellent book for a focus on listening!

## HAPPY NEW YEAR OF LISTENING

January is a good time to review the conditions for listening in the classroom. Some teachers use a little chant effectively, such as:

> *Take a deep breath in . . . and out.*
> *My eyes are on the speaker.*
> *My lips are closed.*
> *My ears are wide open.*
> *My hands are folded.*
> *My feet are together.*
> *I am ready to listen.*

# FOCUS ON SPELLING

## CUISENAIRE® ROD SPELLING

Borrow several sets of Cuisenaire® Rods from a lower-grade classroom teacher if you do not have them in your own classroom. Students can construct their spelling words with them. First, have students do one word at a time on a flat surface. Next, see if it is possible to construct any in a vertical position. (Good luck!)

Students are learning many things about size, shape, and spacial relationships with this activity. In addition, it is a concrete method of spelling out the word by forming the letters.

## INDIVIDUAL SLATES

Collect a set of four or five of these slates for the classroom. Put them in the Writing Center and have students practice their spelling words with chalk.

## CHALKBOARD PRACTICE

Many students like to practice on the chalkboard, but there is barely enough time during the day to do this. If, however, the class is staying in for indoor recess because of bad weather, mark off a space so that three or four students can work on the chalkboard to practice their spelling words. There will be much erasing and chalk-dust all over, but it will be worth it since students don't forget these opportunities. Quickly have them sponge off the chalkboard during clean-up—the board is now ready to go for the afternoon's lessons.

## SPELLING ILLUSTRATIONS

Encourage students to write the spelling words and illustrate them. This will be easy with nouns, because they represent a person, place, or thing, which are concrete. Have students brainstorm

and use their imaginations for illustrating words that don't fit into those categories. If, for example, the spelling word is "ignite," surround it with orange and red zigzag lines. If the word is "splendid," write it with silver and gold marking pens. Students will come up with some marvelous ideas on their own. Praise them for their inventiveness.

## DICTIONARY CHECK

Look up the spelling word in the dictionary. Which word comes immediately *before* the spelling word? Write it down. Which word comes immediately *after* the spelling word? Write it down. Then compose a sentence using all three of these words and underline the spelling word. Silly sentences are acceptable, and the vocabulary development potential is there for students who are ready.

# FOCUS ON MATH

## REVIEW

After a period of time away from the routine of school and daily learning, students need review. This is an excellent time to review what you have been learning in the area of mathematics so far this year.

- Work with your flashcards daily.
- Work with the commutative property of an algorithm.

  (Hold up a flashcard that says $7 \times 3$ and have students answer $3 \times 7$.)
- Work with small groups that need attention on a particular skill.
- Refresh your Math Center.

## THE LANGUAGE OF MATH

Together with students, make a large chart that shows some of the language we use when working with mathematics. This list can help get you started. It also serves as another way to review:

- inch, and the sign that represents inch  (")
- yard, and the sign that represents yard  (')
- equals, and the sign that represents equals  (=)
- the signs for addition (+), subtraction (−), multiplication (×), and division (÷)
- more than (>), less than (<)
- total
- estimate
- story problem
- how many? (a story problem clue that this calls for addition)
- how many left? (a story problem clue that this calls for subtraction)
- time (seconds, minutes, hours, days, months, years)
- temperature (Fahrenheit, Celcius, high/low)
- volume
- area
- perimeter
- circumference
- patterns
- geoboard
- shapes
- money
- ruler, yardstick, trundle wheel

Include others you will add for your classroom. (See Reproducible Activity Pages.)

## DIVISION TERMS JINGLE

Learn the terms of long division. The *quotient* is the answer. The number being divided is the *dividend,* and it's being divided by the *divisor.* Here's a jingle that may help. Print it on a large piece of paper and have students learn it and say it in sing-song fashion. (See Reproducible Activity Pages.)

## THE THREE DIVISION STARS

I'm the **quotient**
And I'm here to say,
I'm the ANSWER
For you today!

When you do the long division,
I'm right there with the decision.
I'm the one who knows it all . . .
Winter, summer, spring, and fall!

Uh, lookit here . . . I'm the **dividend**
I sit in this house for days on end.
You need me to stay on top,
So settle down. Enough now. Stop!

Aren't you two forgetting me?
I'm the **divisor,** you'll agree.
I'm the one who starts the incision.
Without me, there's no division!

Well, there we are,
    we need all three.
It's a trio that
    makes harmony!

When you do your
    long division,
We all pitch in
    with the decision!

Take a bow—quotients, divisors, dividends.
We're your long division friends.

## DIVISION IS REPEATED SUBTRACTION

Use manipulatives, such as trading chips, and pretend they are doughnuts. Think of one dozen doughnuts that need to be shared equally among four people. How can we do that?

We can give one to each person in a line, then go back to the beginning and give another to each person in a line, and do this a third and fourth time until there are no doughnuts left. In this process, we are dividing by four, or making four equal groups of the doughnuts.

Another way is to note that you have one dozen doughnuts, and wonder how many you could serve if you give three to each person. So 12 divided by 3 is 4. This time we are making groups of a given size. You can say, "Here is a subset of three; here is a subset of three; here is a subset of three" until you run out of doughnuts. How many subsets are there? *4*. So four people can each be served three doughnuts from one dozen (12). *Notice we're taking away doughnuts each time; hence, the concept that division is repeated subtraction.*

The four represents the number of equal groups of a given size that could be made of the dividend. So 12 divided by 3 equals 4.

## TWO TYPES OF DIVISION

There are two types of division: measurement types and partative types.

- *Measurement:* You have a length (15 inches) and want to find how many times a smaller length (3 inches) would be found in the 15 inches. (15 divided by 3 equals 5)

- *Partative:* You are trying to find the size of a given number of subgroups that can be made from a certain amount. Say there are 20 cards in a pack. Four people are to share the cards equally. How many cards will each person have? (20 divided by 4 equals 5) To demonstrate this, you can actually have a pack of 20 cards and deal them out, one at a time, to 4 people. How many did each one get? (5)

## THE JANUARY SNOWMAN

If each student makes a January snowman from construction paper circles, how many will the class make? How many scarfs, shovels, and hats does that amount to? (See Reproducible Activity Pages.)

Suppose we have a nice snowy day and the snow is good for packing. Let's make a snowman and do some problem solving along the way.

- What could we use for eyes? (stones, rocks, seashells, buttons)

- What could we use for a nose? (stick, celery stalk, parsnip)

- What could we use for a mouth? (radishes, food coloring)

We can make snowmen to hang from the overhead lights. Use three circles and either glue them together, or staple a string between each circle so that the circles can rotate gently with the indoor air currents. Decorate them with hats, boots, arms, mittens, and facial features, and enjoy them overhead. An excellent picture book that can help with this project is *Snowballs* by Lois Ehlert. Students will be motivated to bring in bits of string, yarn, materials, buttons, and so on for their delightful snowmen.

Make an edible snowman using white bread and cookie cutters. Raisins and nuts can be used for faces and buttons. Save the crusts for arms and legs and the crumbs for the birds outdoors.

Students can eat their snowman treat while listening to a good snowy day story such as *Old Man Winter* by Stephen Gammel or *Snowflake Bentley* by Mary Azarian.

## ADJUSTING NUMBERS IN YOUR HEAD

When you are doing mental math and see a problem like this one, there is something that you can do.

$$\begin{array}{r} 105 \\ +42 \\ \hline \end{array}$$

*Round off* these numbers so that one is larger and one is smaller, and they will be easier to add. Adjust these numbers this way in your mental calculation:

$$\begin{array}{r} 100 \\ +47 \\ \hline \end{array}$$

You took 5 away from 105 and made it an even 100. Then you added the 5 to 42 and made it 47. So, right away the numbers are easier to handle and you can say that 100 + 47 is 147.

Try doing this with more examples in class. Students are mentally using their addition and subtraction facts for this process, and it's quicker.

# FOCUS ON SOCIAL STUDIES

## JANUARY CITIZENSHIP FOCUS

During this month, in honor of Martin Luther King, Jr.'s birthday on January 15, our focus will be

upon *nonviolence*. Dr. King believed in settling differences peacefully.

Engage students in discussions regarding conflict resolution that can be managed by peaceful means. This refers to using our words, *not* our fists or hands. Encourage students to "talk it out" on the playground or during recess when there is a difference of opinion.

Perhaps you will need to take time twice a week to discuss conflicts that keep occurring, and work toward a solution.

## GIVE AND TAKE

Explain to students that sometimes we have to come in second, not always first. Sometimes we want chocolate cookies and there is only maple left. Do we shout? Do we rage? No, that's what an infant does who cannot talk it out. Becoming violent only adds to the problem; it does not solve anything. Students need to discuss this and believe it, and put it into effect in their everyday dealing with others. Have them take the Nonviolent Pledge. Use both hands and count out each quality required by tapping the fingers on one hand with the forefinger on the other:

Nonviolence requires (1) patience.

Nonviolence requires (2) maturity.

Nonviolence requires (3) cooperation.

Nonviolence requires (4) willingness to "give and take."

Nonviolence requires (5) an "us" attitude, not a "me" attitude.

## THE VIOLENT TANK AND NONVIOLENT TOAD

Here is a read-aloud to share with students.

*A big red tank came down the road*
*And bumped into a little toad.*
*"Get out of the way!" the big tank yelled.*
*"You're in my path—I'll have you expelled!"*

*"Hold on, hold on!" grinned the little toad.*
*"You just think you're king of the road.*
*This is my highway, I'll have you know.*
*I say when you can stop and go."*

*The big red tank grew purple with rage,*
*Stepped on the gas and what do you think?*
*The gas tank squirted purple ink,*
*The tires turned into lollipops,*
*The horn blew music that called the cops.*
*"Howdy, Toady, have we got trouble?*
*I tried to get here on the double.*
*Been watching this bully from up the road.*
*Shall we turn him into a toad?"*

*The police lady opened her toad ticket book,*
*But the red tank apologized.*
*That broke a spell and the tank became*
*Nonviolent in front of their very eyes.*

*So take a lesson from this tale*
*And learn to apologize.*
*You will make more friends that way*
*And they will say you're very wise.*

*REMEMBER:*
*Don't be a bully, or you'll get bumpy.*
*Your face and skin could turn all lumpy.*

*Why you could change into a toad*
*And live alongside a muddy road.*

*So step right up, my friend,*
*Do it today, my friend!*
*Get nonviolent, my friend.*
*It's the only way to stay . . . MY friend!*          *(The End)*

## WEBSITE

Visit this site entitled "Creating Peaceable Families." The focus here is to teach kids to handle conflict constructively. K–12 activities for teaching both conflict resolution and peace-making skills are included. The "Kids' Conscious Acts of Peace Project" shows positive efforts students have taken to resolve conflicts in a nonviolent and creative manner. The site has nice graphics. The address is: http://www.benjerry.com/esr/peaceable-index.html.

# PATRIOTISM

## PROOF OF CITIZENSHIP

Inform students that they each have a valuable document—proof of citizenship. This is their birth certificate. Tell students that this needs to be kept in a safe spot in the home or in a safe deposit box in the bank. Invite them to ask parents about their certificate, but *do not bring it to school.* In your newsletter to parents, remind them to put this document in a special, safe place.

## OUR PATRIOT OF THE MONTH: MARTIN LUTHER KING, JR.

This month we'll take a closer look at Martin Luther King, Jr. But instead of giving students a great deal of information about this leader, have students gather as much information as they can.

Begin with a discussion about where they would go in the library to look up information about a famous American. Would it be the thesaurus, the encyclopedia, the telephone book, the dictionary? Is there a website they can explore? We can also use the newspaper and magazines.

## BIOGRAPHICAL INFORMATION

There are certain facts we want to learn when seeking information about a person. Here are some of them:

- person's full name
- place of birth
- date of birth
- family status (marriage/children)
- occupation (in this case, religion would be pertinent)
- living or deceased
- what does/did this person do to achieve fame
- cause of death (if pertinent)
- legacy (for what do we remember this person?)

Students can work in pairs or in small groups of three or four to get this information. Make a big chart with the above headings, and have students fill in the information as they locate it. (Also tell the source of the information.)

## CORETTA SCOTT KING AWARD

Martin Luther King, Jr.'s wife, Coretta Scott King, established an award in children's literature. This award is given yearly to African-Americans who have made a contribution to children's literature for minority children. The person can be an author or illustrator or both. (This award is given at the same time the Caldecott Award is given for outstanding picture book of the year and the Newbery Award is given for outstanding text of the year.) Since the award is given in January, be on the lookout for all three awards this month. (See the February Author Section for some Coretta Scott King Award winners).

# AREA OF FOCUS: THIS IS MY COUNTRY, THE USA

## LAND WORDS

"From the mountains to the prairies . . ." this great land of ours varies. Here are some words that pertain to the land. Some may be right in your own backyard:

| | | | |
|---|---|---|---|
| canyon | cape | flat lands | highlands |
| low lands | hills | mountains | plains |
| plateau | valley | meadow | fields |
| peninsula | | | |

Students can make a large chart and divide it into sections. Each section can contain a land word, a definition, and a diagram.

## WATER WORDS

The oceans and the seas, as well as the Great Salt Lake in Utah, are made up of salt water. Some bodies of water are called "fresh" water, but this does not mean we can drink this water unless it has been treated. Some water words are:

| | | | |
|---|---|---|---|
| ocean | sea | river | lake |
| brook | marsh | swamp | rapids |
| stream | falls | creek | pond |

How many do students live near? What type of life does each body of water support? For this project, make a chart to accompany the Land Words Chart.

## WEBSITE: TRIP THROUGH THE GRAND CANYON

Take a trip through the Grand Canyon. Beautiful photographs and narrative text provide a glimpse of the beauty and thrill of the 240-mile canyon raft ride. Overflowing with information about the Grand Canyon, you'll want to visit http://river.ihs.gov/GrandCanyon/GCrt.html.

## WEBSITE: A BRIEF GUIDE TO STATE FACTS

A website that has state mottos and birds and quick reference to basic facts about the 50 states is http://www.ecnet.net/users/gdlevin/sstudies.html.

## WEBSITE: "MAPMAKER, MAPMAKER, MAKE ME A MAP"

This introductory tutorial on mapmaking provides a self-paced learning experience. The "Mapmaker Crossword Puzzle" can be printed and used as a cooperative class activity. Visit the following: http://loki.ur.utk.edu/ut2Kids/maps/map.html.

## A FAMILY ALBUM

A 55-page combination picture book and information book, one that you will want the school to acquire for grade three and beyond, is entitled *My Fellow Americans, A Family Album* by Alice Provensen. The author/illustrator states clearly that she is in love with America and refers to the people as her American Family. In this family you will meet inventors, statesmen, founding fathers, poets, musicians, groundbreakers, and much more. This book will enrich your study of the nation.

## A CLASSROOM FAMILY ALBUM

Using the information from the biographical activity, have each student complete a sheet to contribute to the class family album. Students may want to confer with parents regarding what information will go on their page. It can also be decorated with a bor-

Classroom Family Album

der and sketches of pets. When each page is completed, the sheets can be run off on the copier so each student can get a copy of the album and make a cover for it. (This is optional and would depend upon the discretion of the teacher.)

# HOLIDAYS AND CELEBRATIONS

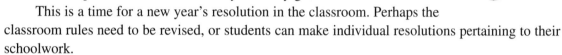

## NEW YEAR'S DAY

Bells ring out the old and ring in the new. The calendar is changed and a whole new year begins.

This holiday is celebrated in the United States and all over the world. In Ecuador people wear new clothes and parade in the streets. They burn their old clothes as a symbol of burning the past and starting anew.

In Europe the "first footers" are the first ones to step over the threshold of the doorstep of the home in the new year. They get to make a wish.

This is a time for a new year's resolution in the classroom. Perhaps the classroom rules need to be revised, or students can make individual resolutions pertaining to their schoolwork.

## GENJITSU—NEW YEAR'S DAY

This is a special festival in Japan. On New Year's morning, the family dresses in new clothes and eats together. After the meal, children receive their special New Year's gifts, usually coins sealed in special gift envelopes. On the second day, the "first writing" or *kakizome* occurs. Every family member uses the art of brush and ink to write a poem or proverb for the home.

## GUNG HAY FAT CHOY (CHINESE NEW YEAR)

This is a time for families to get together. The Chinese add a year to their age on New Year's Day, regardless of the day on which they were born. It's a time for new clothes, time to fill the home with flowers and fruit, and time for families to remember their ancestors. There are money gifts wrapped in red paper for the children, called *lai see*.

At this celebration, the ceremonial dragon winds its way through the throngs of happy people in the streets. It is an honor to be chosen to help hold up the dragon.

## MARTIN LUTHER KING, JR. DAY

This is a national holiday in January in honor of the Civil Rights leader who believed in a peaceful means to attain goals. There are official ceremonies honoring Dr. King, and people gather to listen to speeches about the state of the civil rights movement and freedom for all people everywhere. Choral groups provide lovely music and it is a time for reflection and dreams for a better world.

Perhaps students can talk about their own dreams for a better world, just as Martin Luther King, Jr. did in his "I have a dream . . ." speech.

## CALDECOTT MEDAL AND NEWBERY MEDAL

The American Library Association (ALA) announces the winners of two prestigious awards this month. Be on the lookout for this information in news articles and at the library.

*Caldecott Medal*—This award is named for Randolph Caldecott, British illustrator of children's books. The gold medal is awarded to the outstanding picture book for the previous year. The focus is on excellence in illustrations. Honor books may also be named and they receive a silver medal.

*Newbery Medal*—This award is named for John Newbery, first British publisher of books for children. It is awarded to the book from the previous year that is judged to be the best story. Honor books may also be named.

Set up a Caldecott Corner reading nook in the classroom for sharing these book treasures from previous years. Children can bring in stuffed animals to accompany the books and read to them. Celebrate outstanding books!

# FOCUS ON SCIENCE

## THE SOLAR SYSTEM

Our Sun and the stars that make up the constellations in the solar system are all part of a huge spiral-shaped group that we call the *Galaxy. The Sun is one of the stars in the galaxy.* The galaxy rotates; it is not still.

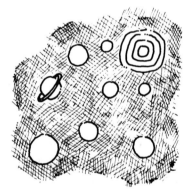

The Sun is at the center of our galaxy and is a blazing ball of gas that gives off heat and light. There are nine known planets that revolve around the Sun at different speeds, and scientists are still searching for more.

Students will need to memorize the names of the planets in order: Mercury, Venus, Earth, Mars, Jupiter, Saturn, Uranus, Neptune, Pluto. (See Reproducible Activity Pages.)

Using a mneumonic device to aid with memorization may help. Try these statements and notice that the first letter of each word represents the planets in order—M,V,E,M,J,S,U,N,P.

**M**y **v**ery **e**legant **m**ouse **J**ames **s**leeps **u**nder **n**ine **p**illows.

OR

**M**r. **V**ick's **e**lephant **m**ay **j**ust **s**teal **U**ncle **N**ed's **p**eanuts.

## THE MORNING STAR, THE EVENING STAR

Planets are not visible to the naked eye, except for a glimpse of Venus in early evening (twilight) and early morning. It appears in the sky along with the stars, and is often mistaken for a very bright star, but the sunlight reflected off of its cloud layer is what makes it appear so bright.

Stars have their own light source, planets do not. A planet is not a star. So, calling Venus a morning or evening star is like a nickname. Do the other planets in the solar system have nicknames? Students can do some research on this.

## THE STARS IN COLOR

Think of glowing hot metal. First it glows a dark red. Then, as it gets hotter, the color changes to orange-red, then to yellow, and eventually to bright white with hints of blue.

Therefore, the coolest stars are red, the warmer and brighter stars are yellow or white, and the hottest and brightest of all are usually blue-white.

Astronomers use a color-code for stars as follows:

| | | |
|---|---|---|
| O, B | = | hottest blue stars |
| A, F, G | = | white, less hot |
| K | = | yellow |
| M | = | red |

The Sun is labeled "G." Students can make a color-coded star guide in the shape of a star.

## ENERGY FROM THE SUN

Are there solar collectors in an area near you? Perhaps your school even has solar collectors on the roof. The purpose is to collect energy from the Sun to help heat the air inside buildings. Students can search through books for examples of solar collectors.

What color should these collectors be? Cut three squares and place them on a sunny window ledge. Make one of black paper, one of white paper, and one of aluminum foil. Ask students to predict which one will feel warmest in five minutes. Then check to see which color feels the warmest. That is the one that traps the most heat from the Sun.

## STARGAZING AT NIGHT

It's almost impossible to study the sky at night with your class, but one book that will serve as a helpful guide for them to do it independently is entitled *Stargazers* by Gail Gibbons.

Students will be introduced to constellations, or a group of stars. They'll see The Little Dipper, with the North Star at the end of the handle, and the Big Dipper. They will learn the shape of "Orion," the famous hunter who is seen in the winter sky. The constellation named "The Greater Dog" has the brightest star in the night sky. That star is called Sirius, or The Dog Star.

One of the best ways to study the nighttime sky, as a class, is to visit a planetarium, if one is in or near your city. Also, contact the Astronomy Department of the local high school or nearby college to invite a guest speaker to address the class about the sky. They can bring instruments and explain their purpose.

## MAKE A PAPIER-MÂCHÉ SOLAR SYSTEM

Work with the Art teacher in your building and, using papier-mâché and balloons or small Styrofoam balls, build a solar system to scale. Some teachers have solved the scale problem by making a bright yellow half Sun (shape of the capital letter D) and taping it to the front wall from the top of the ceiling to the floor. (Remember, the Sun is huge in comparison to the planets.) Then create the planets, paint them, and hang them diagonally from ceiling lights from one corner of the room to another. The classroom is then within a quadrant of the orbiting planets. If it's not possible to hang the planet models from the ceiling in the room, use this same idea for a giant bulletin board.

## SPACE ADVENTURE

Fasten your seatbelts for a trip into outer space with Ms. Frizzle, "the weirdest teacher in school." The book is *The Magic School Bus Lost in the Solar System* by Joanna Cole, with illustrations by Bruce Degen. It's filled with scientific terms and explanations, in addition to being a fantastic adventure that children really enjoy.

## A RAINBOW EXPERIMENT

*You will need:* a sunny day, a shallow see-through container, small mirror, and water.

*Procedure:* Pour water into the container until it is about 3/4 full. Place container on a sunny window ledge or counter area. Place a mirror in the container so that the sunlight hits it directly.

The light passes through the water and bounces off the mirror, making a faint rainbow appear on the wall. If the wall is not light colored, place a white sheet of paper and hold it in front of the wall.

Students need to learn that sunlight is actually made up of all these colors. When it rains, each raindrop acts as a tiny prism. The colors split off to form the colors of the rainbow—red, orange, yellow, green, blue, indigo, and violet.

## TELLING TIME BY THE SUN

In days long ago, even before there were clocks, people told time by the Sun. When it is high in the sky, it's midday or noon. It appears to rise in the east and set in the west, and by looking at the position of the Sun in the western sky, people knew how much longer it would be before "sundown."

People became sophisticated about devising instruments to tell time, and made what we call sundials. Some are very fancy, but we can make a simple one to get the concept across.

*You will need:* a clay flowerpot with a hole in the bottom, a long stick, large piece of paper, and pencil.

*Procedure:* Place the paper on the ground in a sunny spot. Turn the flowerpot upside down, and place a long stick in the hole so that it is upright. Study the shadow and note where the stick is. Every hour make a line on the paper where the stick's shadow is and record the time.

Now, on another sunny day, we'll be able to look at the sundial shadow and see what time it is. If we see a record of 1:00 P.M. and 2:00 P.M. and the sundial shadow is halfway between, then what time would we suppose it is? (1:30 P.M. or half past one)

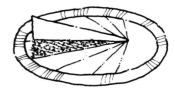

# JANUARY AUTHOR STUDY: JEAN FRITZ

Jean Fritz was born in Hankow, China, the daughter of missionary parents. She has written her delightful autobiography entitled *Homesick, My Own Story*. It tells of a little girl who preferred to be living in the United States if she'd had her way. She enjoyed hearing her parents talk of their school days in Washington, Pennsylvania, and wished that's where she could be with her grand-mother. At an early age she had many questions about the United States, and this may well be the reason that the titles of many of her books are in the form of a question. When her family finally returned to the United States, Jean did live with her grandmother who involved her in such house-hold chores as cleaning, washing, shopping—and Jean was thrilled. In fact, she wrote a glowing letter back to China to a former servant and said that at last "she had become a coolie."

Jean Fritz has done more to enliven the Social Studies curriculum than any other single author. Her books on American history are charming, witty, and informative. She has put a real face on some of the prominent figures in our country's past. Children love the stories, and grade three is a good place to begin with some of them. They can meet up with Jean Fritz again in grades four and five. Many of the books below can be read aloud by you in one or two sittings. So, welcome Jean Fritz into your classroom and make Social Studies come to life.

## BOOKS AND SUGGESTED ACTIVITIES

### *WHO'S THAT STEPPING ON PLYMOUTH ROCK?* (ILLUSTRATED BY J. B. HANDELSMAN)

An amusing account of the history, as far as we know it, of Plymouth Rock. Over the years it has been built into a wharf, moved under a tree, been broken, dropped, mended, dragged, housed, and rehoused. The rock figures into prominent holiday celebrations at Thanksgiving and in summer parades. Many people visit Plymouth, Massachussetts each year to get a look at this famous rock in American history. We can no longer stop to rest on it, or wipe our feet on it as people did for years, but we can at least get a look at it in its lovely setting.

## ACTIVITIES TO ACCOMPANY *WHO'S THAT STEPPING ON PLYMOUTH ROCK?*

1. Act out the story of the landing on Plymouth Rock of the First Comers on the *Mayflower*. We learn that's what they were called before they were referred to as Pilgrims. Students can make up their own script of what was said, since no one was there to record it.

2. *Creative movement.* Have students work together in groups of three or four to reenact some of the experiences this rock has endured. For example, several students can pull the rock in an effort to move it. Students can hold up their arms to simulate a temple built around the rock, and so on.

3. Students can make a tissue-paper collage art version of Plymouth Rock, with the blue sea and sky in the background.

4. How many students in class have been to Plymouth? Locate it on the map. How far away do they live from it now? How close have they come to it in their travels?

5. Students can write to the Chamber of Commerce in Plymouth in an effort to get information about the area, and the rock, for the classroom.

## WHAT'S THE BIG IDEA, BEN FRANKLIN? (ILLUSTRATED BY MARGOT TOMES)

Ben Franklin is portrayed as a man filled with curiosity, good spirit, and many ideas. He founded the first circulating library, a fire department, an almanac, and a postal system. He was curious about electricity. He was an inventor, too, and designed a rocking chair with a fan on top that moved the air around to cool you off as you rocked back and forth. He helped write the Declaration of Independence and was Ambassador to France at age seventy.

Ben had many ideas, and this book also provides many ideas to use in the classroom to enrich the study of early America, and to get an up-close look at a famous statesman and inventor. We've all benefited from this man's contributions to our country.

## ACTIVITIES TO ACCOMPANY *WHAT'S THE BIG IDEA, BEN FRANKLIN?*

1. Read this book aloud to the class in segments. Take at least three or four days to read and digest it.

2. *The naming of streets.* The first paragraph of this book can get you hooked on street names. Ben Franklin was born at a time in American history when streets were just being named and we learn that some were called Cow Lane, Flownder Lane, Turn Again Alley, Half-Square Court, and Milk Street. He was born in the family home on Milk Street. Students can investigate the names of streets in their towns. Were many of them named after people?

3. Benjamin Franklin had many buildings named after him. Is there one in your town, such as a bank, a school, or a store?

4. *Reading.* Ben loved to read "how to do it" books. He liked to know how things worked. Students can find such books in the library and explain to the class how something works or how to make something. If possible, with enough materials and time, students can make one of the items.

5. *Form a Leather Apron Club.* Ben formed a reading club after work hours for the tradesmen who enjoyed reading. They met and discussed good books. Students can do the same thing. Keep track of the book titles on apron shapes.

6. *Rules for good behavior.* Ben made a list of these as follows:

| | |
|---|---|
| Don't eat or drink too much. | Be sincere. |
| Don't joke or talk too much. | Be fair. |
| Keep your things neat. | Keep clean. |
| Do what you set out to do. | Keep calm. |
| Don't spend too much money. | Don't go to extremes. |
| Don't waste time. | Don't show off. |
| Don't fool around with girls. | |

Students can make a big list of these rules for the classroom, and refer to them.

7. *Investigate almanacs in the library.* They are filled with information about lots of things. Ben wrote one called *Poor Richard's Almanack* with one-liners. ("A penny saved is a penny earned.") After reading this book, students may be interested in trying to invent something. So, let's talk about inventions. Find books on inventions at the library.

8. Ben's big idea was that lightning and electricity were the same. In what ways do we use electricity today, and yet take it for granted? Make a list.

9. This book is so filled with ideas that students will need to hear it again and read it again. What main ideas do they take away from this book?

## CAN'T YOU MAKE THEM BEHAVE, KING GEORGE? (PICTURES BY TOMIE DEPAOLA)

When George was just twelve years old, his father died and he became Prince of Wales. He had to get instructions for the time when he would become King, and had many tutors and lessons to learn. He selected his bride from among seven princesses, and even supervised the making of her wedding dress. The author describes the hilarious wedding reception. King George and Queen Charlotte had fifteen children. Things were going quite well for them, but the American colonies started to rebel. How could a King lose a war?

## ACTIVITIES TO ACCOMPANY *CAN'T YOU MAKE THEM BEHAVE, KING GEORGE?*

1. Read the book in two or three stages, so that all of the information can be absorbed. The illustrations help make the book amusing, so point them out.

2. As an author, what information did Jean Fritz need to know before writing this book? Have students talk about it at the end of the book. This is a very different type of writing from fanciful writing. It is called historical fiction. There's an element of truth in it and the author fills in the amusing details. Perhaps students can start out with an outline of truthful information about someone they are studying, and make up a fanciful tale weaving this factual information into the story.

3. As an illustrator, what information did Tomie dePaola need to know before he could begin illustrating this book? What might the notes to him read like—"We need a picture of . . ."

4. Learn to "collaborate." One student can write a story and another can illustrate it.

5. How did the author "hook us" into the story? Read the beginning paragraph again. Read the beginnings of her other books, too. What does an author need to do in order to "hook" her audience like a fish?

6. Learn to share your thoughts. Have students make comments on self-stick notes and put them in the book so others can read their comments. It invites others to think also.

## JUST A FEW WORDS, MR. LINCOLN. THE STORY OF THE GETTYSBURG ADDRESS (ILLUSTRATED BY CHARLES ROBINSON)

A cemetery in Gettysburg, Pennsylvania is to be dedicated to the soldiers who fought in the Civil War. It would be an impressive cemetery, with monuments honoring men from the states in the north and the south. The grandest speaker of the day, Edward Everett, has been asked to speak. It is decided that Abraham Lincoln should also be asked, since he is President. It is a day that is blistering hot, and thousands of people are standing. Mr. Everett is late, and then speaks for two hours! Then President Lincoln gives his Gettysburg Address. It is short (271 words) but electrifying! People are still talking about that speech! (This is a true story.)

## ACTIVITIES TO ACCOMPANY JUST A FEW WORDS, MR. LINCOLN

1. Read and enjoy the book. It, too, is short but electrifying. Then reread it for attention to details.

2. Students will gain more of an understanding of the concept of shaking hands with the president. A hand can become swollen and sore. Have everyone shake hands with classmates. (Then wash them.)

3. Lincoln's son was nicknamed Tad. Have a discussion of nicknames of the classmates, and even of pets.

4. Have students note the folksy expressions used by this president, when he is quoted as saying the speech just needed "another lick" and "it fell like a wet blanket."

5. Even Mr. Everett, who spoke for two hours, wrote a letter to compliment Mr. Lincoln, who said more in two minutes than Everett said in two hours. Talk to students about "quality" vs. "quantity" and how this can apply to many things. Begin to focus upon quality—for example, having a recess of good quality (playing a class game all together), having a quality lunch with friends (eating with a partner or with a threesome), and so on.

## WILL YOU SIGN HERE, JOHN HANCOCK? (PICTURES BY TRINA SCHART HYMAN)

This book gives an account of the early days in New England when the government was just being formed. John Hancock was a wealthy man, good looking, and he wanted people to like him so much that they would elect him to high office. He liked to dress well in fancy, ruffled shirts and buckled shoes and velvet coats. His wigs were rolled and neat. The text gives us good insight into his character. We also get an idea of how he and his wife, Dolly, entertained and lived like royalty.

## ACTIVITIES TO ACCOMPANY *WILL YOU SIGN HERE, JOHN HANCOCK?*

1. Read the book aloud in segments. This is not a book to be read quickly in one sitting. There are many facts to be discussed and digested.

2. Practice handwriting. John Hancock loved to practice writing his name and there is a page in the book showing different styles that he used. Students might be encouraged to practice signing their name with a flourish—underline it, have curlicues on some of the letters. Then all students can use a writing pen to put their newly acquired signature on a large sheet of paper. Use a black, felt-tip pointed pen, and attach a feather to the end of it.

3. Thomas Jefferson wrote The Declaration of Independence, and John Hancock was the first to sign it, which was an act of bravery in those days. What does the book tell us about this? Why do we celebrate July 4 to this day?

4. Students will enjoy the account of the Hancock household serving breakfast to the French officers. Encourage them to draw an illustration of the food and the table, or the cooks scurrying around in the kitchen.

5. *Political cartoons.* Even in his day, John Hancock appeared in political cartoons in the newspaper with long ears like a donkey and with a conceited grin on his face. Have students study the political cartoons in the local newspaper, and bring in those that portray some of our government leaders. What are the political cartoonists trying to say? This creates an awareness of political cartoons in newspapers, magazines, and cartoon pages.

**Note:** There are additional books by Jean Fritz that can be used at this level to enrich the Social Studies curriculum, or just for pure enjoyment and enlightenment. Notice that many of the titles are in the form of a question. They include: *And Then What Happened, Paul Revere?; Why Don't You Get a Horse, Sam Adams?; Where Was Patrick Henry on the 29th of May?* There are additional books such as *The Double Life of Pocahontas; Traitor: The Case of Benedict Arnold; The Great Little Madison; Stonewall;* and so on.

An excellent chapter book to read aloud to the class is the autobiography that Jean Fritz wrote about her early life in China entitled *Biography: My Own Story.* It's a Newbery Medal winner.

# REPRODUCIBLE ACTIVITY PAGES
# FOR JANUARY

## READING/LANGUAGE ARTS

My January Self-Assessment

Baxter and the Blender

Story Outline

Story Character Web

Author Checklist

Handwriting Skills

## MATH

Percy Penguin's Math Slide

Become a Division Star

Snowman Math

## SOCIAL STUDIES

The People's House

Famous Americans Album

## SCIENCE

Our Solar System

Science Tools

## AUTHOR STUDY

Become an Inventor with Jean Fritz

Name _____

# My January Self-Assessment

This is how well I <u>think</u> I'm doing, but, am I on target? After I put an "X" in the square, my teacher will give me some helpful tips.

How can I improve my study habits? Name 2 ways.

©2002 by The Center for Applied Research in Education

| | Very Good | I could work harder | I must work harder |
|---|---|---|---|
| 1. Main Idea—Can I get it? | | | |
| 2. Predictions—Do I sense what's coming next? | | | |
| 3. Independent Reading—Do I read on my own? Do I read at home? | | | |
| 4. Phonics—Can I sound out new words? | | | |
| 5. Listening—Do I listen when others are speaking? | | | |
| 6. Story Time—Can I follow what someone is reading aloud? | | | |
| 7. Spelling—Do I study the words? Am I improving? What can I do to help myself? | | | |
| 8. Handwriting—Do I practice daily? Do I want to be a better writer? | | | |
| 9. Letter Writing—Do I use the correct form? Do I write to anyone? | | | |
| 10. What Is . . . a root word? a compound word? a contraction? | | | |

# Baxter and the Blender

Today Baxter is mixing up a batch of blends. Take the letters from the blender and put them in front of these letters to make words.  Each blend can be used only once.

1.  _____end

2.  _____iend

3.  _____ape

4.  _____acker

5.  _____oon

6.  _____ring

7.  _____ipper

8.  _____ow

9.  _____actice

10.  _____other

11.  _____eater

12.  _____ap

13.  _____itch

14.  _____ack

15.  _____ain

Name _____     Date _____

# Story Outline

| | |
|---|---|
| Book Title | |
| Author/ Illustrator | |
| Main Characters | |
| Setting | |
| Problem | |
| Solution | |

Story Message:

I liked it when

# Story Character Web

Select a character from a story you read. Draw that person below.
Complete the web. Go back and check the story again for more
information.

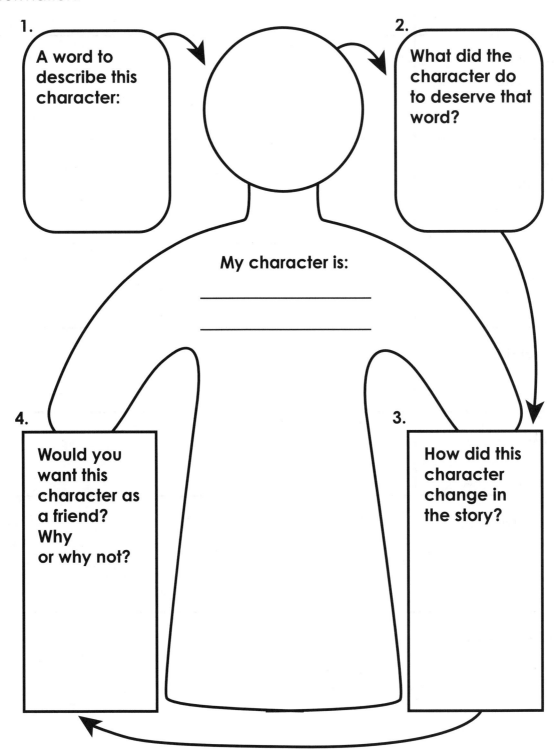

**1.**
A word to
describe this
character:

**2.**
What did the
character do
to deserve that
word?

**My character is:**

_____

_____

**4.**
Would you
want this
character as
a friend?
Why
or why not?

**3.**
How did this
character
change in
the story?

Name _____

Date _____

# Author Checklist

Put an X in each box as you go through this five-step process.

1. ☐ **Prewriting** — What will I write about? A picture I painted, a trip I went on, my pet, or something else? Will I draw pictures to go along with the story?

2. ☐ **First Draft** — This is what I want to let the reader know.

3. ☐ **Revise** — Maybe I should add more information here, and use another word there.

4. ☐ **Proofread** — Did I begin each sentence with a capital letter? Do I need to check any words for spelling? Maybe I will read it to someone else to see if he or she understands what I am trying to say.

5. ☐ **Publish** — It's fine! Now I can carefully print it or type it.

# Handwriting Skills

Practice one row of each letter.  Work slowly and carefully.

*a*  *a* _____

*c* _____

*d* _____

*g* _____

*m* _____

*n* _____

*o* _____

*q* _____

*x* _____

*z* _____

*w* _____

*y* _____

Use these lines if you need further practice with any letter.

_____

_____

_____

_____

_____

# Handwriting Skills

Practice one row of each letter. Work slowly and carefully.

Use these lines if you need further practice with any letter.

# Percy Penguin's Math Slide

Percy fell on the ice and his math words got all jumbled up. Please help him put them together.

1. ottla _____

2. lpsu _____

3. diitando _____

4. ismnu _____

5. unrmela _____

6. bsuttrac _____

7. ermeuas _____

8. iidvde _____

9. tham _____

10. ltmluiyp _____

11. hinc _____

12. loves _____

©2002 by The Center for Applied Research in Education

## Math Key:

| solve | math | measure | numeral | total | minus |
| inch | multiply | plus | subtract | divide | addition |

# Become a Division Star

You've been selected to play on the Bears' team. Help out with the division. Let's score!

$3\overline{)27}$

$7\overline{)28}$

$5\overline{)35}$

$6\overline{)48}$

$3\overline{)9}$

$7\overline{)56}$

$4\overline{)20}$

$7\overline{)42}$

$5\overline{)40}$

$4\overline{)28}$

$9\overline{)81}$

$8\overline{)32}$

$6\overline{)54}$

$7\overline{)63}$

$6\overline{)36}$

$4\overline{)16}$

# Snowman Math

Let's do some counting.  Add carefully.  Record the numbers below.

**TOTAL NUMBER OF:**

snowmen _____

noses _____

buttons _____

hats _____

scarfs _____

eyes _____

shoes _____

mouths _____

shovels _____

brooms _____

mittens _____

Make your own snowman here.

# The People's House

The White House, or "The People's House," is in Washington, D.C.

Unlike a king or queen, the president does not live here forever. It is an elected office.

Go to the library.
Find information books on the White House so that you can answer the questions below. Use another sheet of paper for 4, 5, and 6.

1.  The White House is located in this city.

2.  The name of the current president is:

3.  Name the First Family members:

4.  Draw their pets (if any), and name them:

5.  The president comes from this state. Write it and draw an outline of the state. Locate it on a map.

6.  There are many famous rooms in the White House (Oval Office, Red Room, Blue Room, Lincoln Bedroom, etc.). Select one room and tell something that you found out about it during your research.

Use the other side to list more interesting facts. Compare with classmates.

# Famous Americans Album

If you could help compile a book of famous Americans, who would you like to see there? Use the library. Compare your selections with those of classmates. Tell why you chose them.

Inventor

Name: _____

Statesman or Stateswoman

Name: _____

President

Name: _____

Scientist

Name: _____

My Favorite Person

Name: _____

Name _____

Date _____

# Our Solar System

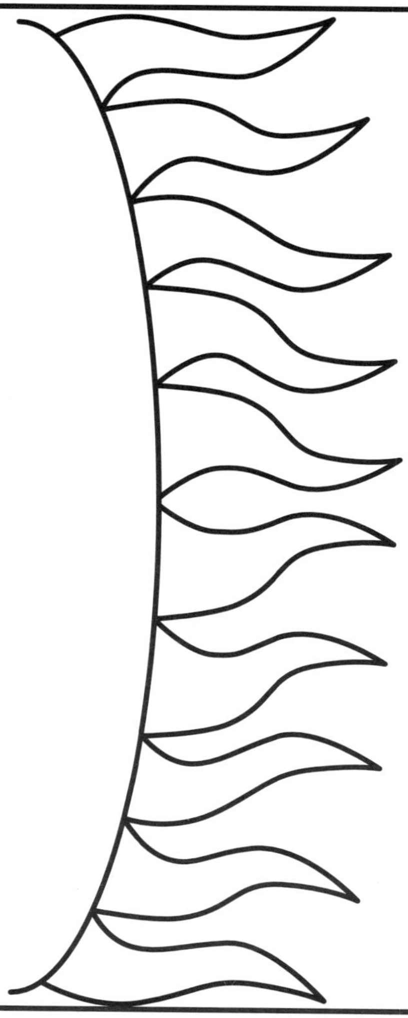

**Unscramble the planets. Write the planet name on the line above.**

1. _____ ruyrmec

2. _____ opult

3. _____ aunsrt

4. _____ rasunu

5. _____ senuv

6. _____ pirjtue

7. _____ smra

8. _____ hrate

9. _____ etnupen

**Now, write the planets in order. Start with the one closest to the sun.**

1. M_____

2. _____

3. _____

4. _____

5. _____

6. _____

7. _____

8. _____

9. _____

Name _____   Date _____

# Science Tools

This scientist is going to set up a new lab. What equipment (tools) will he need in his science lab? Think of six things the scientist could use. Draw them, color them, and label them.

The first one is done for you to get you started.

1. Magnifying Glass

2.

3.

4.

5.

6.

**Perhaps you can set up a Science Tool Table in your classroom, and use it.**

**Name** _____  **Date** _____

# Become an Inventor with Jean Fritz

*What's the Big Idea, Ben Franklin?* is a story that tells of inventions. You, too, can become an inventor. What's your big idea?

You can use clay to show a model of your invention, or draw a diagram.

In this space tell the following:

1. Name of invention:

2. Purpose:

3. What it is made of:

4. How it works:

# FEBRUARY

# FEBRUARY BOOKS

**Adoff, Arnold.** *In for Winter, Out for Spring.* **Illustrated by Jerry Pinkney (New York: Harcourt, 1991).** A collection of poems that celebrates the seasons, the world, and the family through the voice of a young African-American girl. Lovely watercolor illustrations.

**Bender, Lionel.** *Today's World: Birds and Mammals* **(New York: Gloucester Press, 1988).** Each section of the book describes a group of related animals. Throughout the book, charts provide a comparison of the forms and sizes of animals in a particular group. Actual photographs are also used to help investigate the animals and birds.

**Greenfield, Eloise.** *Honey, I Love and Other Poems.* **Pictures by Diane and Leo Dillon (New York: HarperCollins, 1978).** This author is the 1997 winner of the Award for Excellence in Poetry for Children (National Council of Teachers of English). It is said that she writes poetry that nourishes the spirit.

**Kimmel, Eric A.** *Anansi and the Moss-Covered Rock.* **Illustrated by Janet Stevens (New York: Holiday House, 1988).** Anansi the trickster spider finds a moss-covered rock and when he utters the words, "Isn't this a strange moss-covered rock!" a secret is discovered. Anansi is able to hoodwink lion, elephant, giraffe, zebra, and other animals out of their food. But his clever ploy is discovered, and the animals triumph.

**McKissack, Patricia C.** *Ma Dear's Aprons.* **Illustrated by Floyd Cooper (New York: Simon & Schuster, 1997).** Young David Earl knows which weekday it is by the type of apron his mother is wearing. Each day she wears a different one for her work: laundry, cleaning, and so on. This story was inspired by an apron once worn by the author's great-grandmother.

**Polacco, Patricia.** *Pink and Say* **(New York: Philomel, 1994).** The touching story of two young boys, one the color of mahogany and one white, who are Union soldiers in Confederate territory. One, named Say, is left for dead when Pinkus rescues him. He's nursed back to health by Moe Moe Bay, the black boy's mother. A touching war story for boys far too young to fight.

**Provenson, Alice.** *The Buck Stops Here, The Presidents of the United States* **(New York: HarperCollins, 1990).** From George Washington to George H. W. Bush, this picture book traces the presidents. Each portrait page has an abundance of visual information, so the reader can pick up information at a glance. A glossary contains information about each president. This is an excellent teaching book.

**Rogers, Teresa.** *George Washington Carver: Nature's Trailblazer* **(New York: Twenty-first Century, 1992).** This chapter book focuses on Carver's efforts in agricultural research. The summary pages list nearly one hundred products developed by Carver.

**Winter, Jeanette.** *Follow the Drinking Gourd* **(New York: Alfred A. Knopf, 1988).** This is a story about the Underground Railroad and the road to freedom for slaves fleeing to the north, all the way to Canada. The directions for the route were hidden in a song, which is printed on the last page of the book. The "drinking gourd" is another name for the Big Dipper.

**(CHAPTER BOOK) Paulsen, Gary.** *Hatchet* **(New York: Puffin, 1987).** A survival story about a boy who is going to visit his father in a private plane, when the pilot suddenly becomes ill, has a heart attack, and dies. The boy has to keep his wits about him and try to bring the plane down for a crash landing. Then there's the business of surviving with no food or shelter. A thought-provoking story. The sequel chapter book is called *The River.*

# FEBRUARY

February is a delightful month because there is so much going on in the classroom. Our room looks busy because many projects are, no doubt, on display that reflect our studies. We're learning the origins of words and sayings; we're enjoying the stories we read and write; and we have made progress since the beginning of the year in Math, Science, and Social Studies as well as with the computer. We can feel proud of our accomplishments!

That's the good news, and it gets even better as we approach the magic of February with Valentine greetings, the presidents, Black History, and winter. Let's enjoy a good month of learning opportunities.

# FOCUS ON READING

## THE KWL APPROACH

Before students read a book on a particular topic, have them tell or list what they already *know* (K), what they *want* to know (W), and then after they have read it, what they *learned* (L). This has been shortened to the "KWL Approach." It is also useful when studying a topic in another curricular area. Usually, the information is written in the form of a list. The setup of the KWL format is shown here. (See Reproducible Activity Pages.)

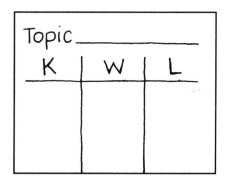

## DECLARATIVE AND INTERROGATIVE SENTENCES

Simply stated, a declarative sentence is used when we "declare" or tell something. It makes a statement. An interrogative sentence is one that asks a question, so we will be certain to use the question mark at the end of it, won't we? Declarative *tells;* interrogative *asks.*

Read the following sentences aloud so that students can determine if each one *tells* or *asks.* If it tells, have students make the letter T with their hands. If it asks, have them put the fingertips of both hands together to form a triangular shape, or the peak of the letter A. Here are the sentences to read:

1. Former President Jimmy Carter is said to be a good listener.
2. Did the first Model T Fords roll off the line in Detroit?
3. "Sputnik" is a Russian word, isn't it?
4. Egypt is mostly a dry, wind-swept desert.
5. I wonder, is Egypt located in Africa?
6. The teddy bear is named after President Teddy Roosevelt.
7. Did you know that you can see Jupiter without a telescope?
8. Your eyes are precious, so take good care of them.
9. Wear gloves or mittens to protect skin in cold weather.
10. Did she say it's time for Science now?

You can make a list of sentences, some declarative (tells) and some interrogative (asks), and students can place the punctuation mark at the end. (See Reproducible Activity Pages.)

## CHANGE THE SENTENCE FROM TELL TO ASK

Change the following sentences from one that is declarative (tells) to one that is interrogative (asks). This is a challenge for some students and an easy activity for others. Once you discover this, pair the students accordingly and have them work together to help each other. (See Reproducible Activity Pages.)

1. Groundhog Day is in February.
   Is Groundhog Day in February?

2. California is a large state.
   Is California a large state?

3. Rhode Island is a tiny state.
   Is Rhode Island a tiny state?

4. A hurricane can cause a lot of damage.
   Can a hurricane cause a lot of damage?

5. Today we're having pizza for lunch.
   Are we having pizza for lunch today?

Be sure to point out to students that in the ask/tell sentences, many of them use the exact words. So, *word order* is important in determining whether the sentence is ask/tell. Also, point out that in many of the ask/tell sentences, those that are asking a question often begin with "is" or "are." Other key words to be on the lookout for are "do," "does," "can," and "could." (See Reproducible Activity Pages.)

## MORE WORK WITH WEBS

Story webbing or mapping was discussed in the January section. This month we can create different types of webs.

**Journey Web.** Create a circular web that recounts the travels a character took in an adventure story, or one in which the family moves from place to place. Use different shapes for each setting.

**Two Comparison Webs.** When you have two opposites in a story, make two webs on the same page to show the differences (homes, food, clothing, and so on). You can also use this for two different books.

**Biography Web.** Draw the person in the center. At the ends of the spokes, draw shapes to represent the person and label them. For example, Abraham Lincoln—log cabin, fireplace light (for reading), books, stovepipe hat, president, and so on. Take the information from the book and use it.

## HOMOPHONES

These words sound the same but have different meanings, and usually different spellings. Homophones add confusion to the language but also some interest. These words are especially helpful in doing rebus stories. Here are some common homophones:

| | | | |
|---|---|---|---|
| bare | I | no | red |
| bear | eye | know | read |
| | | | |
| see | mist | plain | horse |
| sea | missed | plane | hoarse |
| | | | |
| night | rain | shoe | principal |
| knight | rein | shoo | principle |
| | | | |
| dear | made | flour | buy |
| deer | maid | flower | bye |
| | | | by |

Write these on flashcards and have students begin a homophone file. Or the words can be written in their journals, and students can go on a Homophone Hunt in the newspapers, magazines, and ads that are brought into the classroom. Ask your colleagues to save all of their junk mail and bring it to your classroom (set a container by the door). These are good sources of print.

## HOMOPHONE GUESS

Have students turn to their homophone file. Say a sentence using a homophone. If students think they know the correct spelling, they raise their hand. Then you can call upon a person to spell it. If correct, that student becomes the leader and the process starts all over again.

## REBUS STORIES USING HOMOPHONES

Homophones are especially helpful when we want to compose a rebus story. The *Amelia Bedelia* books by Peggy Parish are helpful and students like them. Students can write their own versions and come up with a fanciful rhyming name for this main character who takes everything literally.

The following activity should be helpful for rebus stories. Write the sentences on the chalkboard or chart. Read the first one aloud. Then circle the homophone "I." Next, demonstrate that you are replacing a homophone with a picture of a matching homophone by erasing the word "I" and drawing an "eye" in its place. Print the two words on the chalkboard: I/eye.

Then move on to the second sentence. Point out that the homophone is feat/feet, and make sure students know the meaning of each. Replace "feat" with a drawing of feet, and add these two words to the list. The following will help to get you started:

I like great big dogs. (I/eye)

That was a tremendous feat for the giant. (feat/feet)

Will you be lonely here alone? (be/bee)

Soon night would be here. (night/knight)

Please close the door. (close/clothes)

He ate it all! (ate/eight)

She had to shoo away the cats. (shoo/shoe)

It was a great day for a parade! (great/grate)

Would you put some coal on the fire? (would/wood)

There now, that's a good son. (son/sun)

So, how are you today? (so/sew)

You can do this activity on a chart and make a game of it. Leave the sentences as they are. Make rebus pictures of each homophone on sticky papers or flashcards that fit into a little slit in the chart. Students can take them off, mix them up, and replace them.

For variety, place the rebus homophone pictures in the wrong places and have students move them to the correct spot. Students can choose to do this as an activity during their free time or during indoor recess.

Have students be on the alert for more homophones. Here are some additional ones to work with. Also see Reproducible Activity Pages.

| whole | real | sail | sell |
|-------|------|------|------|
| hole | reel | sale | cell |
| | | | |
| bawl | in | one | meet |
| ball | inn | won | meat |
| | | | |
| byte | road | chilly | bridal |
| bite | rode | chili | bridle |

## WHAT'S A HOMOGRAPH?

Homographs are words that are spelled alike but have different meanings. How can this be? The English language is most flexible, and it is possible to make the same word work for us in a variety of ways.

Make a list of homographs on a chart paper. If there are four meanings, write the same word four times; three meanings, three times; two meanings, two times. The challenge is for students to find the multiple meanings of the same word. This is a good opportunity for them to work with one of their major resources, the dictionary. Perhaps the thesaurus will be of some help in their word explanations as well. When they find an explanation, they can show it to you along with the resource, and print or write it on the chart after one of the words.

The following list of homographs (and explanations) will help get the class started with this fascinating study. Students become word detectives as they search for meanings. This activity also helps students learn that the "context" in which a word is found is essential to its meaning. Therefore, they can work on sentences along with these words.

| | |
|---|---|
| arms: body parts | He had his arms full. |
| arms: weapons | Do they have the right to bear arms? |
| | |
| bat: club | It was Casey's turn at bat. |
| bat: animal | A bat was flying around inside. |
| | |
| clip: cut | Let's clip this out of the paper. |
| clip: fasten | Clip those papers together. |
| clip: hair fastener | Theresa wore a clip in her hair. |
| | |
| dock: cut off | The captain will dock your pay. |
| dock: wharf | The boat inched up to the dock. |
| | |
| fair: honest | The teacher is a fair person. |
| fair: bazaar | The cow won first prize at the fair. |
| fair: lovely | The fair maiden spoke softly. |
| | |
| tip: money | The waiter got a generous tip. |
| tip: the end | It was on the tip of my tongue. |

## USING HOMOGRAPHS

Working with homographs helps students to learn that (1) a word can have more than one meaning, and (2) the context in which a word is used is extremely important.

Write five homographs on the chalkboard and ten sentences. Have students figure out which words to use properly to fill in the blanks. They can make a list of numerals on the page from 1–10 and write the correct word on each line. Then correct these together and clear up any misunderstandings of the multiple meanings of words.

band      bank      left      pitcher      pen

1. "Strike up the _____," called out the conductor.

2. The _____ had three strikes on the batter.

3. Make sure all the animals are back in the _____.

4. At the corner, turn _____ onto Main Street.

5. All he had _____ was twenty-five cents.

6. The _____ closes at 3:00 P.M. today.

7. Some lemonade was poured from the blue _____.

8. "May I borrow your _____?" asked Mr. Marbury.

9. The _____ of the river was quite dry.

10. Was she wearing a wedding _____ on her finger?

The answers are: 1. band; 2. pitcher; 3. pen; 4. left; 5. left; 6. bank; 7. pitcher; 8. pen; 9. bank; 10. band.

## HOMOGRAPH SENTENCE STRIPS

Make sentence strips using the sentences written in the previous activity. Then students can scramble them and sort them so that the homographs are together. Have them read one sentence and then the other so that the double meaning of the word is understood. Be on the alert for homographs; there are many more.

# FOCUS ON LANGUAGE ARTS

## MORE READING OPPORTUNITIES

Some reading skills have been addressed in the previous section and, as we know, many more reading opportunities will present themselves this month as we work in the areas of Math, Social Studies, holiday celebrations, and Science/Health.

## NEWSPAPER CUTUPS

Select a short article from a student magazine or newspaper, and cut it up or mark it up so that when it is read aloud by the teacher, it is out of sequence. It doesn't make any sense. Students are then challenged to make sense of it and tell what information must come first, then second, and then what follows. This is a reading/listening exercise.

This is effective, also, if the article has been typed and cut up. Use the copy machine to make an overhead transparency of the scrambled information. Then read the story aloud and discuss the sequence. Mark on the transparency with numerals which comes first (1), second (2), and so on.

When students all agree, cut the transparency into those sections and rearrange them on the overhead projector. Re-read the article. Does it make sense now?

If you have a class that is off-task, using the projector when they are all attending to the same information may be helpful in getting and keeping them on track.

## CLOSE YOUR EYES AND VISUALIZE

Some students may need warm-up exercises for visualization if they have never tried it before. Ask them to close their eyes and "see" a pond with ducks swimming on it. Have them describe the ducks: What color are they? Where are they? How many are there? Suggest that they look around the pond and add any details that they "see."

Do this with a familiar setting, such as the playground. Have students close their eyes and "see" it and describe it. They can do this with the classroom, the gym, the library.

Once students get the idea of what you mean by "visualizing something in their head," read a short story aloud. Have them close their eyes, listen quietly, and make a mental picture of what is going on in the story as you read. Then talk about it. Give praise to students as they keep adding to the picture. Ask them specifically, "What did you see, Jason?" "What did you see, Kenyon?" "What was in your picture, Addy?"

## CLOSE YOUR EYES, VISUALIZE, AND DRAW

After quite a few exercises with this activity, have students listen to a fable or story and then draw the picture they saw in their mind. Share the pictures. Find the place in the story where the fox was mentioned, for example, or the clouds in the sky and read them aloud again. Have students who didn't draw them into their picture do so now.

Continue to call attention to the rich illustrations in the children's picture books that you are reading aloud. It is well worth the time. It is this ability to make mental pictures of the story, to "see" what is going on, that lays the foundation for the enjoyment of reading when one is reading books independently that do not have illustrations.

## SOME TRICKSTER TALES FOR BLACK HISTORY MONTH

Look for books about Anansi the spider in the library and read them aloud to students this month. Anansi is clever and devious, and sometimes he wins and sometimes he loses. Students enjoy hearing stories about this trickster character. Here are some to get you started: *Anansi and the Moss-Covered Rock* by Eric Kimmel, with illustrations by Janet Stevens; *Zomo the Rabbit: A Trickster Tale From West Africa,* retold and illustrated by Gerald McDermott; and *Anansi the Spider Man: Jamaican Folktales,* told by Philip M. Sherlock, with illustrations by Marcia Brown.

## AN ANANSI RECIPE FOR GOOD EATING

The Anansi tales originated in Africa, and have traveled from there to the Caribbean Islands and to the United States. Because of the settings, there are many animals in the tales such as the monkey, elephant, giraffe, lion, zebra, crocodile, and a variety of birds.

Let's wash our hands and work with the following materials to create an animal. You can use large and small gumdrops, large and small marshmallows, raisins, and soft candy. Licorice, cut into pieces, and straight pretzels can be poked into the soft pieces for arms, legs, beaks, eyes, toenails, and to hold the animal together. What a strange looking array of animals this makes! Gobble them up after story time.

## TALES OF PRESIDENTS

February is the month of presidents and there are good books to read about all of our presidents. Two favorite presidents for the month are George Washington and Abraham Lincoln, because both of them were born in February.

Be sure to check out *Lincoln: A Photobiography* by Russell Friedman. This book contains authentic photos of Lincoln and his time period. Also, the book *George Washington's Cows* by David Small is amusingly told in rhyme. Since George Washington ran a farm, in this book his household is run by animals and the cows have to be pampered or they won't give milk, the pigs are genteel and amiable with manners uncommonly fine, and the sheep are all scholars. This offers many opportunities for a study of rich language.

## COMPUTER IN THE CLASSROOM

Having access to a computer and printer in the classroom is an excellent way for students to compose stories. They can delete (erase) and not have a messy copy. It works wonders for students who have difficulty writing.

There are many commercial computer programs that enable students to write stories, draw pictures to accompany the stories, set up the page format in columns, and so on. The programs are plentiful and too numerous to mention here, but check with your school librarian, the school or district media coordinator, or the public school children's librarian.

The fonts in different styles of print have motivated some students to create stories because they look "real." The ability to control the size of the print is another plus.

## WORLD WIDE WEB

Some classrooms have the ability to access the World Wide Web (www) from their classroom, and they are fortunate. Some schools have this capability in their library setting. In these schools, it is possible to gain a great deal of information by accessing websites of interest, websites that coincide with the course of study, websites of children's authors, and so on. The amount of information and the way it is presented, with an abundance of visuals and options, offers an excellent learning opportunity for students. This medium has increased student interest in reading and writing.

With e-mail capability, the class can find out specific e-mail addresses, and make contact with knowledgeable people all around their community, state, or the country for a wide variety of information that can enrich classroom study.

Students should have a purpose for writing—that has been given your stamp of approval—if they are writing on school time. This is something that needs to be under the control of you or the media specialist. If students want to do additional searching and corresponding on their own time, then that is something parents will have to approve—*and it is something that needs to be handled with a great deal of care.* A good resource is: Cool Sites for Kids, http://www.ala.org/alsc/childrenlinks.html, with categories in reading, writing, and more. (See the Appendix for website information for children.)

## WRITING FOR INFORMATION

Another good way that students can gain information is by writing to:

- state capitals
- government offices
- a classroom in another city, state, country
- the White House (president and other officials)
- state governor

- state senators/representatives
- national art galleries
- national museums
- local library
- local historical society
- local community services
- local zoo
- health services
- economic information (stock reports)
- travel sites
- national news stations
- and many more!

# WORD ORIGINS AND SAYINGS*

By now we are familiar with the monthly routine of introducing sayings or words to students, in an effort to get them excited and interested in the history of words. Introduce the phrase or word at the beginning of the week. Write it on the chalkboard and encourage investigation. By mid-week, have students reveal what they have learned and then give them the meaning contained herein. For the rest of the week, they can enjoy using it in their story writing or journaling.

1. **upside down.** This saying came in at the time of Queen Elizabeth I of England. It means "in a state of disorder." It comes from the English version of "upsedoun," which has the same meaning as "topsy-turvy."

2. **a wild goose chase.** Back in the time of William Shakespeare, this was an actual game played on horse-back with two or more players. It began simply as a race to see which horseman could take the lead. The losers then followed the leader wherever he chose to take them. The reference to goose refers to the follow-ing of the leader, as geese do. It has come to mean "in vain pursuit of some cause or goal that is worthless."

3. **to keep the ball rolling.** No doubt this comes from eighteenth-century England. When playing rugby or bandy (hockey), it was necessary to keep the ball mov-ing, or keep the ball rolling. Today this phrase has come to take on a more social meaning, such as when a hostess tries "to keep the ball rolling" or keep the conversation moving at a dinner party or social gathering.

---

*Source: *A Hog on Ice and Other Curious Expressions,* Charles Earle Funk.

4. **all balled up.** Since the late 1800s, this term has come to mean confused or embarrassed, or all tangled up. Originally, it was a term used with horses. In the winter, when horses were driven over soft snow, the snow would become packed into rounded icy balls on the hoofs of the horses, or "balled up." Sometimes the horses would lose their footing. If they fell, a state of confusion and entanglement broke out on a horse team.

5. **to earn one's salt.** The word "salt" was originally linked to the word "salary." In the days of the Roman soldiers, they received part of their *salarium* (salary) to purchase salt (Latin, *sal*). Salt was not so readily available then as it is today, but people knew that this mineral was valuable for good health and vigor. A soldier "not worth his salt" was worthless. Some people were even paid with salt.

# WRITING SKILLS

## COMPUTER WRITING—EMOTICONS

*When communicating in person,* there is a sender and a receiver. It is possible to get the meaning from the person's facial expression and tone of voice. *When communicating on the telephone,* it is possible to get the meaning by listening carefully to the tone of the person's voice. *When communicating on the computer,* solely in print, we do not get facial expressions or voice cues. This has given rise to a new set of symbols, referred to as *emoticons,* that assist people in the communication process.

## REBUS STORIES WITH EMOTICONS

Here is a set of symbols* for students to use in their own handwritten stories or with computer communication. You can print these emoticons on a large piece of chart paper. Children enjoy these and will learn them quickly. Emoticons will add interest to the children's story writing, and make them more aware of the meaning they are conveying in print. This is a new form of rebus writing. Use this symbol "/" at the end of each thought or sentence. (See the Appendix.)

| | | | |
|---|---|---|---|
| :-) | happy | :-( | unhappy |
| :-D | laughing | ::-) | wears glasses |
| [:-) | wearing earphones | (-: | left-handed writer |
| :-0 | uh-oh | :-& | tongue tied |
| :-] | grinning | :-P | sticking tongue out |

Francine was :-) and was always :-D / That is, until she got ::-) and then she became :-& / Marvin was :-] at her and he was always :-P /

---

*Source of emoticons: *The Reading Teacher's Book of Lists,* 4th ed., by Edward Fry, Jacqueline Kress, and Dona Fountoukidis (Paramus, NJ: Prentice Hall, 2000).

## THE POST OFFICE

February is the month of valentines, notes, and flowers. All of these spell "communication." Work with students to set up a classroom post office. This can be done on a counter, or on a bulletin board, or on the floor. It depends upon what you will use for the mailbox container.

If you use a large manila envelope for each student, the bulletin board could be made into a post office with a red, white, and blue color scheme for the background. Make a pointed roof from

construction paper strips, and cut out letters for "U.S. Post Office" as the title for the board. Students can print or write their first and last names on their manila envelope, and decorate it using blue paper, white paper, and red felt-tip pens. The envelopes can be tacked to the bulletin board. The closer you get to Valentine's Day, the heavier they will be, so staples may be needed at that time.

If you obtain a large appliance box for the floor, the outside can be covered to resemble a post office box. Each student can be asked to bring in a shoe box and decorate it as a letter box (land, sea, or air). Remove one end of the box so that cards and notes can be slipped inside. A little tab that has the student's name on it will need to be visible on the box, and they should be in alphabetical order by last name.

## SET UP A VALENTINE WORK STATION

For the Writing Center or Art Center, the first half of the month can be devoted to valentine making, note writing, and thank-you notes to community service people. Be sure to have a list available of the names of every student in the class. (Some teachers also make photocopies of this list so that students can take them home and work on their addressing and valentines at home.)

Make valentines for family members, grandparents, and area nursing home residents. Students can write a short but sweet greeting. These can be collected in a little basket with a red ribbon tied onto it, and delivered to a local nursing facility by you or a parent volunteer.

## TRACING STENCILS (HAND/EYE COORDINATION)

Place stencils in the Writing Center. Students enjoy tracing around the edges and then coloring them in with a solid color or a design. They can also make their envelopes look attractive by using stencils. These shapes can also be made on colored paper and then cut out with scissors and pasted onto a folded piece of paper to make a valentine.

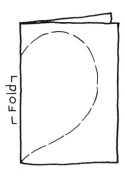

Remind students that when they fold a piece of paper to make a card, they can open it like a book or open it like a flap, from bottom to top. Paper can be folded vertically or horizontally.

Show students how to make a heart shape from a folded piece of paper. Fold paper in half. Place fingers (clutch) on the paper at the fold and cut the side that is open. *Do not cut on the fold.* Demonstrate this for students, then open and show the heart shape. They can make small ones, large ones, and even cut a little one out of a big one to make yet another design.

Stress the importance of writing a clear, friendly message.

## TINY VALENTINE HEARTS

To practice writing, bring in a large bag of candy hearts that have a message printed on one side, and give five to each student. They can write the message carefully that appears on each heart, and draw a heart around it, or cut one out to fit around it. These can then be cut out and used for "stickers" to glue onto their valentine envelopes.

## MAKE POSTAGE STAMPS

Students can design their own postage stamp for February. It can fit in with one of the themes in the holiday section. First sketch the design and determine colors. Then, on 8½- by 11-inch construction paper, draw the design or cut it out and paste it onto the paper. Cut semi-circles around the edges to give it a stamp look.

If you decide to have everyone make a valentine stamp, do this early in the month. Use only red and pink construction paper on a white background. Display the stamps all over the entrance door to the classroom. The heading, written by students, could read, "This class gets a stamp of approval for good citizens."

# SPEAKING SKILLS

## FORM SPEAKING CLUBS

Have the class count off "1, 2, 3, 4, 5" until everyone has said a number. All who said "1" are in that Speaking Club, all who said "2" are together in a Speaking Club, and so on. These five groups are going to be given five minutes to meet and decide on a name for their group. Then one group member will reach into a bag (which you have prepared in advance) for a slip of paper. On that paper will be the name of an animal. That is going to be the subject of the report for that group. How are they going to handle this so that everyone gets an opportunity to speak? It calls for team work, cooperation, and library work.

Students can write and read the report, speak the report using puppets, each draw a picture and tell something about the topic, or each speak a paragraph of the report they wrote. (To appeal to the kinesthetic learners, encourage students to move like the animals; encourage the use of masks, which is helpful for the shy child; encourage singing or making music, which may appeal to some students. It's their Speaking Club, so they should enjoy it as well as learn from their experience.)

## CIRCULAR STORY MAPS

Encourage students to make a circular story map on an overhead transparency of a picture book they have read. Then, using the overhead projector, the students retell the story to the class. This is an excellent, informal way for them to make a class presentation. They may want to use a blank sheet of paper to cover information that has not yet been talked about.

## CLAP, SNAP, SLAP

Have students sit on the floor in a circle. First, you demonstrate the hand movements necessary. Clap (*hands together*), snap (*snap thumb and second finger*), slap (*slap thighs*). Practice this very slowly about five times. (For some, just remembering this order may be a challenge, but eventually they will get it.)

After students get the rhythm moving, they're ready to say a word when they snap their fingers, but go slowly. For starters, try counting by five. Ready? Clap, snap (say "five" simultaneously), slap; clap, snap (say "ten" simultaneously), slap. (Stop when you get to one hundred.)

Do this again, but this time only one student at a time speaks the number on the snap. Go all around the circle. If you get to one hundred, the next person starts all over again with "five."

This speaking/movement activity can be done with different ideas. Students can call out their favorite color, the days of the week, their names, or something in the room. Using words from the word wall may be helpful also. This game helps to develop vocabulary, word categories, coordination of body and speech, and unity of the group. Students will ask to do this again.

## DON'T SAY "AIN'T"*

This activity coordinates verbal and motor performance, and is a challenge for some learners. Even advanced students sometimes have difficulty with coordination. With this activity, students can sit in a circle or stay in their seats. They will clap rhythmically to this old grammar rhyme. (Clap on the X below the word.)

> *Don't say "ain't"; your mother will faint!*
>    *x*         *x*        *x*        *x*
>
> *Your sister will cry, and so will I.*
>          *x*      *x*      *x*      *x*
>
> *Your brother will fall in a bucket of paint,*
>      *x*       *x*       *x*       *x*
>
> *Your father will howl if you say (hum the sound).*
>     *x*       *x*     *x*       *x*

This can be altered and made more complicated by having students:

- Snap on the first beat, clap on the second beat.
- Snap on the first beat, tap foot on the second beat.
- Snap with the other hand on the first beat, tap with the other foot on the second beat.
- Snap, clap, tap, slap.

---

*Source: *Teacher's Handbook of Children's Games* by Marian Jenks Wirth (Parker Publishing Company, 1976).

Students like this because the body movement, along with saying the words, becomes challenging. Encourage them to practice. (See Reproducible Activity Pages.)

Additional lines can be added, such as:

> *Your aunt will sneeze, the baby will cry,*
> *The parrot will blink his one good eye.*
> *Your water won't boil, your bacon won't fry,*
> *Your toaster won't toast, the clothes won't dry.*
> *Your bike won't move, your kite won't fly.*
> *Your cat won't learn how to multiply.*
> *Your bird will shriek, and grandma will sigh,*
> *And all because you said that little word, "_____." (humm)*

# LISTENING SKILLS

Listening is such an important skill that it would be safe to say if you're not listening, you're not learning.

## GIVING DIRECTIONS

Have an able student read a set of directions, slowly and carefully, and then have students follow the directions. They are not allowed to see the directions, but must listen carefully.

At first the directions can be simple, such as "It is now time to put everything in your desk."

A more complex direction would be, "Get out your ruler, and take out your Social Studies project folder."

A still more complex direction would be, "First, get out a piece of paper, then write your addition facts from 1 through 5 on it, check the clock and record the time on your paper, and put down your pencil."

Students need a lot of practice with this. Sometimes being the one to read the directions gives some students a better understanding of what it means to follow directions.

## CAN YOU REMEMBER FIVE WORDS? (ATTENTIVE LISTENING)

First, students must understand that this is a listening activity. Everything is off the desk so there are no distractions. Say five words aloud. Then have students repeat the five in unison. (This enables those who didn't get them to not be singled out.) Do this again and again.

Next, have students get out a pencil and a piece of paper. Wait for everyone to be ready and listening. Then tell students that you will say five words aloud and when you finish, they can write them on the piece of paper. (Let them know that invented spelling is okay.) How many did students get? Praise them for their effort. Try three words. Try four words. Try five again. Then try six. Now seven. Seven is usually the magic number for remembering a set of words. For students, however, they will need to practice this listening activity many times. They must give it their full attention.

Encourage student study buddies to work on this memory strengthening activity together and to make a game of it. Increasing memory span is helpful and carries over when students are studying for tests.

## USING MOVEMENT TO REMEMBER WORDS (KINESTHETIC)

Often when movement accompanies words, it helps students increase their memory and attention span. It adds another dimension to learning. Try this activity:

1. Have students form a fist. You say five words while students listen. Then you and students together say the five words. As students say the five words, have them open up their fist, first by the thumb, and then one finger at a time, in time to the words. Then have them close their fist and try to repeat the words. Can they remember better with this technique?

2. To enable students to get used to the practice of opening their fist and stretching their fingers while saying a word, try some easy words first. Say, "One, two, three, four, five." Then repeat the words as students open their hand, thumb first, then the pointer finger, working their way to the little finger at the end. (There is no talking.)

3. Then close hand into a fist. Say five *unrelated* words while students listen. Have them say the words in time to the opening of their fist. Close fist. Say the words. See if students can remember the unrelated words better this time.

## LISTENING TO RELATED AND UNRELATED WORDS (AURAL)

It is easier to remember words that are related as opposed to words that are unrelated. Try this activity with your students.

First say: snow, mittens, hat, coat, scarf. How many did they remember? Next say: ball, Friday, pencil, cap, door. How many did they remember? Were the words in the second set more difficult to recall? Some students will take to this challenge willingly, whereas others will find it quite difficult. But keep trying it throughout the month, and use it as a "game."

Challenge students to find a way to play it independently. Have them look at five items in the room and say them. Then write them down. Did it work? Good! Do it again. When it's no longer a challenge, add two more words at a time. (Any time you can work to strengthen memory, take advantage of it. It is a "spillover" skill that serves the student well in all areas of the curriculum—memorizing math facts, memorizing spelling words, memorizing information for Social Studies, Health, and Science.)

## WORD PRETZELS* (KINESTHETIC IMPROVISATION)

When students have a list of things to memorize, have them stand and strike a body pose as they say each word, like a quiet statue or a twisted pretzel. Suppose, for example, you want to review the writing of a letter. Print these words on the chalkboard: **Heading**, **Inside Address**, **Greeting**, **Body**, **Closing**, **Signature**. Demonstrate for the students how they might move their body. *No talking, as it breaks the concentration. This is a quiet activity.*

As students say "heading," have them strike a pose and think of the word; say "inside address" and instruct them to change into a different pose, and concentrate on the word as well as their body stance. Encourage students to bend, reach, stretch, twist, and turn as they say each word.

Give students room to move for this one, although they are to stay beside their seat. If feet are moved, make it only one at a time.

Now repeat the words for them, and see if they can remember their pose. If not, they strike a new one and concentrate on the word and the pose. Keep doing this about five times, as students contort like pretzels. Body movement and learning go together like horse and carriage, dog and bone, fingers and gloves. After a time, it will make a difference in increased memory span. Encourage them to do this privately at home. (The tempo can be increased and the rhythm can be altered.)

# FOCUS ON SPELLING

## THE BIG CHALLENGE

This month, challenge students to study from a list that you put together of spelling words from previous lists. A test will be given on 25 of these words. Have students study with a buddy for this one.

## ROLLING IN DOUGH

Use plasticene, Play-doh®, or play clay, and have students roll out long coils. From these coils, they can write their spelling words in cursive writing. Be sure to tell students that the term "rolling in dough" means that someone has lots of money. Check the January word origins for the term "baker's dozen." Could it be that those bakers were rolling in dough (making money) because they were making lightweight bread?

## CONSTRUCTION CHALLENGE

For this activity you will need small balls (tiny) of Play-doh® or play clay, and a lot of toothpicks. Use these materials to construct letters and spelling words in solid capital letters. Students can roll

---

*Source: *Teacher's Handbook of Children's Games* by Marian Jenks Wirth (Parker Publishing Company, 1976).

the clay into little balls so that a toothpick is inserted into one end, and another toothpick in the other end or side. The word "attic," for example, would look like this:

## MAKE A SPELLING HEADBAND

Students can study with a partner by looking at the words spelled out on each other's headband. Also, if the headbands are worn throughout the day on a particular day, students can practice spelling at any time just by looking at someone's headband.

## STAMP IT OUT

You will need a set of letter stamps and a stamp pad. Students can stamp out their spelling words for the week. (Perhaps parents would be willing to donate used stamp pads and letter stamps from games no longer used and worn out.)

## SPELLING SCRABBLE™

Put all of the little cubes from the game of Scrabble™ together in a bag. Shake it up. Reach in and take out ten letters. The challenge is: How close can a student come to constructing one of the spelling words of the week? How many letters are missing? Which ones? This is another way to create interest in spelling.

Also, playing the game of Scrabble™ is a way to improve spelling skills.

# FOCUS ON MATH

## MAKING WINTER SOUP

Br-r-r! It's a cold day and there's nothing more soothing than the smell of soup in the making. So let's make soup in a large crock pot today. We can gain many experiences in counting, timing, temperature, sizes, and so on.

In the crock pot, add:

- one can of chicken soup stock
- cut carrots
- cut celery pieces

- a can of tomatoes
- one onion (diced)
- salt, pepper, a pinch of basil

Fill the crock pot with water (how much?). Let it cook on highest temperature all morning. About halfway through the process, students can be helped to add 2 cups of barley. The lid is hot, so use an oven mitt.

## PROBLEM SOLVING WITH SOUP

After the soup is made, we can turn this into a Math lesson. Determine how it can be shared equally. How many students are there? How much soup is there?

Suppose there are 24 students in class. Put out 24 bowls or cups. Use ½ cup as the measuring tool, and put a half a cup of soup into each bowl. Does there appear to be enough soup? If so, can we put another half cup into each bowl or should we go to the quarter cup measure, or less? We're aiming for an equal amount of soup in each bowl. Enjoy the treat.

An excellent book to read aloud while enjoying the soup is a book about a potluck feast. It's entitled *Alphabet Soup, A Feast of Letters* by Scott Gustafson.

## MENTAL MATH

Ask students to work out problems "in their head" without pencil and paper. You can give them story problems for this type of exercise. Or they can be given a set of problems on the chalkboard. Here are some examples:

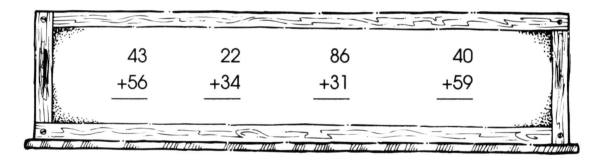

$$43 + 56 \qquad 22 + 34 \qquad 86 + 31 \qquad 40 + 59$$

Fill a basket with empty food containers, soap containers, etc., and put price tags on them. Tell students to shop for two items and add them up, or at least estimate the cost, "in their head."

This is an extremely helpful skill for shopping. People know how much money they have to spend, and when they pick up three items they can add it in their head or at least estimate the cost to see if they have enough money.

To make this little food basket activity more interesting, have students start off with a certain amount of money (draw a ticket from the bank bag) and see what they can buy for that amount of money. No paper and pencils for this. Do it all in the mind. Strengthen those addition skills.

## RULERS AND YARDSTICKS FOR MEASUREMENT

Hold up a yardstick and ask students how many times they think it would go across the room. Write it down. Check it by actually having students place the yardstick on the floor from one side of the room to the other. Then record that number. Check their estimates.

There are three feet in a yardstick. How many feet would that amount to? (Multiplication times three.) To show that there are actually three feet in a yard, lay three rulers on top of a yard-stick to convey the visual message.

Have students measure items with rulers and search for items that are seven inches in length, ten inches in length, four inches in length. Have them record the items on a list. (See Reproducible Activity Pages.)

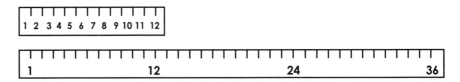

## GRAPHING HEIGHT

This can be a meaningful activity because it relates to the students, and there's an element of prob-lem solving here. Measure each student's height. Then make a graph so that one inch is equal to two inches (or three inches) on the actual graph, depending upon how big you want the graph to be. When constructing the graph from left to right, decide whether you want to work from tallest to shortest or shortest to tallest.

## FIGURE OUT THIS PATTERN

Link the idea of patterns to numbers. For example, if students were given this string of numbers, ask them how they would memorize it:

1 5 9 1 3 1 7 2 1

Many students would try to chunk the numbers either by 159 131 721 or by 15 91 31 721. Or some may look at the number of one's and fill in the numbers in between.

Here is another way to do it by *putting a pattern to work for you:* The above line of numbers is a "plus four" pattern. Look at it this way: 1+4=5, 5+4=9, 9+4=13, 13+4=17, 17+4=21. When you do this, students will look at this pattern in a different way.

**1** (+4 =) **5** (+4=) **9** (+4=) **13** (+4=) **17** (+4=) **21**

Find this pattern: 3 6 9 1 2 1 5 1 8 (plus 3 pattern)

Find this pattern: 1 8 1 5 2 2 2 9 3 6 (plus 7 pattern)

Find this pattern: 4 9 1 4 1 9 2 4 2 9 (plus 5 pattern)

Find this pattern: 1 0 1 5 2 0 2 5 3 0 (plus 5 pattern)

Have students make up their own patterns. Other students can look for the pattern. This is an excel-lent way to work with simple addition facts. Students enjoy this and some get hooked on patterns. You can also do this with subtraction patterns. (See Reproducible Activity Pages.)

## LOOK FOR PATTERNS IN THE ENVIRONMENT

Check the classroom floor, windows, door, etc., for patterns.

Go outdoors and look for patterns in nature on the trunks of trees, in leaves, and in plants. Students can do bark rubbings.

Animals have patterns, too. Check picture books and nature magazines for zebra stripes, tiger spots, jaguar rosettes, bird patterns of color, also patterns on reptiles. Encourage students to paint some of these at the easel, as though they are painting through the zoom lens of a camera.

An enjoyable picture book that entices students to look for patterns is *Hide and Snake* by Keith Baker. The patterned snake slithers through the book and is caught in among shoe laces, wrappings around presents, and napping with the cats. Another enjoyable book for searching is *Who Is the Beast* by Keith Baker. As the tiger prowls through the jungle, we catch glimpses of parts of the tiger on a page.

## LINE UP BY PATTERNS

AB could mean boy/girl. ABC could mean tall boy, short boy, girl. ABC could mean tall girl, tall boy, short girl. ABC could also mean other height patterns, so have students come up with their own.

Students can also sit in patterns.

## SETTING A TABLE

Set up a table right in the classroom, or on a desk, with a checkered tablecloth, stacks of paper plates, and packages of plastic utensils. Let students work on their multiplication tables this way. They can make aprons from kraft paper and wear waiter or waitress "hats."

Have a set of activity cards with instructions such as:

- Set up the table for 5.
- Set up the table for 6.
- Big party today. Set up for 7.

They can also draw pictures of the forks, knives, spoons, and plates needed for each place setting. (See Reproducible Activity Pages.)

## ANTONIA'S RISTORANTE

Set up an area in the room for a restaurant. Different students can be chosen each day to set up the table before lunch. An activity card can be placed on the table that reads: "Reserved for four." So, how many plates, forks, knives, spoons? Perhaps the knives, forks, spoons can be put into "sets" so that four sets can be taken from a container at one time (times four).

Have students diagram the solutions and show their work on paper for these directions on activity cards:

- "It's going to be busy today. Set up four tables for four."

- "Big party today! We need three tables for six in the back."

- "Busy day! We need three tables for five in front, and two tables for two in back."

Notice that when setting up the restaurant tables, we find that our multiplication process comes in very handy.

# FOCUS ON SOCIAL STUDIES

## FEBRUARY CITIZENSHIP FOCUS

Along with Black History Month, February is often referred to as the "Month of Presidents." The President of the United States is a strong leader. This month we will focus upon the qualities of *leadership*.

### WHAT DOES IT TAKE TO HAVE LEADERSHIP SKILLS?

First, engage students in a discussion of the question. What is it that they are looking for in a person *they* vote for as class president or class secretary? Listen to students voice their opinions and seek to clarify some of the opinions.

One thing you need to make sure of is that students end up with the awareness that a strong leader is one who displays all or most of the skills we have mentioned so far in our citizenship sections, plus more. That person has to have outstanding qualities, and yet show compassion and consideration for others. A good leader also needs to have self-confidence. Some people have so many qualities going for them that it is called "charisma." (This is a new vocabulary word to learn.)

### SET UP A CLASS GOVERNMENT

Do you have a class president, vice president, secretary? If not, this may be a good month to set up a class government system. What are the duties and responsibilities of each office? Have students work this out, and learn to compromise. This is a good lesson in the democratic process and concept that the majority rules. Also, the person holding the office must abide by the rules of the office and not step out of bounds, or he or she can be removed from the position. Once the positions have been defined, go to the next step of electing the officers.

You can put the titles of **President, Vice President**, and **Secretary** on the chalkboard. Then ask who would like to nominate someone for president (this can also be done using secret ballot). Use the same procedure for the other two offices. Make certain that those nominated are willing to accept the office. Determine how long these people are to serve—one month, two months? Use the chalkboard to write candidates' names and for tally marks. Use the secret ballot for final voting.

Make sure students learn the behavior that one expects in a democracy. Even if their candidate does not win, they will abide by the majority rule and support the candidates who won. This is a valuable lesson for young children to learn.

## CITIZEN OF THE MONTH

Select a Citizen of the Month—one boy and one girl. This is something that you can do, or students can vote on it (depending upon the group). Take a photo of the citizens and post them on a piece of chart paper. Do this monthly. Is it possible to have the names of these two students announced over the school intercom system? If not, perhaps the principal could be invited to stop by at a convenient time and congratulate them. Also, you can have a Citizen's Hall of Fame that goes back to the beginning of the year. Nominate and vote on classmates with outstanding qualities for an honored spot.

## LOOKING FOR OURSELVES IN STORIES

When students are doing their independent reading this month, have them be on the alert for the character traits we have worked with up to this point. When they find them (honesty, respect for authority, trustworthy, dependability, and promptness), students can record the situation in their journals. Also, a class chart can be made for this purpose. Then students can introduce the book character and the situation where the character displayed (or did not display) these characteristics.

An updated version of *Aesop's Fables* entitled *Yo, Aesop! Get a Load of These Fables,* by Paul Rosenthal, with illustrations by Marc Rosenthal, is written in a style that appeals to third-grade students. The illustrations will attract their attention for these tales with a moral.

## GOOD CITIZENSHIP BRACELETS

Assign a color to each trait we have discussed to date. When students are "caught in the act" of using one of these admirable traits this month, they can receive a colored ribbon to wear as a bracelet for the day.

# PATRIOTISM

## GEORGE WASHINGTON AND ABRAHAM LINCOLN

Our two patriots this month are George Washington and Abraham Lincoln. They are selected this month because both of these men were born in the month of February, are two of our most well-known presidents, and were both strong leaders. They lived at different times in our nation, but each made a contribution.

Make a timeline and record the dates during which each man held the office of the presidency. Determine how many years are between the two presidents. Also, determine what was going on in the country at the time these two men were elected president.

Students can select either president for their biographical sketch this month. Have them work in groups of three or with a partner. They can "go digging" in the library for information that would be necessary and interesting for their biography.

In the classroom, have a large stovepipe hat cut out of white construction paper (and outlined in black), so that students can record their information on the hat. Actually, Abraham Lincoln did carry papers *under* his hat, so you might want to make a flip-up hat. Record George Washington's facts on red circular pieces of paper and tack them to a large green tree with a brown trunk. Explain to students that the saying "I cannot tell a lie, I cut down the cherry tree" is a legend. The purpose of it is to instruct children in the concept of honesty.

# AREA OF FOCUS: OUR COUNTRY

## THE PEOPLE'S HOUSE

Locate Washington, D.C. on the map. Explain that this is the home of the president and first family, who live in the White House, otherwise known as "the people's house." Students should know:

- The name of the current president and first lady

- How many children (if any) live in the White House

- Family pets

- What state the first family is from

- The president is elected by the people and does not live forever in the White House (unlike a King or Queen)

Since the president and the first family are in the news daily, have students bring in news articles from newspapers and magazines to report on the first family. They should be able to identify the president by photos in the news.

## GETTING READY FOR A VISIT TO ANOTHER CITY

Students should be taught that when they are going to visit a different place, they should make a plan with parents regarding what to do if they get separated. If a student is in a public place or park, he or she can go to a uniformed guard or police officer. If in a mall, the child can go to a cashier behind a counter in one of the stores, who in turn will get in touch with security. If on the street, he or she can look for a police officer. Also, if a student is lost and frightened, he or she can dial 911 from a phone. Some parents do keep in touch with their children via cell phone when on trips. Mention this important topic in your newsletter to parents. Having students role-play this situation will help reduce the stress level if it should happen because they will be prepared.

## 1600 PENNSYLVANIA AVENUE, WASHINGTON, D.C.

This is the address of the White House. The five state rooms on the first floor are the best preserved part of the house. A tour of these rooms begins with the largest, the East Room, then the Green Room, the Blue Room, the Red Room, and through the State Dining Room. The famous Lincoln bedroom is on the second floor. The second and third floors are off limits to visitors because the President and his family live there.

The White House has a total of 132 rooms. It is run by the first lady and her staff. Entertaining guests has always been an important part of life at the White House. It is a record of joys and tragedies, weddings, births, and deaths.

A good resource book is *The White House* by Cass R. Sandak (New York: Franklin Watts, 1981). It gives many interesting facts about the families, the pets, and functions at the White House over the years.

## MONUMENTS AND MEMORIALS

The city of Washington, D.C. is a wonderland of memorials to people and/or events in our history. Some of the more well-known ones for students to be on the alert for as they search through library books on the subject are: Lincoln Memorial, Jefferson Memorial, Washington Monument, Vietnam Memorial Wall that reflects its surroundings and the people walking by, Korean Monument (a field of soldiers walking carefully through a field), Franklin D. Roosevelt Monument (in four sections), memorial to nurses who served in the war, as well as other important memorials too numerous to mention here. Students can make a class Big Book of Monuments and Memorials.

Some of the holiday events held in the nation's capital are listed in the Holiday section of this book.

## MAP AND GLOBE SKILLS

Show students where Washington, D.C. is located on a map and on a globe. Is it in the N, S, E, or W area of the country? Create an awareness of directions when moving about on the playground, or while on a field trip, or even inside the school building. Have several compasses in the classroom so that students can use them for this purpose.

Students should be working on location skills and memorization skills in relation to the United States. They need to locate the *shape* of the USA on a map and globe. They need to know that the eastern coastline of the USA runs alongside the Atlantic Ocean, and that the western coastline is adjacent to the Pacific Ocean. The USA is bordered by another country to the north (Canada) and another country to the south (Mexico). Some students may be interested in getting picture books from the library on these two countries.

- *Turning to the north:* Some students may have visited Canada with their family. We have had peaceful relations with this country, and are able to cross the border with relative ease. The "Peace Bridge" connects the two countries at Niagara Falls in New York State. Our cultures are similar in many ways, and the fact that both countries have a common language (English) makes communication relatively easy.

- *Turning to the south:* We have an influx of immigrants from Mexico, so the Spanish language is spoken increasingly in many areas of our country. Students need to be made aware of this. Mexico has a history of wonderful arts, crafts, and music. Students can be on the lookout for picture books at the library.

Use kraft paper to make a large map outline showing the three countries. One that is readily available as a guide is the weather map located in the newspaper *USA Today*. On this large map students can draw symbols and scenes for each country around the borders. Important information can be printed in the middle.

## WEBSITE: VISIT THE WHITE HOUSE ONLINE

The history of the White House and information on past presidents and their families can be found at this attractive website. Students can send messages to the president and vice president, and someone from the staff usually does send some form of response. The site is structured around major sections, so try the following: "The President & Vice President" and "White House for Kids." Log on at http://www.whitehouse.gov/WH/Welcome.html.

## OTHER WEBSITES FOR OUR VISIT TO THE NATION'S CAPITAL

**U.S. CAPITOL.** This is the official home page of the nation's Capitol building, and includes an account of the construction of the Capitol, its architectural features, the Capitol grounds, treasured works of art housed at the Capitol, the U.S. Botanical Garden, and current and recent projects at the Capitol. Log on at http://www.aoc.gov/.

**U.S. SENATE.** Special features of this site include a virtual tour of the U.S. Capitol, and Senate art and historical collections. Log on at http://www.senate.gov/.

**SMITHSONIAN: AMERICAN TREASURE HOUSE FOR LEARNING.** The online version of "America's attic" offers a wide variety of educational exhibits and resources. Rummage through the extensive collection of Americana. Log on at http://www.si.edu/newstart.htm.

**CONSTITUTION OF THE UNITED STATES.** A record of the U.S. Constitution, the Bill of Rights, and other amendments, as well as annotations of cases decided by the Supreme Court. Log on at http://www.access.gpo.gov/congress/senate/constitution/index.html.

# HOLIDAYS AND CELEBRATIONS

## GROUNDHOG'S DAY

February 2 is a day when attention is focused on the weather. In Punxatawney, Pennsylvania, Punxatawney Phil the Groundhog is one of the official weather predictors. If it's cloudy, the groundhog will not see his shadow when he crawls out of his burrow, and that means there will be an early spring. If it's a sunny day and Phil's shadow can be seen, he will be frightened and retreat for another six weeks of winter weather.

Make a Groundhog Badge and put the weather prediction on it.

## PRESIDENTS DAY

A day is set aside to honor all past presidents of the United States, but especially two who were born during this month—George Washington and Abraham Lincoln. Both men were considered strong leaders. Can we find them on our currency (money)? If so, what denominations? Make a list of the people on our coins and paper money. Were they all presidents?

Students can select a past president to research. They can also learn more about the current president of their country. All information can be shared with classmates.

## VALENTINE'S DAY

February 14 is a time for sending valentines and flowers as a gesture of love. Saint Valentine was a patron saint of lovers in Italy. At one time, valentines were sent by men and boys only but today everyone sends valentines as a gesture of love and friendship. At one time, young people drew a name from a vase, and that person was to be their true love.

Each student can put his or her name on a heart-shaped piece of paper. Collect these in a bag and shake the bag. Then each student can withdraw a "secret pal" for Valentine's Day. They need to do something nice for that person, and try to remain anonymous.

## MARDI GRAS

This celebration is held in New Orleans, Louisiana just
before the beginning of Lent. People eat, drink, and parade
in costumes during a carnival atmosphere—a street party.

The Trinidad Carnival (Caribbean) two days before
Lent, known as "Mas" (mask), is held with singing, dancing, and festivities. Carnival costumes are
sometimes outrageous, with headpieces as large as 6 feet high, representing biblical characters,
primitive-looking people, or present-day famous people. A Queen of the Carnival is chosen, and
there is a competition for the best band.

## BLACK HISTORY MONTH

The United States holds celebrations this month to honor those African-Americans who made contributions to this country. There are celebrations, art festivals, speeches, and parades.

Students can celebrate this month by reading African folktales and having a storytelling festival. How many different Anansi stories can be located? Students can check the newspaper for
events in their own area. Log on to www.surfnetkids.com/blackhistory.

## DENTAL HEALTH AWARENESS MONTH

This is the month to be on the alert for good dental health habits. Brush twice a day. Floss once per
day. Visit the dentist regularly, at least once or twice a year for a check-up. Also, in honor of this
special attention to teeth, parents can be reminded that students need to keep changing their toothbrush regularly for good hygiene.

# FOCUS ON SCIENCE

### HOW HIGH CAN YOU JUMP?

This month we will take a look at animals in nature and compare ourselves to some of them.
Students can measure how high they can jump from a standing position. Then, outdoors, they can
run and jump. Is the jump longer outdoors when motion and speed are involved?

We can measure and compare jumps that students make to jumps made by a variety of animals. For example, an impala, from the deer family, can spring 10 feet in the air and lurch forward
by 30 feet. How can students compare with that record?

### WHERE ARE OUR EYES LOCATED—FRONT OR SIDE?

People see out of two eyes located on their face. The eyes do have some peripheral vision. Students
can work with a partner for this experiment. One can stare straight ahead and the other can slowly
move an object around the person's head. Have a signal, such as finger up/finger down, when the
objects can be seen and when it fades from view.

Students should find that their field of vision ends where their arms are straight out on both sides
of their body.

Some animals in nature, such as a frog, have eyes on the sides of the head that protrude, or stick out. This enables them to see what is behind them without making a move. It serves as a built-in hunting device for catching food, and it helps protect the frog from danger, too. Students can go on an "eye hunt" through such nature magazines as *Ranger Rick* and *National Geographic World.*

## HAWK EYES

Stand at one end of the room and look at something across the room. Now, look through binoculars. This is how hawks, eagles, and many other birds of prey can see so well from far away. Often "Hawkeye" is a nickname for people who are quick to spot things. Students with this quality make good bird watchers!

## MY, WHAT BIG FLICKERING EARS YOU HAVE!

Can people flick their ears? Not really. But some animals can, and they also swivel their ears around to hear better, without moving their head. This enables animals like the fox or wolf to hear sounds in the night and to catch their food more easily.

Notice that rabbits have long ears that flick around to catch sounds. Animals with big ears have a built-in "air conditioner" since more heat escapes through ears faster than anywhere else on the body. Find photographs of animals with large ears (elephants) and small ears, and classify them. (See Reproducible Activity Pages.)

This month encourage students to wear hats or earmuffs, since they are losing heat through their ears and also their head when they go outdoors.

## ANIMALS USE SOUND TO COMMUNICATE

Animals communicate through sound. Sound carries a long way so animals do not have to see each other to communicate. The pitch and length of a warning cry can tell whether an approaching predator is a bird or an animal.

Many animals use song to communicate. There are howling monkeys, croaking frogs, chirping birds, howling dogs, meowing cats, roaring tigers, roaring seals, and singing humpback whales.

## PEOPLE USE SOUND TO COMMUNICATE

Boys and girls have the ability to create such sounds as speaking, humming, hissing, crying, calling, yodeling, and so on. Have students demonstrate and identify the versatile sounds they are able to create.

People also have devised other ways of communicating. By blowing air into a variety of instruments, and by pressing the right keys that represent notes and tones, people can "make music." No doubt this originated with early man blowing through the hollow bones of birds, such as vultures. Carving holes in the bones, and alternately covering the holes with fingers and releasing the air by removing the fingers, creates a flute. Stretching animal hide over an earthenware vessel and striking it with a stick may have been the forerunner of our modern-day array of drums.

## COMMUNICATION AND TECHNOLOGY

If there is a computer in your classroom, and the class has access to the World Wide Web (www), then students can readily and easily gain access to a world of information available to them. The web, as well as e-mail (electronic mail), has opened up the world of communication for all people. If you do not have access in your classroom, then perhaps there is a computer lab in the building so that students can gain information. If not, direct them to their local library for this experience.

Have students list other electronic devices that are used for communication, from the early phonographs to cellular phones. Even though they may not use "record players" today, students need to know that these were important in the developmental process. Construct a timeline to show how we evolved to the present state of communication. Where are we headed next? Students may come up with some good invention ideas.

## DO PEOPLE SLEEP MORE IN WINTER?

We're in the winter season in February. Students can keep a record for one week of how much sleep they get per night. What is the average? Make a graph of the sleep that the class is getting each night. What are some of the things in our environment that affect the amount of sleep students get? List them. (Often students get more sleep in winter because it gets dark earlier and they are indoors earlier.)

## DO ANIMALS SLEEP MORE IN WINTER?

Some animals *hibernate*. In that state, they may not awaken for a long time. Most hibernating mammals prepare for the long winter by eating and storing body fat. That fat is broken down into energy during the sleep. Hibernation is a protection against the deep, cold winter. There are deep sleepers and those who tend to wake up now and then, and then go back to sleep.

Have students locate books that give information about hibernation so that they can list the names and habits of the true deep sleepers, such as the jumping mouse, some bats, some bears, skunks, raccoons, frogs, turtles, and so on.

## GROUNDHOG'S DAY

It's a tradition. On February 2, people gather in Punxatawney, Pennsylvania to see if the groundhog, named Punxatawney Phil, sees his shadow. If Phil sees his shadow, supposedly he returns to his burrow to sleep through six more weeks of the winter season. If Phil doesn't see his shadow, then spring is just around the corner. The groundhog is also called a woodchuck or a marmot. (See Reproducible Activity Pages.)

# FEBRUARY ILLUSTRATOR STUDY: FLOYD COOPER

Our Coretta Scott King Award winner this month is Floyd Cooper. Mr. Cooper began his art career by illustrating greeting cards for Hallmark. He also worked as a commercial artist. Then he began to illustrate books for children, and eventually to write his own stories. This month we're going to be focusing upon his art work and the stories he has illustrated.

Mr. Cooper's technique is unusual. He begins with a canvas washed in oil paint, usually brown in color. Then he takes a "kneadable" gum eraser, rather than a paintbrush, and dabs it against the background, pulling off the paint. For example, rather than painting a face *on* the canvas, he is removing paint *from* the canvas that eventually reveals a face, or a person, or a tree. He is working from positive to negative space. It is fascinating to watch!

Floyd Cooper began painting on wood scraps thrown aside by his father, who was a builder. Once, as a youngster, he decorated the side of his family's house with a big duck. He drew all through elementary and high school, and credits his second-grade teacher for his interest in art. When she hung up his picture of a sunflower, it made him feel like he was an artist.

In 1999, he received the Coretta Scott King Award for *I Have Heard of a Land* by Joyce Carol Thomas. This month we salute the talent of an artist and a gentleman, Floyd Cooper!

# BOOKS AND SUGGESTED ACTIVITIES

## *GRANDPA'S FACE* BY ELOISE GREENFIELD

Tamika loves her Grandpa and the stories he tells. She loves his gentle manner and the way he can change his face from funny to sad to worried, without saying a word. She also enjoys their "talk walks" where they talk about things. Grandpa likes to act in summer theatre, and one day Tamika unexpectedly sees him practicing his lines before a mirror and trying out a mean face. This frightens her and she's not herself. Finally, Grandpa tells her it's time for a "talk walk."

## ACTIVITIES TO ACCOMPANY *GRANDPA'S FACE*

1. Not many books deal expressly with Grandpa, so take time out for a class discussion of Grandpa. What's he like? What does he do? How many do the children have? What's their favorite thing about Grandpa, and can they describe his face?

2. *Taking a "talk walk."* This is a good discussion topic. Do young children have an older person in whom they can confide? Do they have someone who they can talk to about their fears and concerns? Ask students who they wish they could take a "Talk Walk" with in their family. Then perhaps they could explain what it is to someone at home and actually take one.

3. *The role of the illustrator.* When the illustrator is given the text, he or she receives "words only" and must paint the pictures to accompany the text. In this book, the challenge was to draw the many faces of this loving Grandpa. Find the faces and study them carefully. Encourage students to trace over the lines with their finger. Then have them draw a Grandpa face.

4. Ask students to draw something that is mentioned in the text but not shown in visual form.

## *LAURA CHARLOTTE* BY KATHRYN O. GALBRAITH

This is a touching story about a little girl who is not sleepy and tells her mother she wants a bedtime story—but, not just any bedtime story. She wants to hear the one her mother has told many times before. It's the story of her mother as a little girl and Charlotte, the hand-sewn elephant, who was given to her as a birthday present from her Grandmother Laura.

## ACTIVITIES TO ACCOMPANY *LAURA CHARLOTTE*

1. First, read the story without showing any of the drawings. Point out that this is how Mr. Cooper, the illustrator, first read the story. The drawings didn't exist. Then he had to make the drawings for the story. Ask students to identify certain items, people, scenes that they think need to be illustrated for this story. Then go through the book, read it again, and show the illustrations. If a picture is not there for something the children wanted to see, they can draw one of their own and share it.

2. *Time for drawing.* Have students draw themselves with their favorite stuffed animal. Does it have a special story? Who gave it to them?

3. *What's in a name?* Laura Charlotte was named for her grandmother and for her mother's favorite girl's name. Ask students how they got their name. Who named them? Who was there to welcome them into the world? (Include a note in the newsletter that goes home to parents so that they can expect to be asked these questions in the spirit of sharing "name stories.")

## *MIZ BERLIN WALKS* BY JANE YOLEN

This is an intergenerational story of a friendship that develops between a little African-American girl and an older, white-haired woman who walks by her house each day. Soon the girl falls into step behind the woman and hears the most wonderful, and sometimes magical, stories. Because the girl is only allowed to go to the end of the block, the story is often picked up the next day without missing a beat. This is written by the award-winning author of *Owl Moon*.

## ACTIVITIES TO ACCOMPANY *MIZ BERLIN WALKS*

1. Have students put themselves in the role of an illustrator and make their version of a drawing of some of the scenes that are being described. Share these with classmates.

2. Again, remind students that Mr. Cooper, the illustrator, received the text (words) and had to put them to music (pictures). When two people create a song (one writing the words and one writing the music), can this be compared to two people collaborating on a book (one writing the words and one painting the pictures)? This would be a good discussion question.

3. *Loss of a friend.* In this book, Miz Berlin falls and is bedridden and eventually passes away, so the little girl loses her friend. But the ending is upbeat, for the woman is alive and "walks" in her memory. Sometimes students who have had a family loss feel the need to express how they feel about this. It's a sensitive subject.

4. "Well, child, I recall once upon a time an old woman lived on our street, oldest woman I'd ever seen . . ." These are the last words in the book and invite the reader to make up a story that Miz Berlin might have told. Classroom storytellers might want to tell one while walking around the room.

## *MANDELA, FROM THE LIFE OF THE SOUTH AFRICAN STATESMAN* BY FLOYD COOPER

This book is written and illustrated by Floyd Cooper. It is the story of Nelson Mandela, from his boyhood days in the South African countryside to his time as a leader of the African National Congress, and through his twenty-seven years in prison and eventual release to become the first black president in South Africa's history. Mandela's father was Chief of the village. Because he stood firm for his beliefs, he lost his title and land and had to move his family to another village. This is a story of hardship and triumph.

## ACTIVITIES TO ACCOMPANY *MANDELA, FROM THE LIFE OF THE SOUTH AFRICAN STATESMAN*

1. Before reading the book, locate the continent of Africa on a map, or preferably on a globe. Note that it is a huge body of land. Explain to students that there are many different countries within this vast continent. These countries contain different tribal villages, with their own language and set of customs.

2. *Brave men.* Nelson Mandela's father stood up for what he believed and lost his title and land. Nelson Mandela stood up for what he believed and spent twenty-seven years in prison. Talk

to students about "ideals" and "dreams" that some people have at a young age to enable them to endure hardship rather than give up or give in. Do they have that kind of grit? Discuss this.

3. *Making the world a better place.* What can students do at this level to help make the world a better place in the future? Talk about the traits of good citizenship that we have been stressing throughout the book in the Social Studies area each month.

4. *Note the illustrations in this book.* This is one of the first books that Mr. Cooper has both written and illustrated. Does it make it easier to illustrate your own work? Compare the illustrations in this book to some of his other work. What do you notice?

5. *Setting goals.* Do students have something in mind for their future? The future begins today. Have students read other works of famous people and begin to note what they did as young people—their study habits, their hobbies, their friends. How can we plant the seeds today for the person we want to be tomorrow? Discuss these ideas to see what students are thinking, and to help direct and inspire them to be all they can be.

6. *Keep the dream alive.* Encourage students to keep a diary of their dreams and ambitions for the future. Guide them to books, and if they choose to share their diary, offer written encouragement and even suggestions on sticky notes.

## BROWN HONEY IN BROOMWHEAT TEA; GINGERBREAD DAYS; I HAVE HEARD OF A LAND BY JOYCE CAROL THOMAS

These three books show the browns, golden tones, and wheat tones of Cooper's first works. In each of these works the theme of nurturing through familiar songs, rhymes, and family stories melds with Cooper's style of letting the imagination of the viewer fill in the details.

## ACTIVITIES TO ACCOMPANY THESE THREE BOOKS

1. Paint with only three colors at the easel: brown, tan, and the color of honey (or use three shades of construction paper that match this description). Then, after one of the books is read aloud, students can make a picture using just these three tones.

2. Serve tea with honey and honey graham crackers and listen to a story that Floyd Cooper has illustrated.

3. Have each student become an author and write a poem and put it in a box. Then each student can become an artist and withdraw that poem from the collection, and illustrate it. If the artist would like to meet with the author to ask what images that person had in mind, it might help the illustrator with this assignment.

**Note:** Other books written by Floyd Cooper include *Coming Home: From the Life of Langston Hughes,* a poet. Also, the traditional African-American folk song "Cumbayah" has been made into a picture book and illustrated by Mr. Cooper. He traced the origins of the popular song to a hymn in the Gullah dialect of the Sea Islands of Georgia.

Mr. Cooper is making a fine contribution to excellent children's literature for children of all cultures.

# REPRODUCIBLE ACTIVITY PAGES
## FOR FEBRUARY

## READING/LANGUAGE ARTS

The KWL Cake

Ask and Tell Sentences

Don't Say Ain't

Homophone Fun

Story House Web

## MATH

Working With Rulers

Carlos Sets the Table

Putting a Pattern to Work

## SOCIAL STUDIES

Coretta Scott King Awards

Meet Benjamin Franklin

## SCIENCE

My! What Interesting Ears You Have!

Science Bookmarks

## AUTHOR STUDY

The Floyd Cooper Design Team

# The KWL Cake

When you are beginning to study a new topic, you can use a layered cake approach. Work from the bottom up.

1. K—List what you KNOW about the topic (bottom layer).
2. W—List what you WANT TO KNOW (middle layer).
3. L—List what you actually LEARNED (top layer).

**What I LEARNED:**

**What I WANT TO KNOW:**

**What I KNOW:**

Name _____ Date _____

# Ask and Tell Sentences

Zippy hit a speed bump and all the punctuation marks fell off the end of the sentences. Can you please help him put them back on? Thank you!

1. The state of Maine is along the east coast

2. Is it time for Science now

3. When do we go to lunch

4. I read that former President Carter was a good listener

5. Benjamin Franklin was a man of many good ideas

6. The inside of the seashell is pink

7. Who is your favorite author

8. Who is your favorite illustrator

9. I'm going to wear a hat and mittens

10. Will we ride the bus on the field trip

11. Nick and Tony live on the same street

12. Do you have a pet dog or a pet cat

13. What do you want on your hamburger

14. Do you know all of your times tables

15. Carrots are a good source of vitamin A

Turn over the page. Change all of the "turtle" (tell) sentences to "alligator" (ask) sentences. Write carefully.

# Don't Say Ain't

This is a chant that requires talking and movement. You can clap on the word with the X below it. Snap your fingers on the word with the O below it. Ready?  Go!

Don't say "ain't"; your mother will faint!
X    O    X    O    X    O    X

Your sister will cry, and so will I.
O    X    O  X    O  X    O X

Your brother will fall in a bucket of paint,
O    X    O  X  O    X    O    X

Your father will howl if you say _____!
O    X    O    X  O X    O    (humm, rather than say the word)

Now, for this verse, clap on the X and slap your thigh on the O.

Your aunt will sneeze, the baby will cry,
O    X    O    X    O    X    O    X

The parrot will blink his one good eye.
O    X    O  X    O  X    O    X

Your water won't boil, your bacon won't fry
O    X    O    X    O    X    O    X

And all because you said that little word (whisper it _____)
O  X    O  X    O    X    O    X    O

I like to snap, clap, tap, slap.

©2002 by The Center for Applied Research in Education

# Homophone Fun

Use each rebus word in a sentence **OR** write a story below, using the 10 rebus symbols.

_____

_____

_____

_____

_____

_____

_____

_____

_____

# Story House Web

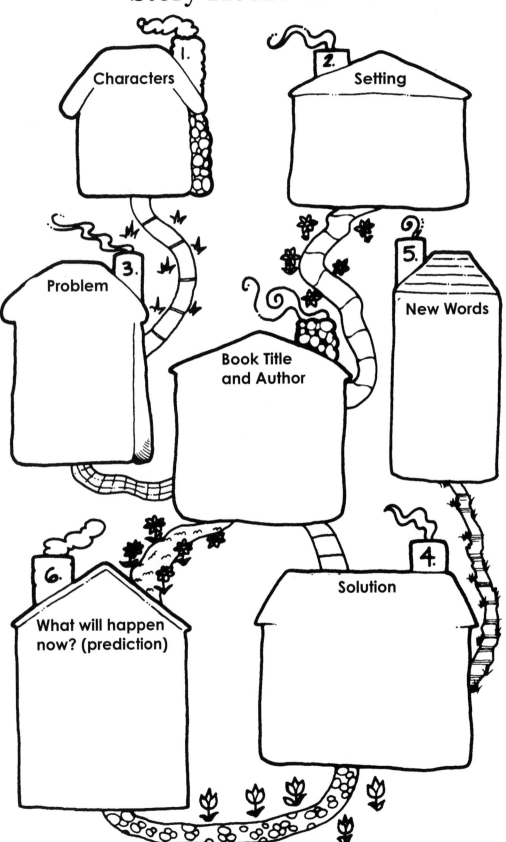

Characters 1.

Setting 2.

Problem 3.

New Words 5.

Book Title and Author

What will happen now? (prediction) 6.

Solution 4.

**Name** _____   **Date** _____

# Working with Rulers

1. **Find an item in the room that is 8 inches in length. Draw it here.**

2. **Find an item in the room that is 5 inches in length. Draw it here.**

3. **Find a 3-inch item. Draw it here.**

4. **Find a 12-inch item. Draw it here.**

5. **Find a 8-1/2-inch item. Draw it here.**

6. **Find a 2-inch item. Draw it here.**

Name _____     Date _____

# Carlos Sets the Table

This bird has a new job setting tables. He says he's done. But is he?
Can you help set the table so he can learn from you? Thanks!

**This is how it should look.**

©2002 by The Center for Applied Research in Education

Color Carlos. If he has four place settings to set up, what instructions
would you give him? On the back, set up a table for six.

# Putting a Pattern to Work

Look at this row of numerals. Can you remember it?

1  5  9  1  3  1  7  2  1

Now look at the pattern. It's called a "+4" pattern. Now it's easier to remember.

1 (+4=) 5 (5+4=) 9 (9+4=) 13 (13+4=) 17 (17+4=) 21

There are other patterns below. Find them and show the math.

| 6 | 1 | 0 | 1 | 4 | 1 | 8 | 2 | 2 |
|---|---|---|---|---|---|---|---|---|

**What's the pattern?**

+_____

| 7 | 1 | 2 | 1 | 7 | 2 | 2 | 2 | 7 |
|---|---|---|---|---|---|---|---|---|

**What's the pattern?**

+_____

| 1 | 7 | 1 | 3 | 1 | 9 | 2 | 5 | 3 | 1 |
|---|---|---|---|---|---|---|---|---|---|

**What's the pattern?**

+_____

Make up your own pattern on the back.

What's your favorite pattern?

+5

# Coretta Scott King Awards

The Coretta Scott King Awards are given yearly to African-American artists and writers of children's books. Go on a library hunt. Find a book and read it. Report on it to the class.

**MY WINNER IS:** _____

**Title**

**AUTHOR/ILLUSTRATOR:** _____

**SETTING:**

**MAIN IDEA:**

**TYPE OF ART:**

**WHY DO YOU THINK THIS BOOK IS OUTSTANDING?**

**Some award winners to look for:**

Jerry Pinkney
Andrea Pinkney
Brian Pinkney

Floyd Cooper
Patricia McKissack
Virginia Hamilton

# Meet Benjamin Franklin

Benjamin Franklin was the tenth son in his family. He was also the youngest. His father was a soapmaker. One son drowned in a tub of his father's soap suds.

Ben, as he was called, was a smart boy. He liked to read and write and took on the pen name of "Silence Dogood" as he grew older. One of his older brothers was a printer and had his own newspaper. Ben worked for him as a young lad, but the brother would not print his articles. That's why he took on a pen name.

Ben made up a list of "Good Behavior Rules" and checked them weekly. He also formed a "Leather Apron Club" that met every Friday.  Men who worked in the shops wore leather aprons to work, not fancy suits and a tie. But Ben found that tradesmen liked to read just as he did, and so the Leather Apron Club met to discuss books they had read.

Ben was an inventor, and is famous for his experiments with kites. He also invented the Franklin stove, and suggested ways to light the streets at night, and to dispose of garbage. He liked "sayings" such as "a penny saved is a penny earned" and published them in a book called *Poor Richard's Almanack*.

**How many questions can you answer? Re-read if necessary.**

1.  What did Ben's father do for a living?

2.  What was the name of the club Ben formed?

3.  What was the purpose of this club?

4.  What was Ben's pen name?

5.  Why did he take on a pen name?

6.  Can you name two of his inventions?

7.  What was the title of the book that he wrote?

*Read *What's the Big Idea, Ben Franklin?* by Jean Fritz.

# My! What Interesting Ears You Have!

Find animal photos in magazines and examine their ears. Some are large, some are small. Large ears are the "air conditioner" and allow air to escape to cool the animal.

    Select four animals—two with large ears, two with small ears. Draw them below. Make the ears from construction paper and let them "fly off the page."

| _____with small ears. | _____with large ears. |
|---|---|
| _____with small ears. | _____with large ears. |

# Science Bookmarks

Here are three bookmarks showing a prairie dog, a squirrel, and a beaver. Color each bookmark and write your name at the top of each one. Then cut each one out and write three facts about the particular rodent on the back of the bookmark. Use these bookmarks in your books as you read stories about these and other rodents.

# The Floyd Cooper Design Team

Before becoming a children's book illustrator, Floyd Cooper designed greeting cards. Today you're invited to become a member of the company. Create two greeting cards. Make (1) a get-well greeting, and (2) another of your choice. Share the cards with classmates.

# MARCH

# MARCH BOOKS

**Aardema, Verna.** *Pedro and the Padre.* **Pictures by Friso Henstra (New York: Dial, 1991).** In this tale, Pedro is a picaro (PEE car o), a mischievous person. He will not work, so his father sends him out into the world. His laziness is soon found out, and in the end he changes his ways.

**dePaola, Tomie.** *Fin M'Coul: The Giant of Knockmany Hill* **(New York: Holiday House, 1981).** The retelling of an Irish folktale is about Cucullin, the strongest giant in the land, and Fin M'Coul, another popular Irish giant. In this version, M'Coul's wife proves to be the heroine. Cleverness and bravery win out over brawn.

**Gerberg, Mort.** *Geographunny: A Book of Global Riddles* **(New York: Clarion, 1991).** In this riddle book, the answers all relate to geography. There are maps and hints in the pictures to help with solutions. An answer page is at the back of this funny book.

**Gibbons, Gail.** *Dinosaurs* **(New York: Holiday House, 1987).** A good introduction to dinosaurs and paleontologists. We see a wide variety of the beasts, with information about each one and a pronunciation guide. A section on dinosaur footprints is informative. (This author has a wide variety of books on many topics appropriate for this grade level.)

**Keller, Holly.** *Island Baby* **(New York: Greenwillow, 1992).** A young boy named Simon helps nurse a baby flamingo back to health, and in the process learns a lesson in independence.

**Morris, Ting and Neil Morris.** *Sticky Fingers: Dinosaurs.* **Illustrated by Ruth Levy and Joanne Cowne (New York: Franklin Watts, 1993).** Step-by-step instructions for dinosaur crafts. Make a tyrannosaurus hobby horse, catch a diplodocus, or make a pop-up pliosaurus.

**Nozaki, Akihiro.** *Anno's Hat Tricks.* **Pictures by Mitsumasa Anno (New York: Philomel, 1985).** The reader is introduced to binary logic, which is the basis of mathematical problem solving. The pictures are a series of puzzles that cause the reader to think critically. A challenging book. Students can work out the problems with concrete objects.

**Prelutsky, Jack.** *Tyrannosaurus Was a Beast.* **Illustrations by Arnold Lobel (New York: Greenwillow, 1988).** Meet fourteen different dinosaurs in rhyme. For example, "Allosaurus liked to bite, its teeth were sharp as sabers, it frequently with great delight, made mincemeat of its neighbors."

**Schlein, Miriam.** *The Puzzle of the Dinosaur-Bird. The Story of Archaeopteryx.* **Pictures by Mark Hallett (New York: Dial, 1996).** Archaeopteryx has puzzled scientists for many years. With a long tail, claws, and teeth, this little skeleton looked like a dinosaur with one exception—feathers!

**(CHAPTER BOOK) Dalgliesh, Alice.** *The Courage of Sarah Noble* **(New York: Simon & Schuster Children's Books, 1991).** When the west was settled, there were many trails that people traveled by foot and horse backpack. It's difficult to imagine the thousands of men, women, and children who followed these rough trails. This is an excellent book that informs the reader of the character development that Sarah experienced.

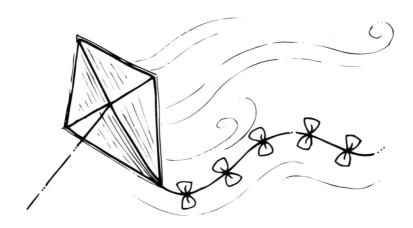

# MARCH

There's no doubt about it: March is a magical month. This is the month when the grass begins to turn green, the trees begin to bud, and bulbs planted deep in the earth begin to poke their noses through the ground.

There's plenty going on inside, too! The class has been together for over half a year now. Think of it! Half a year! We've grown, too. This month, take some time to look back to the autumn, and see how far we've come . . . in all subjects, in all ways. The achievements make us feel good and that's what contributes to the self-esteem of students—being able to gain mastery over subject matter and over their own behavior. But, hang on! The March winds are swirling up some good activities! It's the month for leprechauns and fairies, so we never know what's going to happen.

# FOCUS ON READING

## READ ACROSS AMERICA WITH DR. SEUSS

In early March, teachers, parents, children, and others join in this yearly celebration which honors the birthday of children's author Dr. Seuss. This event is sponsored by the National Education Association (NEA). Some ideas the NEA suggest are:

- Enlist community leaders to come to school to read.
- Turn off TV—"Pull the Plug and Read."
- Green eggs and ham for breakfast (use blue flood coloring).
- Carry a favorite book around all day. At a designated signal (bell ringing), there will be a DEAR drill (Drop Everything And Read).
- Give a certificate of participation to students.

- Make tall hats to wear in the *Cat in the Hat* style and color.
- Other ideas are welcome.

See www.nea.org/readacross or www.drseuss.

## SYLLABLE TAPPING

A syllable is often described as a unit of pronunciation, or a part of a word (or even a short word) with one, sustained, uninterrupted sound. Teaching students to listen for syllables is like teaching them to listen to the beat of the drums. You can have a stick or ruler available when teaching about syllables and tap out the sounds. Students can tap their two pointer fingers together.

It's easy for students to recognize a word with one syllable and two syllables. You almost have to teach these concepts together so that students can hear or feel the difference between one tap and two taps.

Tap first a "one-tap" and then a "two-tap" word, so students get the idea. Remember: One tap is equal to one syllable. Pointer fingers ready. Tap where the "X" is:

cat, sleeping                         dog, jumping

  X    X   X                            X    X   X

bird, singing                         mouse, running

  X    X   X                            X        X   X

Now try a sentence of one-syllable words with one tap per word, so that students understand this and can do it. Go slowly, and enunciate distinctly:

  I    can    see    the    dog    jump.

  x      x      x      x      x      x

Change the sentence as follows and have students pick out the word with two syllables:

  I    can    see    the    poodle    jump.

  x      x      x      x      x  x      x

*Poodle* has two taps, or two syllables. Continue to change the format of the sentence so that students can tap out the syllables and distinguish between the one- and two-syllable words.

  I    am    seeing    the    poodle    jump.
  I    am    watching    the    poodle    jumping.

## HOW MANY SYLLABLES?

Once students get the hang of syllables, they like to try to figure out how many are in longer words. This is where the dictionary will prove helpful as a resource. Try this. Use a word list. Say a word, one at a time, and have students tap the syllables. Do they all agree on the number of syllables? If so, is it correct? Someone will have to be the one responsible for going to the class dictionary to check this one out.

Scramble the words so that not all of the syllables are the same. Here are some you can use:

| | | | |
|---|---|---|---|
| goat (1) | plentiful (3) | cranky (2) | poison (2) |
| evergreen (3) | maple (2) | oak (1) | birch (1) |
| consonant (3) | motorcycle (4) | vowel (2) | syllable (3) |
| miraculous (4) | hurricane (3) | hullabaloo (4) | dime (1) |

Then try these tongue twisters for some fancy syllable taps:

antidestablishmentarianism (12)

supercalifragilisticexpialidocious (14)

## WORKING WITH PLURALS

"Plural" means more than one. Make sure students know the term. Usually, the plural form of most nouns is made by adding the letter *s* to the end of the word. Here are some examples:

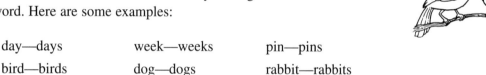

| | | |
|---|---|---|
| day—days | week—weeks | pin—pins |
| bird—birds | dog—dogs | rabbit—rabbits |

If the word already ends with an *s* (whether one or two), then you will need to add the letters *es*:

| | | |
|---|---|---|
| bus—busses | plus—plusses | fuss—fusses |
| class—classes | pass—passes | kiss—kisses |

"Change *y* to *i* and add *es*" is an old vowel rule that works most of the time. Here are some examples. Have students look for more:

| | |
|---|---|
| carry—carries | city—cities |
| vary—varies | family—families |

If the word ends with the letters *sh* or *ch,* you can make it plural by adding the letters *es*:

| | |
|---|---|
| shush—shushes | church—churches |
| splash—splashes | crutch—crutches |
| dish—dishes | patch—patches |
| fish—fishes (different species) | latch—latches |

Knowing these rules helps students with spelling, writing, and decoding new words. Also, since there are exceptions to the rules, it is always an eye-opener when students find one. They enjoy being word detectives. So, have a special place on the word wall or on a different chart for "exceptions to the rule."

Isn't it better to have a rule that can help you more than 50% of the time, than having no rule at all? *When you have a rule and it doesn't work, at least you know that much information, and it's a signal to try something else. Don't overlook vowel rules.*

## TIME FOR A CHECK-UP

Recheck district, state, and national standards for reading proficiency this month and every month. Work on these skills over and over again so students will become good readers.

## VISUAL LITERACY

This term refers to the use of graphic aids, such as Venn diagrams, webs, charts, illustrations, story maps, KWL charts, and the types of activities in which we have been engaged all year long. Keep doing this to enhance visual literacy and learning.

Read a story to students and have them select the way in which they will represent and retell the story using one of the forms in the paragraph above. It is often helpful to work with partners for this type of project in the beginning. Later, make sure students can do it independently using all of the above formats.

## REVIEW PARTS OF A BOOK

See November's Author Section for the book *The Stinky Cheese Man and Other Fairly Stupid Tales* by Jon Scieszka and Lane Smith. You can do a complete review of the parts of a book with the Little Red Hen who is totally confused.

## WORDS THAT CAN SCARE UP SOME FEELINGS

These words can't really scare people, but they do describe people's fear. A fear is called a *phobia* (FO bee ya). Since we're interested in word origins throughout the month, the root of this word is from the Greek *phobos*, or *fear.*

Write these words on the chalkboard and have students copy them. Then have them look up each word in the dictionary and write a short description next to the word. At a designated time, have students get out this list so that the word can be pronounced and the meaning explained.

Students can be motivated to use these words in their story writing and storytelling, and it will enrich their vocabulary as well as liven up the stories. For example, supposing a prince with arachnophobia (fear of spiders) meets a princess with brontophobia (fear of thunder). Could they help each other? Would a bus driver who woke up with amaxophobia (fear of driving and vehicles) be able to go to work today?

Sometimes when students write about phobias, and know that other people have them too, it helps to lessen their own and offers a great sense of relief. Here are some known phobia words* to use for your vocabulary list, and to promote realistic or fanciful writing:

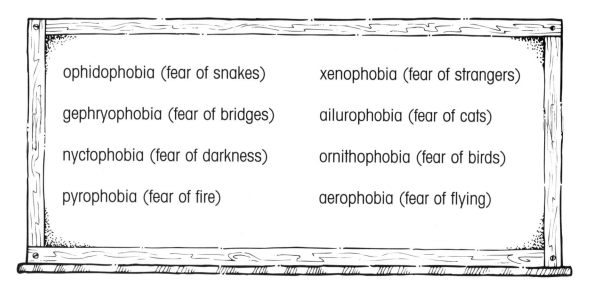

ophidophobia (fear of snakes)     xenophobia (fear of strangers)

gephryophobia (fear of bridges)     ailurophobia (fear of cats)

nyctophobia (fear of darkness)     ornithophobia (fear of birds)

pyrophobia (fear of fire)     aerophobia (fear of flying)

## ONCE UPON A TIME (PHOBIA STORIES/PROBLEM SOLVING)

Have "story starters" for students in the fairy tale genre. They must read the sentence starter (printed on a 3- by 5-inch card), determine the phobias, then think about how they can solve this problem. The story must have a beginning, middle, and satisfying ending.

Once upon a time . . .
    . . . there was a giant who came upon a wounded man in the forest. "Help!" cried out the man. "I've been shot in the leg by a hunter." Now even though the giant was gentle and kind, and also big enough to carry the man in one hand, he had hemophobia (*fear of blood*) . . .

Once upon a time . . .
    . . . the queen invited a handsome prince to lunch at the castle to meet her daughter, the most beautiful princess in the land. She served her famous peanut butter and jelly sandwiches, but what no one knew was that the prince suffered from arachibutyrophobia (*fear of peanut butter sticking to the roof of your mouth*) . . .

*Source: Fry, Edward, et. al., *The Reading Teacher's Book of Lists*, 4th edition (Paramus, NJ: Prentice Hall, 2000).

Once upon a time . . .

. . . the King told two of his men that he wanted to surprise the Queen with a beautiful garden. "Plant it at once!" he commanded in a booming voice. Now one of the men had anthophobia (*fear of flowers*) and the other had chromophobia (*fear of color*), so they were both worried . . .

## IDENTIFY TIME SEQUENCE IN A STORY

Most stories that students are reading at this level do not begin and end on the same day, and if they do, there is still the passage of time in the day. So, make sure students can determine the passing of time by drawing a timeline, or a circular story map for each season, day, or week in the book.

Chapter books are more apt to have a greater length of time from the beginning to the end of the book. Perhaps students have not thought of "time" as a vehicle the author uses as a way to move the story along. The author may use words such as "months later" or "soon thereafter" for an indeterminate amount of time that has passed, but they can also be more specific as well. So have students be on the alert for the concept of time in their books.

## LEARNING TO EVALUATE THROUGH TESTING

Students can be introduced to different forms of testing. You might give "trial" tests with psychologically neutral, or nonthreatening, material. (Folktales, fairy tales, and familiar books serve as good subject matter when exposing students to the experience of testing.)

Students need to learn the various forms of testing. They need to be comfortable with them, so that the format of the test itself does not get in the way of evaluating what a student knows. Therefore, use a variety of evaluation measures throughout the month as a way to prevent the possibility of "test anxiety" that causes students to freeze up during the testing situation. These are some of the forms of testing to use with the class. First, address the entire class and work with them, and then see to it that students can work independently. Frequently revisit the following types of testing:

- *matching*—Match one column, or list, of terms with those in another list.

- *underlining*—Look for the correct word, or the synonym, or a name.

- *multiple choice*—Find the correct answer among others.

- *circling the correct number*—Put a circle around the number that shows which answer is being chosen.

- *filling in the correct circle*—Select the answer. What number is it? Find that number to the left of the question and, if it is enclosed in a circle, color it in carefully with a pencil.

Also, have students construct their own test questions in a variety of formats. This is a skill that needs to be developed over a period of time. Student questions can be collected and read aloud (without mentioning the name of the student) to see if the question is *clear* to others. Encourage students to listen carefully and to offer help and suggestions in the spirit of cooperation. (See Reproducible Activity Pages.)

## SUMMARIZING CHAPTER BOOKS

Students can learn to write summary sentences for each chapter in a story. Give them a small square for writing, and tell them that the summary of each chapter will have to fit on that small piece of paper. This prevents students from writing a long summary paragraph and gets them into the habit of sifting and sorting through words and information in an effort to select pertinent information.

This is one place where computers are helpful because not only can the font be made smaller, but it is of great assistance to the student who writes large. Otherwise, you may have to make some squares larger than others for those whose writing still takes up a great deal of room.

**Procedure.** Count the number of chapters in the book, and give students that many squares (or have students take them from blank squares that are available at the Reading Center). Teach students the importance of writing the summary sentence as they read through the book, rather than waiting until the end. Often chapter titles are of assistance in this exercise. Students can keep the squares in a small white envelope at their desk while they are reading the chapter book.

## PRESENTING INFORMATION IN A VISUAL FORMAT

Once the chapter book has been read and the summary squares are approved by you, students can plan a way to present their material through a visual medium. They can make a story map; make a story condominium (different chapter per floor); construct a story quilt (different chapters interspersed with colored squares of wallpaper); or make a picture or diagram of something that is representative of the book itself and have the chapter squares be an integral part of the design. (For example, if the story centers around an airplane, the squares can become the windows, and the aircraft is drawn around them.)

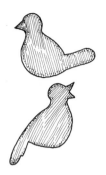

These squares can be placed on other shapes to go with the mood and setting of the story. If, for example, the migration of birds figures heavily into the story, or if the story is about birds, students can cut out bird shapes, place a chapter summary square on each bird, and arrange them on the page. Encourage the drawing of borders and additional visual information, including the title of the story and the author.

# FOCUS ON LANGUAGE ARTS

## MORE READING OPPORTUNITIES

### CHARACTER DAY

Have a Spring Character Day for which students make and wear the mask of their favorite book character. Perhaps they can make a headband to wear that identifies the character. They can wear their masks in the classroom on the afternoon of the designated day. This generates much excitement about books and book characters. Students can be encouraged to introduce their favorite character and tell of the admirable quality or qualities that caused this character to be selected among all of those available, thus giving students an opportunity to speak before the group. (Check with the librarian to see if he or she has a moment to drop by the classroom to enjoy these character masks.)

### BUILDING A STORY GRAPH BY GENRE

This is a good way to see to it that each student has read something in each genre (zhahn' ruh, or category). Make a graph with a variety of genres listed along the bottom. Have students use squares to build the graph and to write the title, author, and their name on the square. Here is an example:

| | | | | |
|---|---|---|---|---|
| **OUR CLASSROOM GENRE GRAPH** | | | | |
| X | | X | X | |
| X | X | X | X | |
| X | X | X | X | X |
| X | X | X | X | X |
| Folktale | Biography | Humor | Information | Adventure |

Some students may be motivated to make an individual story genre graph. They can make one graph per book, or, later, one graph for every three books. They can use color-coded circles of red, blue, and orange to represent a particular book.

| MY GENRE GRAPH | | | | |
|---|---|---|---|---|
| F  x | Charlie | many | ridiculous | boy/father |
| B  x | Mr. K. | horse | frivolous | girl/school |
| P  x | Taffy | cats | sympathy | cats/Mr. B. |
| <u>Book Titles</u> | <u>Character</u> | <u>Animals</u> | <u>New Word</u> | <u>Conflict</u> |

Key: F = fiction, B = biography, P = poetry

## INDIVIDUAL CONFERENCES

Periodically, have a short, quiet time with the students individually, so that you can get some feedback from them regarding their independent reading and the information that is in the reading portfolio. This can be done while students are all working quietly on a writing project or even a research project for a Social Studies topic. It's a special time to enjoy the personal interaction with a student.

## AND THEN WHAT? (STORY PREDICTIONS)

When students finish a chapter book, they usually have questions about the character and what is going to happen next. First discuss the topic and all of the possibilities. Then have the students, either independently or with a partner, outline another chapter for the book after the conclusion. It could take place one month later or two years later.

## CHARACTER CHANGES

One of the qualities of a good chapter book is to see evidence of growth in one or two of the characters, and especially the main character. When you finish a chapter book that is being read aloud to the class, have a discussion about how a character changed. How did the person grow in his or her thinking and actions?

Challenge the students to portray this change visually, so that someone who has not read the book will know that the character changed and in what way.

Change is usually gradual and is not always easy. Encourage students to talk about their own change in attitude or actions in a particular situation.

## A STORYBOOK DIORAMA

A diorama is usually a 3-D depiction of a scene. Students can select a favorite book and make a diorama of that scene. A medium-size box turned on its side can be used as the setting. The inside and outside need to be painted or covered with some type of paper or material. If the class is making a diorama of a chapter book just completed, perhaps three or four committees can work on different diorama scenes.

First, students can make a sketch of the scene.

Second, determine what materials (scissors, felt pens, construction paper, pencils, ruler, clay, real items, etc.) will be needed for the project.

Next, students will need to determine how the "props" in the setting will stand up. They can use tape to put cardboard strips on the reverse side of the paper character (or tree or house) to make it more sturdy, and then determine how it will stand.

The "floor" or bottom of the box is important to the 3-D effect, especially if it is in the woods. Students may use "realia" (real items) in this section, for example, grass, sand, tiny tree branches, and so on.

Be flexible with this project. Students get inspiration as they go along, and new ideas can emerge as they're working on it. Encourage this type of flexibility and fluency of ideas, otherwise known as creative thinking.

## INDIVIDUAL DIORAMAS

Once students get involved in the diorama project listed above, many of them will become motivated to do their own small diorama either at home or in school during their free time. Encourage this. Ask for shoe boxes or other small boxes to be donated to the class so that students have a head start with their setting. When these dioramas are completed, students will enjoy having them displayed in a showcase or in the library for other classes to enjoy.

## VIDEO AND TEXT COMPARISONS

You can make a trip to the public library, children's section, to see what videotapes are available that are made from children's stories. It may be easier to select the video first and then find the book to go along with it, rather than the other way around.

Once the story has been read and discussed, show the video of the story. Make this a special treat for the students, as if they are going to a movie. They can arrange their seats in rows in front of the monitor and popcorn can be served. They can take notes of something in particular that they will later share.

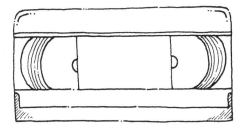

When this is over, it's time for a discussion and comparison of the video and the text. Not only do you want to know which one the students enjoyed more, but why. How were the characters portrayed in the video? Were they true to the text? Was the setting accurate? Did the video version "measure up" to the pictures the students had in their mind? This is an invaluable comparison experience and one worth discussing.

# WORD ORIGINS AND SAYINGS*

1. **OK.** A colloquial (common) expression widely used. It is believed that this expression came from The OK Club, a group that was supporting Martin Van Buren for a second term in the White House. Van Buren was born in *Old Kinderhook, New York and his nickname was the "Red Fox of Kinderhook." This led to Old Kinderhook, or OK.

2. **clue.** In Greek mythology, a "clewe" (clue) was a piece of thread given to Theseus to guide him out of a labyrinth (series of paths) after he had slain a monster. The word "clue" then came to mean anything that guides a person through a perplexing situation. We "thread" our way through a puzzling situation.

3. **confetti.** This is an Italian word for candies or sweets. The corresponding French word is *bonbon.* Centuries ago on carnival days, people used to throw candies at each other in celebration. Later, imitation sweets or *confetti,* made from colored paper, was thrown at weddings and parades. It is a symbolic offering, often used when heroes ride by in a parade.

4. **basin.** This means a soldier's helmet. The word *basin* began in Roman times with the Latin term *bachinus,* "an eating bowl." Later, knights wore cone-shaped metal caps or helmets. The word for helmet was *bacin* or a bowl for the head. Many a soldier has eaten out of his hat and washed his socks in his basin.

5. **Video.** A Latin word that means "see" or "look." It also appears in the forms *vid* and *vis.* The word *video* is a synonym for *television* (*tele*—far away, *vis*—see).

   *Vis* and *vid* are used in other words, such as in*vis*ible stars and a super*vis*or, one who oversees.

# WRITING SKILLS

## SORTING WORDS INTO CATEGORIES

Students can take out a piece of paper and fold it so that there are three columns. At the top of each column they are to write the word given by you. For our purposes the words to use are:

### Animals, Outer Space, and Foods

Then you say a word aloud from a list prepared in advance. Give students time to think about the word and then write it in the proper column, or category. For this exercise, spelling is not an issue. Have students use invented spelling. At the end, go through the list together and write the words on the chalkboard in the appropriate columns, as dictated by the students.

---

*Source: *Word Origins and Their Romantic Stories* by Wilfred Funk.

This list of ten words can get you started, using the categories mentioned above. Say these words slowly one by one:

tiger            lettuce            bread            moon            bear

star             Pluto              rabbit           carrot          rhino

They should end up on the chalkboard, and on the student's list, as follows:

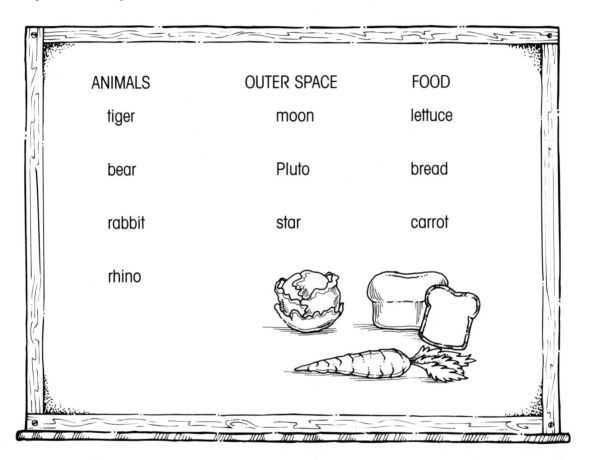

This strengthens listening skills, provides the opportunity to categorize information, helps build vocabulary, and teaches students to organize meaningful information rather quickly. When three categories are mastered, try four, then five, to make it more challenging. Students will want to play the game of "Categories" on their own during choice time or during indoor recess.

## WHEN DO WE USE CAPITAL LETTERS?

When writing information on the chalkboard, you can informally point out the capital letters that are used. Thus, teaching this skill can be an ongoing process as students read and write. However, there are some helpful hints for using capitals. Make a chart of this information so students can use it as a beginner's reference:

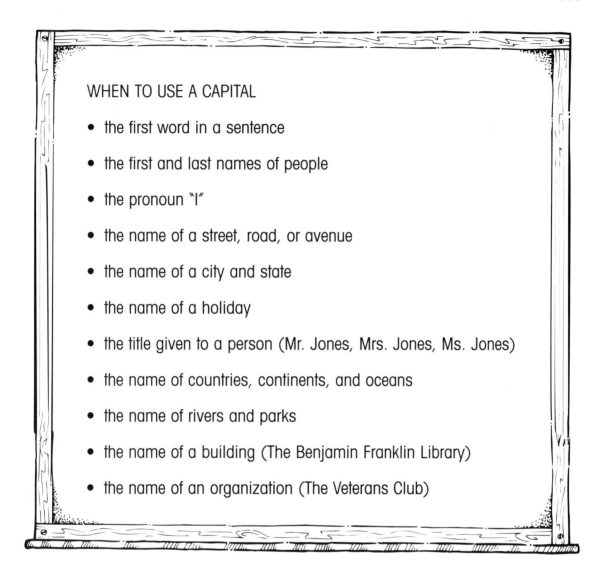

WHEN TO USE A CAPITAL

- the first word in a sentence

- the first and last names of people

- the pronoun "I"

- the name of a street, road, or avenue

- the name of a city and state

- the name of a holiday

- the title given to a person (Mr. Jones, Mrs. Jones, Ms. Jones)

- the name of countries, continents, and oceans

- the name of rivers and parks

- the name of a building (The Benjamin Franklin Library)

- the name of an organization (The Veterans Club)

## SILLY LEPRECHAUNS WRITE STORIES

Since this is the month of elves and fairies, anything can happen. Write a short story on a chart with some of the capital letters in the correct place and some in a ridiculous spot. Students enjoy finding the errors.

## WRITE A NEWS FLASH

Students can write a news flash about an incident in a book that they have read, or are reading, for "Today's News Program." The information has to read as though the incident happened today, not yesterday, so students have to swing into the present and write a short, fresh, version of an incident in their story. All of the verbs have to switch from past to present tense. This is a challenging activity and a different type of task for many students.

## MORE WORK WITH EMOTICONS (REBUS, PUNCTUATION)

Emoticons draw students into the use of computer keyboard symbols that represent quite a range of information and emotions. These are extremely helpful in reading a message and in writing or constructing a rebus sentence to convey meaning.

Here are some emoticon sentences for students to complete. A key is at the top of the four sentences. Which emoticon, or word, should be used in the blanks below? Write this information on the chalkboard. Students can copy them and fill in the blanks.

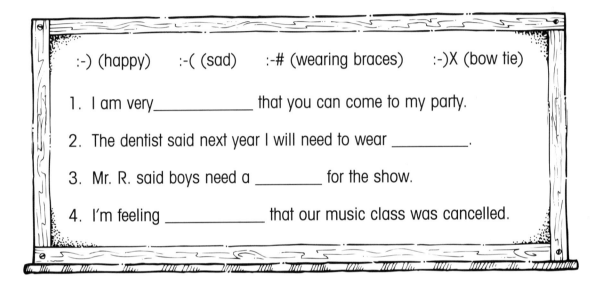

:-) (happy)     :-( (sad)     :-# (wearing braces)     :-)X (bow tie)

1. I am very_____ that you can come to my party.

2. The dentist said next year I will need to wear _____ .

3. Mr. R. said boys need a _____ for the show.

4. I'm feeling _____ that our music class was cancelled.

## STILL MORE WORK WITH EMOTICONS

This time, using the same four emoticons, incorporate the emoticon into the sentence and have students write the word on the line just in front of the number of the sentence:

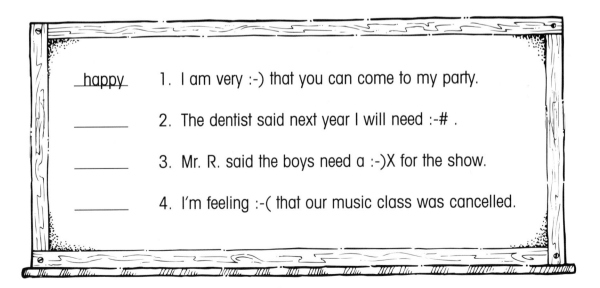

_happy_     1. I am very :-) that you can come to my party.

_____     2. The dentist said next year I will need :-# .

_____     3. Mr. R. said the boys need a :-)X for the show.

_____     4. I'm feeling :-( that our music class was cancelled.

## THE LEFT-HANDED WRITER

This person should be given the same consideration as a right-handed person. Sometimes writing seems to be more awkward in the beginning for the left-handed person. These tips might help:

- Slant the paper to the right.
- Try to use a pencil with a hard lead as it's not so apt to smear.
- Some left-handed students use an upside-down hand style while others curve their hand under. What makes this happen? Apparently it is a function of the brain. Encourage the left-handed student to get comfortable with a position.
- Grasp the pencil the same way as that of a right-handed writer.
- Place a piece of tape or a rubber band well above the pencil point to help the student know how far away from the point the grip should be. This often allows the upside-down writer to be able to see where he or she is going.
- In *printing,* many strokes are more comfortable if they are reversed. For example, printing an "o" by a right-handed person requires a curved stroke to the left and down, whereas many left-handed writers make the curved stroke to the right and down.
- Allow for a wide variation and be patient. Fine-motor skills are still developing in many students.

# SPEAKING SKILLS

## GROUP DISCUSSION "TALK TICKETS"

When groups are formed for discussions, distribute three squares to each student to be used as "talk tickets." When the student speaks, he or she deposits the ticket into a container located in the center of the group. This does two things: (1) It sets the expectation for all students to contribute and empowers the reticent student with an action, and (2) it limits the speaking of the students who are apt to enjoy center stage and who will speak repeatedly.

This same technique can be used for total class discussions. Each person is given one ticket. When students have spent their ticket, they have taken their turn, and must wait until all students have spent their tickets to speak again.

## ROUND-ROBIN STORY

Start a story and have students "pick up the ball" and continue the story. Students can sit in a circle and take turns adding information to the story, and then roll a ball to another person who must continue the story.

When used in small groups, students can use a Styrofoam ball or a Nurf ball in their groups. They have to listen carefully because they don't know when they will be called upon to speak.

## HELPFUL HINTS FOR GIVING A BOOK REPORT

Book reports are useful in all areas of the curriculum. When dealing with subject matter of various types, students still need to keep these specific points in mind:

- Organize the information.
- Stick to the topic.
- Use visual aids if they will enrich the speech.
- Check the facts.
- Practice the report repeatedly before giving it.
- If someone in the audience is distracting you, do not get pulled in by their behavior. Instead, turn your attention to another section of the audience.

## ANTONYM ACTION

An *antonym* is the name given to words that mean the opposite, or almost the opposite, of one another. Students often use these words while working in pairs, and can do a beanbag toss between them, or they can jump rope to antonyms, or bounce a ball to antonyms. One student says one word, the other student says another.

For the whole class activity, students can make two lines in the classroom. One side whispers one word, the other side responds with the antonym. Here are some to get you started:

| | |
|---|---|
| before/after | up/down |
| night/day | black/white |
| cold/hot | give/get (or receive) |
| big/little | fat/thin |
| loud/soft | happy/sad |
| huge/tiny | winter/summer |

These are a bit more challenging:

| | |
|---|---|
| plain/fancy | hero or heroine/coward |
| better/worse | positive/negative |
| praise/criticize | seldom/often |
| sour/sweet | speechless/talkative (or chatty) |

## MAKING PUPPETS, MAKING CONVERSATION

Working with puppets is an excellent motivation tool for promoting speech. Have materials available so that students can make puppets. You will need:

| | | |
|---|---|---|
| paper plates | paper bags | felt-tip pens |
| string | glue | construction paper |
| scissors | towel rolls | cylindrical food containers |
| fabrics | yarn | string |

Once the puppet character is made, it looks like it wants to say something. Students can make conversation by introducing their puppet to someone else's puppet. They can ask the puppet questions, opinions, and so on. The puppet is a good promoter of informal speech. This month's puppets could be green elves and leprechauns.

## OVER-THE-HEAD PUPPETS

These large brown paper bag puppets can be made at holiday time, or can be characters in books, or characters from Social Studies and Science topics that students are studying.

Make sure to have large eye holes so that students can see well while wearing these puppets.

## TALKING HEADS

Visit your local ice cream store and ask what the proprietor does when all of those wonderful, large, sturdy cylindrical containers that hold the ice cream are empty. Many of them toss the containers away. Ask if they will save them for you, and be diligent about picking them up daily or every other day.

Students can use these to make puppets. They can be the "talking heads" of television broadcasters or radio commentators. This puts new zest into speaking aloud while behind a comfortable shield. It is a bonus for the insecure or shy child, and some of them really shine with this project. (This becomes a good storage space, too).

# LISTENING SKILLS

## AUDITORY PROBLEMS?

Check with the school psychologist, speech teacher, or special needs team if you suspect that a student has difficulty with hearing what is being said in the classroom. Some students who have learning disabilities are very distracted by noise in the classroom. Get some direction from the team of special needs people regarding where the student should be seated in the classroom, and whether there are study carrels available for students who want to go to a different place to work where it is quiet with less distractions.

## MAKE A QUIET WORK STATION

A special station, or stations, can be made for the students who choose to go there (or are requested by the teacher to go there) to complete work. Obtain a medium-large appliance box that can be placed on the desk. Make the outside attractive, and label it with a title such as "Shh! Leprechauns at Work" or "Only Listening Allowed." If there is a favorite book character that students enjoy, label

it as "_____'s House." This portable station can be placed on a table or desk top out of the line of traffic and commotion. Some students will visit it often.

If you have your students sitting in clusters or groups, and they begin to pile up books or make a paper wall for privacy, it is a direct hint that some seating rearrangements need to be made.

## INFORMAL INVENTORY FOR LISTENING

Check to see if students hear beginning sounds that are the same and different. They can take out a piece of scrap paper and number it from 1–10. Then you can slowly say a set of ten words. If they begin with the same sound, have students print the letter that makes the sound. If they begin with a different sound, have them leave the space blank. Here are some words to use:

| | |
|---|---|
| said/sunny | make/muffin |
| took/book | funny/fake |
| Eskimo/elephant | plum/grape |
| yarn/yellow | bank/butter |
| desk/finger | hi/helicopter |

Check to see if students can hear differences in ending sounds, such as: had/hat, pin/pit, pat/pad, skip/skid, band/bank, and so on.

Check to see if students can hear words that have a rhyming sound, such as: tell/bell, cramp/stamp, pick/stick, rung/sung, sweet/meet, crash/dash, toy/ boy, jam/ham, chop/stop, and so on.

Check to see if students can hear the differences or similarities in vowel sounds internally or in the middle of a word, such as:

| *Different* | *Same* |
|---|---|
| pin/pen | rain/pain |
| bag/big | get/met |
| hit/hat | cat/sat |
| tub/tube | pill/fill |

Remember, if a student is having difficulty with speech and articulation of sounds, it may mean he or she is having difficulty hearing these sounds. Check student records for any evidence of ear infections or other problems, such as constant colds, where the child's ear/nose/throat passages are semi-clogged. When having a parent conference, ask about the child's early health record if it is not available. This is solely in the interest of determining whether or not the student might benefit from having an ear check-up by a physician. The inquiry should be in a nonthreatening manner.

## LISTENING AND SUMMARIZING

Read a very short paragraph to students, and have them summarize the information. This is a skill that can be developed through the process of attentive listening to the speaker.

Read a very short list of directions that include an orderly procedure, such as 1, 2, 3. Then ask students if they can recall what to do first, second, third, and have them repeat it. This is a skill that can be developed.

## GIVING DIRECTIONS

If you find that you have to repeatedly give directions to a class, then perhaps you have, in fact, been giving directions more than once and students don't listen until about the third or fourth time. Tell students you need to have their attention . . . and get it. Tell them you are only going to say this once. Then say it. If a student later asks what to do, say that you have already given the directions and if they were listening they would know that you are not going to repeat them. (But offer the student an "out" and say that some kind soul in the classroom may be willing to give them the directions and, if so, that's fine, but it won't be you.) There is usually someone in the beginning of your effort to change listening patterns who will willingly step into the teacher role to help out a classmate. If not, ask someone to say the directions since it won't be you.

Students soon get the message that when you ask for their attention, the room is quiet and they are listening to what you are saying. Review the information once. Ask if there are any questions. Then proceed. Also, it is most helpful to write procedural information on the chalkboard so students have a handy reference.

# FOCUS ON MATH

## WHAT IS MATH, ANYWAY?

Students need to know that math is not just something in a book, it is something that they use every day. Hopefully we're doing that each day in the classroom. A helpful discussion starter would be to make a chart with this title: "How Did You Use Math So Far Today?" You can start the list and, through discussion, help students come to the realization that they can't do without math. Here are some items for the list:

- alarm clock rang (has numbers and can be set)
- got dressed (clothing sizes important)

- ate breakfast (what size glass? what size dish? was microwave or stove involved—how many minutes? what temperature?)
- left the house at a certain time (clock)
- got on the correct bus (buses use a numbering system)
- already walked up and down how many steps?
- bus driver knew the route (map); do students know the route and how far it is?
- how much money do they have for lunch?

Extend this list to make students aware that math is in their everyday life. Have them keep a log of every time they use math today (counting papers, using the clock to know when to go to the next lesson, lunch money and change, etc.).

Make badges that say "Caught Using Math" and have students earn the right to wear them because they got "caught in the act of using math."

Another day, use a hand stamp or stickers. (See Reproducible Activity Pages.)

## JINGLE, JANGLE

Coins make a jingling sound in our pockets. Let's take a good look at the four major coins we use in our money system: penny, nickel, dime, and quarter. (We also have a half dollar and a dollar coin.)

Which of the four major coins is the largest? (quarter)

Does this largest coin have the most value of the four? (yes)

Which of the four major coins is smallest? (dime)

Does this smallest coin have the least value? (no, the dime has more value than either the nickel or penny)

Our coin system is based on a system of tens. Students can fill in the blanks as these statements are read aloud:

- Five one-cent coins are equal to a . . . (*nickel*)
- Ten one-cent coins are equal to a . . . (*dime*)
- Twenty-five one-cent coins are equal to . . . (*quarter*)
- Fifty one-cent coins are equal to . . . (*half dollar*)
- One hundred one-cent coins are equal to . . . (*dollar coin or dollar bill*)

Ask students to line up their four coins according to *size*. Ask students to line up their four coins according to *value*.

## WORKING WITH COINS

Students like to figure out these problems, especially if there is real money (coins) in a little cash register for them to work with. When working with the coins at the Math Center, students need to sign in and out. They need to sign in, count the money to see if it is all there, and then sign out. The next person does the same thing. This generally prevents problems with the money.

Have activity cards to go along with the money, such as:

---

Mary bought a hat for 5 cents and an ice cream cone for 16 cents. Show how she paid for it. (Students can also draw their answer.)

---

How many ways can you pay for popcorn that costs 25 cents?

---

How many ways can you pay for ice cream that costs 19 cents?

---

Lay out coins worth 25 cents. Take away the least amount of coins to end up with 15 cents.

---

Have students make up their own activity cards and sign them. They can put the answer on the reverse side so that students can check their own work when they finish. (See Reproducible Activity Pages.)

## LEPRECHAUN MATH

It's the month of March and soon it will be St. Patrick's Day. We all know what that means! There will be tomfoolery with the money in the pot at the end of the rainbow. Leprechauns love to get people confused about money. Put these examples on the chalkboard and have students figure out how those busy leprechauns changed the signs around to try to trick us. But can they? Students can copy these down and change the signs. Ask for volunteers to come to the chalkboard one at a time to change the signs.

Use light green chalk today for all math work on the chalkboard.

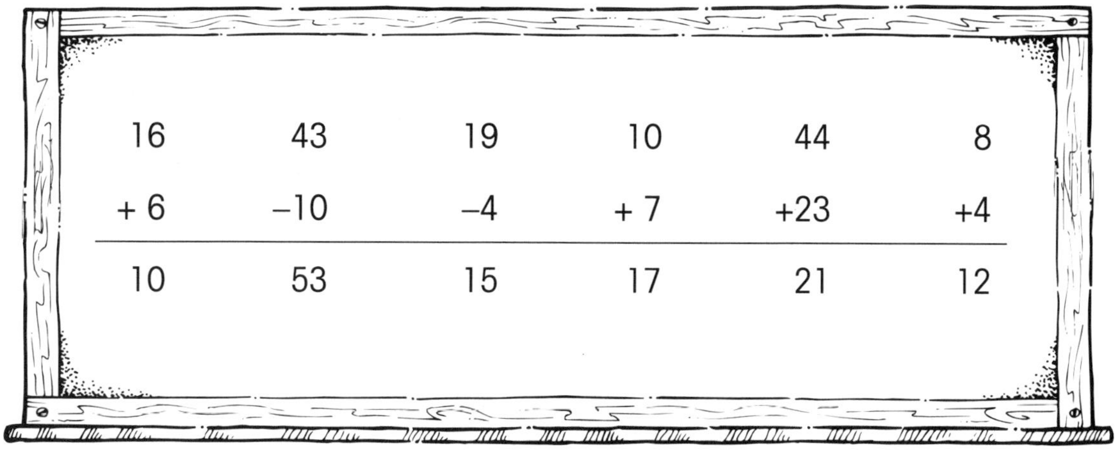

| 16 | 43 | 19 | 10 | 44 | 8 |
|---|---|---|---|---|---|
| + 6 | −10 | −4 | + 7 | +23 | +4 |
| 10 | 53 | 15 | 17 | 21 | 12 |

## LEPRECHAUN STORY PROBLEMS

Well, once again those tricky leprechauns are trying to mix us up by using the wrong words in story problems. Can we find the words that don't belong and correct them? Those leprechauns won't have the last laugh now, will they?

1. Tony had six alligators. Two had toothaches. How many alligators does he have all together? (*It already says six.*)

2. Ann Marie picked twelve purple plums. She put six in the basket, five in her pocket, and one in her bag. Now how many plums does she have? (*still twelve*)

3. Heather H. McGolly had sixteen candies, by golly. She ate one on the trolley. She gave one to friend Polly. How many does she have in her jar at home, by golly? (*16 – 1 – 1 = 14 that Heather has. How many she has in her jar at home is not part of the problem.*)

Students enjoy making up their own silly story problems. They can write them up, or tell them, and then show the math answers and how they arrived at the solution. (See Reproducible Activity Pages.)

This type of silliness creates a resurgence in interest in math story problems this month.

## 'CAUSE I'M THE SUBTRAHEND, THAT'S WHY (SUBTRACTION JINGLE)

Long ago in a land far away, people were missing things. One boy couldn't find his good pencil. One girl's ribbon was missing. Now one day, a woodsman spied a little elf in a green suit, dancing under a tree and saying this rhyme in sing-song fashion. The elf was moving in rhythm to the words, and enjoying all of the things that it had stored up, or *taken away,* from animals and people. This is what someone heard, anyway. Do you believe it? Can you learn it? (See Reproducible Activity Pages.)

*You got it? I like it.*
*I'll take it. Why?*
*'Cause I'm the Subtrahend.*
*Yeah, yeah! Just call me Subtrahend.*

*Suppose you have ten pieces of pie.*
*Seven of them catch my eye.*
*I take seven, now you've got three.*
*'Cause I'm the Subtrahend,*
*Yeah, yeah! The hungry Subtrahend.*

*What's that you say?*
*You've got seven rats?*
*I'll take six, feed them to my cats.*
*I get six, and you get one.*
*'Cause I'm the Subtrahend,*
*Yeah, yeah! The mighty Subtrahend.*

*Farmer Bill was very sad.*

*His ten pounds of taters all went bad.*

*I took all ten, now he has none.*

*'Cause I'm the Subtrahend,*

*Yeah, yeah! The helpful Subtrahend.*

*You got it? I like it! I'll take it! Why?*

*'Cause I'm the Subtrahend.*

*Yeah, yeah! I'm the "take away guy."*

Hmmmm. What does the word "subtrahend" stand for? (The subtrahend is the name given to the number that is subtracted from another number. The sign that indicates this is the minus sign.) Where does it live in a computation problem? What is its sign? Read this jingle aloud to students. Print it on a large chart. Have them learn it this month in sing-song rhythmic fashion, with their own motions and movements.

# FOCUS ON SOCIAL STUDIES

## MARCH CITIZENSHIP FOCUS

### THE TCAA FORMULA

A good citizen *accepts responsibility for his or her actions.* This is a difficult concept for many youngsters. Accepting responsibility is a complicated process that involves several steps. Refer to it as TCAA.

**T**—*Think* about what it is you are going to do, or are being asked to do. In your mind, think it through to the end. Is this something that will make you feel proud, or is it something that will make you feel awkward? Don't make a hurried decision.

**C**—*Consequences* of your decision. If you do/don't do this, what could be the result in the short term and in the long term? Work this out.

**A**—*Act* on what you have determined is right for *you,* not what is right for someone else.

**A**—*Accept* the responsibility for your actions. Take the "high road" and own up rather than cover up.

Here are two general discussion starters for a warm-up:

1. Leon was working at the Writing Center and there were many scraps of paper on the floor, and nothing had been put back in place. In a moment, the teacher was going to announce that it was time to clean up and get ready to go to gym. So, Leon left the Center and went to his seat. When the teacher called time, there was no one to clean up the Writing Center so he asked for volunteers. Darren and Keith said they'd help. Discuss this:

   • Darren and Keith had not worked at the Writing Center and yet they volunteered to help. (They took on responsibility.)

- Leon left the Writing Center so he would not have to clean up. (Leon avoided any responsibility.)
- How could Leon have handled this in a different way? (He could have asked for additional help, thus accepting responsibility, in general, for keeping the classroom in shape.)

2. Melody accidentally spilled milk on the floor in the cafeteria. Barry didn't see it and slipped and fell. "Who spilled this?" asked the cafeteria worker. No one spoke up. "Will someone please help me out and stand here and direct traffic away from this spot until I can get a mop?" asked the cafeteria worker. Susan and Diane volunteered. Discuss this:

- What makes these two girls *good citizens*?
- Did they spill the milk?
- Did they *have* to help?
- What opinion does the cafeteria worker have of the girls?
- Should you try to help others who are asking for help?

Try to instill this message in children: "Accepting responsibility" often means that you do something for the general good, even though you weren't the one who caused the problem. This is something that needs to be learned and needs to be worked on this month.

## WORKING WITH TCAA

Now that the discussion has "warmed up" and is done on a nonthreatening note, we can turn to more personal issues with the realization that children are faced with any number of choices. This is where the TCAA formula needs to be applied. Here are some situations that could be discussed in class. Remember, you as the teacher are the moral compass:

- A student asks you to sneak out of the cafeteria at lunch time and go to his house.
- Three students tell you they have no intention of doing the assignment and want you to join in.
- A student tells you she knows where the teacher keeps her purse, and asks you to stand watch at the door while he or she looks for lipstick (or money, etc.).
- One of your friends tells you there is a plan to gang up on a student after school and wants to know if they can count on you to be "in."
- A student tries to hand you a small package and asks you to keep it for him or her in your desk.

Stress with students that sometimes accepting responsibility may mean that you accept the responsibility of being unpopular with an "in" group. Find your own "in" group—one that is more attuned to leadership guidelines and principles. Again, this is not easy, so it needs to be addressed on a regular basis. Give students some ammunition phrases, even if they sound silly; they could be helpful. Ask them to add some statements that give a "no way" message:

- "Sorry, not today."
- "Have to run after school, have an appointment."

- "Don't count on it."
- "It's not my style."
- "My mom has me wearing a wire so she'd know."
- "The doctor says I'm contagious (cough)."
- "My ears are clogged up and I can't hear you."
- "My grandmother is with the secret police."
- "I keep seeing flashing lights. Do you?"
- Stomp imaginary bugs on the floor, repeatedly and loud.
- Start scratching your arms, legs, hands, and roll your eyes.

# PATRIOTISM

## WHAT IS YOUR PATRIOTISM I.Q.?

Let's check. How many students can write out the Pledge of Allegiance?
How many know what the red/white/blue colors of the flag stand for?
How many know how many stripes are on the flag?

## WHAT IS YOUR SYMBOL I.Q.?

Let's check. How many students know the national bird? (*Bald eagle*)
How many students know the nation's capital? (*Washington, D.C.*)
How many students know the "nation's attic"? (*Smithsonian*)

## A WEEKLY I.Q. CHECK-UP

Students can write more questions for patriotism and symbol facts and then give a weekly check-up each Friday. Reward students with food at the end of the week. Try something *as American as apple pie* or a hot dog in a roll. Scores will soar!

# AREA OF FOCUS: WHO WORKS IN OUR CITY AND COUNTRY?

In a good community, we're all "worker bees" and have a contribution to make to keep the community running. The community can be a city, a nation, a town, or a school.

## WHO HELPED YOU GO TO SCHOOL TODAY?

This is an eye opener for students, especially those who are still in a self-centered mode. Some insist that they got themselves to school. But, let's take a closer look and see if they got help from other resources:

- family
- clock in the home (electricians)
- breakfast (microwave, food shipments, mother/father)
- washed face and hands (water department provided safe water for drinking and bathing)
- clothing (manufacturers, parents or other adults)
- lunch (who packed it or gave money for it?)
- how did you arrive at school (bus driver, car, on foot, other).

Students will begin to supply a longer list.

## COMMUNITY WORKERS

Begin to make a list of those who keep our city running smoothly. This list will help get you started. It is helpful if the workers are clustered in groups (or you can use a web). Keep adding to the list and make new categories:

### *Health Providers*

| | | |
|---|---|---|
| family doctor | health specialist | dentist |
| eye specialist | paramedic | dental hygienist |
| ER personnel | nurse | medical center worker |
| pharmacist | nursing home personnel | in-home assistant |
| veterinarian | | |

### *Safety Providers*

| | |
|---|---|
| police officer | road construction workers |
| crossing guard | water treatment workers |
| firefighter | utility workers (phone, electricity) |

### *Business Providers/Services*

| | | |
|---|---|---|
| grocery store | clothing store | florist |
| restaurant | dry cleaner | bank |
| hotel | bookstore | gas station |
| mall | library | fast-food restaurant |

## WRITE TO COMMUNITY WORKERS

Have each student select a community service that he or she is interested in, or one he or she thinks he or she would like to work in when grown up. Then students can write a letter asking that community worker something about his or her job, such as: How much education is needed for the job?

What do you like about the work? What is a day like on the job? and so on. Inquire within the school building and among parents and friends for names of people to send the letters to, so that you are more apt to get a response. However, it is amazing the local community people who do respond to letters like this and even send materials (especially if there is a cover letter from you explaining that a unit of study is going on in the classroom).

Students are getting an opportunity to write and mail a letter and they look forward to a response. Set up a Center in the classroom for Community Workers where students can post their letters. Have letters addressed to the school (*no home addresses given out*). This is always a lively Center and a hub of activity as the responses come in.

## FIELD TRIPS

A field trip that contributes to your study of the community is one that students will always remember. Some school districts have recommendations for trips at third-grade level, so be sure to check with the office before initiating anything on your own. Go through channels for correct field-trip procedure. (Don't mention any field trips to the students until plans are underway.)

## GUEST SPEAKERS

Be sure to invite some community workers to the classroom to give a talk to the students about their work. This is always fascinating and a memorable learning experience for the students (as well as the visitors!).

## THE BEHIND-THE-SCENES HEROES AND HEROINES

Many people have interesting and unusual occupations or jobs, that we often take for granted. They don't have a glamorous title or a high profile like a TV announcer or a star athlete, but they're just as important. Make a list of some of these people and put them into a hat. Students can pull the name out of a hat and investigate it at the library. Then they come back and tell all about these important people. You might find that the Yellow Pages of the telephone directory (one of our resources) is very helpful. Here are some to get you started:

- dry cleaning machine operators—sort, load, clean, some specializing
- insulation workers—install special materials in homes and buildings to save energy
- industrial machine repairers—keep machines in factories in good condition, and fix them when they break down
- payroll and time-keeping clerks—keep accurate records so people can get paid, computer work
- interviewers for new accounts—help people fill out forms, and they check information (hospitals, credit checks, banks)
- insurance repair people—are called during emergencies to board up windows, put roofs back on, etc.
- caregivers—work with senior citizens, activity directors, cafeteria workers

# HOLIDAYS AND CELEBRATIONS

## "READ ACROSS AMERICA" DAY

This special event is sponsored by the National Education Association (NEA). *The Cat in the Hat* by Dr. Seuss is the mascot for this emphasis on reading activities. Everyone gets into the excitement of reading a good book. Contact: Read Across America, c/o NEA, 1202 16th St. NW, Washington, D.C. 20036; websites: www.nea.org/readacross or www.drseuss.

## IDITAROD (ALASKAN SLED DOG RACE)

This international sled dog race is 1,049 miles in length, stretching from Anchorage to Nome, Alaska, along mountains, rivers, and the icy shores of the Arctic. It simulates the trail that was blazed long ago by pioneers who raced serum from one city to the other during an outbreak of diphtheria. For classroom information, write to Iditarod Trail Committee, P.O. Box 870800, Wasilla, Alaska 99687.

## ST. PATRICK'S DAY

March 17 is a day when Irish people wear green, but others join in the fun and also wear green. Ireland has lush green landscapes because of the favorable climate. In some cities in Ireland and in the United States there are parades, bands, and celebrations. It is a time for storytelling, dished up with corned beef and cabbage. So, put on the Irish music and read a fanciful Irish folktale.

## SMITHSONIAN KITE FESTIVAL (NATION'S CAPITAL)

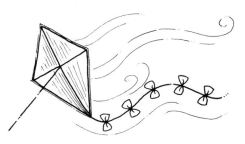

Students can make kites from construction paper. Affix a string to one end and crepe-paper streamers for a tail to the other end. These make a colorful doorway display.

# FOCUS ON SCIENCE

## IT'S DINOSAUR MONTH!

Make a Dinosaur Study Area where you can house books, supplies, and projects. This can be done by securing a large appliance box (refrigerator or dishwasher box). Cover it with green tempera paint or green construction paper. Make wavy designs with a black felt-tipped pen on this outer cover to represent scaly skin. Another box placed on top can be the head, and can also be a storage area. Cover that box with green paper, and draw a giant mouth with teeth, eyes, and nostrils. Glue green strips or ribbons of paper from the mouth to represent grass. This can be the hub of activity for your study.

## RESOURCES

There are many picture books available at the library for students to look through. From this, they can gain helpful information, such as the names given to these giant, and not so giant, lizards. They can also learn how big they were and what they ate, as well as other interesting information.

Some helpful books are *Dinosaur,* Eyewitness Books, by David Norman and Angela Milner; *Dinosaurs* by Gail Gibbons; *The Era of the Dinosaurs,* by Andreu Liamas, illustrations by Luis Rizo; *New Questions and Answers About Dinosaurs* by Seymour Simon, illustrations by Jennifer Dewey; and *Digging Up Dinosaurs* by Aliki.

## SCIENCE FOLDERS AND ACTIVITIES

Make a folder for the dinosaur study. Students can decorate the cover, and keep notes, written materials, and stories inside the folder. Here are some activities students can do.

## FROM ANKYLOSAURUS TO TYRANNOSAURUS REX

Make a list of the many dinosaurs and alphabetize them. These are some to include in the list:

| | |
|---|---|
| ankylosaurus | anatosaurus |
| brontosaurus | brachiosaurus |
| coelurosaurus | elasmosaurus |
| iguanodon | megalosaurus |
| ornitholestes | proteceratops |
| triceratops | tryannosaurus rex (king of the giants) |

Note that many of the names end with "saurus" which is Greek for "giant lizard." There are many more to locate in books, such as "ultrasaurus" and "compsognathus."

## LIST THE BEASTS ACCORDING TO THEIR CHARACTERISTICS

Here are some dinosaur facts to get you started:

- *Compsognathus:* name means "fancy jaw." It was about the size of today's chicken, was swift, and moved on hind legs.
- *Torosaurus:* means "piercing lizard." It was a horned dinosaur, with a head about nine feet in length.

- *Anatosaurus:* means "duck lizard." It had a bill like a duck but had many teeth. It was about 30 feet in length.
- *Supersaurus:* It was 100 feet in length.
- *Seismosaurus:* means "earth shaker." It was120 feet in length.

## INTERVIEW A DINOSAUR

Students can do research on a particular dinosaur after they have looked at books that show pictures and tell interesting facts about each. Often students will select one that interests them. They should have a Dinosaur Fact Sheet that includes the name, the size, what the dinosaur ate, and any other interesting tidbits of information about the beast. (See Reproducible Activity Pages.)

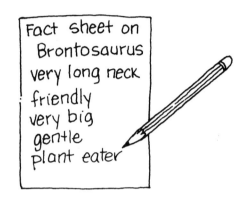

Then students can interview one another, asking the questions from their research papers.

For this project, students may want to make masks or puppets to represent their favorite dinosaur.

## SMALLEST TO LARGEST

Make a graph of dinosaurs from smallest to largest. Decide how this will be represented to scale, in terms of how many feet are represented by one inch. (See Reproducible Activity Pages.)

## DID DINOSAURS FLY? WHO IS ARCHAEOPTERYX?

It is generally believed that dinosaurs did not fly, but scientists are now questioning this theory. However, there were gigantic flying reptiles during the time of dinosaurs. Some names are Eudimorphodon, Dimorphodon, Pterodactylus, and others.

As for Archaeopteryx, with its long tail, teeth, and claws, it had something else: feathers! Look for more information in the Science section next month entitled "Are Birds Really Today's Dinosaurs?"

A good resource book is *Let's Go Dinosaur Tracking!* by Miriam Schlein.

## MAKING FOSSIL PRINTS

*You will need:* modeling clay, paint, construction paper, stick, tempera paints, and sponge.

*Procedure:* Roll the clay into a ball. Then flatten it with the palm of the hand. To make a foot, taper the end of one side of the ball of clay to represent three toes. Bring these three triangular shapes to a sharp point for claws. Use the stick to make ridges.

When the foot is complete, press the flat end on a sponge soaked with tempera paint. Then march the prints across the sheet of construction paper.

Students can also make designs on paper or cloth. They can make stationery or a cover for their very special dinosaur research paper.

## DINOSAUR BONES!

Many of the picture book illustrations include skeletons of dinosaurs. For this activity, you will need an abundance of straws cut into different lengths.

Students can outline their dinosaur skeleton on a sheet of paper using chalk. Place the "bones" (straws) on top of the skeleton, and glue one section at a time. Work slowly and carefully.

What can students do to make the area look like Earth? Start with brown construction paper. Cut long strips of green construction paper to glue around edges representing grass around the pit, and so on. Let students solve this problem.

## PAPIER-MÂCHÉ MODELS

If time permits, students can make their own dinosaur models. Perhaps students can work in small groups for this activity. Determine how large the beasts will be. Here is an opportunity to use Math in conjunction with this project by determining the number of feet that will be represented by an inch or a foot.

## ANOTHER RECIPE FOR DINOSAURS

Cook up a batch of instant potatoes. Add a little green food coloring. Give each student a dollop in the middle of a green or red small paper plate. Using a plastic spoon, they can mold it into a dinosaur shape. Use olives, cut-up pickles, green pepper pieces, carrot slices, and tomato wedges to make a dinosaur treat. Then devour the beast while also enjoying a good dinosaur story or video.

# MARCH AUTHOR/ ILLUSTRATOR STUDY: JOANNA COLE AND BRUCE DEGEN

*The Magic School Bus* series is a hit with children at a variety of grade levels. The fascination with these books is doubly appreciated because they deal with a variety of science topics that children are studying in school.

*Joanna Cole,* the writer, is a former elementary school librarian who became a full-time writer in 1980. All of her books have been named "Outstanding Science Trade Books for Children." She writes in a frank, easy style that makes the subject matter seem easy to younger children. The off-beat science teacher, Ms. Frizzle, is modeled after the author's own science teacher in elementary school (although her teacher was more conservative). It seems that all children love "the Friz."

*Bruce Degen*, the illustrator, is also a writer, as well as an illustrator, and has taught both. He's also been a scenery painter, printmaker, and a teacher of life drawing as well as calligraphy. He has received many prestigious awards and honors for his work. Along with this series, he is also known for his illustrations for the *Commander Toad* series with author Jane Yolen.

Welcome this creative, dynamic, entertaining, educational, and talented team into your classroom this month!

## BOOKS AND SUGGESTED ACTIVITIES

This month we're going to take a new approach to our author study. Several of the books from *The Magic School Bus* series are listed below. Then a technique for using the books will be explained. Finally, a general section of activities for using the series will follow.

The series includes:

*The Magic School Bus at the Waterworks*

*The Magic School Bus Inside the Earth*

*The Magic School Bus Inside the Human Body*

*The Magic School Bus Lost in the Solar System*

*The Magic School Bus on the Ocean Floor*

## HOW CAN I USE THESE BOOKS IN MY CLASSROOM?

*First,* introduce Ms. Frizzle, the teacher who will be taking the students on field trips. Note her clothing, jewelry, and shoes. They match the subject being studied. She is fearless, and students who go on her field trips end up having the experience of their life. We learn a lot from Ms. Frizzle.

*Second,* point out that there are several things going on at once in the books. Direct students' attention to the background text, to the words in the bubbles that indicate what people are saying, to the many posters and report sheets on the pages, and to the art work that helps explain what's going on. The books are busy.

You should be familiar with the book before reading it to your class. Then give them some hints about what they can expect on this field trip through the book. You can then: (1) Read the background text aloud. (2) Read the reactions of the students to what is going on (words in bubbles). (3) Point out the art work on the school buses. The school bus is apt to change into a rocket ship, for example, so keep alert. Keep an eye on the art work throughout the book. It helps explain what's going on.

You can go through the book again, after the book has been read, to read the many diagrams and charts in more detail. At first, just point out to students that they are available.

*Third,* make sure that the book or books are available to students after they are read aloud. They are available in paperback editions and you can secure them from the school library or children's section of the public library. Students need to pour over the books again and again. Each time they will find something new.

## SOME GENERAL SUGGESTIONS FOR USING THE BOOKS IN THE CLASSROOM CURRICULUM

### Science

1. Use the book as a field trip to supplement the study of the solar system, rocks, water, human body, etc. In addition, use other information books.

2. Students can go through the book and learn three facts from the charts or diagrams they see. Write the three facts on small cards. Quiz their fellow students on these facts.

3. Make the same chart or diagram or model found in the book.

4. Start a rock collection or a seashell collection. Begin to label everything.

5. Begin to focus on "Nutrition." Keep track of information on food labels and start a calorie-count chart.

6. Read the "Notes From the Author" section in the back of each book that does give factual information.

### Math

1. How long is a year on different planets?

2. How much would you weigh on another planet?

3. Name the largest and smallest planets in the solar system.

4. Learn to convert from miles to kilometers.

5. Learn to convert temperature from Fahrenheit to Centigrade. Find out what *Fahrenheit* and *Centigrade* mean.

6. Find out the depth of a body of water necessary to enable you to navigate the waters in a paddle boat, steamship, ocean liner.

## *Art/Music*

1. Create a new outfit for Ms. Frizzle for another trip.

2. Paint a mural of a science process, such as the one in the trip to the waterworks.

3. Design a school bus so that it can be determined where it's headed by the pictures on the outside.

4. Create a life-size Ms. Frizzle. Make a fancy dress, earrings, jewelry, shoes, etc., for her, and place her in the Science Center so that she can oversee the discoveries being made there. She can send written messages to the students.

5. What background music would be suitable for the pages as the students take their trip?

6. Make a picture (paint, chalk, felt-tip pen, construction paper) of something from one of the books, only in greater detail. For example, an underwater sea scene with sea creatures; a picture that focuses upon the sky with clouds, birds, bugs; and so on.

## *Reading/Language Arts*

1. Write a journal entry about one of the magic bus trips.

2. Read about an entirely different subject and take a magic bus ride there. Record the information in the form of charts, diagrams, drawings, and text. Work in small groups or with partners.

3. Write a letter to Ms. Frizzle telling what you learned by taking the magic bus trip.

4. Students can make masks of the students shown in the book, and wear them as they read the information in the bubbles, after a narrator has read the background text. Make a Ms. Frizzle mask, too.

5. *The Magic School Bus Video* series would complement the books. They should be available at the public library. Play one after reading the book, then reread the book. Which do students prefer? From which medium do they learn more?

## *Other Activities*

1. Keep a list of the scientific words found in each book.

2. Learn to spell at least three of the words.

3. Begin a classroom rock collection. Start looking for fossils.

4. Use a grinder and tiny pebbles, small earth chunks, and little twigs to make soil in the classroom.

5. Study sculptures that have been carved from marble and granite that is found in the earth.

6. What material is the school building made from? Does it come directly from the earth and, if so, in what form?

7. How are certain products (a wooden table, a porcelain vase, an alabaster statue, and so on) made from natural items found on Earth?

8. Foster curiosity and safety, too. Find out what people need to wear for certain occupations (safety goggles, safety shoes), and what astronauts need to do and wear to get ready for space travel.

9. This series answers questions and leaves us wondering about more. Students can list three questions they'd like to ask Ms. Frizzle, the science expert. Maybe we can go on a library hunt to find the answers or write to a scientist. Hmmm . . . now where would we find a scientist? (Write to a high school science department, or a research department at a local hospital, university, plant, and so on.)

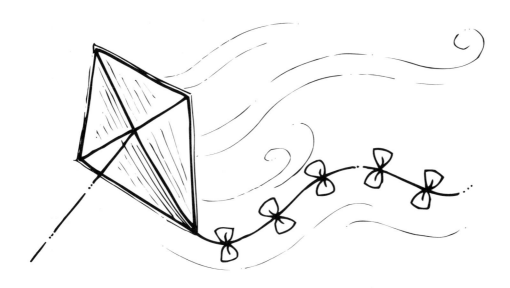

# REPRODUCIBLE ACTIVITY PAGES
# FOR MARCH

## READING/LANGUAGE ARTS

Read Across America with Dr. Seuss

Are you a Good Test-Taker?

Brer Rabbit Tries to Trick Anansi

Homer Has ENDophobia

Tap, Tap, Tapping for Syllables

## MATH

I Was Caught Using Math

Making "Cents" with Math

Leprechaun Math

'Cause I'm the Subtrahend

## SOCIAL STUDIES

What Is Your Patriotism I.Q.?

Community Worker Link-up

## SCIENCE

Interview a Dinosaur

The Eighteen-Foot Dinosaur

## AUTHOR STUDY

Ms. Frazzle Explores Under Her Feet

Name _____    Date _____

# Read Across America with Dr. Seuss

Join The Cat in the Hat for the reading celebration!  Color the red stripe
when you complete the activity.

**Select 2 good books.  Read them.**

**Green Eggs and Ham for Breakfast.
(Cook it or paint it.)**

**Carry a book under your arm all day long.
When the DEAR bell rings....read.**

**Make a tall "Cat in the Hat" hat and
wear it for reading.**

**"DEAR" BELL  (Drop Everything and Read.)
If you don't have a bell, use a
different signal.**

**Listen to someone read aloud
a good story.**

**What else?**

# Are You a Good Test-Taker?

Anansi the Spider is a trickster, but don't let him trick you! He's making up some test questions. See how well you do.

## MATCHING

Draw a line from words in A to words in B, that are opposites.

| A. | | B. | |
|----|----|----|----|
| day | | awake | |
| up | | walk | |
| stop | | night | |
| sleep | | go | |
| crawl | | down | |

## CIRCLE THE ANSWER

1. March is the _____ month in the year.

   first          second          third

2. Baseball season begins in _____.

   spring          winter          autumn

## MULTIPLE CHOICE

Put an "X" in front of the correct answer.

1. A rose is a . . .

   ____fruit

   ____flower

   ____bulb

2. This is a type of dirt.

   ____shell

   ____clay

   ____cement

3. Apples contain ____.

   ____pits

   ____seeds

   ____bulbs

What are the 3 types of questions? Learn them. Write one of each on another paper. Exchange tests with a partner.

Name _____  Date _____

# Brer Rabbit Tries to Trick Anansi

Brer Rabbit and Anansi both like to take tests. These two tricksters are having fun with circles today. Don't let them trick you!

Brer Rabbit says, "Circle the *number* of the answer!"

A.  Horses have big _____.
    1.  wings
    2.  fins
    3.  teeth

B.  *Cinderella* is what kind of story?
    1.  biography
    2.  fairy tale
    3.  realism

C.  We can hear this sound during storms.
    1.  thunder
    2.  lightning
    3.  swaying

Anansi Says: Fill in the correct circle.

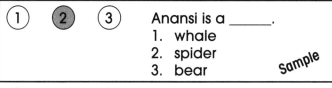

( 1 )   ( 2 )   ( 3 )   Anansi is a _____.
                        1.  whale
                        2.  spider
                        3.  bear            *Sample*

( 1 )   ( 2 )   ( 3 )   Dogs can be _____.
                        1.  frisky
                        2.  fried
                        3.  bunch

( 1 )   ( 2 )   ( 3 )   Spider webs can catch this.
                        1.  elephant
                        2.  fly
                        3.  bird

1.  Read the question.
2.  Select the answer.
3.  What # is it?
4.  Find that # in the circle to the left.
5.  Shade it in with your pencil point.

( 1 )   ( 2 )   ( 3 )   You can get a rash from this plant.
                        1.  vines
                        2.  poison ivy
                        3.  violets

( 1 )   ( 2 )   ( 3 )   March is followed by which month?
                        1.  February
                        2.  May
                        3.  April

# Homer has <u>End</u>ophobia

Homer G. Xytlefry has a *phobia.* A *phobia* is a fear of something. Homer is afraid to write the <u>end</u>ing to a story. Can you help by doing this? Thank you! As you will see, there's a *phobia* in the story, too. It calls for some problem solving.

Title:_____

Once upon a time, the queen invited a handsome prince to lunch at the castle to meet her beautiful daughter. She served her famous peanut butter and jelly sandwiches. What no one knew was that the prince suffered from "arachibutyrophia"—the *fear of peanut butter sticking to the roof of the mouth.*

So, when lunch was served

_____

_____

_____

_____

_____

_____

_____

_____

_____

_____

There are many phobias. Oh oh! Homer has another one! It's ophidophobia, a fear of snakes. Can you write a story about this phobia and perhaps help him learn to deal with it? Do YOU have any phobias to write about?

# Tap, Tap, Tapping for Syllables

All month, the spriggins are tapping in the mines. These little elves know their syllables. Do you? Tap out the words and put the number of syllables on the line in front of the word.

____goat

____evergreen

____consonant

____maple

____plentiful

____motorcycle

____vowel

____syllable

____dime

____hurricane

____cranky

____hullabaloo

____birch

____telephone

____miraculous

Try these. Do they add up to 26 or 28?

_____antidisestablishmentariasm

+_____supercalifragilisticexpialidocious

Name _____     Date _____

# I Was Caught Using Math

Show six ways you used math today.  Share this information with the class.
Use pictures and words

**1.**

**2.**

**3.**

**4.**

**5.**

**6.**

# Making "Cents" with Math

Let's work with four coins. You can use them more than once.

How many ways can you pay for popcorn that costs 25¢? Show the coins.

There's a special today on ice cream. How many ways can you pay for it? Show the coins.

How many ways can you pay for this? Show the coins.

How many ways can you pay for this? Show the coins.

# Leprechaun Math

Get out your green pencil and correct this Math page. The leprechauns are trying to play tricks on us. Circle the correct answer. Do it over if it is not correct.

**A.**

| 76 | 16 | 61 | 42 | 34 |
|----|----|----|----|----|
| + 12 | + 53 | + 38 | + 36 | + 22 |
| 89 | 46 | 99 | 41 | 56 |

**B.**

| 22 | 54 | 35 | 93 | 29 |
|----|----|----|----|----|
| + 16 | + 24 | + 63 | + 4 | + 35 |
| 3♣ | 78 | 98 | 96 | 10 |

**C.**

| 36 | 42 | 85 | 24 | 32 |
|----|----|----|----|----|
| + 32 | + 26 | + 13 | + 75 | + 46 |
| 79 | 68 |  | 99 | 69 |

**D.**

| 81 | 76 | 67 | 42 | 25 |
|----|----|----|----|----|
| + 20 | + 23 | + 22 | + 35 | + 41 |
| 61 | 99 | 88 | 77 | 66 |

Oh oh! They changed the + and − signs. Watch out! Change the signs if they need it.

| 63 | 54 | 89 | 43 | 75 |
|----|----|----|----|----|
| + 41 | − 22 | + 17 | −56 | + 23 |
| 22 | 32 | 72 | 99 | 52 |

# 'Cause I'm the Subtrahend (Chant)

What does the word "subtrahend" stand for?  Where does it live in a computation problem?  What is its sign?

You got it? I like it.
I'll take it. Why?
'Cause I'm the Subtrahend,
Yeah, yeah! Just call me Subtrahend.

Suppose you have ten pieces of pie.
Seven of them catch my eye.
I take seven, now you've got three.
'Cause I'm the Subtrahend.
Yeah, yeah! The hungry Subtrahend.

What's that you say!
You've got seven rats?
I'll take six, feed them to my cats.
I get six, and you get one.
'Cause I'm the Subtrahend,
Yeah, yeah! The mighty Subtrahend.

Farmer Bill was very sad.
His ten pounds of taters all went bad.
I took all ten, now he has none.
'Cause I'm the Subtrahend,
Yeah, yeah! The helpful Subtrahend.

You got it? I like it! I'll take it! Why?
'Cause I'm the Subtrahend.
Yeah, yeah! I'm the "take away guy."

Learn this chant. Make up your own motions and movements.

# What Is Your Patriotism I.Q.?

| | |
|---|---|
| Draw the national bird. | Show a monument in the nation's capital. |
| Design this space with the three colors of the flag. | Show something from the "nation's attic" (Smithsonian). |
| Do a crayon rubbing of a quarter. | Do a crayon rubbing of a dime. |

Do you know the names?  Write them below.

_____   _____   _____
    (President)              (First Lady)           (Vice President)

# Community Worker Link-up

Match the job with the symbol. Select one of the workers and write a paragraph about his or her work. Color the items.

# Interview with a Dinosaur

Name:

Size:

Weight:

Food:

Special Information:

_____

_____

_____

_____

_____

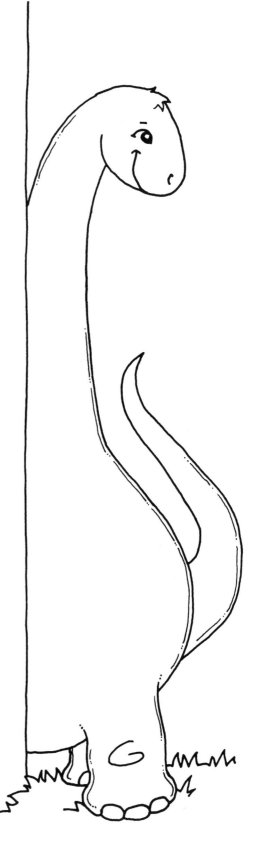

# The Eighteen-Foot Dinosaur

The Styracosaurus was 18 ft. long. Use your yardstick to measure this length.

How many yardsticks does it take
to measure 18 feet?

_____

Find books on dinosaurs.
Can you find one bigger
than me?

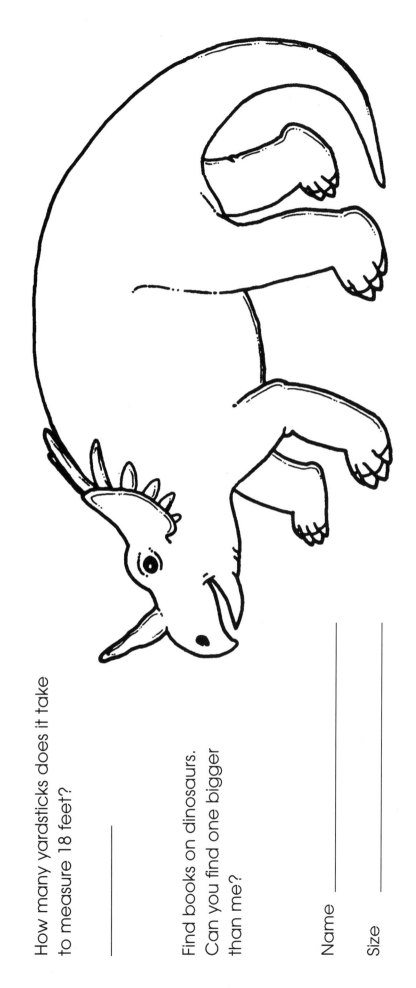

Name _____

Size _____

# Ms. Frazzle Explores Under Her Feet

We think Ms. Frazzle is the sister of Ms. Frizzle from "The Magic School Bus" series. She likes to dress up and explore right around home. Today she's going to explore the earth under her feet—and you can too.

Use your crayons to make Mrs. Frazzle look colorful. Don't forget her shoes.

Stake out a 2- by 2-foot spot under a tree. Examine it closely. Draw and label everything you see.

Move to a different spot. Examine it closely. Record your findings below.

# APRIL

# APRIL BOOKS

**Dewey, Ariane.** *The Narrow Escapes of Davy Crockett* **(New York: William Morrow and Co., 1990).** A series of tall tales that tell of Davy's escapes from rattlesnakes, bears, tornadoes, along with other larger-than-life adventures. Action-packed with fanciful stories that children will enjoy retelling.

**Ehlert, Lois.** *Moon Rope, Un Lazo a la Luna* **(New York: Harcourt Brace Jovanovich, 1992).** This Peruvian tale is printed in English and Spanish. The striking pre-Columbian illustrations were inspired by ancient Peruvian designs and are a study in themselves. The story begins with Fox asking Mole, "If you could have anything in the world, what would it be?"

**Grimm, Jacob and Wilhelm.** *The Six Servants.* **Pictures by Sergei Goloshapov (New York: North-South Books, 1996).** Amazing illustrations! Amazing story! A prince sets out to try his luck at winning a princess with a cunning queen mother who lures men to their doom. Along the way, the prince enlists the aid of six servants who have extraordinary attributes. This is one that keeps children on the edge of their seats, even the second time around.

**Heller, Ruth.** *Chickens Aren't the Only Ones* **(New York: Grosset and Dunlap, 1981).** An award-winning story, in rhyme, that moves from chickens to other creatures of nature that lay eggs. The illustrations, rhymes, and concepts will enrich your spring curriculum. Don't miss this teaching opportunity.

**Macaulay, David.** *The Way Things Work* **(Boston: Houghton Mifflin, 1988).** This is a good picture book to have in your library so that students can browse through it again and again. This author/illustrator also has a series of books that are visual treats. They are: *Pyramid; Castle; Cathedral: The Story of its Construction;* and *City: A Story of Roman Planning & Construction.*

**Maestro, Giulio.** *Riddle Roundup: A Wild Bunch to Beef Up Your Word Power* **(New York: Clarion, 1989).** Wild and whacky word play that children enjoy. For example, "What woke up the rooster? His alarm cluck." This is one in a series of riddle books by this author.

**Polacco, Patricia.** *Thundercake* **(New York: Philomel, 1990).** On a sultry day, the air gets damp and heavy and storm clouds begin to form. Grandma keeps her granddaughter, who is frightened of thunder, so very busy helping to bake a cake, that the little girl believes it when grandmother tells her she's very brave. A recipe for this cake is at the end, and it's a treat, just like the story.

**Silverstein, Shel.** *Where the Sidewalk Ends* **(New York: Harper and Row, 1974).** This poetry book is a classic. For the first time, some children enjoy poetry when they listen to these catchy, zany rhythms and rhymes. A favorite with children of all ages.

**Westervelt, Linda.** *Roger Tory Peterson's ABC of Birds.* **Pictures by Roger Tory Peterson and Seymour Levin (New York: Universe Publishing, 1995).** Go on a bird hunt through the alphabet with colorful birds portrayed realistically from all over the globe. Contains much information about the birds.

**(CHAPTER BOOK) Lewis, C. S.** *The Lion, the Witch and the Wardrobe* **(New York: Amereon, 1976).** Four children enter the world of Narnia through a wardrobe, and their life is never the same. Children are enchanted with this story.

# APRIL

A new season is here! The birds are back, the daffodils are waving, and the outdoors is calling to all of us. Bring as much of the outdoors inside as you can. This month can provide a wealth of learning opportunities in the Science Center with growing things. Put shades of green and yellow at the easel and liven up the indoors with fresh paintings or an art mural. Read stories and poems about springtime and have students create their own from their shift in activities and sports that enable them to be outdoors more. Take stock of the Learning Centers. Are they still inviting? Perhaps this is the time for a spring cleaning, with fresh signs and new characters to be in charge of the centers.

We still have an exciting classroom right here, and students need to know that it is just as inviting indoors when there's learning going on. There is a lot to learn. Instill in students the idea that that's part of the joy of learning . . . to know that there's always more . . . a second helping, more pies to cut into, and more cookies to chew. Learning never lets you down; you finish one thing and go on to the next. There's always more to investigate and there always will be. The pay-off is that students keep getting better, more knowledgeable, and more capable. School does that to (and for) you!

# FOCUS ON READING

## SPRING GROWTH

As if by magic, many students enjoy a spurt of growth in reading in the spring. Skills that you have been working on all year are getting easier for students, but many still need review work.

When students return from spring vacation, you need to check, once again, the guidelines for grade three that have been prepared at the district and state levels. Have all of the skills been addressed this year in this classroom? If not, plan to do so in the few months that remain. That needs to become a priority.

## HIPPITY HOP INTO NATIONAL LIBRARY WEEK

Each April, libraries across the United States promote reading and libraries. This is sponsored by the American Library Association (ALA). Contact www.ala.org/events/promoevents/.

Also, bring in Easter stories from the library for students to enjoy. They can construct a large paper basket for their folder, and print the book titles on egg shapes.

## MAKE BUNNY BOOKS

Students can cut out a white, brown, or tan rabbit shape and decorate the rabbit with construction paper clothing. Be sure the bunny is carrying a basket of eggs. Make a flip-top book of the egg basket.

## ASSESSMENT TIME

Once again, it's time to assess student skills in reading. It is possible to use the same assessment tool that was used previously so that student growth can be measured and comparisons made.

If a student has not made the desired progress and is not keeping up with the class, *this is the time to have a parent conference.* Do not wait any longer. Prepare parents now for what they can do to help the student. Just alerting parents to the possibility that the student may face retention or summer classes sometimes causes parents to double their efforts at home. They see to it that school work is still a priority in the life of the child. This can make a big difference in outcome.

## MONTH OF POETRY (IDIOMS)

"Idioms" refer to the rather unusual way that words are put together in a sentence, either verbal or in writing, to convey a thought. They are rather colorful and are used in informal speech.

How do we learn these? Often native English speakers learn them as children, by hearing them said in a particular setting over and over again. They crop up repeatedly in literature, so reading also helps. They're second nature to us, and even though people use idioms all the time, they might not know the word *idiom* itself. Teaching idioms to a non–English-speaking person who is just learning the language is challenging.

Students do enjoy working with idioms, and they like to draw the visual interpretation of an idiom. It's a good interplay of the visual and verbal connection between art and language because with the art students can portray a "literal translation" of the saying, which tickles their fancy. Listed below are some examples of idioms that students can illustrate:

- I can't go to the ballgame today, but *I'd like a raincheck.*
- Avery was in a grouchy mood and Tammi asked him if he *got up on the wrong side of the bed.*
- Karlisha's mother was angry and *jumped down her throat.*
- Carl has *a nose for news* and came back with the story.

- Everyone missed the answer so we were *in the same boat.*
- Gage got a new parakeet and *is on cloud nine.*
- Be sure to *drop me a line* when you get back from your trip.
- The third time Raymie's camera broke, everyone agreed *it was a lemon.*
- Hussein has scooters *on the brain.*
- Brandon *bent over backwards* to please the teacher.

The "Amelia Bedelia" stories by Peggy Parish and *The King Who Rained* by Fred Gwynne are good examples of the use of idioms in storytelling. Urge students to be on an "Idiom Alert" this month. Copy them on a chart when they're found. Use them to liven up story writing.

## MONTH OF POETRY (SIMILIES)

A similie is a colorful phrase or term that uses the word "as" or "like" frequently in making something clear. Students can devise their own similies, once they catch onto the method. When they read poetry this month, they'll need a big piece of chart paper on which to write down all the ones they find.

Here are some to read to students so they understand the concept:

---

### Similies using "like"

- The lights *sparkled like diamonds.*
- He *cried like a baby* when he got the news.
- When she's excited, she *chatters like a monkey.*
- In her muddy dress, she *stood out like a sore thumb.*

---

After reading these aloud to students, write just the similie on the chalkboard. Give students an opportunity to make up their own similies. Ask them what could sparkle like diamonds (water, a waterfall, night sky, fireworks, etc.).

---

### Similies using "as"

- My tire was *as flat as a pancake.* (Ask students what else could be that flat that isn't supposed to be, such as a basketball, football, and so on.)
- The bananas were *as green as grass.*
- The puppy was *as cute as a button.*
- His snore was *as loud as thunder.*

---

There are many similies in fairy tales, folktales, and fables. Reread some of the short Aesop's fables for an abundance of them. Some include: as dry as a bone, as happy as a lark, as hungry as a bear, as quick as a wink, as sly as a fox, as sweet as honey, and as strong as an ox.

## COMPOSING SIMILIES

Students can be encouraged to compose their own similies. You can write incomplete ones on the chalkboard and students can fill in the spaces with one word or with a phrase. Accept all attempts. Some students do well with this, and for some it takes a little longer. This is where the student who has read a great deal, or the student who has been read to, usually has the edge.

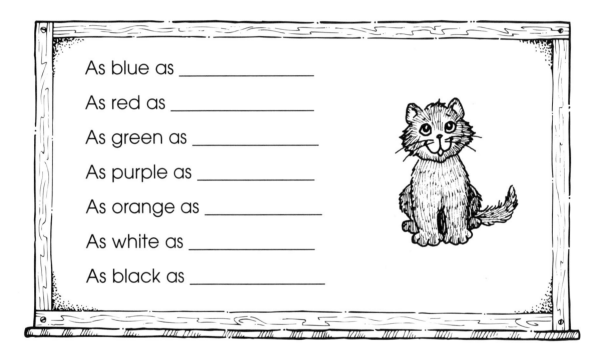

As blue as _____

As red as _____

As green as _____

As purple as _____

As orange as _____

As white as _____

As black as _____

In the beginning, students will usually try to complete the similie with just one word, such as "as white as snow" or "as black as night." That is fine for a beginning. Next, move the students to phrases, such as "as white as fresh snow on the rooftops" or "as white as a blank sheet of paper."

## CREATE A CHARACTER USING SIMILIES

Students can create story characters using similies and then make that character come to life by writing a short story about him or her. It can be an animal or a person. Think of the character in this way:

| | | | |
|---|---|---|---|
| as tall as | eyes as big (or small) as | ears as | neck as |
| teeth as | skin as | hands as | fingers as |
| lips as | hair as | arms as | legs as |

When students paint or draw this character, it should be colorful indeed because they have all of these descriptions as clues.

## READ-A-STORY (MEDIA)

Give students an opportunity to read aloud a favorite short story into a cassette tape recorder microphone. They will need to go to a quiet area of the room, and other students should be notified that this area is "off limits" to them for the time being. A large appliance box, decorated as "The Recording Studio" and turned around so that the entrance/exit is facing the wall, works well as a special place to read and record stories.

Students can use the following format. SAY: "The title of this book is _____. The author is _____ and the illustrator is _____. Your story reader is (student's name)." They can read the story and, when it is finished, say, "The End."

Put several stories on a tape, or use one tape per story. Some students may be interested in making up a story quiz sheet for all who listen to the story.

# FOCUS ON LANGUAGE ARTS

## MORE READING OPPORTUNITIES

Some reading skills have been addressed in the previous sections; however, many more reading opportunities will be available this month in the area of Language Arts and in other sections of the book as we go through the month and the year. Always be on the alert for reading links to other subject areas.

## RICKY THE RASCAL RACCOON (R-CONTROLLED VOWELS)

Raccoons are frisky rascals! In the case of the vowels, the letter "r" changes the sound of them. A vowel followed by an "r" takes on a different sound. Listen carefully to the long, short, and r-controlled vowel sounds:

| *Long* | *Short* | *R-Controlled* |
|--------|---------|----------------|
| a | aah | ar |
| e | eh | er |
| i | ih | ir |
| o | ah | or |
| u | uh | er |

There have been many stories about how Ricky the Rascal Raccoon got the upper hand on the vowels and how they come to share their sound with him. Have you heard this one? Settle back and listen.

## Ricky Raccoon and the Vowel Dogs

One day, the vowels decided to take their dogs for a walk. The dogs were named after the vowels (the long sounds). Vowel A's dog was called "A," Vowel E's dog was called "E," Vowel I's dog was called "I," Vowel O's dog was called "O," and Vowel U's dog was called "U." They all wore little plaid dog coats with the big letter sewn on the side of the coat.

The vowels decided to play a game of volleyball, and they tied their dogs to a nearby tree so they could have a rest and yet be safe. Well, little did the vowels know that Ricky the Rascal Raccoon was watching from behind a bush, and when the vowels were in the middle of their game, he changed the coats on the dogs. Ricky also cast a spell on the dogs so they were quite groggy.

When the vowels returned and greeted the dogs, the dogs didn't jump up and wag their tail like they usually did. When Vowel A took the dog with the vowel "A" on its coat and said, "Come along, little A," the dog wouldn't budge. Instead, it went over to Vowel O. When Vowel O took the dog with the vowel "O" on its coat and said, "Come along, little O," the dog wouldn't budge. Instead, it went over to Vowel U.

This had never happened before, and so the vowels were puzzled. Their pets wouldn't come when they were called. Once Vowel E called to the dog with the letter "E" on its coat, and the dog with the letter "I" on its coat came over and whimpered. What could be the matter?

Along came Ricky, swaggering down the path with a black bag in his hand. He told the vowels that he was going to nursing school and was going to become a pet specialist. The vowels told him of the strange behavior of their dogs, and Ricky stood on his hind legs, scratched his chin, furrowed his brow, and walked all around the dogs, pretending to look them over very carefully.

"Well, for one thing," said Ricky, "dogs don't wear coats. Those coats don't fit well, either. Try changing them around." They changed them and changed them again until two dogs perked up a little when their sound was called.

But Ricky the Rascal Raccoon shook his head and told the vowels he had heard of a case like this once before, and it would take a lot of nursing to get the vowel dogs back on their feet.

"Will it take a week?" asked Vowel A.

"Longer than that," answered Ricky.

"Will it take a month?" asked Vowel E.

"Longer than that," scowled Ricky, licking his chops.

"Will it take a year?" asked Vowel I.

"Oh, much longer than that!" sighed Ricky.

"How can we afford a nurse? asked Vowel O.

"Maybe I can help you out so you won't lose all your savings," cooed Ricky.

"Anything! Anything!" said Vowel U.

"OK. I'll stay close to them, and watch over them, but you will have to feed me AND let me use your vowel sounds."

"Agreed!" said the vowels at once.

Ricky passed his hand over the vowel dogs and took away just enough of the spell so that the dogs jumped up and ran to their masters. They looked better already, but still not completely well. It would take a long time for Ricky to cure them, if he ever did.

So that is how we have Ricky the Rascal Raccoon controlling the vowel sounds. He follows the vowels around with their pets. He's on their heels! Sometimes the dogs seem to get well and the vowels wonder if they need Ricky's services any longer, and as soon as they mention it to him, the dogs get sluggish again.

"Oh, we're so fortunate to have Ricky for our dog nurse," the vowels all agree. "He has a magic touch." Ricky just eats his meal and howls, "ar, er, ir, or, ur." The End.

## SILENT LETTERS (KN, WR, GH)

Be on the lookout for silent letters such as kn, wr, gh. At one time, in days gone by, all of these letters were pronounced out loud. "Knight," derived from German, was said as "k.nah.guht." Now, "kn" says "n," "wr" says "r," and "gh" says "f."

Students may be able to make up some fanciful tales, like the one above with Ricky the Rascal Raccoon, using these letter patterns.

## "YOU HAVE REACHED THE READING HOT LINE"

A chart can be made for the classroom in the shape of a telephone answering machine. A message, supposedly coming from the tape inside, can be printed in large letters with quotation marks around the phrase "You have reached the Reading Hot Line." Then listed on the space below can be instructions to press the appropriate number for help when trying to figure out a word (much as we hear when using the telephone):

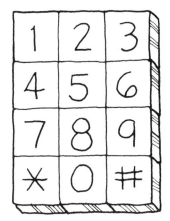

Press 1—Look for little words in big words.

Press 2—Look for the rimes (*ack, act, an,* etc.).

Press 3—Look for the root word.

Press 4—Look for the blends.

Press 5—Is Ricky controlling the vowels? (*ar, er, ir, or, ur*)

Press 6—Is the beginning letter silent? (*kn, gn*)

Press 7—What word would make sense?

Press 8—Check your word file or word bank.

Press 9—Ask a friend or ask the teacher.

Press 10—Goodbye. Leave it for now. Call back later.

(See Reproducible Activity Pages.)

## SCRAMBLED OR SUNNY SIDE UP?

Cut out egg shapes from construction paper and place them in a toy frying pan. On some egg shapes, print words that are scrambled so that students have to figure out the word puzzle.

Cut out yellow and white egg shapes from paper, and place them in another frying pan. Staple the yellow egg on top of the white egg, or vice versa. Print a word on the top one. Print a synonym for that word on the one underneath. How many can students guess?

They can "cook up more eggs" for this project. Making real egg salad for sandwiches (check for food allergies) could be a good treat this month. Students can help with the preparation, which requires reading, listening, speaking, and then writing about it. This could be made into a little book, for which they would be using their language arts skills.

# WORD ORIGINS AND SAYINGS*

1. **neither head nor tail.** This means "neither one thing nor another," or something that is not clear. The expression dates back to the seventeenth century. The word *head* means "beginning" and *tail* means the end. So, it means that you can't make sense of either the beginning or the ending of a story. It's all tangled up. Today we say, "I can't make heads or tails of this."

2. **itching palm.** This means you have your hand out and are ready for some money, or a desire for gain even if it means taking a bribe. It is believed to come from William Shakespeare. Even before Shakespeare's time, other body parts were used in sayings, such as: "itching tongue" (craving to repeat gossip); "itching foot" (craving for travel); and "itching ear" (craving to hear something new).

3. **other fish to fry.** This means "to have other things to do." The German version is *andere Dinge zu tun haben,* and the French version is *il a bien d'autres chiens a fouetter,* which means "he has many other dogs to whip." This first appeared in print in English around the late 1600s, but it had been familiar in spoken English before then.

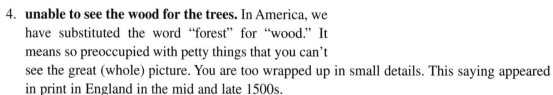

4. **unable to see the wood for the trees.** In America, we have substituted the word "forest" for "wood." It means so preoccupied with petty things that you can't see the great (whole) picture. You are too wrapped up in small details. This saying appeared in print in England in the mid and late 1500s.

5. **to save face** or **to lose face.** This means to save (or lose) one's prestige, one's dignity. If you try to save face, you are trying to avoid humiliation or disgrace. You can avoid losing face by doing the same. The Chinese use only *tiu lien,* which means "to lose face." The English coined the phrase "to save face."

# WRITING SKILLS

## A SPRING CHECK-UP (SPACE AND SLANT)

Time for a spring tune-up for writing skills. These are some of the things we need to be aware of with writing, and they can be improved upon daily. Students need to take the finished product seriously and move their pencil across the page slowly, and with the same amount of pressure throughout. Writing is a skill that improves with practice. Have models in the Writing Center for them to trace over and copy. Determine which skills students need to work on after the check-up.

Check up on the following:

- formation of letters
- slant of the letters

---

*Source: *Heavens to Betsy! And Other Curious Sayings* by Charles Earle Funk.

- spacing within words
- spacing between words
- speed of writing
- posture while writing

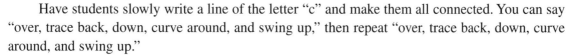

## FORMATION AND SLANT

Have students slowly write a line of the letter "e" and make them all connected. You can get them started by saying "under, up, over, down; under, up, over, down" in a measured tone.

Have students slowly write a line of the letter "c" and make them all connected. You can say "over, trace back, down, curve around, and swing up," then repeat "over, trace back, down, curve around, and swing up."

## OPEN AND CLOSE "TUNE-UP" GARAGE

Just as a garage mechanic opens and closes valves, tightens some and loosens others, so too do we need to become like a garage mechanic for our writing. *Pretend that the student is the driver, the pencil is the car, and the paper is the road.* Try the following ideas for working with the skill of handwriting as a spring tune-up:

- *Letter e*—Is it open or closed? Is it opened too wide (loop too large)? If so, close it. If it looks more like the letter "i," then we need to work on opening the loop. It requires a movement up, around a curve to the left, and back down.
- *letter i*—Is it open or closed? It needs to be shut tight. The letter "i" requires a movement up and back down the same line—no loop.
- *letter o*—Is it closed or open? It needs to be shut tight at the top so nothing can escape from within. This requires an overstroke from the bottom line to the middle of the line above, then a retrace part way down to the bottom line, around the curve, and back up to meet the stroke and close it.

## DRIVING PRACTICE—WATCH THE ROAD, WATCH YOUR SPEED

Make a lined reproducible page. Put one letter on a line and skip a space before placing the next letter on the line. (Students can then practice two lines of the letter.) Run off enough copies so that each student can slowly practice the letter formation. Run off extras for the Writing Center, and make a master copy that is covered in a transparent folder.

It will be most helpful if you use the analogy and students understand that *the pencil is the car, the paper is the road, and they are the driver.*

## DRIVING PRACTICE TERMS

Refer to writing as "driving practice." Use the following terms:

- "right turns" and "left turns"
- "back up straight"
- "you stopped too soon right here"
- "look here, you crossed over the line—good thing a truck wasn't coming"
- "this is a straight road—no curves"
- "this is a hilly road—watch it"
- "you've got to back up on the same road—you're in the ditch here"
- "you're driving much too fast—slow down or you'll get a ticket"

This will put some renewed interest in writing. Give out tickets for speeding (writing too fast). Decide what to do when a student receives three tickets. Give out badges for good "manuevering," and so on.

# LISTENING SKILLS

## LISTEN TO POETRY

Students can listen to many types of poetry this month, in addition to those in the "Author/Illustrator Section." Write short poems on a chart and have students memorize them. Then say them in groups of four or five, while others listen. Get cassette recordings at the local library of poets reading their own poetry, and also recordings of interviews with poets. Students can have the experience of listening to the authors in this way.

## WHO'S THAT KNOCKING AT MY DOOR?

You can make a cassette tape of sounds in the environment. Take the recorder home and record the sounds of the following: telephone ringing, the doorbell, someone knocking at the door, the sound of the car's engine revving up, the dog barking, door slamming shut, music on the radio, news broadcast, keys jingling on a key ring, and so on. Then play it for students and see if they can determine what these sounds are. Many are "background sounds." We get so used to them that we don't pay much attention to them.

Encourage students to go home and listen for one minute to sounds in their environment and then share them the next day. We can get many more sounds to add to a list, such as: microwave bell, baby crying, tea kettle whistling, coffee perking, alarm clock bell, and many more sounds that students will hear when they are listening for them—even where the creaks are on the stairs (like the third one from the top).

## LISTENING TO FUNNY STORIES (SERIES BOOKS)

Students need a good dose of humor in their book reading, and if you have an abundance of good books in your classroom library that rotate regularly (about every three weeks), chances are students will have an opportunity to laugh at a character, or laugh at some impossible situation, or amusing descriptions, or even laugh when the author surprises everyone with something unexpected! Be sure to check with the children's librarian for good books that are humorous.

Series books are often enjoyable when read aloud by you to the entire student group.

Some excellent BOOKS IN A SERIES are the "Ramona" books by Beverly Cleary. They include *Ramona, the Brave; Ramona and Her Father;* and *Ramona Quimby, Age 8.* Beverly Cleary also has an excellent series on "Henry Huggins."

Students enjoy the "Blossoms" books by Betsy Byars, such as *Blossoms Meet the Vulture Lady* and *Blossoms and the Green Phantom.*

Also, the "Anastasia" series by Lois Lowry is amusing. These books include *Anastasia Krupnik; Anastasia Has the Answers;* and *Anastasia at Your Service.*

## WORDLESS PICTURE BOOKS INVITE LISTENING

Have a variety of wordless picture books that you obtain from the school library or the community library. Go through them with the students, one frame at a time, and "listen" for the sounds going on in the story, and "listen" for what someone could be saying.

Then have students tell the story, or write text to go along with the wordless picture book.

Students can make wordless picture books on their own, and tell the story that accompanies the pictures.

# SPEAKING SKILLS

## A SPRINGTIME LISTENING/SPEAKING WALK

It's that time of year when outdoors the birds are singing, squirrels are scampering over dry leaves, car horns are honking, and trees are swishing in the breeze. Or maybe it's just a very, very quiet day when you can hear your own self breathing. Go on a walk around the playground and listen for the nature sounds and for the manmade sounds.

Then come back into the classroom and talk about the sounds heard. Have students imitate the sounds while others try to guess what they are. A good book to accompany this experience is *The Listening Walk* by Paul Showers, illustrated by Aliki.

## READERS THEATRE

Informality is one key in Readers Theatre. Students read from scripts that they write, based on selections from stories they especially enjoy. The lines can be spoken rather than read, and certainly are not meant to be memorized. There are no sets or lighting or scenery to develop. Students don't enter and exit the "stage." Rather, they focus upon a retelling of the story.

Determine what book students are interested in working with and count the number of characters needed, as well as the number of readers for narration. If six are needed, then those six will form a Readers Theatre group for that particular book. Other students will work on other books. Later, different people can work together on another set of favorites. Determine the time frame for the production, which includes preparation and presentation.

Select a story that has a lot of dialogue, so that the readers move the plot along. The narrators can fill in where needed to indicate passage of time, or any other events that are not heavy with dialogue. The readers can stand or sit in front of the class. When not reading, they may wish to turn around. This will depend upon the decisions made by the group.

Some of these are so successful, that Readers Theatre groups may wish to become a traveling group that performs for the first and second graders, and perhaps for fourth graders.

At times when it is difficult to sign up an interested audience, perhaps students can go to the main entryway or in an alcove in the main hall, and perform their Readers Theatre for those who are passing by.

By all means, use videotape to record these groups. They are priceless.

Some good "starter" stories for inexperienced Readers Theatre groups can be familiar short folktales like "The Little Red Hen" and fairy tales like "Cinderella." There are many multicultural versions of the Cinderella tale, such as *Mufaro's Beautiful Daughters* (African-American version), by John Steptoe; *The Egyptian Cinderella* and *The Korean Cinderella,* both by Shirley Climo, illustrated by Ruth Heller; *Ye-Shen, A Cinderella Story from China,* retold by Ai-Ling Louie, illustrated by Ed Young; *The Rough Face Girl* (Native American), by Rafe Martin, illustrated by David Shannon; and, of course, many versions of the European tale with lovely illustrations. Look for *Cinderella* illustrated by Susan Jeffers.

## WHEN WE GO HOME, WHAT DOES THE DESK SAY TO THE CLOCK?

To generate speech that revolves around what is going on in the classroom, ask students what they suppose one object would say to another object if they "came to life" in the classroom at night when we were all at home. What, for example, did they learn since September? What did they learn this month? What are they good at? What do they need to work on? What do they say about us?

For a more fanciful approach, some students like to tell stories about pencils that go to the cafeteria kitchen in search of food, or rulers that go to the gym and play volleyball, and so on.

## PICTURE BOOK COMPARISONS

Have students compare art styles of different picture books. Start them off with one, and talk about the colors. Are they bold, bright, and loud? Or are they muted and quiet? Are the lines soft and flowing or are they straight and angular? Go part way through a book looking at the art style. If you could hear music playing in the background, would it be loud or quiet?

Then select a book that is very different in terms of color and design and talk about that. Before long, students will be making their own comparisons and will be more attuned to the art and how it goes along with the text.

Some possible book comparisons are: *Miss Rumphius* by Barbara Clooney (soft lines, gentle colors); *Dots, Speckles and Stripes* by Tana Hoban (bright, bold shapes); *Where the Forest Meets the Sea* by Jeannie Baker (collage with rough textures); and *Cukoo* by Lois Ehlert (cut paper, bright bold shapes).

Give each student a picture book to study. Then have them work with a partner to make a comparison of the art work in the two books. The room will be buzzing with conversation about an interesting topic—styles in art. When students do this, their own art work is more detailed and they are apt to take more time with their work.

## CARTOON TALK

Word bubbles that appear above cartoon characters in comic strips contain words that are spoken or words that the character is thinking. Have students examine a variety of comic strips (bring in the Sunday paper for several weeks) so they can get the idea of writing within the bubbles, and that the writing is "conversation" or "talk."

Cover up the words within the bubbles of several cartoons, run them off on the copier, and have students fill in the conversation. This sounds easier than it is, so give students time to examine the action taking place and the facial expressions. Then they can share the comics with the rest of the class. They will all be different, so telling them should be interesting and fun.

## CUMULATIVE TALES

These repetitious tales, where the same words are repeated over and over again, offer an excellent opportunity for speaking aloud. Read *There Was an Old Lady Who Swallowed a Fly, Old MacDonald Had a Farm, The Gingerbread Boy, The Little Red Hen,* and others. Make a cassette recording of these tales. Soon students will be able to retell them by heart.

# FOCUS ON SPELLING

## WRITE THE WORD 100 TIMES?

Make a very long strip of narrow paper for each spelling word of the week. Eventually this paper will be hung from ceiling to floor, or hung on the wall or bulletin board. Put a spelling word in large letters at the top of each strip. Then, for example, if there are 20 students in the class, each student writes the spelling word five times. When you reach 100, hang it up. Do the math. If there are 25 students, figure out how many times each student must write the word in order to reach 100. (When the paper is taken down, use the other side in the Writing Center or Math Center for scrap paper.)

## SPELLING RABBITS

Cut out a rabbit shape for each student. They can write the spelling words in the center of the rabbit. Decorate the edges with the words intertwined with flowers. This calls attention to where the flower vine needs to bend and twist for tall letters and short ones. Study, using this colorful rabbit.

## GEOBOARD SPELLING

Students can use the geoboard and colored rubber bands to shape their spelling words. Try this kinesthetic approach.

## BOUNCING-BALL SPELLING

Students can bounce a big ball as they spell out a word. Say the word on the first bounce. Say each letter on one bounce. Then say the word again on the last bounce. (For example, The word "April" would have seven bounces.) If the ball is missed, have the student start over again until he or she does this with success.

## SPELLING KITES

Make diamond-shaped kites and decorate them for spring. Spelling words of the week can be written on bow shapes and attached to a string. Then attach the string to the diamond-shaped kite and hang them from a high place in the room.

## CRAYON-RESIST SPELLING QUILT

On an 8½- by 11-inch piece of white manila paper, students can write or print their spelling words using crayons. Encourage them to make thick lines, press hard, and color in the fat letters. Then, using a brush, watercolors and water, have students brush over the sheet with a watercolor wash. It's okay for the colors to run together. Use bright, spring colors—no dark colors. After these are dry, they can be hung up on the bulletin board close together. Make vertical and horizontal strips of pink or green paper to separate the student work. It's a colorful and exciting way to study spelling.

# FOCUS ON MATH

## FRACTIONS

A fraction may be thought of as part of a whole or as part of a group. It's important for students to recognize that a term such as "one half" refers to a part of a whole. They need to learn that one half is one of two equal pieces, or one of two equal parts of a group. Halves must be the same size.

Students need continual work with manipulatives to show fractional parts of units and groups. Have cardboard circular pies and cardboard circular cakes in the Math Center this month. There are many commercial items of this sort available, but you can also easily make them. Students can take them apart as they work with $\frac{1}{2}$, $\frac{1}{4}$, and $\frac{3}{4}$.

Also have rectangular cardboard cakes and candy bars, so that students can work with $\frac{1}{3}$ and $\frac{2}{3}$. Students can work with clay and plastic knives, and cut circular pie shapes or rectangular cake shapes into one half and one quarter shapes. Remember, fractions have to have *equal* parts.

When writing a fraction, the number on top (*numerator*) of the line tells how many parts, and the number on the bottom (*denominator*) of the line tells how many all together.

So, if we see $\frac{1}{6}$, we know there are six pieces all together, and we are focusing upon one of them. The fraction $\frac{1}{6}$ can also be thought of as *one of the six* pieces.

Hold up fraction flashcards and have students say the fractions as follows:

| *Hold Up* | *Students Say* |
|-----------|----------------|
| 2/3 | Two of the three pieces |
| 11/16 | Eleven of the sixteen pieces |
| 2/7 | Two of the seven pieces |
| 4/9 | Four of the nine pieces |

## FRACTIONS GO WELL WITH FOOD

Cut a candy bar into thirds, or three equal pieces. Hold up one piece and say, "This is one of the three pieces and we write it this way: $\frac{1}{3}$." Hold up two pieces and demonstrate for students that it is written this way: $\frac{2}{3}$.

Cut an apple in half, or two equal pieces. Hold up one piece and say, "This is one of the two equal pieces and we write it this way: $\frac{1}{2}$."

Keep cutting up food pieces so that everyone has a morsel of a fraction to eat. (See Reproducible Activity Pages.)

## FRACTIONS AND DIVISION

There is a relationship between these two functions. We *divide* a cookie into two equal parts. Demonstrate this and write it as ¹/₂. Using trading chips, marbles, buttons, and so on, have students work with dividing the whole into parts. For example, divide 16 marbles in half and you will have ⁸/₁₆, or 8 in each group. Divide each of the two groups of 8 in half and you will have ⁴/₁₆, or 4 in each group. Later you can show students how to reduce these fractional parts into lower, common denominators.

## FRACTIONS COME BEFORE DECIMALS

Work with fractions *before* working with decimals. A fractional part is represented in writing, to the *right* of the decimal point. We are working with a base ten number system so .25 is the same as 25/100 or ¹/₄. A diagram for decimals might look something like this:

| hundreds | tens | ones | **decimal** | tenths of one | hundredths of one |
|----------|------|------|-------------|---------------|-------------------|

Thus, .03 is the same as ³/₁₀₀. When we say numbers to the right of the decimal point, they always have "th" endings.

## WORKING WITH CALCULATORS

If you have a calculator, it is easy to demonstrate and easy for students to follow. Introduce the calculator, the buttons, and their functions. Show where the "C" or "Clear" button is and explain that this needs to be pressed when a transaction is over, or else the numbers remain "on duty" and the calculator will give a wrong answer for the next problem. Distribute the calculators and do some warm-up exercises:

- Press phone number and then clear.
- Press street number and then clear.
- Press age and clear.
- Press ages of family members and clear.
- Press numbers in the room (windows, desks, sinks) and clear.

## CALCULATOR DIRECTIONS

When asking students to press the number 46, for example, say "Press four, press six." When asking them to press 139, say "Press one, press three, press nine." Or, "press one, three, nine." Give directions slowly and deliberately.

You cannot say "Press one hundred thirty-nine, because students don't see a button that says 139." So it has to be distinctly stated as "Press one, press three, press nine." Then have them notice that the number "139" does show up in the viewer.

## CALCULATOR EXERCISE

Work with small groups of students or with the whole class and give all students the same directions. Make sure they know where the plus, minus, and equal keys are. Here is an example:

- Turn on.
- Press the Clear button.
- Press 1, 6.
- Press the plus sign (+).
- Press 3, 1.
- Press the plus sign (+).
- Press 4, 2.
- Press the equal sign (=).

Ask students what answers they got and record them on the bulletin board. The correct answer is 89, but all students may not have that number. Some may have pressed a different key or a different function along the way, so do the same exercise again. Then ask for the answer again. Are more students closer to the answer of "89"?

If one or two students are consistently missing the mark, then watch them during the process in order to determine what it is they are doing incorrectly. Some students have worked with calculators up to this point, some may have one or two at home, and some students may never have had an opportunity to work with one. They need practice.

## MATH CENTER CALCULATORS

Have several calculators in the Math Center so that students can check their own work when they do activity pages there. Also, during the day when they are working with math at their own seat, they may be able to go to the Math Center to check their answers for accuracy. This is a good way for them to get immediate feedback.

If each student has a calculator, determine whether these will be kept at their desk or in a prescribed location in the room.

## USES FOR THE CALCULATOR

Make a series of activity cards for use at the Math Center, such as:

- Count to 100 by 5's.
- Count to 100 by 2's.
- Count to 100 by 10's.
- Add 56 + 42. What is your answer?

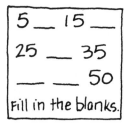

- Add 56 + 42 again, and this time keep track of how long it took using the calculator.
- Add 63 + 41 by doing mental math. Record your answer. Now check it on the calculator. (You can have many activity cards of this type at your Math Center.)
- Make an estimate. Take three numbers and write them down. Decide "about how much the total will be." Write it down.
- Check your estimate using the calculator.

Calculator activities can be done independently or with a math buddy. Students enjoy using them. But, remember that calculators do not take the place of learning the math facts. Students need to be able to operate without them.

Students can write short stories about an imaginary character who was dependent upon the calculator. This day he really needed it! The story can be entitled "The Day Brewster's Batteries Died" when Brewster was absolutely counting on the calculator, AND couldn't do the math without it. Then what? Have students share their stories.

## LESS THAN/MORE THAN

Students are used to having the largest number win, and can easily pick out a number that is "more than" another. Periodically work with "less than" and have the one with the number "less than" another number be the winner.

The spinner in many math games provides a good manipulative and thus a good opportunity for two students to play "Less Than." (See Reproducible Activity Pages.)

# FOCUS ON SOCIAL STUDIES

## APRIL CITIZENSHIP FOCUS

Being a good leader takes *courage*. Sometimes a good leader must make a decision that is not popular with his or her best friend. It is not easy. Here are some examples of leadership courage in our third-grade classroom.

*Discussion #1.* (Read aloud to students.)

---

You have been called upon to be the leader of the debate team. Your team will debate the students in the class across the hall. You may select one debater. Now, you want to get an able student, one who studies hard and answers quickly. Your job is to bring honor to your class. You must choose now and the hand of one of your best friend's is in the air and waving wildly. You think about it for a minute but don't select your friend. Instead, you select a straight-A student. You can't help but notice the mad look on your friend's face. Did you do the right thing?

Discuss this in terms of:

- what is good for everyone
- the job that the teacher gave to you to carry out
- not always selecting your best friends but giving others a chance
- how this is going to work out with your friend

*Discussion #2:* (Read aloud to students.)

It's Springtime and the class votes to enter into a Spring Mural Art Contest for the third grades. Ms. Whan has selected you to be the head of the committee and tells you to select three classmates to help you. Your best friends are calling out to you. How should you select your mural committee?

Discuss this in terms of:

- what is good for everyone
- your responsibility to help win the contest
- the basis for selection of the three classmates (good artists but also good at getting along with others)
- not always selecting best friends but giving others a chance
- the sinking feeling you get when your best friends are unhappy with you and think you're not fair

The idea of not always selecting best friends is one that needs to be conveyed to third graders, and might also get some students "off the hook" when the hard decisions have to be made.

# PATRIOTISM

## PATRIOTIC POETRY

Cinquain (sin cané) poetry is a good vehicle to use for writing a patriotic poem. Try this formula:

1. One subject word
2. Two words that describe the person or thing named
3. Three words ending in "ing" that further describe it
4. A four-word sentence pertaining to subject word
5. One "oomph!" word to sum it all up

Here is an example:

> *Flag*
> *Stars, stripes*
> *Waving, flying, protecting*
> *Long may it wave.*
> *GLORIOUS!*

Try this technique for some of the symbols we have discussed in the Social Studies sections, such as the Liberty Bell, Bald Eagle, Uncle Sam, and so on. Use some of the colorful, descriptive words from the songs and pledges, too.

## PATRIOTIC RIDDLES

Try the "I'm thinking of something that . . ." formula for a riddle.

- "I'm thinking of something that has broad stripes." (*flag*)
- "I'm thinking of something that cracked." (*Liberty Bell*)
- "I'm thinking of something that's our flying symbol." (*eagle*)
- "I'm thinking of something that almost became our national bird." (*turkey*)
- "I'm thinking of the fourth word in our national anthem." (*you*)

## PATRIOTIC RIDDLE BOARD GAME

Students will enjoy making up their own riddles. Perhaps they can make them in the form of a board game. For example: Make a pathway of squares across a map of the USA. Put the riddles on cards. Two students can play. Stack the cards in a pile, and a student draws a card. If he or she gets the answer, he or she advances. If the player misses, he or she goes back. The number of squares to be gained or lost can be written on the riddle card.

# AREA OF FOCUS: JOBS AND LIFE IN EARLY AMERICA

## DAYS OF LONG AGO

In Colonial days, or days of long ago, young children did not go to school. Wealthy families might have had tutors for the boys. Girls were instructed in needlework and table settings. For the common family, however, the boys were apprenticed to a tradesman and learned how to work. They also were taught to write and do arithmetic if they were capable. But they had to be loyal and faithful to the craftsman. These were some of the rules a good youngster had to follow:

- You could not speak unkindly of your master.
- You could not allow anyone else to speak ill of your master.
- You could not buy or sell anything without permission.

- You worked as an apprentice from sun up to sun down, then went home and did your chores and your homework.

Have students contrast this with the life of children today. There was no such thing as after-school sports, or clubs, or teams. There were no facilities for children. Parents had to work extremely long hours just to make ends meet. There were no restaurants, no such things as radio, computers, or TV. Toys were handmade from items in the environment (rag dolls, rolled-up rag balls, sticks, and so on).

## WIGMAKERS

Being apprenticed to a wigmaker meant steady work. Wigs were very popular in England and among the colonists. The wigmaker not only made the wigs from animal hair, but colored them, curled them, and fitted them. There were many styles. Business was good since almost everyone wore a wig, and it was best to have two. While one was being cleaned and reworked, the man or woman could wear the other. The higher the person's station in life, the bigger the wig, hence the saying "big wig." (That's a saying to add to our Word Origins this month.) Young children wore caps or bonnets.

The wigmaker had to be an artist of sorts, because sometimes ribbons were added to the wig or woven in, and the wigs were perfumed and styled.

Students can make wigs from rolls of cotton batting. Also, long strips of construction paper can be glued to a swim cap or shower cap. Engage students in a discussion of "hair" and "hair care." People in many cultures around the world have been inventive with hair styles. Look for them in books.

## HATMAKERS

This was another popular trade in Colonial days. Women and men wore hats over their wigs. Most of the hats were made from felt, but animal pelts were used as well.

An apprentice had to learn how to shape the hat, roll it, clean it, mold it, and so on.

In class, girls can make and decorate hats from paper plates with ribbons that tie under the chin. Boys can make tricornered hats from newspapers. Have a "Hat Day" and wear the hats in the afternoon. Serve a fancy treat, such as pineapple chunks or berries—both delicious treats in Colonial days.

## FARRIERS

These men and apprentices put shoes on horses' hoofs. Old shoes had to be removed and foot tissue had to be cleaned. New shoes were nailed on, and often horses kicked and would bite. This was not a job for the weak-hearted. Students can simulate this very active job.

## BLACKSMITHS

This was an important trade. The blacksmith made and repaired all of the tools that other people used in their trades. There were also silversmiths and goldsmiths. In fact, these people were referred to as "Smiths." How many people with Smith as a last name do we know?

## NAMES OF TRADES

People were often known by their trade. So if you were a barber, you would be called "Barber." Have students speculate about the trades of people with these last names. Then search for more.

|              |               |                 |
|--------------|---------------|-----------------|
| Mr. Baker    | Mr. Weaver    | Mr. Shoemaker   |
| Mr. Cooper   | Mr. Mason     | Mr. Carpenter   |

Often "son" at the end of a name was given to the son of a tradesman. For example, if a man was a clerk (often pronounced clark), his son might be called "Clarkson." How many names can we find with "son" as a suffix? What resource should we check—the encyclopedia or the Yellow Pages or a directory?

Encourage students to select their name (featuring their favorite occupation) and make a nametag for the day. What might Dr. Cavity do? Or Ms. Gemstone? Or Mr. Graves?

## MAKING SOAP

Colonists took a bath once a week, on Saturday, and had to make their own soap. Soapmaking was a lot of work for them but here's a recipe for us that's quite a bit easier. You will need:

bits and pieces of old bar soap

water

container with a lid

Put the bits of bar soap in a container. Cover soap with water. Keep adding more soap and water if necessary until it all dissolves. Then shake it up or mix with a long-handled spoon. Add some fragrance. This can be placed in a liquid soap dispenser for all to enjoy.

## WHAT'S IN A FIRST NAME?

Ask students if they were named after someone in the family. Who chose their name? What name would they choose?

In early Colonial days, some children were named after a family member but many were named after people in the Bible. Some were named after traits that were considered important, such as Humility, Patience, Charity, Thanks, and so on. (These would go along with some of the good citizen traits we are discussing each month, such as Honesty and Trustworthy.) Perhaps students can take on a "trait name" for the day and live up to it. These names can be put on a slip of paper and students can draw them out of a container. Several students could have the same trait name.

## THE 13 COLONIES ON A MAP

Locate the 13 states that made up the original Colonies. Students can memorize these states that are rich in our nation's history. They are often referred to geographically as the New England Colonies (MA, CT, RI, NH), the Middle Colonies (NY, NJ, PA, DE), and the Southern Colonies (VA, MD, NC, SC, GA).

Another way for students to memorize them is to put them in alphabetical order. Memorize them in a week: three each day plus one more on Friday.

## SAYINGS THAT PERTAINED TO CHILDREN (THEN)

Students need to know that Colonial children did not have "status" in the family. They did primarily what they were told to do. Here are some sayings and thoughts that are revealing. Discuss their meaning with students:

- Children should be seen and not heard.
- Don't speak unless spoken to.
- Stand still while you're eating your dinner. (The adults sat.)
- Don't use a fork, use your fingers. (Forks were only used to procure food from a common dish, not to be put into the mouth.)
- Sit not while others stand.
- In the presence of others, sing not.
- In company, every action should be respectful.
- Let your countenance be pleasant.

## SAYINGS THAT PERTAIN TO CHILDREN (NOW)

What rules for good behavior and good manners can students come up with for life as it is today? What is acceptable behavior when with adults, or when eating in a restaurant, or when eating in the cafeteria, or when riding on a public bus, or when asked a question by someone, or when asking for something to be passed along to you?

## RESOURCE BOOKS

Two good resource books for teachers are *Colonial American Craftspeople* by Bernardine S. Stevens, and *Colonial Kids, An Activity Guide to Life in the New World* by Laurie Carlson.

# HOLIDAYS AND CELEBRATIONS

## PASSOVER

This important Jewish holiday is celebrated about the same time as Easter and lasts for eight days. It is a celebration of freedom. At one time, the Jews were slaves in Egypt until they got their freedom. Today, they remember this important time in history by gathering together and celebrating their freedom. They tell stories and make some of the traditional food for this holiday: horseradishes are eaten at the dinner and represent the bitterness of slavery, roasted eggs symbolize life, and charoses symbolize the sweetness of freedom.

## EASTER

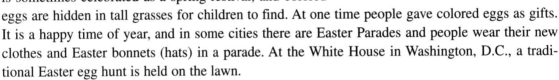

This Christian holiday, which follows Lent, is marked by family gatherings and get togethers. People decorate and color eggs, which are a symbol of life and growth, and put them in baskets with artificial grass. The Easter Bunny, representing abundance, is the one who delivers eggs in the basket, along with candies.

This holiday came to the new world via Europe. It is sometimes celebrated as a spring festival, and colored eggs are hidden in tall grasses for children to find. At one time people gave colored eggs as gifts. It is a happy time of year, and in some cities there are Easter Parades and people wear their new clothes and Easter bonnets (hats) in a parade. At the White House in Washington, D.C., a traditional Easter egg hunt is held on the lawn.

## EARTH DAY

This day is celebrated in the United States on April 22 in an effort to make the Earth a healthier and safer planet on which to live. Everyone the world over needs to become more aware of water and air pollution, overpopulation, energy, endangered species, natural resources, and people's relationship to their environment. Children in school renew their efforts to recycle items.

Students can become inventors. Have a contest to see who can make a new product using recycled items.

## NATIONAL LIBRARY WEEK

Encourage all students to apply for a library card at the local library if they have not already done so. A note to parents in the newsletter will help facilitate this. Libraries have many summer programs and special Saturday programs, so it's never too late to visit the library. Check the website: www.ala.org/events.

## NATIONAL CHERRY BLOSSOM FESTIVAL (NATION'S CAPITAL)

Over 3,000 cherry trees (a gift from the Japanese government) are planted around the Tidal Basin. Look for newspaper articles about the cherry blossom festivals. What trees are blooming in your own neighborhood?

# FOCUS ON SCIENCE

## BACK IN THE NEIGHBORHOOD

What a treat! One day you look out the window and there in the backyard is a robin pecking the ground for seeds. Welcome back! Many birds come back to the very same spot year after year after their long migration toward the south and warmer weather.

Some birds that leave cold climates to fly south will fly just far enough to locations where it will be warm and where they will have a winter food supply. Not all birds migrate to the very same place, nor for the same distances.

Some birds do take exotic trips, though. Many birds from southern Spain spend the winter in Morocco because of the increased warmth. Locate these two areas on the globe to see where the birds decide to go. The point to get across is that bird migration occurs all over the world.

## A WELCOME-BACK NEST-BUILDING BAG

It's a time for birds to build their nests. To help birds feather their nest, prepare a net bag (one that is used for onions or potatoes). In the bag place pieces of string, fluff from clothes dryers, dried grasses, soft cotton, and so on. Hang the bag from a tree limb, and birds are sure to find it and take some of the materials off in their beak. They line their nest with soft items and even use the dried grasses and twine to help hold the nest together. After a time, take the bag down and replace it with a feeder.

## NEW NEST, NEW BABIES

When birds are building their nests in the spring, it is a time for observation, *but not a time for touching.* Birds may desert their nest if a human has tampered with it. So sit quietly and wait and watch—*but do not touch bird nests.*

A clue for finding nests is that birds will build close to their food source. Since a woodpecker eats insects that live in trees, for example, it is apt to make a nest in tree holes. Birds that eat fish and other food from the sea will build close to the shore, but not in the woods and not in your backyard.

Robins often nest in bushes close to houses or in trees. They have even been known to make their nest in grapevine wreaths that hang on houses. Bluejays often nest in park trees, but they could choose an evergreen right in your backyard. Doves like evergreens, too.

The shape of a nest is a clue to its inhabitants. Robins build bowl-like nests using mud to help fortify it. The Baltimore Oriole's nest is tightly woven in an elongated shape. It is built at the edge of wooded areas with the top strands of dried grasses woven over several branches. This nest sways in the breeze and provides a gentle rocking motion for the baby birds. (See Reproducible Activity Pages.)

## MAKE BIRD NESTS

For a Science unit on birds, have students try to build a bird nest in the style and shape of a particular bird. Display these on the window ledge, and be sure to make eggs from rolled pieces of clay to place inside.

## MAKE BIRD FEEDERS

Use commercial feeders to clamp or stick to your windowpane, or make one from a milk carton. Fill it with sunflower seeds and hang it from a branch near the classroom window. Then be prepared to watch and wait.

## FEATHERS ARE SPECIAL

Only birds have feathers. No other living thing has feathers! If you spot a bird feather on the ground, pick it up, brush it off, and keep it for good luck. Make a feather-shaped bookmark with bird feather facts written on it. For example, birds comb their feathers to keep them clean. Some birds have a special gland to oil their feathers to help make them waterproof.

## ARE BIRDS REALLY TODAY'S DINOSAURS?

Some people see many comparisons between birds and dinosaurs. One thing they have in common is their feet. Most birds have four toes; most dinosaurs did, too. The most common bird foot has three toes pointing forward and one pointing back (so did flesh-eating dinosaurs). Some birds have two toes pointing forward and two pointing back, so their footprints resemble the letter "X." Some birds have only a total of three toes, with two pointing forward and one back to resemble the letter "Y." Waterfowl have webbed feet, which are a tremendous help in swimming. (See Reproducible Activity Pages.)

Secure a copy of the picture information book *The Puzzle of the Dinosaur-Bird, The Story of Archaeopteryx* by Miriam Schlein, with pictures by Mark Hallett. What makes a bird a bird and a dinosaur a dinosaur? Should the way we classify dinosaurs be changed? The author has a section entitled "You Be the Scientist," which allows readers to think about what they have learned and to then draw their own conclusions. It's a golden learning opportunity.

## LET'S DO A BIRD WARM-UP EXERCISE FOR SPRING

Students can relax and think of their favorite bird. Picture it in their mind. Then we can do some bird warm-ups:

- Flap your wings (arms) ten times.
- Flap your right wing five times.
- Flap your left wing five times.
- Flex your shoulder muscles back and forth.
- Scrunch your neck down into your shoulders three times.
- Turn your head to the right and look over your shoulder.
- Turn your head to the left and look over your shoulder.
- Bend your knees seven times.
- Jump on your right foot ten times.
- Jump on your left foot eight times.
- Fly away to the count of ten. (Flap wings and move forward three steps.)
- Stop in the tree.
- Fold in your wings (arms) slowly.
- Use your fingers to grip the branch.
- Slowly bend your knees and settle down to rest.

## BIRD PUPPETS

Help students make large paper-bag puppets. Have students slip the puppets over their heads and use them for creative play. They can also interview the birds, and give bird reports using these huge puppet heads.

## BIRD SEED SPROUTS

Bring in bird seed and sprinkle it on a large wet sponge, in an aluminum dish filled with water. The seed will sprout. Students are often very surprised that bird seed will actually sprout!

# APRIL AUTHOR STUDY: J. PATRICK LEWIS

April is the "Month of Poetry" and J. Patrick Lewis is our author selection for his versatile poetry that makes us laugh, wonder, and think, too. Mr. Lewis lives in Ohio, and for many years was a college professor of Economics. He said when he grows up, he still wants to write poetry for children to enjoy. He has an innate sense of rhythm and rhyme, and a fanciful view of the world on the one hand, and a serious view on the other. So this month we are in for a treat as we read both poetry and stories written by this author. You can also visit Mr. Lewis on his website to gain information about him and his family, as well as a listing of upcoming publications. He invites classrooms to send photos of his work that has been illustrated by students, or classroom art displays inspired by his poetry. These may even appear on his website. He is a guest speaker at many conferences and enjoys making school visits. (Log on at www.jpatricklewis.com.)

Now, swing open the door and welcome this imaginative, award-winning writer into your classroom for Poetry Month and enjoy the images that he creates with words.

# BOOKS AND SUGGESTED ACTIVITIES

*First,* for our study this month, we will take a look at some of the poetry books. They will be listed with a brief annotation. These poems are to be read aloud and savored. Enjoy the rhythm and the rhyme, and also the art work that accompanies them. One poetry book asks questions of the reader and invites interaction; another has art work interwoven with the riddles; another is a continuous story. As you will see, the style of writing is quite different.

*Second,* after the poetry books are listed, there will be a section with suggested activities for use in the classroom.

*Third,* we will take a quick peek at several picture book stories written by J. Patrick Lewis, who is every bit as skillful at story writing as he is at turning a phrase in poetry.

## *DOODLE DANDIES, POEMS THAT TAKE SHAPE* (IMAGES BY LISA DESIMINI)

These delightful poems are written in shapes, such as a dog or a giraffe. Or, as in the case of the poem "Lashondra Scores!" the poem about basketball, the words are flung from the hand, up into the air, and land *kerplunk*! right into the basket for a score. The well-chosen words contain the letter "O" which serves as the round basketball. In some poems the words are written around an object, or descend from the sky as raindrops. Here is an example of a shape poem called "Dachshund."

```
                                              g  g      r
     H                                        n  n      i
       e                                       i  i  a
         r                                     r  r  e
           e    comes the lady with the diamond t  h
              walking a dog like a sausage on a  s  t
           there goes the dog with his nose  in
           walki      the  l  with the pur    h
                n            a           p    a
                  g            d           l  i
                    y              e    r
```

## THE LITTLE BUGGERS, INSECT & SPIDER POEMS (PICTURES BY VICTORIA CHESS)

From yellow jackets to termites, praying mantises to doodlebugs, no "little bugger" has been overlooked in this collection of clever verse.

There's "The Ladybug" who "wears no disguises. She is just what she advertises: A speckled spectacle of spring, A fashion statement on the wing . . . in Nature's polka dots."

And "The Marriage of the Spider and the Fly" with Monarch caterpillar bridesmaids in so many pairs of shoes. And we meet Daddy Longlegs, who caught the garter, and Miss Cicada, the bouquet.

> *But the honeymoon was over long before the webs were cleared*
> *And the spider-bride was smiling—the groom had disappeared!*

Other side-splitters include "School Lesson" by a termite and "The Love Song of the Rhinocerous Beetle."

## FREEDOM LIKE SUNLIGHT, PRAISESONGS FOR BLACK AMERICANS (ILLUSTRATIONS BY JOHN THOMPSON)

This celebration takes a serious look at the experience of courage and human struggle in the lives of thirteen inspiring Black Americans, including steadfast Rosa Parks, track star Jesse Owens, Jazz legend Louie Armstrong, tennis pro Arthur Ashe, and others. This book received a nomination for the Coretta Scott King Award.

## THE FAT CATS AT SEA (ILLUSTRATED BY VICTORIA CHESS)

This book has twelve verses, like twelve chapters in a book, that tell the saga of "The Voyage of the Frisky Dog," a ship of fat cats who are off on an ocean adventure aboard the ship in search of sticky-goo buns for the Queen. Meet Hillary Hollery Q. McQatt the Captain ("I'm Hillary-dillery, Hollery-dollery, Hillary Hollery over the sea! A potbellied cat, Delightfully fat, There's no one as tubby as me!"); First Mate Razor-Toes Jerome; Cook Rotten Stew; and others. Will they make it to the island that has tons of sticky-goos? Read the hilarious verses to find out.

### *JULY IS A MAD MOSQUITO* (ILLUSTRATED BY MELANIE W. HALL)

From the raw days of January to the red-hot days of July to the migration of geese in October, this collection of superbly crafted poems illuminates nature and the months of the year. Read it for the images, sounds, smells, textures.

### *RIDDLE-ICIOUS* (ILLUSTRATED BY DEBBIE TILLEY)

This is a guessing game, and anyone who likes a good riddle or rhyme will enjoy these twenty-eight poems. For example:

> *It rambles through mountains, It rumbles through town,*
> *It whistles whenever It wants to slow down.*
> *When you are near it, It hisses and steams,*
> *But once you get <u>on</u> it, How gentle it seems.*     *(train)*

And see if you can guess this one:

> *The tall handsome lady, On Uncle Sam's porch*
> *Stands still as a statue, Holding a torch.*     *(Statue of Liberty)*

Other poetry books include the best-selling *A Hippopotamusn't*; *Ridicholas Nicholas, More Animal Poems*; *The La-di-da Hare*; *Black Swan/White Crow, A Book of Haiku,* and many others.

## SUGGESTED USE IN THE CLASSROOM

For poetry, it's a good idea to read and enjoy the poems again and again. Be sure to point out the illustrations that go along with the poems that tickle your fancy, especially many of the animal poems. After reading a book aloud, leave it in the Reading Center so that students can read the poems on their own and examine the drawings more thoroughly.

After students become familiar with poetry and the rhythm and the rhyme, and the way similies and idioms are used, they may want to try writing their own poetry. Students can:

- Create a shape poem.
- Illustrate a poem.
- Write idioms.
- Review homophones.

- Create a riddle.
- Write haiku.
- Write more similies.
- Write a cinquain poem.

- Paint a mural of the poems in a particular book.

- Paint large pictures at the easel of animals in a poem. When they are dry, students can outline them in black paint using a broad brush. Wait for the paint to dry and cut out the figures. Now arrange them around the room, or on the door, or on a mural and paint in the background.

- Read a poem without looking at the illustration. How does the illustrator know what to draw? Students can experiment with this interplay of words and art.

- Look at the art work. How does the poet know what to write? Students can experiment with the interplay of art and words from this point of view.

- Make art displays of the poetry using different media, such as papier-mâché, tissue-paper art, construction-paper 3-D animals, clay models, etc.

- Work with descriptive words to define an animal (use the thesaurus).

- Review alliteration and use it in poetry.

- Look through the books for examples of "playing with words," such as *butterfly* and *flutter by*.

- Examine the illustrations done by different artists to determine how this affects the poetry.

- Make stick puppets of characters and critters and memorize a short verse about them.

# PICTURE BOOKS BY J. PATRICK LEWIS

## THE TSAR AND THE AMAZING COW (PICTURES BY FRISO HENSTRA)

The setting is far away in Russia where an old couple own an extraordinary cow that begins to speak, and tells them to drink her magic milk. They do and become young again. They are transported back "to the green time of their years." The Tsar gets wind of the magic cow and must have the milk, and it's then that amazing things happen.

## THE CHRISTMAS OF THE REDDLE MOON (PICTURES BY GARY KELLEY)

On Christmas Eve, a young boy and his sister set out across the heath to exchange presents with their cousins. On the way back home, a shortcut leads them into a swirling blizzard and they become hopelessly lost. The last thing they remember are the eyes of the cat of Wee Mary Fever, a strange old woman who lives on the heath. Mary lights up the sky with a red glow and, with the aid of a welcome stranger, the children make it home safe in their beds in time for Christmas—but with the most unusual tales.

## THE BOAT OF MANY ROOMS, THE STORY OF NOAH IN VERSE (ILLUSTRATED BY REG CARTWRIGHT)

This is a retelling in verse of the story of Noah's Ark. Each poem appears on a spread with richly detailed artwork. The collection offers a continuous narrative of the story and the mission of the many animals, such as:

Let the spider embroider the air

Let the zebra buck and clatter in the cage of his skin

Let the panther surround the quiet panic she has made

Let the hippos squat and the antelope lope

Let the turtle be

## OTHER BOOKS

Other books by this author include a retelling of *The Frog Princess, The Night of the Goat Children* (Germany), *The House of Boo (A Halloween Rubaiyat), The Moonbow of Mr. B. Bones,* and others. Log onto the website for a list of the author's many publications.

**Note:** This author may lead students to search for poetry books in the library so they can read other poems as well. The books are a treat for the students in terms of being exposed to exemplary use of the language. Above all, if they come away from this experience with a love of words and phrases, and a good feeling about poetry, it will be well worth the time and laughter, and the good feelings left long after.

# REPRODUCIBLE ACTIVITY PAGES
# FOR APRIL

## READING/LANGUAGE ARTS

Flip-Top Bunny Book

Homer Is Ba-a-a-ck! More Phobias

Idiom Alert!

Similies Using "Like" and "As"

Using Similies to Create a Story Character

"You Have Reached the Reading Hot Line"

## MATH

Fraction Food

More Than, Less Than

## SOCIAL STUDIES

Colonial Days vs. Today

Patriotic Coins and Stamps

## SCIENCE

Classify Birds by Feet

Nature's Weavers

## AUTHOR STUDY

J. Patrick Lewis Writes Poetry that Sings

# Flip-Top Bunny Book

Make a book about rabbits and staple it to this spot.

It can be an information book or a fantasy tale.

Color and cut out the big bunny. Share your book.

Name _____   Date _____

# Homer Is Ba-a-a-ck! More Phobias

Remember Homer G. Xytlefry? He's the one who had the fear of ending a story and you helped him! Thank you! He's calling on you again today. This calls for more of your good thinking, good writing, and problem-solving skills.

Title _____

ONCE UPON A TIME the King told two of his men that he wanted to surprise the Queen with a beautiful garden. "PLANT IT AT ONCE," he roared! Now, one of the men had *anthophobia* (fear of flowers) and the other had *chromophobia* (fear of color).

"I'll be back at 3 o'clock," said the King and he was off.

_____

_____

_____

_____

_____

_____

_____

_____

_____

_____

P.S. Homer has a cat with ornithophobia (fear of birds). The cat can't go out in the yard and feel the grass under his feet. What can Homer do for him?

# Idiom Alert!

"Idioms" refer to the unusual way words can convey a thought. They are colorful, and provide a rich visual and verbal connection.
Below are spaces that contain idioms. Draw a picture (literal) to go with each one.

| | |
|---|---|
| **Carl seems to have "a nose for news."** | **Gage got a new parakeet and "is on cloud nine."** |
| **Be sure to "drop me a line" when you return.** | **Hussein has scooters "on the brain."** |
| **Kalisha's angry mother "jumped down her throat."** | **Grouchy Tammy "got up on the wrong side of the bed."** |

# Similies Using "Like" and "As"

A similie is a colorful phrase often used in poetry. It makes the meaning *as clear as a bell,* and the descriptions *lively like a string puppet.* Make up similies, using descriptive words.

**Similies using *like*.**  Here are two samples.

> The lights sparkled **like diamonds.**

> She cried **like a baby** when they said goodbye.

Now you try.

1. The bear was big like a _____.

2. The house was run down like a _____.

3. The candle glowed in the dark like _____.

**Similies using *as*.**  Here are two samples.

> The tire was **as flat as** a pancake.

> She was **as happy as** a singing canary.

Now you try.

1. His boots were as _____.

2. The grass was as _____.

3. The morning sky was as _____.

Write more similies using color words:

as red as _____        as orange as _____

as yellow as _____        as green as _____

as blue as _____        as violet as _____

as black as _____        as white as _____

Name ______________________ Date ______________________

# Using Similies to Create a Story Character

Describe an unusual character using similes. Then write a story using that very same character and the descriptions.

| | |
|---|---|
| **as tall as** ____________ | **eyes like a** ____________ |
| **teeth as** ____________ | **skin like** ____________ |
| **lips as** ____________ | **hair like** ____________ |
| **ears as** ____________ | **neck like a** ____________ |
| **arms as** ____________ | **feet like** ____________ |

**Picture of character:**

**TITLE** ______________________

**(continue on the other side)**

Name _____  Date _____

# "You Have Reached the Reading Hot Line"

Press 1:    Look for little words in big words.

Press 2:    Look for the rimes (*ack, act, an,* etc.).

Press 3:    Look for the root word.

Press 4:    Look for the blends.

Press 5:    Is Ricky controlling the vowels? (*ar, er, ir, or, ur*)

Press 6:    Is the beginning letter silent? (*kn, gn*)

Press 7:    What word would make sense?

Press 8:    Check your word file or word bank.

Press 9:    Ask a friend or ask the teacher.

Press 10:   Goodbye. Leave it for now.
            Call back later.

What number would you tell
the caller to press?

____A.  I can't read "singing."

____B.  How do you say t-h-a-t?

____C.  What rhymes with sand?

____D.  I can't read "knight."

____E.  I need help with "order."

____F.  Please help with short vowels.

____G.  What rhymes with "play"?

____H.  Where can I find "splish"
        and "splash"?

____I.   How do you say "Mississippi"?

____J.  Should I say, "The boat is big"
        or "The boat is fig"?

____K.  Is it a little "flower" or a little
        "flour" for a cake?

Do you have a Word Bank?
Start one today!

# Fraction Food

Divide the food as directed. Remember, fractions mean the parts are equal. Color the food to make it look delicious.

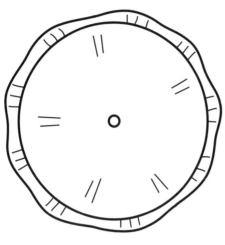

**Divide to serve 4.**

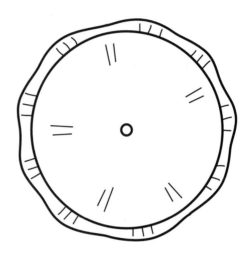

**Divide to serve 8.**

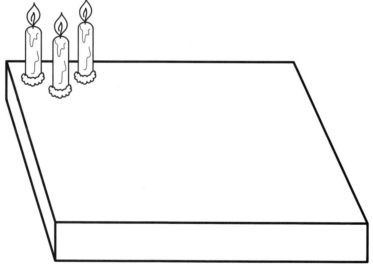

**Divide the cake to serve 12.**

**Divide to serve 6.**

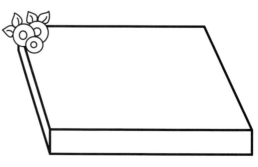

**Divide to serve 10.**

Name ______________________ Date ______________________

# More Than, Less Than

Smitty has to sort the potatoes into two groups. You can help.

Color those over 50 — green. Color those under 50 — tan.

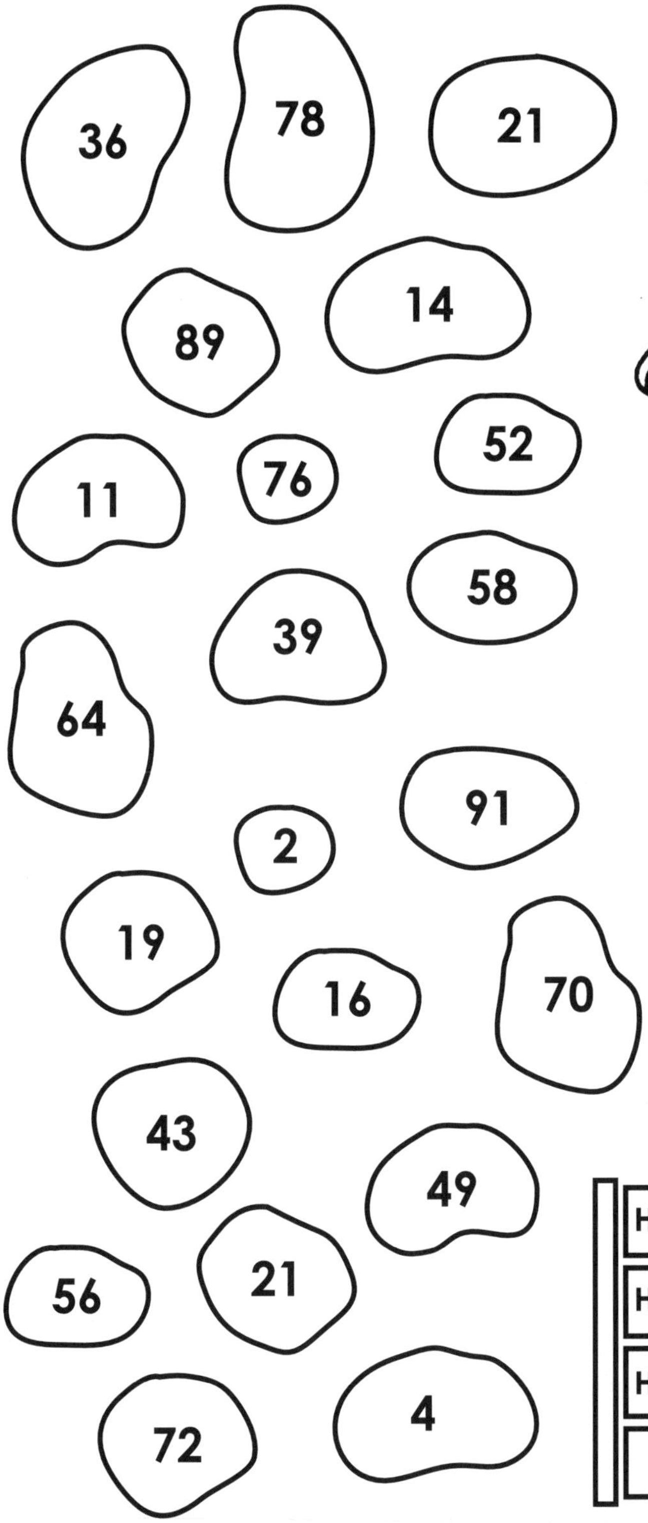
36
78
21
89
14
11
76
52
58
39
64
91
2
19
16
70
43
49
56
21
72
4

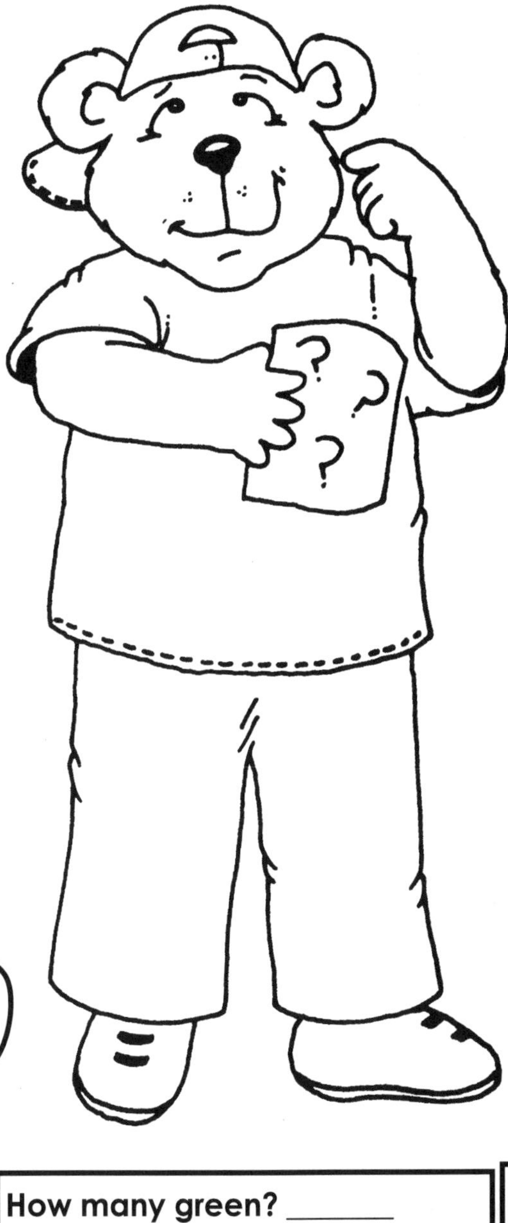

How many green? ______

How many tan? ______

How many all together? ______

POTATOES! POTATOES! POTATOES!

# Colonial Days vs. Today

"How was life different in early America from life today as we know it?" Use this as a focus sheet. Find information in the library on these topics and make notes in the spaces provided. Then, share your information with the class to make a big profile chart of LONG AGO and NOW. Select one of the categories and draw a picture that shows the difference.

| | LONG AGO | TODAY |
|---|---|---|
| Food | | |
| Jobs | | |
| Games and Toys | | |

# Patriotic Coins and Stamps

Do you know what the patriotic quarter from your state looks like? Examine the symbols on coins.

Now you can design a new patriotic coin for the USA. Choose your symbols carefully.

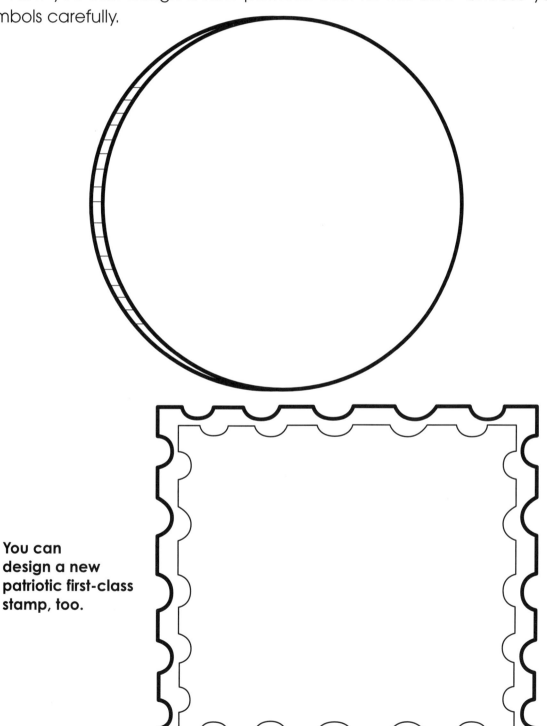

**You can design a new patriotic first-class stamp, too.**

# Classify Birds by Feet

Most birds have four toes, but there are other varieties of feet. Bird feet are useful tools for building nests and for catching food. Below are three different types of bird feet. In the appropriate column, draw, color and label at least three different kinds of birds in each category. Make the male bird so that you can show the bright, beautiful feathers. Be sure to emphasize the feet!

| Birds of Prey and Perching Birds | Tree Trunk Walkers | Water Fowl |
|---|---|---|
| | | |

# Nature's Weavers

Birds are natural weavers. They use natural items such as grass, twigs, reeds, and dried leaves to weave into their nests. The robin uses mud to make a bowl-shaped nest.

In the spring, birds are out looking for soft items to weave into their nests. YOU can help. Hang a mesh bag from a tree branch that contains items such as string, cotton, fiberfill from clothes dryers, and yarn.

In the spaces below, show the nests built by four different birds. Show the birds and eggs also.

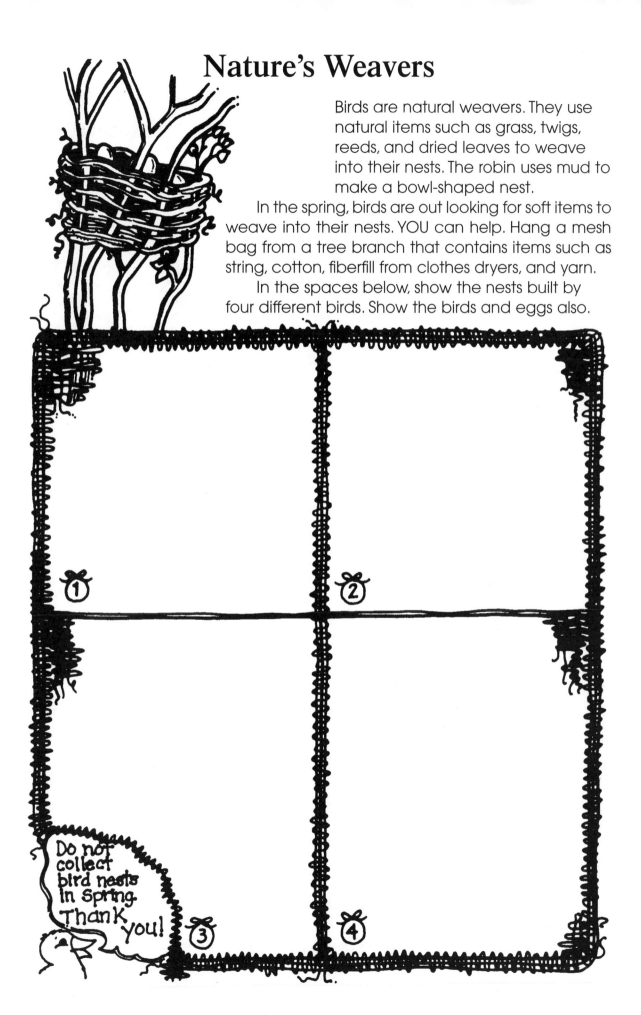

Do not collect bird nests in Spring. Thank you!

1
2
3
4

# J. Patrick Lewis Writes Poetry that Sings

Perhaps you can become a "word wizard" like J. Patrick Lewis.
Use any form of poetry that you like to write two poems about birds.
Write them on the birds in straight lines, or around
and around in a circle. Remember to
use colorful words.

# MAY / JUNE

# MAY/JUNE BOOKS

**Cherry, Lynne.** *The Great Kapok Tree, A Tale of the Amazon Rain Forest* **(New York: Harcourt Brace Jovanovich, 1990).** This is a story of the endangered forest and how the saving of just one tree can save a network of rare and wondrous animals who depend upon the tree for food and shelter. The message is delivered by animals to the man who has come to cut down the tree. Timely.

**Greene, Carol.** *The Old Ladies Who Liked Cats.* **Pictures by Loretta Krupinski (New York: HarperCollins, 1991).** Aside from being a good story, this book has an important message. It is a timely ecological folktale that shows in no uncertain terms that plants and animals are interdependent, and that each has its special job in the community.

**Huff, Barbara A.** *Greening the City Streets.* **Photographs by Peter Ziebel (New York: Clarion, 1990).** All over the country, community gardens are thriving and greening city streets. Overgrown lots are being transformed into gardens. The book lifts your spirits.

**Jonas, Ann.** *Reflections* **(New York: Greenwillow, 1987).** Read this book, turn it upside down, and continue the story. In each full-color picture, there is another picture reflected. A marvelous visual treat.

**Munro, Roxie.** *The Inside-Outside Book of Washington, D.C.* **(New York: EP Dutton, 1987).** An excellent visual picture of Washington. You see the outside of a building and are led into the interior to view the activities that go on there.

**Raschka, Chris.** *Simple Gifts: A Shaker Hymn* **(New York: Holt, 1998).** A new interpretation of this well-loved Shaker hymn. The lushly colored art and information of the history of the Shaker community, along with musical notations for the song, make this book a rich, multi-layered experience of the arts for all children.

**Ryan, Pam Munoz.** *The Flag We Love.* **Illustrated by Ralph Masiello (Watertown, MA: Charlesbridge, 1998).** A picture book about the flag with beautiful illustrations that evoke good feelings about the flag of our nation.

**Sharmat, Marjorie Weinman.** *Hurray for Father's Day!* **Illustrated by John Wallner (New York: Holiday House, 1987).** Sterling and Monica Mule vow to make this the best day yet for Dad. One wants to do things for Dad; the other wants to buy presents. They are in competition, but at the end of the day Dad calls a halt to it and decides how to best end the day.

**Wynot, Jillian.** *The Mother's Day Sandwich.* **Pictures by Maxie Chambliss (New York: Orchard, 1990).** Ivy and Hackett surprise their mother with breakfast in bed on Mother's Day. But the kitchen is a mess! Oops, make that two messes, for when mother is awakened from a sound sleep, she overturns the tray in the bed and the food flies.

**(CHAPTER BOOK) Byars, Betsy.** *The Summer of the Swans* **(New York: Puffin, 1981).** Touching story about a girl who has to take care of her little brother during the summer. She's a bit resentful until there is a near mishap. She comes to appreciate the brother and what it means to care for someone other than yourself.

# MAY/JUNE

If the class has been attentive and well disciplined throughout the year, it no doubt means that you have been working at it and it's paid off. During this time of the year, don't let the standards slip. The class will get off track and it takes a lot of effort to get back to the business of what we're here for.

Work doubly hard on class management so that learning can take place throughout the year. Practice *waiting* until everyone is ready and on task. Don't talk while others are talking among themselves and not listening. Send out the signals verbally and nonverbally that school is in session.

If you have not had a class "team" approach, it might be a good time to start one. Review the classroom rules and rewrite them. Get a class structure in place with a president, vice president, and so on. Do things that unite the group, such as working toward a goal (a science project fair, an art fair). Perhaps it's time to make large characters from cardboard to be in charge of the Learning Centers. These can be painted and decorated. Make new nametags for the desks. Create new bulletin boards. Put up a daily schedule so that students know what is expected of them. Distribute responsibility for classroom jobs among the students.

Praise students' good effort and good work habits so that others will follow. We still have a lot of work to do before the year is over. Motivate students so that they will be excited about what's coming up next. Link up with a first-grade teacher and have third graders become assistants. Keep on target!

# FOCUS ON READING

## SPRING GROWTH

Plant seeds in the classroom, and bring in starter kits for plants or herbs. This generates interest and results in a lot of learning. Students can learn to spell the various items being planted, and can write their own experience chart story about the procedure for planting seeds. They can track down books in the library that deal with plants in all types of climates.

They can link Reading to Math by graphing the plant growth.

## GRASS SEED/BIRD SEED LETTERS

Grass seed or bird seed will grow on a wet sponge. Students can draw the initial of their first name on a flat sponge. You or an aide can use an X-acto® knife to cut out the letters. Students

can wet the sponges, place some grass seed or bird seed on them, and then place them on aluminum trays that have the bottom covered with water. Soon, you'll be growing a garden of letters. Now, how many words can we make? What can be made with the sponge pieces that were cut away? (bird shapes, flower shapes, etc.).

## VOCABULARY FLASHCARDS

Make a classroom set of flashcards for Reading vocabulary, Social Studies words, Science words, Health words. Put a rubber band around them and store them where students have access to them. They can work with them individually or with a partner. They can work with the sets in groups of three, with one person acting as the teacher. Be sure to use flashcards daily with the group.

## ARTICULATION OF SOUNDS

When students are pronouncing letters, have them do this process very slowly while they assess what's going on inside their mouth. Where is the tongue—on the roof, the floor, touching the front teeth only, touching the side teeth? Is the mouth open or shut? This exercise is helpful for all, and especially for students who are still having some difficulty with articulation, or formation of the letters and sounds.

## FORMULA OF THE DAY

Create some plastic bag puzzlers. Select several items, such as real objects, photos, pictures, etc., that are related to a particular theme, and let students have the opportunity to figure out the formula. Some ideas are as follows:

*Everything in the packet*

- begins with the same letter
- ends with the same letter sound
- begins with the same blend
- rhymes except for one item
- begins with the same letter except for one
- contains the letters "gh" in the word

Students can be encouraged to make up their own Formula-of-the-Day puzzlers.

## EXPERIENCE CHART STORIES

Continue to write class experience chart stories throughout the year. It helps with organization skills, sequence, main idea, synthesizing information, summary skills, and review. By this time of year, students can be in charge of writing the story on large paper and drawing the illustrations.

At the end of the year, what will you do with all of those experience chart stories? Many of them can be "auctioned off" to the students who will use them over the summer months. Some students are thrilled to get the large materials they have been using in class. Put them to good use—don't throw them away. Make sure the student or students who don't appear to be overly enthusiastic about the process also get something to take home from the classroom.

## BOOK JACKETS

When you get library books, make a photo copy of the front of the book jacket. Start a collection. Student volunteers can color them carefully with felt-tip pens. Laminate them. Now you have a growing collection of books used in the classroom. Students can classify these book jackets in many ways:

- fiction and nonfiction
- same author
- subject matter
- order of preference
- identify main characters

- one they'd like to hear again
- class can vote on TOP 10
- students can retell story
- identify the main idea
- identify setting

## REVISITING STORIES

If the class is reading stories from a basal reader, have them read stories that they read last September or October. Do they seem easier now? Are there still words that are sticklers? If so, write them down and try to learn them.

## REVISITING ACTIVITY PAGES

Use some of the activity pages from this book that were used in the early months of this school year for review. Do students find them easier? Are they still having difficulty? These can help pinpoint problems that students need to address.

## COMPOUND-WORD CHALLENGE

Give the students the beginning of a compound word and have them write the next word. For example, say the word "school." Students then write the word *school* and also another word so that it becomes a compound word. Ask students to either say the word or write it on the chalkboard. Students learn from each other this way. (*Some possibilities:* schoolyard, schoolhouse, schoolbag, schoolbook, schoolmate, schoolroom, schoolwork, schoolmarm.)

Students can make up their own compound-word challenges. A good place to look to begin a list is in the dictionary.

## RESEARCH AND REFERENCE MATERIAL PUZZLERS

Continue to give assignments that enable students to gain skills using the following resources: dictionary, pictionary, glossary, thesaurus, encyclopedia, telephone book, directory, newspaper.

There can be a puzzle of the day written on the chalkboard to which students need to find the solution. Have them write down the solution and the source, including page number. Some suggestions are:

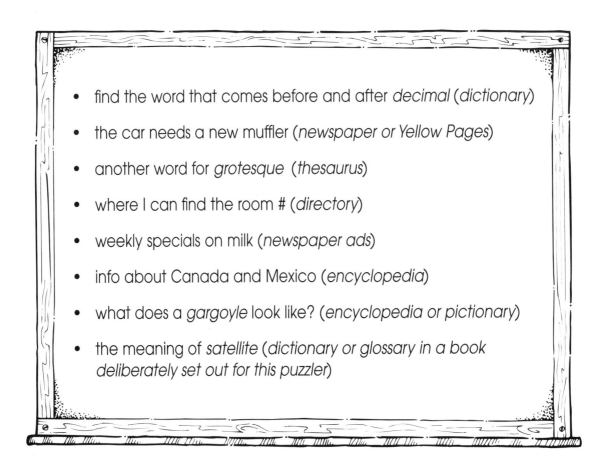

- find the word that comes before and after *decimal* (*dictionary*)

- the car needs a new muffler (*newspaper or Yellow Pages*)

- another word for *grotesque* (*thesaurus*)

- where I can find the room # (*directory*)

- weekly specials on milk (*newspaper ads*)

- info about Canada and Mexico (*encyclopedia*)

- what does a *gargoyle* look like? (*encyclopedia or pictionary*)

- the meaning of *satellite* (*dictionary or glossary in a book deliberately set out for this puzzler*)

## VOCABULARY BUILDING—FROM SIMPLE TO COMPLEX

On the chalkboard, write the sentence: Mr. Jones was <u>mad</u>. Tell students they need to find another word for the word that is underlined. There can be a number of sentences on the chalkboard that students can work with. In this exercise, go from simple, recognizable words to more complex words. They can copy the entire sentence OR just the underlined word followed by another word that is a synonym. (For example: mad—aggravated, or mad—angry).

## VOCABULARY BUILDING—FROM COMPLEX TO SIMPLE

This exercise is just like the previous one except that you use more complex words to underline. Have students find a synonym that would be understandable by more people. For example, "The <u>truculent</u> beast roamed through the woods." (truculent—fierce)

After students have identified the meaning of the word *truculent* (fierce, savage, ferocious), they can write (after the sentence on the chalkboard) a sentence that could possibly come next in a story. The next sentence will show that the student understands the meaning of the first word, in this case *truculent*. (Best source for this exercise is the dictionary because meanings are given.)

**Remember:** When building vocabulary, it is important to not only go from complex to simple, but to also go from simple to complex words, so that students understand that the words are on *a continuum of word possibilities*. Sometimes it is important to look up words that we do not understand in an effort to make sense of the information on the page. This is especially true in nonfiction writing.

## AM I ASKING? I AM TELLING!

Work with punctuation marks at the end of sentences. Remember that the three major ones are the period (.), question mark (?), and exclamation point (!). Write a list of sentences on the chalkboard and have students put the correct mark at the end of the sentence. (Put all three there, one at a time, so students see that some don't make sense. In other cases, you might use one or the other depending upon the context clues.)

## READING ROAD SIGNS

Look upon punctuation marks as reading "road signs" on a page of print. The sentences can be likened to pathways or roads. Some are short and some are long. You always stop at the end of the road (*period*). But what else could the road sign be telling us? (*asking a question? shouting!*)

> *Remember the road signs*
> *Along the way*
> *Stop (.) is a dot*
> *Pause (,) says slow down*
> *The ? asks a question*
> *The ! shouts hip hurray!*

Students can say this sentence in three different ways, using the inflection that the ending road sign is telling them to use:

> *Mary is going to the party?*
> *Mary is going to the party!*
> *Mary is going to the party.*

## FIND LITTLE WORDS IN BIG WORDS

Write "Tyrannosaurus Rex" on the chalkboard and
have students see how many little words they can
find in this name. Remember, for this you can mix
the letters around, so that, for example, the word
"rest" would be a possible word.

Students enjoy working with a partner and in teams for this
exercise. Do one regularly. Make it a learning game.

## TEST TAKING: MULTIPLE-CHOICE VARIETY

Give students exercises so that they will have ample opportunity to answer in a variety of ways.
Here are some examples using the same term "trumpet creeper." If we don't know what a trumpet
creeper* is, this is an opportunity to have someone look it up and read the information. Then
demonstrate these techniques for students.

- Multiple Choice: *Underline the answer* that best describes the underlined word or words:

> The <u>trumpet creeper</u> was coming over the fence.
>     big dog
>     climbing vine
>     fierce cat

- Multiple Choice: *Circle the letter* in front of the answer that best describes the underlined
  word or words:

> The <u>trumpet creeper</u> was coming over the fence.
>     a.  big dog
>     b.  climbing vine
>     c.  fierce cat

- Multiple Choice: *Fill in the bubble (or circle)* in front of the answer that best describes the
  underlined word or words:

> The <u>trumpet creeper</u> was coming over the fence.
>     O  big dog
>     O  climbing vine
>     O  fierce cat

-----

*Trumpet creeper is a climbing vine.

Students get opportunities to do these exercises in workbooks. If you are using workbook pages with your reading program, this process is being taught naturally. If you are not using a special program, then you will need to have many exercises for students to do so that they can gain practice with vocabulary AND test taking.

## TEST TAKING: HOW IS THIS TEST DIFFERENT?

The examples given below are also multiple choice; however, there is a difference. In this exercise, the answers are written in linear style (all in a row). This is different from having the answers listed underneath each other. It is a skill to be taught; it doesn't just happen.

*Fill in the blanks* with the correct word. (This can also be *circle* the correct word. Teach these skills using sentences written on a large chart, or with the overhead projector, or worksheet pages.)

---

Anna Marie and Tiffany both like to make doll _____.

closet     clothes     close

I hear _____ and that means a storm.

barking     thunder     footsteps

---

## TEST TAKING: FINDING THE MAIN IDEA

Read a short paragraph to students, or have them read it. Then ask what the one thing is that stands out. If they were going to write it in a headline for the newspaper, what would they need to pick out as the main subject?

---

Late one day when the sun was going down, a big noise could be heard coming from the town water supply. What was it? People started running toward the sound. Soon, water was flowing down the street and into the sewer. Two water pipes had burst! The water shot way up into the air.

Circle the letter in front of the main idea of this paragraph.

   a. a big noise sent people running

   b. water shot into the air

   c. two water pipes had burst

---

Talk about the main idea. Some students may have selected the first one. Discuss them as follows:

   a. This choice leaves the reader still wondering. What's the noise? It doesn't tell the main idea, or the most important thought.

   b. OK, but if we know this, we don't know how water shot into the air. Was it from a water pistol? A balloon? We don't have a main idea.

   c. This is it! Two water pipes burst. That's the main idea. That tells us why there was a noise, why water was flowing down the street, and why it shot up into the air.

Selecting the main idea is not simple. It requires repeated teaching and practice, practice, practice before students are able to sift through the information. Once again, use the analogy of sifting sand through a strainer—one grain of sand is too big to go through and stays in the sifter. It's the main one—the big idea.

   Sometimes students benefit from going at this in just the opposite way. Give them the main idea and let them fill in the facts in a paragraph. Either way, they need experience with this concept.


## THE PUPPETS HAVE THE ANSWERS

Students may be quite familiar with TV quiz shows. Making three hand puppets—Puppet A, Puppet B, Puppet C—could be helpful in teaching the concept of *multiple choice* or *true/false,* or *main idea.* Each puppet could have an answer pinned onto it, and students could turn it into a quiz game.

   However, you need to focus upon the written word as well. How can we do this? Perhaps using the overhead projector, or chalkboard, or individual chalkboards to write, circle, and underline at the same time as the game is going on would help students with the visual component of test taking.

## END-OF-YEAR WRAP-UP STATEMENTS FOR RECORDS

Make sure to write professional evaluation statements on the reading records. Do not "editorialize." Just write factual information, *not* your personal opinion. There may be some other avenue for you to voice your concerns, but be professional with permanent records.

| *Professional example* | *Unprofessional example* |
|---|---|
| "James has made progress this year with reading comprehension." | "James still doesn't get the main idea. He'd rather daydream." |
| "James needs to continue to work on building listening skills." | "James just doesn't listen. I don't think he gets enough sleep." |
| "James needs reminders about personal hygiene when handling books." | "James comes to school with dirty hands, so he wasn't allowed to handle the picture books. He always looks like he needs a bath." |

Sometimes permanent records can convey the negative attitude of the teacher toward the students in the class. This train of thought is easy to detect when reading numerous class records.

# FOCUS ON LANGUAGE ARTS

## MORE READING OPPORTUNITIES

### MAKING STORY CHARACTERS

Read stories and draw large outlines of the body shapes of story characters. Fill in information on the arms, around the neck, on the fingers, on the legs, and so on, that tell the components of a story: characters, setting, problem to be solved, attempts to solve, solution. Make the facial features with felt-tip pens, the hair from yarn, and the clothing from colorful cloth swatches or wallpaper sample patterns. Perhaps the character could have a photocopy of the front of the book jacket tucked under an arm or stapled to a wristwatch.

These story characters could accompany the author study section, or could be children's "All-time Favorite Story Characters from Grade Three." Place them on a large bulletin board with a lively title and relive the stories. Share them with schoolmates by lining them along the wall in the hallway. Write a short explanation to accompany the story character and be sure to have the students print their own names at the end of this. (See Reproducible Activity Pages.)

### REVISIT AND RETEACH CONSONANT BLENDS

Check the January Reading section for information about teaching consonant blends. This is an opportune time to revisit and reteach the blends. Find them in the beginning and middle of words. Assign a particular blend to each student, and see how many words they can find in a magazine in one minute, two minutes.

## READING CLOTHS

Cut out a 9- by 12-inch piece of felt for each student. They can make a story cloth illustration for a particular book by cutting out swatches of felt, or shapes from varieties of material. Burlap could be the rough texture used for a log cabin or a hunter's jacket. Satin material could be selected as the texture for a dress or for draperies. Encourage students to bring in a wide variety of materials that can be cut up for this project.

## STORY WALL HANGING: ARPILLERA

An applique sewing process in some countries in South America, such as Peru and Chili, is called *arpillera*. For this process you need many swatches of material, needle, thread, and a large cloth for the background.

Draw a sketch of a story scene with buildings, people, animals, trees, background, etc. Cut the materials and sew them onto the larger fabric. Sometimes cotton can be stuffed behind the shape of an animal or a tree trunk so that the items look puffy and stand out, thus taking on another dimension.

Once the arpillera is completed, students can write something about the story they selected and place it under the story cloth for display purposes. These are items that students will want to keep.

## POETRY READING

Students can find poetry about spring to read aloud to the class. Challenge them to find a poem about something from the following list to share with the class:

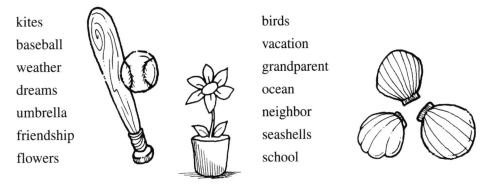

| | |
|---|---|
| kites | birds |
| baseball | vacation |
| weather | grandparent |
| dreams | ocean |
| umbrella | neighbor |
| friendship | seashells |
| flowers | school |

## READING A STORY VS. WATCHING A VIDEOTAPE

Enlist the aid of the school librarian or another third-grade teacher for this experiment.

Select a short story that has been made into a videotape to read to the class. Randomly divide the class in half, with each group consisting of an equal number of boys and girls. Half the class listens to the story being read aloud and sees the illustrations. The other half of the class watches the videotape.

Bring the two groups together and discuss the story. What do you notice about the differences in the discussion between the two groups? (This will vary with groups.) Also, have students draw the characters or a scene from the story and see if there are any noticeable differences in detail in the drawings.

The videotape paints the story visually with pictures. The book paints the story verbally with words. At the end, switch the groups: Those who heard the story can now watch the videotape and vice versa. It will be interesting to note their comments on ways vocabulary was used, ways they were able to spot good/bad characters, and so on. Can both groups find the main idea? Can both groups note predictions of things to come in the story? (Varies with the story and with groups, but it is a good learning experience.) *Be careful not to have students overwhelmingly favor one method over another, for both have value and this needs to become a main point of the lesson. Teacher selection of the story will be important. Also, to make a good teaching analogy, use food as an example. You need a balanced diet—not the same type of food over and over again.*

## LINK READING TO ALL SUBJECTS

Point out to students that reading is essential. We read stories and information in Social Studies, Science, Health, Math, etc. So, reading is a key factor in our success.

Students can make a Social Studies folder, Science folder, and/or Math folder, and make a key vocabulary list for each folder. These words can be kept on a sheet of paper cut in half vertically and stapled to the inside cover of the folder. Each time a new subject is studied, it's time to add to the list. Have students review their lists and challenge them to learn to spell a certain number of the words.

## LINK READING TO SPORTS

Our author study for June involves many sports stories. After students read a story about someone playing tennis, for example, have them look up a book on tennis and learn about it. Put key facts on shapes made to look like a tennis racquet. Make a crossword puzzle of words in the square netting of the racquet for a challenge.

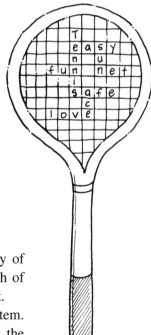

After reading a story about a boy playing a particular sport, the girls can go on a hunt for a story about a girl playing that sport. Check the newspaper for stories about men's and women's sports that are the same and different.

## PULL A STORY OUT OF A HAT

Check through magazines and newspapers and cut out a variety of items, such as a baseball, basketball, football, tree, house, bunch of bananas, monkey, tiger, dog, and so on. Put these items into a hat.

Students then can reach into the hat and each pull out an item. Their challenge is to find a good storybook (picture book) at the library to go with that item, read it, and share it with the class. This will present a wide variety of topics for discussion and liven up the classroom learning connections.

# WORD ORIGINS AND SAYINGS*

1. **hold the ketchup.** *Ketchup,* the word and the sauce, came into English use via Dutch traders. Dutch called the sauce *ketjap.* They got it from the Chinese who called it *ketsiap.* Chinese ketsiap was a spicy sauce of fish broth and black mushrooms. Tomatoes were added by the English to make the sauce less spicy. So "hold the ketchup" means that a person prefers to do without it.

2. **something to marvel at.** Today, a monster is an ugly, scary creature. This word is from the French *monstre,* taken from the Latin meaning *monstrum,* or "something marvelous" or "something to marvel at." Thus, today's meaning has changed from something frightful to something filled with wonder.

3. **Where did we get the word "alphabet" (ox house)?** *Aleph* is the first letter in Hebrew languages. It means "ox." Since the ox provided food and clothing, *aleph* or *ox* was very important. The second letter, *beth,* means "house" or shelter, which was also important. So *aleph* and *beth* were combined together to stand for the Hebrew written letters used to make words.

4. **Are you being a wet blanket?** A *wet blanket* is a person who takes all the fun and the spirit out of everything. You may have an exciting plan for a game of ball and someone ruins it by saying he or she won't play. The expression comes from throwing a wet blanket, or heavy cloth, on a fire to put it out.

5. **flex your muscle.** When you flex your arm muscle, for example, it means that you tighten the muscle and then let it relax or go limp. The Romans thought that this movement looked like a little mouse running under the skin. Their word for little mouse was *muscalus,* which today we called *muscle.*

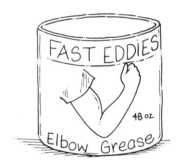

6. **Use a little elbow grease on that.** In the 1700s someone might be sent to get some elbow grease on April Fool's Day. Actually, elbow grease means to work hard. How do you polish furniture? With a little elbow grease or hard rubbing.

# WRITING SKILLS

## SCHOOL PEN PALS

To foster writing and communication, start a friendly pen pal letter-writing venture with another third-grade classroom. The classroom can be right in the same building or in the same school district. Remind students that their handwriting represents them so they need to put their best foot forward. This is unlike an e-mail pal where all of the letters in the body of a message are uniformly typed.

*Source: *Words* by Jane Sarnoff and Reynold Ruffins.

## PENMANSHIP AWARDS

"And the penmanship award for the week goes to . . ." Start a campaign so that each week students submit a piece of writing to be evaluated by outside sources (teachers, school secretary, older students). Have the work numbered with no names visible so that those doing the evaluating do not know whose writing it is.

## STORY STARTERS FROM WELL-KNOWN BOOKS AND WRITERS

On 3- by 5-inch cards, write the characters, setting, and problem to be solved, with a particular book in mind. For example, on one card, you might write:

---

Main Characters: little girl and grandmother

Setting: farm

Problem: a storm is brewing and the little girl is afraid of thunder

---

Students can write a story about this situation. They can work independently or with a partner, and try to help the little girl to manage her fear. Share the stories aloud.

Then bring out the book that also used this situation and review it with students or read it aloud. In this case, the book is *Thundercake* by Patricia Polacco.

Make a set of these "story starters" using some of the class storybook favorites.

## READ, STOP, AND WRITE

1. Begin reading a story aloud to students and stop about a third of the way through it.
2. Students can continue the story by writing an episode or a paragraph of what might happen next, being careful not to end the story. (Share several of these with the class.)
3. Continue reading aloud another third of the book.
4. Students can continue the storyline from there, in writing, and end the story. (Share several of these with the class.)
5. Finally, finish reading the book aloud.

Students will have had an opportunity to become personally involved with the story, and to write at least twice in conjunction with the story being read aloud to the class. They can sharpen their skills of prediction, use of colorful vocabulary, and show that they are able to further the story and yet stay within the framework already set up.

When the storybook is finished, students can be encouraged to rewrite their version of it, using some of their own ideas or some of the ideas that were shared in class. All of them will be slightly different, which adds to the joy of reading and writing

You can accompany this activity on the chalkboard by webbing the possibilities written by students. They will see how rich and varied the ideas are, and this will help them in their own writing.

## SPRING WRITING SLOGAN

Students need to continue to work on penmanship. They can submit a catchy slogan for writing improvement. The class can vote on the slogan of their choice and this can be the spring writing slogan for everyone. They can write the class slogan in their best penmanship and decorate it.

# SPEAKING SKILLS

## I SPEAK, YOU LISTEN. YOU SPEAK, I LISTEN.

Set up rules for speaking in the classroom, or during assembly programs, or on field trips. Use the *5 W Approach: Who* is speaking? *What* are they saying? *When* should you be talking? *Where* do you talk or not talk? *Why* are these speaking rules necessary?

Once students understand the rules and the necessity for them, they are generally more cooperative about using the rules. It's more effective to know the reason for the rules than to just be told words like *don't* and *no*.

*To get the point across, simultaneously* turn on a radio program, an audio cassette, or a recording, and give verbal directions for something students need to know. Confusing? You bet! What is the lesson? There's a time to speak and a time to listen. If everyone is talking at once, who's listening?

## ARE YOU A TALKING MACHINE?

Some students like to talk a lot. However, that does not mean others always enjoy hearing what these people have to say. Have students think of speaking or talking in terms of taking up space. How much space (and time) does their talking take up? Are some students using too much talk-time? If so, others aren't getting their fair share of talk-time. This needs to be pointed out to students because they may not realize that they are trying to do all of the talking, or are interrupting, or are overriding the speech of someone else by talking louder.

Distribute "talk coupons" during class discussion time that have a certain amount of time written on them. Students who talk a lot will have to pace themselves. To check up on this, two students, with a stopwatch, can be monitors to keep track of the number of seconds students are speaking. Sometimes this is an eye-opener for the talkative student, especially when he or she is in charge of the stopwatch and is in a position to make comparisons.

This is also a good activity to do at this time of year because classroom management of the talking outloud and talking out of turn may benefit from using a different approach.

## INDOOR/OUTDOOR VOICES

Often children's voices sound louder at this time of year because, especially in colder climates, they are outdoors more and are running and shouting while at play. When coming indoors from recess, students are still in "outdoor voice" mode.

To help with this, make a large cardboard thermometer used for teaching temperature. Adjust the ribbon upward and downward to show "too noisy" (temperature is way up at the top in the red zone). Get the temperature (sound meter) down to a reasonable level before moving indoors with students. This extra time gives them an opportunity to settle down.

## PLEASANT SPEAKERS

Students have seen their share of people speaking on TV. Tape some examples of people who are considered to be good speakers and play them in class. What are some of the qualities that these people display in their speech? Create a list. Begin to use the information when talking before small groups and larger groups.

- Look directly at people when speaking (not looking at the floor).
- Sound lively (interested in the topic).
- Look friendly (smile, don't frown).
- Give others a chance to speak (good listener).
- Use hand gestures when appropriate.
- Speak up (no mumbling).
- Avoid repeated mannerisms (brushing hair aside, shuffling feet, pointing).
- Use pleasant voice (not too loud or soft, not shrill).
- Avoid use of "uh" and overuse of certain words ("like").

## HAVE A DEBATE, OR A PRO/CON PRESENTATION

Give students the opportunity to talk on topics that are being studied in Health, Social Studies, or Science. Encourage students to line up on one side or the other of an issue and teach them how to debate the issues, which at this level means presenting their point of view, sticking to the topic, and putting into practice their good speaking and listening skills.

During this time, students in the audience are practicing their listening skills.

If time is allowed for questioning and a student does not know the answer, make a rule that allows them to say: "I'll get back to you on that." Then, later, they have to look up the information that the student in the audience is calling for. This helps to eliminate unnecessary tension for those engaged in the debate or presentation.

Keep this in mind also when a student is giving an individual report to the class. Students don't have all the answers. Make it a part of the learning situation and reassure students before-hand that this is a natural state. Explain to them that when they see people on television who seem to have a great deal of information and who never seem to be at a loss for words or for answers, they may be wearing a little electronic device in their ear. Someone is "feeding them information" through this device. (It is extremely reassuring for students, especially those having difficulty with speaking, to know this information.)

# LISTENING SKILLS

## LISTENING FOR LETTER SOUNDS (RIDDLES)

*You hear me in party,*
*But not in rain.*
*You hear me in kite,*
*But not in plane.*
*Who am I?* (letter **t**)

*You hear me in eskimo,*
*But not in pet.*
*You hear me in asking,*
*But not in forget.*
*Who am I?* (letter **k**)

*You hear me in trouble,*
*But not in carry.*
*You hear be in bubble,*
*But not in merry.*
*Who am I?* (letter **b**)

Students enjoy guessing the letters. Have them raise their hand if they know the answer. They are not to shout it out, because the same person could be doing all of the answering. Students who need to hear the verse a second time, or who need more time to figure it out, simply are not getting this opportunity if answers are shouted out.

In the verses, notice that the last word in lines 2 and 4 match. None of the other words have to rhyme.

## "AMERICA" ("MY COUNTRY 'TIS OF THEE")

*Say* this verse while students listen. When you pause, students can fill in the silence. Do it repeat-edly so that those who didn't learn it can have another opportunity. Then, at the end, sing it together.

*My country, 'tis _____ thee,*
*Sweet land of _____,*
*Of _____ I sing.*
*Land where _____ fathers died!*
*Land of the _____ pride!*
*From every _____ side,*
*Let freedom _____ !*

Now listen for a different purpose. This time students can locate the words that rhyme:

*My country this of THEE,*
*Sweet land of LIBERTY,*
*Of thee I SING.*
*Land where my fathers DIED!*
*Land of the Pilgrims' PRIDE!*
*From every mountainSIDE,*
*Let freedom RING!*

## ANIMAL SOUNDS

Students are familiar with many animal sounds if they have had an opportunity to read and listen to many picture books. Also, from their home environment they may be familiar with the bark of a dog, the purr of a cat, the chirping of a bird, and so on.

Make flashcards of the following phrases, or write "The _____ of the wolf" on the chalkboard. Ask students to *listen* when the phrase is read, and then tell the sound they hear. After the first one is completed, erase the word *wolf* and write in the word *bear,* and so on.

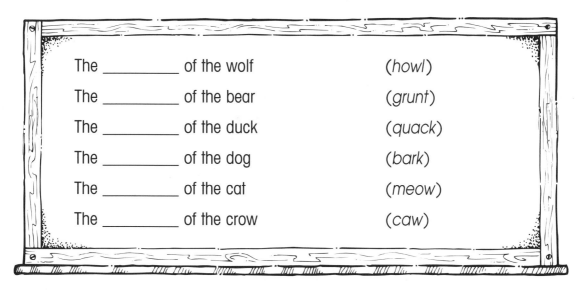

The _____ of the wolf          (*howl*)

The _____ of the bear          (*grunt*)

The _____ of the duck          (*quack*)

The _____ of the dog           (*bark*)

The _____ of the cat           (*meow*)

The _____ of the crow          (*caw*)

If you make flashcards, use this follow-up activity. Hold up the phrase and just have students make the animal sound.

Next, have half of the students (Group A) sit facing away from you and the other half (Group B) facing toward you. You can hold up the saying for Group B to see. Group B then barks, and this is the cue for Group A to listen and say: "The bark of the dog." Repeat this using all of the cards. Then you can have groups reverse positions, so Group A becomes Group B. Shuffle the flashcards and do this listening/speaking activity again.

## SOUND STORY MAKERS

Bring in at least three items that make a sound and place them in a little basket. Hold up the item, and shake it or ring it. Make sure students are familiar with the item and the wide range of possible places they could hear the sound. For example:

- bell ringing—bicycle bell, church bell, ice cream truck, bell over a shop door, doorbell, telephone ringing

- music box—in a shop, on a dresser, in a music store

- castanets—clicking while dancing, crickets calling, clattering of shoes on pavement

- baby rattle—a baby, rattling of broken dishes, snake rattler, orchestra, crowd cheering

Then students can write a short story making sure that the three items appear in the story. Remember, they will need characters and a setting, and the sounds can take them wherever they want to go. Encourage students to read their story aloud and physically use the sounds while others listen.

It is interesting and informative for students to see how many different ways these three sounds can be incorporated into a story.

## INCORPORATE LISTENING WITH MUSIC AND ART

Use the picture book *Looking at Paintings: Musicians* by Peggy Roalf. In this book, the author has selected a series of paintings that show musical instruments. It is a personal tour through a collection of a variety of art styles as well. The author gives us a new art vocabulary to sharpen our seeing. Some good words to learn are:

| | | |
|---|---|---|
| highlights | shading | background |
| foreground | textures | designs |
| egg tempera | contrast | portrait |
| chiaroscuro | embellished | fresco |

In each portrait by a different well-known artist, different instruments are portrayed, such as cithara (harp), fiddle, banjo. Students will be interested to find out what these instruments sound like. Check the videotapes in the children's section of the local library for introductory instrument and orchestral experiences.

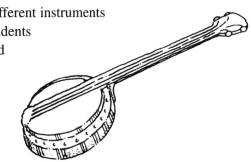

Also, be on the lookout for the recording of *Peter and the Wolf* by Sergei Prokofiev. Here the instrument sounds represent the characters in the story. It provides a rich listening experience.

# FOCUS ON SPELLING

## SPELLING POETRY

For springtime when poetry is in the air, let's link it to Spelling. Use the spelling words for the week in a cinquain poem. Or, write phrases using three words for alliteration. For example, if a spelling word is "fabulous," the phrase could be "*f*abulous, *f*antastic, *f*unny clowns."

## SPELLING SPORTS

Write spelling words on shapes made to look like sports equipment. For baseball, for example, make cutouts of ball, bat, mitt, cap, base, and so on.

## SPELLING CHAMPS

Link spelling to the author study for May/June. One message is that you need to practice to be good in sports. That's true for spelling, also. To be good in spelling, students need to continually practice—in writing, in their head, verbally with a partner, etc. Think of spelling this spring as you would think of baseball practice. You're up to bat—now hit a homer!

## SHAPE POEM

Make a shape poem using the spelling words.

## SPELLING BASEBALL

Divide into teams. Play Spelling Baseball in the classroom with different areas of the room designated for the dugout, home plate, and the bases. Batter up! Here's the pitch. (Say a spelling word.) If the student up at bat spells it correctly, he or she goes to first base. Then it's time for the next batter. Play until there are three outs. But, if the team is especially

"hot" and the game is running long, you can always call time because of rain. Then start it up again, with the other team up at bat.

Play Spelling Baseball with the entire class acting as one big team.

## P.A. ANNOUNCEMENTS

The office P.A. system can be turned on to your classroom only, and the spelling champs for the week can have their names read aloud. Or, a spelling champ can be interviewed and asked for tips.

An occasional word of congratulations at this time from the principal is always seen as a big boost.

If it is not possible to use the P.A. system, then simulate this in the classroom with a cassette recorder or on videotape.

# FOCUS ON MATH

## SUSTAINED SILENT MATH

Give students 20 minutes at least two days per week to engage in math activities. They can play  card games, work with puzzles (shapes), play chess, read a math book, work with Cuisenaire® Rods or any other commercial material, do an extra math activity worksheet, work with geoboards, and so on. Give students the freedom to choose to do this and to have a quiet atmosphere in the classroom for Math Time.

## ALL OCCUPATIONS REQUIRE MATH

Some students may have picked up the "Why do we have to do this anyway?" attitude about Math, and that attitude needs to be adjusted. One way to approach it is to enable students to gain an awareness that people use math in their daily lives, no matter what their occupation.

List some obvious occupations where math is necessary:

| | | |
|---|---|---|
| banker | financial planner | accountant |
| tax consultant | tax collector | bookkeeper |
| sales clerk | cashier | waiter/waitress |

## DOES A TAXI DRIVER NEED MATH?

Students need to recognize that a taxi driver must have an acute awareness of math. How does the cab driver use math?

- needs to have a knowledge of money (even if there is a meter)
- needs to make change
- needs knowledge of number of miles from Point A to Point B
- needs knowledge of fuel costs
- needs to know how many miles to the gallon the cab gets
- needs to be able to read the meter and odometer in the cab
- needs to read signs that indicate miles per hour (speed)
- needs map knowledge (north/south/east/west)
- needs to recognize house numbers
- needs awareness of time—when to pick up a passenger
- other

## PLAY "OH, YES, YOU DO!!"

Have a variety of activity cards made up that read "I'm a hairdresser. I don't use math," or "I'm an animal vet. I don't use math," or "I'm a florist. I don't use math," and so on. Have one student select an activity card from the little container of cards and read it aloud. All students answer in unison, "Oh, yes, you do!"

Then have students brainstorm and come up with all of the ways that that person DOES use math in daily life.

This usually helps to convince students that they will be using math processes throughout their life, and they can learn to enjoy it too! Math makes your life easier. (See Reproducible Activity Pages.)

## "MY GRANDMA DOESN'T USE MATH"

Some students are convinced that they can stump the "Oh, yes, you do" response. A student may say, "My grandma doesn't use math. She watches her favorite TV programs and then makes the supper."

Think about it. Does Grandma use math? Talk about it in small groups and then share the information. For example:

- Grandma has to watch the clock to see when her favorite TV programs come on (time).

- If it's cold or hot in the home, Grandma adjusts the thermostat (temperature).

- Grandma does the cooking, so she has to count, prepare the right amount of food, set the table (counting), have dinner at a certain time, etc.

- When the doorbell rings and it's the paperboy, Grandma pays him (money).
- Grandma uses the telephone to call a friend (numbers).
- Grandma listens to the radio, too (numbers for stations).

Students will also come up with many more ways that Grandma uses math.

## HAVE STUDENTS KEEP "CATCHING THEMSELVES" USING MATH

Use "math currency" for this activity. Have students keep a list of every time they catch themselves using math today, and they can turn this in for a reward:

- Caught 5 times is good for a one-star coupon.
- Caught 10 times is good for a two-star coupon.
- Caught 15 times is good for a three-star coupon.

Now, determine what the coupons are worth.

- one star: Read a math picture book of your choice.
- two stars: Do anything you want at the Math Center for ten minutes tomorrow.
- three stars: Get three pieces of candy.

## WORKING WITH WEIGHT

Have a set of scales in the classroom so that students can weigh items and begin to get a sense of what "one pound" and "two pounds" feel like. They will also get a sense of "ounces" as well.

For an activity at the Math Center, students can weigh small cans of food and record the weights. They can weigh a group of apples, a bunch of bananas, a squash, a bag of potatoes, and so on.

Work with estimation and weight. Have students lift something that is known to weigh a certain amount, say a two-pound bag of sugar. Feel it; get the sense of two pounds. Then:

- Find two things in the classroom that also weigh two pounds.
- Lift an item and determine whether it is *more than* or *less than* two pounds. Then check the estimate by actually weighing the item.

Another activity is to have students take off a shoe and weigh it. Then their challenge is to find five things in the classroom that weigh as much as their shoe.

Have them discuss their findings. For example, do small items always weigh less than large items? Do large items always weigh more than small items? (See Reproducible Activity Pages.)

## END-OF-THE-YEAR ASSESSMENT . . . COMING UP

Use the materials from the basic Math program to determine the progress students have made throughout the year. Hopefully, you have been assessing student progress in Math throughout the months, and keeping track of them with their Math Portfolio.

Some teachers take representative samples from the portfolio. Others keep the Math Portfolio in the classroom and send it along with class records for the next year so the teacher can see at a glance what the student has mastered, and where the student is placing in Math.

## SUMMER WORK IN MATH

Make sure that in your newsletter to parents at the end of the year you include a variety of math activities for students to engage in over the summer months. They need to keep up their math awareness. They need to keep using those flashcards so the skills they worked so hard to maintain will not fade away. List them for parents. (See Reproducible Activity Pages.)

# FOCUS ON SOCIAL STUDIES

## MAY/JUNE CITIZENSHIP FOCUS

One area of our citizenship focus that requires continuous work is that of *diversity*. Students need to be made aware of the fact that although someone may look different, dress different, or talk different from them, it does not mean that at the core of the person they are any less. Students need to be told that to laugh or to poke fun at another person is to show their own lack of compassion.

"He who is laughed at, gets the last laugh." Explain this saying to students. (It means, laugh at someone and it will come back to haunt you.)

Sometimes reading aloud good books that deal with diversity will help teach us lessons that need to be learned. Here are three good ones:

- *Chicken Sunday* by Patricia Polacco. An innocent threesome of children are blamed for throwing eggs at the door of Mr. Kodinski, a Jewish shopkeeper. Mixed races of children. (picture book)
- *Amazing Grace* by Mary Hoffman. It's unheard of! Grace, who not only is a girl, but a black girl, wants to play the role of Peter Pan in the school play. (picture book)
- *Bicycle Man* by Allen Say. The setting is Asia, after World War II, and two soldiers visit an elementary school. One soldier has white skin but red hair, and the other one has black skin. Soon the children's fears are put to rest by some magic bicycle tricks. (short story, some pictures)

# PATRIOTISM

Songs (and food) often bind people together. Here are songs of America that are often sung in groups, and some good recipes to try, too. It helps for you to try the snacks at home the first time through.

## "YANKEE DOODLE"

This song is from the Colonial American period. At first it was a song to poke fun at the new colonists who looked scruffy and couldn't afford "macaroni wigs" (big wigs) so stuck a feather in their cap instead. A "doodle" was a nitwit.

*Yankee doodle came to London*          *Yankee doodle keep it up*
*Riding on a pony*                       *Yankee doodle dandy,*
*Stuck a feather in his cap*             *Mind your manners and your step*
*And called it macaroni.*                *And with the girls be handy.*

## MAKE "YANKEE DOODLE" SNICKERDOODLES

1$^3$/$_4$ c. all-purpose flour
1 tsp. baking soda
$^1$/$_2$ tsp. nutmeg
$^1$/$_3$ c. sugar
1$^1$/$_2$ sticks butter
2 eggs (large)
2 tbsp. sour cream
raisins

*Topping:*
cinnamon and sugar mixed together

Mix flour, baking soda, and nutmeg together. (Dry mixture.) Mix butter and sugar in another bowl to make batter. Add eggs and sour cream to the batter a little at a time and stir until smooth. Add the dry mixture to the batter a little at a time. Keep stirring. Add raisins. Onto a cookie sheet, scoop 1 tbsp. of mixture, placing the dough about an inch apart. Sprinkle a bit of cinnamon and sugar (topping) over each cookie. Bake at 350 degrees until brown (approx. 10 min.).

## "SHE'LL BE COMING 'ROUND THE MOUNTAIN"

This is a "transportation song." People would wait for the train to come into view to bring goods and visitors. "Toot! Toot!" is accompanied by two gestures of pulling the whistle cord on a train.

*Stanza 1:*

She'll be coming 'round the mountain when she comes, *Toot! Toot!*

She'll be coming 'round the mountain when she comes, *Toot! Toot!*

She'll be coming 'round the mountain, she'll be coming 'round the mountain,

She'll be coming 'round the mountain when she comes, *Toot! Toot!*

*Stanza 2:*

("Whoa, back!" is accompanied by arms pulling back the reins.)

She'll be driving six white horses when she comes, *Whoa, back!*

She'll be driving six white horses when she comes, *Whoa, back!*

She'll be driving six white horses, she'll be driving six white horses,

She'll be driving six white hoses when she comes, *Whoa, back!*

*Toot! Toot!*

*Stanza 3:*

("Hi, Babe" is accompanied by a wave of the hand.)

Oh, we'll all go out to meet her when she comes, *Hi, babe!*

Oh, we'll all go out to meet her when she comes, *Hi, babe!*

Oh, we'll all go out to meet her, oh, we'll all go out to meet her,

Oh, we'll all go out to meet her when she comes. *Hi, babe!*

*Whoa, back!*

*Toot! Toot!*

There are four more stanzas. Keep repeating the last two words.

- **Stanza 4:** Oh, we'll kill the old red rooster when she comes, *Cockadoodle-doo!*
- **Stanza 5:** And we'll all have chicken and dumplings when she comes, *Yum, yum!*
- **Stanza 6:** Oh, she'll have to sleep with grandmaw when she comes, *Snore, snore.*
- **Stanza 7:** And she'll wear red flannel pajamas when she comes, *Wheee-whooo!*

## TASTY CHICKEN SALAD SANDWICHES

4 cooked chicken breasts
chopped celery
creamy salad dressing
carrot sticks (for tail and neck)
green olive (for head)
potato chips
beverage

Cut chicken into chunks. Mix with chopped celery and salad dressing for a spread. Spread mixture on hamburger buns. Place buns on a paper plate. Construct the "chicken." Serve with potato chips and beverage.

## "AMAZING GRACE"

*Amazing grace! How sweet the sound*
*That saved a wretch like me.*
*I once was lost, but now am found,*
*Was blind but now I see.*

*'Twas grace that taught my heart to fear,*
*And grace my fears relieved.*
*How precious did that grace appear,*
*The hour I first believed.*

*Through many dangers, toils and snares,*
*I have already come.*
*'Tis grace hath brought me safe thus far*
*And grace will lead me home.*

## MAKE AMAZING FRUIT POPS

$1/2$ c. berry juice blend
1 tbsp. unflavored gelatin
2 c. nonfat vanilla yogurt
$1 1/2$ c. frozen berries
small, waxed paper cups
plastic wrap
craft sticks

Combine juice and gelatin in a pan and cook over slow heat, stirring constantly. Add yogurt and berries and stir. (Everyone can get a chance to stir if you don't use a blender.) Spoon or pour mixture into cups. Place plastic wrap over cups and insert a stick through the plastic into the mixture. Freeze. Remove plastic and tear away paper cups. Turn upside down. Amazing!

# AREA OF FOCUS: CONSUMERS

## CHILDREN AS CONSUMERS

After discussing some of the issues in last month's Social Studies section, it will be enlightening for the students to see what privileges they enjoy today. Some children have an excess of material things but are still not happy. Work with students to determine the difference between wants and needs.

## WANTS AND NEEDS

Let's talk about toys, clothing, and TV ads that are aimed at children. Help students to determine that some things are needed, but other things are not. Have they ever wanted something and then when they got it, they didn't like it? This is a good discussion question. Did they really need it in the first place? Can it be returned, and if not, what happens next? You need to listen carefully but must also bring the discussion back to the concept of wants versus needs.

Make a list of items, some personal and some for the home, and put after them either a "W" for want or an "N" for need. Which items are essential (needs) and which can we do without (wants) if we have to?

soap                       ice cream sundae      bed blanket

comb                       chair                  lamp

scooter                    toothbrush             mittens

## WANTS AND NEEDS STATEMENTS

Make a list of statements. Read them to students. Do they consider them *wants* or *needs*? There will be a difference of opinion on some items, so let students discuss their feelings. Remember, you need to be a good listener and a thoughtful guide.

1. Tom asks for a new scooter because Tony got one. (W or N)
2. Allyson is tired of her green coat and sees a blue one that she says she can't live without. (W or N)
3. RJ is saving his money for a new hockey stick. (W or N)
4. Mary Jane asks for a new backpack she saw on TV. (W or N)
5. Joanne sits down in the last chair, and Granny has to stand. (W or N)
6. "I absolutely *need* a new bracelet," says Tiffany. (W or N)

## ADVERTISING TECHNIQUES

Appealing to children is "big business." Getting children to buy products is important to the life of some companies. Here are some advertising techniques that students need to become aware of when they see them on TV so they can become "smart shoppers." If they recognize the technique, they will think twice about whether or not they actually want/need the product.

1. *Bandwagon approach:* Everybody's doing it! Join in! Don't be left out! Don't be the only one without this!
2. *Snob appeal:* A rich or famous or popular person is doing the talking. Implication is: Get this and you'll be just like me.
3. *Slogans:* Catchy tunes, or logos, or signs are attached to the product to get your attention.
4. *Plain folks talk:* Sounds like something said around the kitchen table; homey.
5. *Derogatory words:* This product is better than the other one.

Students watch a great deal of TV and are bombarded with ads. Have them watch TV with a purpose. Identify some of these techniques in ads. Can they find different techniques? (humor, statistics, etc.) Have students record this information in their journal writing and share it with the class on a designated date.

## COMPARISON SHOPPING

Use the newspapers and a shopping list for groceries. Have students compare the cost of a product at one store versus another. What happens if they use coupons—does it lower the price? Work in teams with a set list of groceries and see who can get the best value for their money. This is often an eye-opener for students, and they begin to encourage their parents to use grocery coupons if they don't already do so.

In the home, that could be one role a student could play. They could be in charge of cutting and filing the coupons for the family grocery trips. What a contribution to the family that would be!

## LET'S "DO" LUNCH

Make this a learning experience, a field trip, and a food treat at the same time.

1.  Decide on a simple menu for lunch at school, such as: sandwich (bread, and whatever they decide goes inside—meat, tomatoes, cheese, peanut butter—in other words, vote on the choice of sandwich), drink, chips, dessert.

2.  Work in teams to decide how much (quantity) of drink and food will be needed by the number of students in class. Then paper products (napkins, cups) and plastic utensils will need to be purchased. Once the list is made, students are ready to "go shopping" in the local newspapers for this week. Turn to the grocery ads. Are coupons available? What about "two for the price of one" or "buy one, get one free" coupons? This will help.

3.  Student teams need to submit their list of items and costs. Now, how do we raise the money? Will each student be asked to bring in money? Is their money for this type of activity in an office petty cash fund? Will class mothers be asked to collect money?

4.  If a field trip cannot be taken to the grocery store (although this is a good experience), then you, an aide, or parents will have to be asked to assist with the shopping. On the morning of the big luncheon, the food can be delivered to the classroom.

5.  Student teams need to pour drinks, make sandwiches, serve food, clean up. This work should be designated in advance. Students gain practice in organization skills, math, planning, problem solving, and nutritious food choices. Then they have the added enjoyment of a fine social lunch with their classmates.

They also gain an awareness of the time, effort, and energy that goes into meal planning for a group and for a family. Link this activity to your Math program so students can gain a real-life experience.

# HOLIDAYS AND CELEBRATIONS

## MAY DAY (LEI DAY IN HAWAII)

May Day (May 1) is another opportunity to celebrate Spring. This custom
came to the United States via Europe. In many little towns in European
countries, there are contests to see which community can create the
most attractive pole. People work on this for a month in advance,
and even stand guard so no one from a neighboring community
can take a peek and get an idea. It's a time for singing, dancing,
eating, and selecting a May Day King and Queen. Streamers are
placed around the pole, and people hang onto a streamer and
weave over and under until they can't weave any more, and then
the job is to reverse their steps and unweave the streamers. It is
a day for merriment.

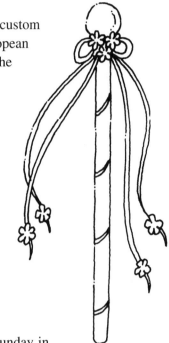

   Use an old-fashioned clothes tree or a stand from the
gym to make a classroom May Pole. What music will you play
as students weave around the pole?

## MOTHER'S DAY

We honor mothers (and grandmothers and aunts) on the second Sunday in
May. The special flower for Mother's Day is a carnation. Anna M. Jarvis
(1864–1948) was the founder of Mother's Day. It was *her* mother's idea.
The purpose of this day is: (1) to honor our mother, (2) to bring families together, (3) to make us
better children, and (4) to brighten the lives of good mothers everywhere.

## MEMORIAL DAY

This day, observed on the last Monday in May, is a day set aside to honor the soldiers who died in
any war in which the USA was a part. It is a day marked with parades, patriotic speeches, and flags
waving in the breeze. Often, Veterans of Foreign Wars and American Legion organizations place
flags on cemetery graves of those who fought for the United States, even if they did not lose their
life in the war.

   Students should be made aware that men and women join the armed forces to protect our
country. Can students name the branches of the military?

   A Memorial Day Concert is held at the Nation's Capitol.

   The National Symphony Orchestra gives a free concert at the West Front of the U.S. Capitol.
It is attended by people who come together especially to celebrate freedom.

## "READING IS FUN" WEEK

Check with the school librarian or the district reading consultant to find out what information is
available at the state level or district level for this week. Many schools invite career people from
the community (bank president, state representative, mayor, nurse, dentist, retired teachers, etc.)

into the classroom to read a storybook aloud. Sometimes parents are invited to come in to read a favorite story to the children, and it makes a student proud to have mom or dad or a relative read a book (practiced beforehand) to their classmates.

This is also a good week to have students decide which of their favorites they'd like you to read over again. It's also a good time to invite a published author to read his or her work.

Take the time to go back over the author sections and find a reading activity to do that will be fun!

Check out the Reading Is Fun (RIF) website at www.rif.org.

## FATHER'S DAY

Since a father plays an important role in the family, we set aside a Sunday in June especially to honor him, and to let him know that we care. What are the ways that students can show their appreciation for their dad? Have a class discussion and make an I.O.U. for dad (I.O.U. help with the lawn; I.O.U. help with a car wash; and so on).

For families who don't have a dad in the home, greeting cards can be made for an uncle who is a dad, or for someone else in the family who is a dad. Then, too, there's always grand-dad.

## FLAG DAY

June 14 is a day to honor the flag, a symbol of our country and the freedoms we enjoy as a nation.

Make flags in school and have a class parade. A good resource book is *Patriotic Holidays and Celebrations* by Valorie Grigoli.

## CELEBRATE SUMMERTIME READING

Compile a list of books to send home to parents that are available at the local library. This list can be by author, or subject matter, or favorite books. Be sure to include a variety. Include some of the books mentioned at the beginning of each month or in the bibliography.

Celebrate reading by encouraging parents to procure a library card for their child if they have not already done so. Some libraries have fantastic summer programs for students—check it out! Promote a weekly trip to the library and a quiet time for reading at home.

Make a grid for the months of July and August and in the squares print simple activities. For example: Get a good book about bugs! Read a book about butterflies. Put on a puppet show of a favorite story. Draw a picture of your favorite villain. How many books have you read so far? Find a poetry book about summer at the library.

By all means, encourage reading over the summer so that students will keep their skill level, and even increase it!

For more ideas, check the website www.ed.gov.

# FOCUS ON SCIENCE

## MIXTURES AND SOLUTIONS

A *mixture* consists of two or more substances that retain their separate identities when mixed together. A *solution* is the name given to substances placed in liquid that become part of the liquid.

Get containers or jars for water. Also have a container to house items to submerge and mix in the water. For example, put paper clips, toothpicks, and bits of paper in one jar of water and a spoonful of sugar in another jar of water. Which becomes a mixture? Which is a solution? (Try other substances such as sand, olive oil, powdered milk, and so on.) Have students try to identify mixtures and solutions before putting items together. Then record results. Explain the differences. Students can experiment and make a list of mixtures and solutions that they find in their natural environment, such as sand, dirt, pebbles, grasses, and so on.

## BENDING LIGHT

*You will need:* a glass half filled with water and a pencil.

*Procedure:* Place the pencil in the glass. Look at the pencil from the top and sides. It appears to be bent.

The reason for this is that light travels slower through water than air. So, as light enters and leaves the glass of water, and the glass itself, it changes speed and direction; thus, the pencil looks bent!

## BECOME AN INVENTOR—MAKE A SIMPLE INSTRUMENT

Students can make simple instruments. For a start, they can drum on the plastic lids on coffee cans. What else can they devise? Have them bring in an assortment of tubes (paper toweling tubes), string, trinkets, cans, jars, sticks of varying lengths. Create an instrument they either strike or through which they blow air.

## CLASSIFYING SOUND

First, have students make a list of all the sounds they hear during the day and even when they go home. The next day we will work with the lists. Compile the sounds and make a huge chart of all the sounds. Let's aim for 50 sounds! (See Reproducible Activity Pages.)

Next, we will classify the sounds. Put a green check in front of nature sounds and a red check in front of man-made sounds. Then you can talk about pleasant and unpleasant sounds, or noise. Have students vote on whether they find the sound pleasant or unpleasant (and why), and use a tally mark after the sound.

Now that we've gone down the path of pleasant and unpleasant sounds, students can make another list of sounds that fit those categories that may not have been on the first list (a baby cooing, a cat purring, garbage can covers clanging, and so on). Find out where students differ and why.

## HEALTH WATCH—FEED YOUR BONES

People don't think in terms of "feeding their bones," but for bones to grow strong and healthy, people need to eat foods that contain vitamins C and D. These include dairy products (have students make a list of dairy products, including milk and cheese products), fresh fruits, green vegetables, and fish.

## HEALTH WATCH—TEETH

These are the same foods that are needed to grow healthy teeth. Remind students to see their dentist for a "spring check-up." Include this information in a newsletter for parents.

Cutting, tearing, grinding, chewing—this is the work of teeth! The incisors (front) cut and bite, the canines (side) tear, and the premolars and molars (back) are for grinding and chewing.

List the types of teeth and the food that they help people to eat. Make sure at least 32 foods are listed, for that is the number of healthy teeth the students should eventually have.

## HEALTH WATCH—SKIN

Students need to learn at a young age to protect their skin from sunburn. It is wise for them to slather on lotion when they are playing outdoors in the sun. Sunscreen protection lotions are available with different levels of protection. Again, this is something to put in your newsletter to parents. Remind parents to replenish their supply in their medicine cabinet for the spring and summer months.

## HEALTH ALERT—WEIGHT

Remind students that some foods tend to put more weight on the body than it needs in terms of fat. Therefore, a diet of pizza, doughnuts, sweets, ice cream, and soda is not what the doctor ordered for good health. Again, remind parents of this in your newsletter. Students need a balanced diet with the five food groups represented. They also need exercise such as running, jumping, playing ball, swimming, bicycle riding, and so on.

## PROTECTION IN THE OUTDOORS

Explain to students that a squirrel makes good use of its natural protection—its tail. A squirrel uses its tail as an umbrella in the rain, to wrap around as a blanket when it is asleep, or as a sunscreen to shade itself from scorching hot sun. (The tail also helps squirrels maintain balance as they jump from a rooftop to a tree, or from tree to tree.)

Discuss with students the needs of people for outdoor protection when they are (1) at the beach, (2) on a camping trip, (3) in the desert, (4) on a picnic, (5) in a swimming pool, and (6) in a snowstorm or in a rainstorm with thunder and lightning.

Take large sheets of paper and cut them into shapes that represent the weather picture (giant beach ball, huge tent, enormous sun, raindrop, and so on). On the shapes that represent the settings mentioned, students can draw protective clothing or items needed. As an alternative to drawing, students can locate pictures of items in magazines, cut them out, and paste them on the appropriate shape.

## SPRING SAFETY

Now that daylight hours are longer, students are more apt to be playing in or near a street. Take time for a discussion of bicycle safety, scooter safety, skate safety, and so on. These are important topics and time spent discussing safety will be time well spent.

Check student newspapers and the local newspapers and magazines for safety tips. There is usually an abundance of safety articles at this time of year to help keep students safe.

Safety Rules
No running
No pushing
No diving
Have fun!

# MAY/JUNE AUTHOR STUDY: MATT CHRISTOPHER

Matt Christopher has been called the "author of the #1 sport series for kids." He has written over 80 chapter books for children and, now in his 70's, is enjoying new-found and well-deserved popularity and fame. He began his writing career in 1940. He was very good in sports as a youngster and played many of them. Since age fourteen, he wanted to write. Actually, he wanted to write mystery stories but found his niche writing sports stories for children. His first book was *The Lucky Baseball Bat,* written in 1952, and he's been batting homeruns ever since.

He has won numerous awards over the years. It is not uncommon for parents to say they learned to read by reading his books, and now their children are saying it, too. Hats off to Matt Christopher! For a look at some of his books related to baseball, football, soccer, and so on, and to read chapters of select books online, visit his website at www.mattchristopher.com.

## BOOKS AND SUGGESTED ACTIVITIES

This month we will take a look at several books by Matt Christopher and present an annotated bibliography. Then we are going to suggest a different study approach. The students can select which sports category they want to read. Divide the group into smaller interest groups such as Soccer, Football, Basketball, Baseball, and so on.

During silent reading, the Soccer group will read in one area of the room, the Basketball group in another, etc. Students within groups may or may not be reading the same book. But once they finish one, they are invited to pick up another in the same sports category. It should not be difficult for students to secure the books from the school library or the public library (they're the dog-eared ones). Also, they are available through The Trumpet Club at a minimum cost. Or, two students can work together as partners and take turns reading aloud through the same book.

As stated above, certain chapters of select books are available on this author's website at www.mattchristopher.com.

Suggested activities will follow the short annotated bibliography. (We don't have room for 80 books, but students have been known to have contests to see how many Matt Christopher books they can read and talk about.)

## BASEBALL

### ALL-STAR FEVER: A PEACH STREET MUDDERS STORY

Bus Mercer, shortstop for The Peach Street Mudders baseball team, would give anything to be picked for the county all-star team. Everything looks good and is going his way. But then his concentration is broken by his new mountain bike. Actually it's not the bike, but what he did. The day after he got it he broke one of his parents' rules for using it and it's beginning to bother him. He's got a guilty conscience and it's beginning to affect his game. Will Bus set the matter to rest and prove he's an all-star both on and off the ball field?

## THE DOG THAT CALLED THE PITCH

Harry, the Airedale with ESP, and his best friend Mike, pitcher for The Grand Avenue Giants, are back! Mike and Harry discover that someone else has mental telepathy—Mr. Grimley, the umpire. When Mr. Grimley's glasses are accidentally broken, suddenly it's up to Harry the dog to call the pitches. This is a winner.

## OTHER BASEBALL BOOKS INCLUDE:

*Stranger in Right Field; Prime Time Pitcher; Double Play at Short; Shadow Over Second; Baseball Pals; Baseball Turnaround; Challenge at Second Base;* and *The Reluctant Pitcher,* among others.

# FOOTBALL

## LONG ARM QUARTERBACK

Cap Wadell loves football but he lives in a rural area and there's no team. His grandfather suggests that Cap organize a local six-man team and play other surrounding small towns. There's one major problem—who will be the coach? Cap thinks his grandfather would be perfect, but when his grandfather suggests that Cap be the quarterback, another team grandfather says he's playing favorites. This heats up an old-time rivalry between the grandfathers that's played off the field while Cap and the other grandson battle it out on the field.

## THE DOG THAT STOLE FOOTBALL PLAYS

Harry the talking Airedale steals the show in this funny football book. Mike's football team is put to the test when Harry, his telepathic dog, has to stay home. Can the team possibly win without Harry's supernatural advice? Fast paced and humorous.

## FOOTBALL JOKES AND RIDDLES

Football bloopers, puzzlers, wacky stories, and fun facts are included in this zany collection for fans of pigskin-tossing action.

## OTHER FOOTBALL BOOKS INCLUDE:

*Football Fugitive; Great Moments in Football History; Crackerjack Halfback; Touchdown for Tommy; Tough to Tackle; The Great Quarterback Switch;* among others.

# SOCCER

## *SOCCER HALFBACK*

Jabber Morris has his heart set on playing soccer, but his family is putting on the pressure for him to play football. Football is the sport his dad loved and played before he died. It's a tough decision made more difficult when suspicion of stealing a wallet falls on Jabber's shoulders. Will Jabber give up soccer for football?

## *SOCCER CATS #5: MASTER OF DISASTER*

This is one in a series of "Soccer Cats" stories. Jason is better known for his wisecracks than his goalkeeping ability. But that had better change fast because the Soccer Cats' starting goalie is going on vacation and Jason is taking his place. Will Jason be able to learn all there is to know about goal-keeping before the big game with the tough Panthers?

## OTHER SOCCER BOOKS INCLUDE:

*Soccer Duel; Soccer Scoop;* and The "Soccer Cat" series which includes *The Hat Trick; The Captain's Contest; Operation Babysitter;* and *Soccer Cats #6: Heads Up.*

# TENNIS AND OTHER SPORTS

## *TENNIS ACE*

Steve just wishes he had as much drive to win at tennis as his older sister Ginny. The truth is, she's better at the game but their father ignores her and pushes a reluctant Steve even harder. Will Steve and Ginny finally get up the courage to have a talk with their father?

## *SNOWBOARD MAVERICK*

Dennis O'Malley is a master on the skateboard. In the winter he likes to ski until his accident leaves him afraid to try skiing again. Then Tasha, his friend, gets a new snowboard and Dennis begins to develop his winter skills on that. Can the snowboard help him to overcome his fear on the slopes?

## OTHERS IN THIS CATEGORY INCLUDE:

*Mountain Bike Mania; Snowboard Showdown; Skateboard Renegade; Roller Hockey Radicals; Wheel Wizards; Wingman on Ice; Zero's Slider;* and others.

# ICE SKATING/ICE HOCKEY

## *ON THE ICE WITH . . . WAYNE GRETSKY*

This hockey player was called "The Great One" and was without a doubt the most dominant athlete ever to play the game. Matt Christopher goes "on the ice" for an inside look at the triumphs, troubles, struggles, and statistics of superstar Wayne Gretsky.

## *ON THE ICE WITH . . . TARA LIPINSKI*

A close-up look at this superstar athlete who won the Olympic gold medal in figure skating at age fifteen. She dazzled the world with her agility, difficult combinations, and an unbridled enthusiasm.

## OTHERS IN THIS SERIES INCLUDE:

Biographies of famous sportspeople of today: *At the Plate With . . .* series; *In the Huddle With . . .; On the Field With . . .; On the Mound With . . .; On the Track With . . .; On the Court With . . .; On the Course With . . .;* and many others.

# SUGGESTED ACTIVITIES

1. Read books aloud so that the class catches the flavor of the action and pulls together as a unit.
2. Students can form Sports Groups, and read books from a particular category. Then they can report to the class on their book. Make a poster advertising the book.
3. Sign up another student to read the book you just read, so that students read in different categories.
4. Use the newspaper to keep track of real sports—the teams, the sports, the players.
5. Keeping track of baseball game scores and performance scores at this time of year (runs batted in [RBI's], batting averages, etc.) will foster graph making and interest in math.
6. Play organized games during outdoor recess.
7. All of the books revolve around a problem to be solved. What's the problem and how do the different characters go about solving the problems?
8. What is the message that the author is giving to the reader?
9. Keep classroom charts of the books read in different sports categories.
10. Make an illustration for the part of the story for which there was none.
11. Make puppets of the dog with supernatural powers and have him tell the stories.
12. Interview sports figures from the biography series. That is, have a student read a book and agree to act as the character and be interviewed using the information in the book.
13. Form a "Readers Theatre Group" and have different students read aloud from various parts of the book. Practice this before the class and then travel to other classrooms to present the material.

14. Visit the website <u>mattchristopher.com</u> and report to the classroom about videos, interviews with the author, shopping, how to send an e-mail message to the author, and more.

15. *Discussion time.* Ask the question "What did you learn today?" after Sustained Silent Reading (SSR) time. Students learn an amazing amount of information about the sports, and also how the main character is thinking his or her way through a problem.

**Note:** This is a good time of year to introduce books on outdoor sports because students are spending more time outdoors and summer is just around the corner. Perhaps these books will be helpful in many ways since they present sound values. Encourage students to read the books throughout the summer. There are more than enough to go around! They can form a Matt Christopher Fan Club and meet and read during the summer. Matt Christopher is still writing and knocking them out, so be on the lookout for new titles, too. Hats off to Matt Christopher for the hard work he's done to make our reading pleasurable and informative!

# REPRODUCIBLE ACTIVITY PAGES
# FOR MAY/JUNE

## READING/LANGUAGE ARTS

Homer Likes to Read and Write

Meet a Story Character—Girl (two pages)

Meet a Story Character—Boy (two pages)

Consonant Blend Search

## MATH

"Oh, Yes, You Do Need Math!"

Working with Weight

Baseball Math  (Answer Sheet on p. 503)

Basketball Bears  (Answer Sheet on p. 503)

Tennis Teddies  (Answer Sheet on p. 503)

## SOCIAL STUDIES

Wants and Needs

## SCIENCE

Listen for Sounds of Spring

Let's Go Digging for a Graph

Write a Bird Report

Spring Tree Graph

## AUTHOR STUDY

Spin a Story with Matt Christopher

Name _____     Date _____

# Homer Likes to Read and Write

Remember Homer Xytlefry?  He has taken up writing.  But there is one problem.  Homer is having trouble with the "reading road signs."  Can you circle the errors and correct them?  Homer will learn from you and he says, "Thanks!"

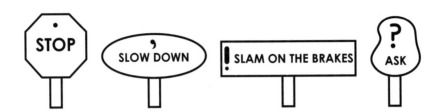

Max J. Pennybroth was a good baseball player.  Some said Max was the best?   That is, until Penny B. Maxwell, a new girl came to town.

When Penny stepped up to the plate?   Max just grinned,   He threw a curve ball and Penny swung hard and missed!   Max just grinned?   Then he threw another ball to Penny?   and the Ump yelled, "STRIKE?"   This was it.  It was now or never, for Penny B. Maxwell,

Max grinned and threw a fast ball.   Penny swung the bat"   and hit the ball hard,   It was a line drive to first, but she ran fast and made it to second,

The crowd cheered.   The trumpets blared,   It was the first hit of the season that anyone got off of Max?   Even Max looked surprised?

After the game.   Grandpa said, "Gee Whillikers, Max?   Hot dog?   You got yourself some competition!"

# Make a Story Character—Girl

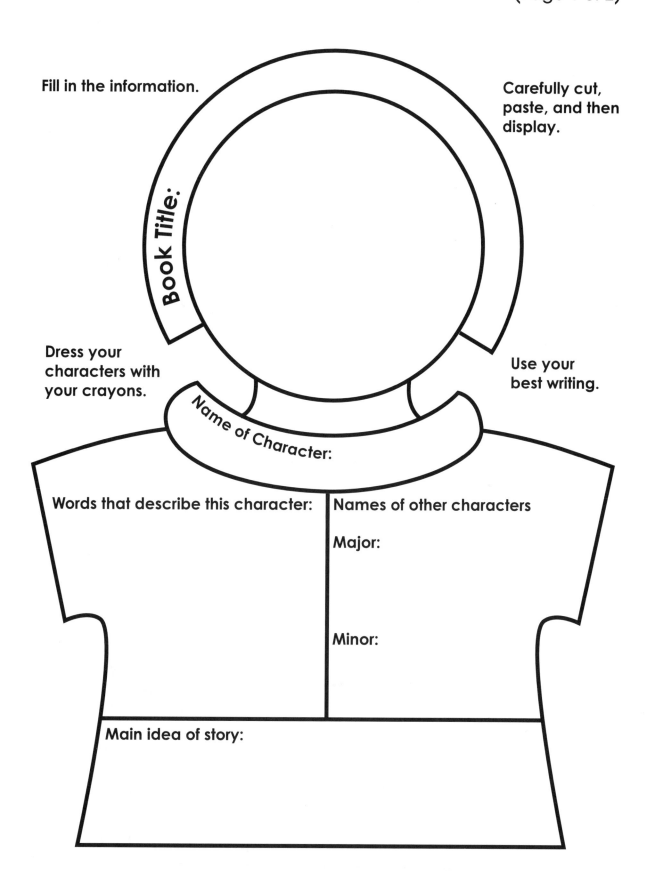

Fill in the information.

Carefully cut, paste, and then display.

Book Title:

Dress your characters with your crayons.

Use your best writing.

Name of Character:

Words that describe this character:

Names of other characters

Major:

Minor:

Main idea of story:

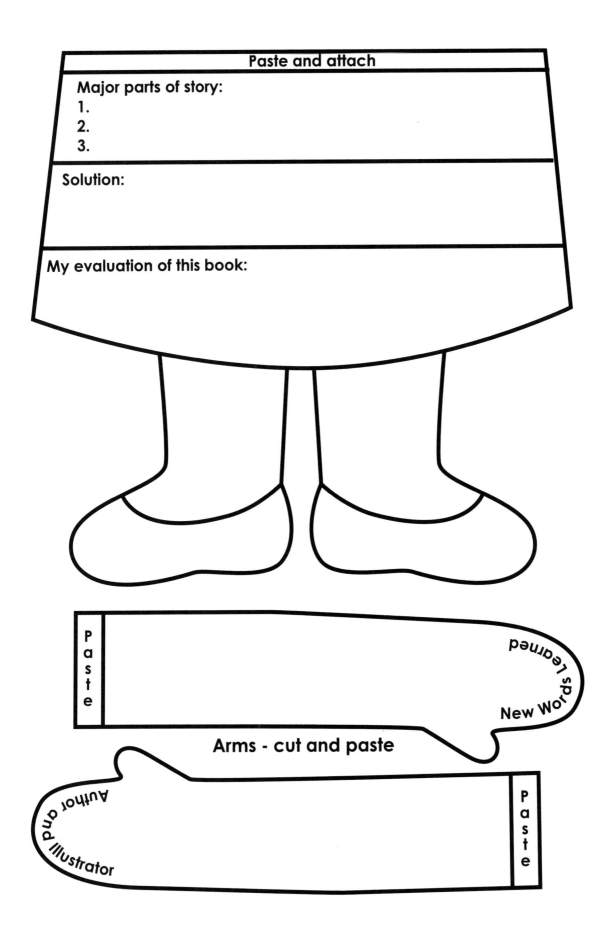

**Paste and attach**

Major parts of story:
1.
2.
3.

Solution:

My evaluation of this book:

Paste

New Words Learned

Arms - cut and paste

Author and Illustrator

Paste

# Make a Story Character—Boy

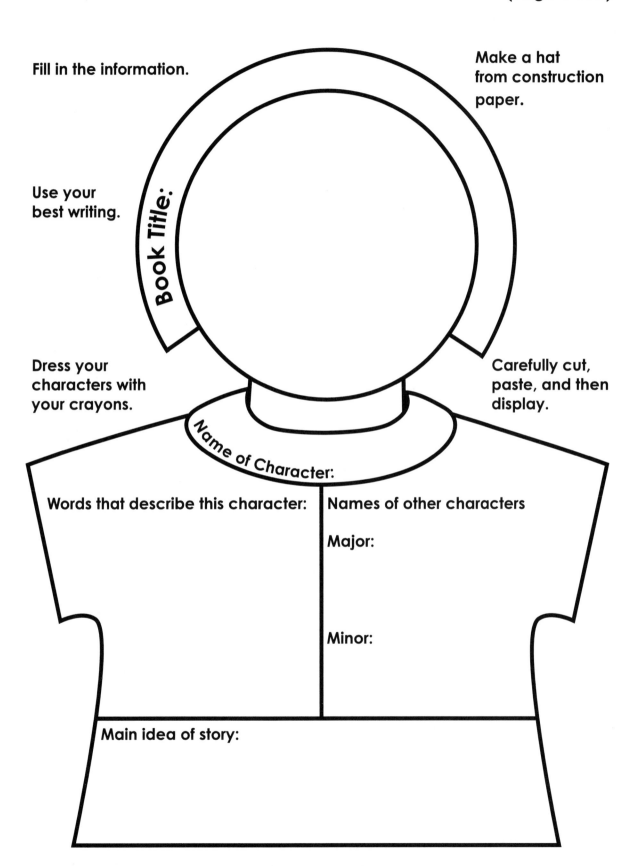

Fill in the information.

Make a hat from construction paper.

Use your best writing.

Dress your characters with your crayons.

Carefully cut, paste, and then display.

Book Title:

Name of Character:

Words that describe this character:

Names of other characters

Major:

Minor:

Main idea of story:

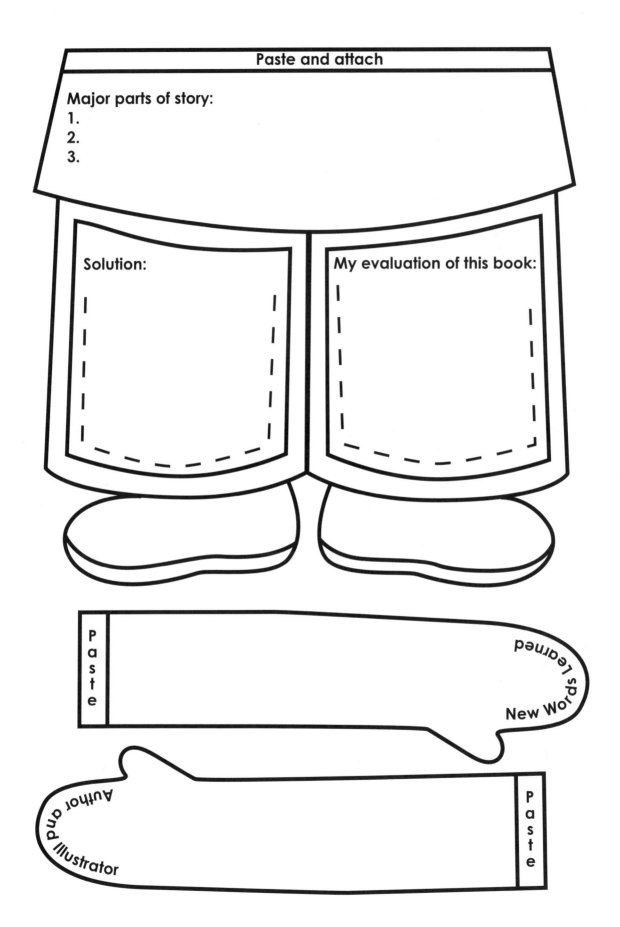

**Paste and attach**

Major parts of story:
1.
2.
3.

Solution:

My evaluation of this book:

Paste

New Words Learned

Author and Illustrator

Paste

Name ____________________ Date ____________________

# Consonant Blend Search

Go on a search for consonant blends through newspapers, magazines and mail. Cut out and paste some interesting ones to fit these spaces.

Space 1

2

3

4

5

6

7

8

9

10

11

# "Oh, Yes, You Do Need Math!"

Macaroni the Monkey dreams of being a truck driver. "I don't need Math," he says. "Oh, yes, you do!" answer his friends.

List 10 ways that he will need to use math.

1.
2.
3.
4.
5.
6.
7.
8.
9.
10.

Name _____    Date _____

# Working with Weight

Find two things that weigh more than the books. Draw them here.

Find two things that weigh less than the books. Draw them here.

Name _____     Date _____

# Baseball Math

This member of the "Baseball Bears" team claims you have to know a lot about math to play the game. How many questions can you answer? Find information books about baseball and read them. Now how many can you answer? Keep score!

1. How many teams are needed to play a game of baseball? _____

2. How many players are on each team? _____

3. How many bases are used in the game? _____

4. These bases form what math shape on the field? _____

5. If a player gets a base hit and goes to first base, it's called a _____.

6. If a player gets a base hit and goes to second base, it's called a _____.

7. It takes _____ strikes, and the batter is OUT!

8. Each team stays at bat until _____ players are out.

9. When both teams have had a turn at bat, it's called an <u>inning</u>. There are _____ innings per game.

10. The baseball is in the shape of a _____.

11. The bases are canvas bags and are shaped like a _____.

12. How far does the pitcher stand from home plate? _____

13. A pitcher can pitch a "fast ball" that can travel _____ miles per hour.

14. To keep fans informed during the game, _____ are flashed on the scoreboard.

15. The official baseball weighs approximately _____.

16. Explain this phrase: "It's the bottom of the 5th." _____

17. After the _____th inning, the fans get up and stretch.

What's Your Score? _____

Usually the baseball season runs from April to September. What is the name of a major league team near you? _____ Follow the news about the team daily on the Sports Page of your newspaper. Learn about RBI's, and averages, and who is winning. You'll enjoy using your MATH! "Batter up!"

See Answer Page—back of book

Name _____    Date _____

# Basketball Bears

Basketball is a very fast game that is played in a small area. It was first played in Massachusetts with "peach baskets" fastened high on the wall at each end of the gymnasium. That's where we get the term <u>basket</u>ball. Let's find out some Math Facts about this peach of a sport!

1. The season is usually from the month of _____ until the month of _____.

2. Standard court size is _____ by _____.

3. Distance from floor to basket rim is _____ ft.

4. How many players are there on each team? _____

5. The basketball is shaped like a _____ and weighs approximately _____.

> **SPORTS BEAR TIMEOUT FOR ESTIMATION.** Hold a basketball in one hand and another item in the other hand. Which is heavier? Can you find something that you estimate to be the same weight as the ball? Weigh the items to verify your hypothesis (estimate).

6. Timing is very important in this game. The clock runs at all times except for 4 reasons. Name them.

   a. _____     b. _____

   c. _____     d. _____

7. How long is "timeout"? _____

8. A professional basketball game is how long? _____

9. Each game is <u>divided</u> into <u>four</u> _____.

10. There is a _____-minute rest period between <u>halves</u>.

11. OBSERVE A GAME OF BASKETBALL and use tally marks to keep score on this sheet:

| | team A | team B | team A | team B | A | B |
|---|---|---|---|---|---|---|
| | 1st half | 1st half | 2nd half | 2nd half | | |
| fouls | | | | | | |
| fouls | | | | | | |
| timeout | | | | | | |
| timeout | | | | | | |

# Tennis Teddies

This Sports Bear claims that tennis is both physically and mentally demanding. Also, you should know some math facts about tennis in order to be able to play the game. How many questions listed below can you answer? Let's find some information books about tennis and skim them for the answers. "Match" these questions with the correct numbers.

1. The first point scored by a player is worth _____.

2. The second point scored by a player is worth _____.

3. The third point scored by a player is worth _____.

4. Add up the three consecutive points from above and what do you get? _____ + _____ + _____ = _____

5. In a tennis match, is the server's score announced first or second? _____

6. How many games are in a set? _____

7. The first player to take _____ games wins the set.

8. The average tennis racket is about _____ inches long.

9. The standard weight for a tennis racket is approximately _____ ounces.

SPORTS BEAR TIMEOUT TIP: Bring in a real tennis racket and weigh and measure it. Then find things that are the same length. Find things that are the same weight.

10. When waiting for the ball to come your way, your feet should be about _____ feet apart.

11. To "volley" is to return the ball before it touches the ground, instead of waiting for it to bounce. How many times is the tennis ball allowed to bounce before you return it? _____

12. What is the length of the tennis court? _____

13. What is the width of the tennis court? _____

14. After the first game, the players change sides of the net. Then how often do they change sides of the net? _____

SPORTS BEAR MATH FLASH: "Love" means no score. It's from the French word "l'oeuf" which means ZERO.

©2002 by The Center for Applied Research in Education

Name _____  Date _____

# Wants and Needs

Circle your **needs** in red.  Circle your **wants** in blue.
Carefully color the items on display.

©2002 by The Center for Applied Research in Education

**Name** _____  **Date** _____

A membrane called the eardrum is located inside the ear. It vibrates when sound waves enter the ear. This sends signals to the brain, and we hear sound.

Go for a "Spring Listening Walk." What are the sounds you hear over your head and under your feet? Do you hear some high sounds and some low sounds? Do you hear some pleasant sounds and some sounds of alarm? When you come back from your walk, have a class discussion and draw or list items in the spaces provided below. Keep listening every day.

| | |
|---|---|
| **High Sounds** | **Low Sounds** |
| **Pleasant Sounds** | **Moving Sounds** |

Name _____     Date _____

# Let's Go Digging for a Graph

We can find many things at a sandy beach.  Below are symbols to show four different things that we can find.  Count how many there are of each kind in the large sand pile.  Graph that number by coloring in the correct number of boxes above each one.

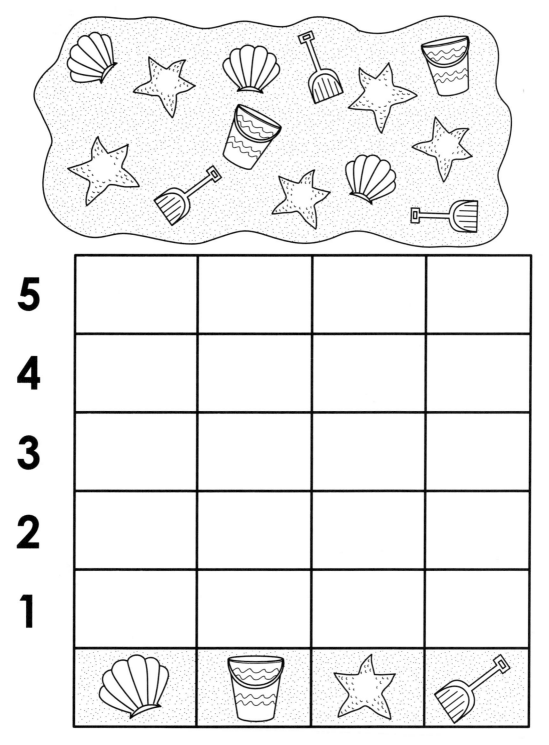

Name _____     Date _____

# Write a Bird Report

Use several resource books or nature magazines from the library to complete this bird report.

The name of the bird I am reporting on

is the _____.

1. On a separate page, draw a picture of the bird in flight.

2. **Bills and Beaks:** A bill is usually pointed and a beak is usually curved. Birds use their beak, or bill, as a tool to get and handle food.

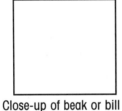

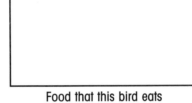

Close-up of beak or bill          Food that this bird eats

3. **Feet:** Most birds have four toes, with three pointing forward and one pointing backward. It would make this shape footprint Ⴘ . Some birds have two toes pointing up and two pointing down. It would make this shape footprint ✕ . Some birds have only three toes, and their footprints may look like this Ⴘ . Some have web feet.

Close-up of bird's feet          Footprints

4. Tell some special things about this bird (where it lives, how it got its name, etc.). Write them on another sheet of paper.

Use the back of this sheet to write more interesting facts about this bird. People who study birds are called ORNITHOLOGISTS.

# Spring Tree Graph

Count the number of kites in the tree. Find the kite column on the tree trunk. Color in the same number of squares above the kite. Do this for the birds and the bird nests, too.

Use your crayons to make the tree colorful.

Of which items does the tree contain the most? the least?

Are there more or fewer bird nests than kites?

Go outside and look way, way up into a large tree. Make another tree graph of your own.

# Spin a Story with Matt Christopher

Cut out the spinner and attach it to the middle of the wheel with a paper fastener. Then spin until the spinner lands in Section A—that is your major character. Spin until the spinner lands in Section B—that is your setting, or where your story will take place. Spin again, until you land in Sections C and D.

Make up a story with the help you got from the story spinner. Keep spinning again and again for more good stories. Later, use a paper plate and a spinner to create your own story wheel.

There is always a problem to solve and a lesson to learn in Matt Christopher's stories. Use that formula for your stories.

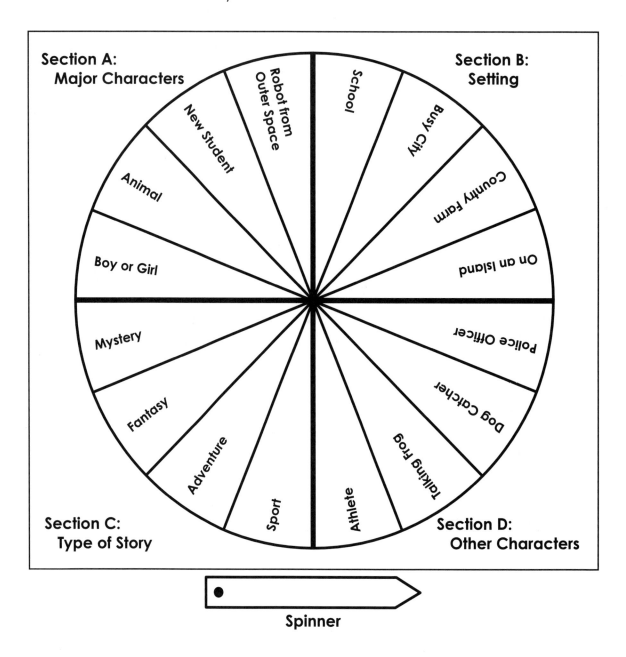

**Spinner**

A "spinner" of tales, or a "spinner" of yarns, means that a person is a good storyteller. Be prepared to write or tell your story, just like Matt Christopher.

# Answers for May/June
# Math Activity Pages

## "BASEBALL MATH" (page 494)

1. two
2. nine
3. four, including home plate
4. diamond
5. single
6. double
7. three
8. three
9. nine
10. sphere
11. square
12. 60 ft. 6 inches
13. 90–100 miles per hour
14. numbers (scores)
15. five ounces
16. It's the 5th inning, and the first team is out, and the second team is at bat.
17. seventh

## "BASKETBALL BEARS" (page 495)

1. October, May
2. 94 ft. L × 50 ft. W
3. 10 ft.
4. 5
5. sphere, 20–22 ounces
6. foul is called; jump ball is called; too much time to put ball back into play; when a timeout is called by a player or by an official
7. one minute
8. 18 minutes
9. quarters
10. fifteen

## "TENNIS TEDDIES" (page 496)

1. fifteen
2. fifteen
3. ten
4. 15 + 15 + 10 = 40
5. first
6. six at the minimum
7. six
8. twenty-seven (27)
9. 14–15 oz.
10. 1½ (one and a half)
11. once
12. 78 ft.
13. 27 ft.
14. after every two games, or the odd-numbered games

# TEACHER RESOURCE
# BIBLIOGRAPHY

## ART

Bolognese, Don and Elaine Raphael. *The Illustrator's Library: Charcoal and Pastel* (New York: Franklin Watts, 1986).

Butterfield, Moira. *Fun With Paint* (New York: Creative Crafts, 1994).

Mainprize, Virginia (Ed.) *Craft Workshop: Fabrics* (New York: Thumbprint Books, 1998).

Martin, Judy (Editorial Consultant). *Painting and Drawing* (Brookfield, CT: Millbrook, 1993).

McGill, Ormond. *Chalk Talks!,* drawings by Anne Canevari Green (Brookfield, CT: Millbrook Press, 1995).

Roalf, Peggy. *Looking at Painting Series* (New York: Hyperion, 1993). The artist has a series of 12 books that look at famous paintings of the following subjects through the eyes of different painters: Families, Dancers, Children, Dogs, Cats, Seascapes, Circus, Self-portraits, Horses, Landscapes, Flowers, and Musicians.

Stevens, Bernardine S. *Colonial American Craftspeople* (New York: Franklin Watts, 1993).

Zubrowski, Bernie. *MOBILES, Building and Experimenting With Balancing Toys,* illustrated by Roy Doty (New York: Morrow, 1993).


## GENERAL

http://www.phedu.com (Complete listing of helpful books for teachers)

Bigham, Vicki Smith and George Bigham. *The Prentice Hall Directory of Online Education Resources* (Paramus, NJ: Prentice Hall, 1998). (www.phdirect.com)

Dreikurs, Rudolf and Pearl Cassel. *Discipline Without Tears,* 2nd Edition (New York: Penguin Plume Books, 1991).

Foster, David R. and James L. Overhold. *Indoor Action Games for Elementary Children,* illustrations by Ron Schultz (West Nyack, NY: Parker Publishing, 1989). (www.phdirect.com)

Wirth, Marian Jenks. *Teacher's Handbook of Children's Games: A Guide to Developing Perceptual-Motor Skills* (West Nyack, NY: Parker Publishing Co., Inc., 1976).


## READING/LANGUAGE ARTS

Block, Cathy Collins. *Teaching the Language Arts,* 2nd Edition (Boston: Allyn & Bacon, 1997).

Fry, Edward Bernard, Jacqueline E. Kress, and Dona Lee Fountoukidis. *The Reading Teacher's Book of Lists,* Fourth Edition (Paramus, NJ: Prentice Hall, 2000). (www.phdirect.com)

Funk, Charles Earle. *A Hog on Ice & Other Curious Expressions,* drawings by Tom Funk (New York: Harper Colophon, 1985).

———. *Heavens to Betsy! & Other Curious Sayings,* drawings by Tom Funk (New York: Harper Perennial, 1986).

———. *Thereby Hangs a Tale* (New York: Harper Colophon, 1985).

Funk, Charles Earle and Charles Earle Funk, Jr. *Horsefeathers & Other Curious Words,* drawings by Tom Funk (New York: Harper Perennial, 1986).

Funk, Wilfred. *Word Origins and Their Romantic Stories* (New York: Bell Publishing, 1978).

Norton, Donna E. and Saundra Norton. *Language Arts Activities for Children,* Fourth Edition (Upper Saddle River, NJ: Prentice Hall, 1999).

Steckler, Arthur. *101 Words and How They Began,* drawings by James Flora (Garden City, NY: Doubleday, 1979).

Stull, Elizabeth Crosby. *Let's Read* (Paramus, NJ: The Center for Applied Research in Education, 2000). (www.phdirect.com)

Wheeler, Cindy. *More Simple Signs. (Sign Alphabet Words)* (New York: Viking, 1998).

## MATHEMATICS

Burns, Marilyn. *This Book Is About Time* (Boston: Little, Brown, 1978). (This is one in a series of popular books for teachers including the *I Hate Mathematics Book.*)

Haskins, Jim. *Count Your Way Through . . . Series* (Minneapolis: (The Lerner Publishing Group, 1987–1990). (Includes counting your way through the Arab World, China, Japan, Russia, Africa, Canada, Mexico, Germany, and Italy.)

Kaplan, Andrew (interviewer). *Careers for Number Lovers,* photos by Eddie Keating and Carrie Boretz (Brookfield, CT: Millbrook, 1991).

Kennedy, Leonard and Steve Tipps. *Guiding Children's Learning of Mathematics* (Belmont, CA: Wadsworth, 1991).

Lobosco, Michael L. *Mental Math Challenges* (New York: Sterling Publishing, 1991).

*Math Matters* (Danbury, CT: Grolier Educational Publishing, 1999). (Series of 13 short books includes *Numbers, Adding, Subtracting, Multiplying, Dividing, Decimals, Fractions, Shape, Size, Girls and Grapes, Chance and Average, Tables and Charts, Mental Arithmetic.*)

Rancussi, E. R. and J. L. Teeters. *Creating Escher-Type Drawings* (Palo Alto, CA: Creative Publications, 1977).

Reys, Robert E., Marilyn N. Suydam, Mary M. Lindquist, and Nancy L. Smith. *Helping Children Learn Mathematics,* Fifth Edition (Needham Heights, MA: Viacom, 1995).

Stenmark, Jean Kerr, Virginia Thompson, and Ruth Cossey. *Family Math,* illustrated by Marilyn Hill (Berkeley: University of California, 1986).

*The Case of the Missing Zebra Stripes* (Alexandria, VA: Time-Life Books for Children, 1992).

Wells, Robert E. *Can You Count to a Googol?* (Morton Grove, IL: Albert Whitman & Co., 2000).

Whitin, David J. *Read Any Good Math Lately?* (Portsmouth, NH: Heinemann, 1992).

Wyatt, Valerie. *The Math Book for Girls and Other Beings Who Count,* illustrated by Pat Cupples (Niagara Falls, NY: Kids Can Press, 2000).

## MUSIC

*An Illustrated Treasury of Songs, National Gallery of Art, Washington* (Milwaukee, WI: Hal Leonard Publisher, 1991).

Blackwood, Alan. *The Orchestra* (Brookfield, CT: Millbrook, 1993).

Hudson, Wade and Cheryl (selected by). *How Sweet the Sound, African-American Songs for Children,* illustrated by Floyd Cooper (New York: Scholastic, 1995).

Husain, Shahrukh (retold by). *The Barefoot Book of Stories from the Opera,* illustrated by James Mayhew (New York: Barefoot Books, 1999).

MacDonald, Margaret Read and Winifred Jaeger. *The Round Book, Rounds Kids Love to Sing* (New Haven, CT: Linnet, 1999).

## SCIENCE/HEALTH

Baldwin, Dorothy and Claire Lister. *The Structure of Your Body* (New York: Bookwright, 1984).

————. *Your Body Fuel* (New York: Bookwright, 1984).

Bonnett, Bob and Dan Keen. *Science Fair Projects: Physics,* illustrated by Frances Zweifel (New York: Sterling, 1999).

————. *Science Fair Projects: Energy,* illustrated by Alex Pang (New York: Sterling, 1997).

Brimner, Larry Dane. *Animals That Hibernate* (New York: Franklin Watts, 1991).

Garvy, Helen. *The Immune System: Your Magic Doctor,* illustrated by Dan Bessie (Los Gatos, CA: Shire Press, 1992).

Gibbons, Gail. *Stargazers* (New York: Holiday House, 1992).

Hickman, Pamela and Pat Stephens. *Animal Senses* (Buffalo, NY: Kids Can Press Ltd., 1998).

Krupp, E. C. *The Big Dipper and You,* illustrated by Robin Rector Krupp (New York: Morrow, 1989).

Lauber, Patricia. *How Dinosaurs Came to Be,* illustrated by Douglas Henderson (New York: Simon & Schuster, 1996).

Markle, Sandra. *Outside and Inside Birds* (New York: Bradbury Press, 1994).

Porter, Keith. *Discovering Science: How Animals Behave* (Sussex, England: BLA Publishing Ltd., 1987).

Savage, Stephen. *What's the Difference? Birds* (Austin, TX: Raintree Steck-Vaughn Publishers, 2000).

Scagell, Robin. *Space Explained. A Beginner's Guide to the Universe* (New York: Henry Holt, 1996).

Selsam, Millicent E. and Joyce Hunt. *A First Look at Bird Nests,* illustrated by Harriett Springer (New York: Walker & Co., 1984).

Simon, Seymour. *New Questions and Answers About Dinosaurs,* illustrations by Jennifer Dewey (New York: Morrow, 1990).

Tolman, Marvin N. *Hands-on Science Activities for Grades 3–4* (Paramus, NJ: Parker Publishing, 1999). ([www.phdirect.com](www.phdirect.com))

## SOCIAL STUDIES

Brandt, Sue R. *Facts About the Fifty States* (New York: Franklin Watts, Inc., 1988).

Climo, Shirley. *City! Washington, D.C.,* photography by George Ancona (New York: Macmillan, 1991).

Clouse, Nancy L. *Puzzle Maps U.S.A.* (New York: Henry Holt & Co., 1990).

————. *Mapas rompecabezas de los Estados Unidos* (New York: Henry Holt & Co., 1990).

Giblin, James and Dale Ferguson. *The Scarecrow Book* (New York: Crown, 1980).

Henderson, Kathy. *I Can Be a Geographer* (Chicago: Childrens Press, 1990).

Knowlton, Jack. *Geography from A to Z,* picture glossary by Harriett Barton (New York: Thomas Y. Crowell, 1988).

Partin, Ronald L. *The Prentice Hall Directory of Online Social Studies Resources* (Paramus, NJ: Prentice Hall, 1998). ([www.phdirect.com](www.phdirect.com))

West, Delno C. and Jean M. West. *Uncle Sam and Old Glory,* woodcuts by Christopher Manson (New York: Atheneum, 2000).

APPENDIX A

# JUMP THROUGH JULY WITH JULIUS J. JAYBIRD

Julius J. Jaybird has 25 activities for you to do during the month of July. Do one a day. Color the box when you finish the activity. If you finish early, enjoy a good book. If July has 31 days, how many days off is Jaybird giving you?

| | | | | |
|---|---|---|---|---|
| Read a book about birds. | Draw all of the math shapes you know. | Make a calendar for July. | Write and illustrate your own story. | Find a good mystery book and get lost in it. |
| Start a daily journal of your summer. | Check out your local library activities. | Make an ABC Book of Summer. | Start a rock collection. | Plant some flower seeds. Water with care. |
| Make a paper bag puppet. Act out a story. | Sit under a tree and daydream. (5 minutes) | Find 3 books on the same topic and read them. | Practice the multiplication facts. | Watch the clouds. What pictures do they remind you of? |
| Pretend you're a weather reporter and do a news report today. | Make an ABC Book of Sports. | How many words can you read on a cereal box? | Collect and classify 25 pebbles. | Keep a record of the books you're reading. |
| Read a story in the newspaper. | How many zoo animals can you list? | Play a board-game with a friend. | How many fruits can you name? | Jump rope in time to the multiplication tables. |

# APPENDIX B
## AMBROZE APPLEBEE'S AWESOME AUGUST ACTIVITIES

This busy bee wants you to spread out these activities throughout the month of August. Color the box when you finish the activity.

| | | | | |
|---|---|---|---|---|
| Read a picture book about an animal. | Make a list of 10 spelling words and learn them. | Create a picture using only 3 colors. | Make up two story problems. | Write a letter and mail it. |
| Take a survey of people's favorite summer sport. | Keep a weather chart. | Count the different colored flowers you see. | Do some comparison shopping in the paper. | Eat something green today. (celery, grapes, green pepper, lettuce) |
| How can you help around the house this week? | Catch yourself doing math today. | Find 10 items that begin with "B." Put them in ABC order. | Read a book by your favorite author. | Make a big mask from a grocery bag. |
| Practice your division facts. | Practice handwriting slowly. | Make a set of picture flash-cards for 10 weather words. | Can you sit still for 5 minutes? Time it. | Make a greeting card and send it. |
| Draw a map of your street. | Draw your state bird inside the shape of your state. | It's a day for poetry! Read some. Write some. | Find a snowy day book. Read it today. Do you feel cooler? | Play a game of ball. |

# APPENDIX C
# HANDWRITING CHARTS

Have you ever needed a handwriting chart for a student and couldn't quickly locate one? The Zaner-Bloser and D'Nealian manuscript and cursive alphabet charts are here to help you out in just such a situation.

**Zaner-Bloser Manuscript Alphabet**

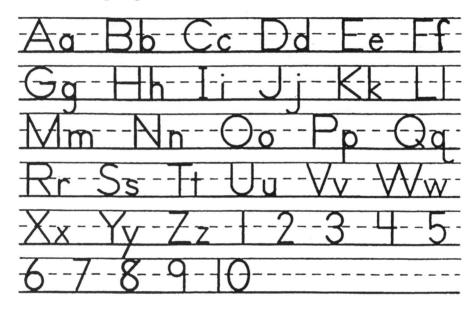

**Zaner-Bloser Cursive Alphabet**

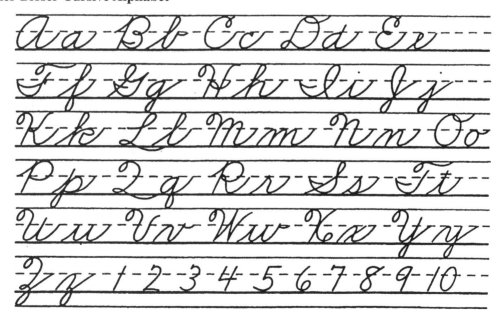

**D'Nealian® Manuscript Alphabet**

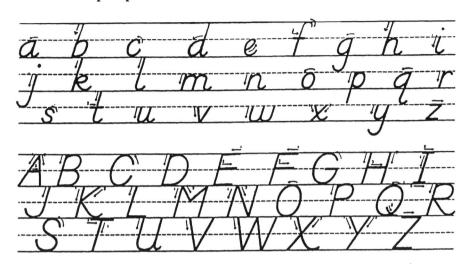

**D'Nealian® Cursive Alphabet**

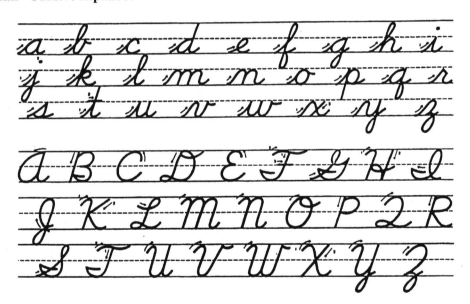

**D'Nealian® Numbers**

# APPENDIX D
# EMOTICONS

Getting your ideas across on the Internet—in e-mail, chat rooms, or discussion groups—is helped by the use of emoticons that let your readers know how you feel about things. The word "emoticon" is a portmanteau formed by combining the words *emotion* and *icon*. They are formed using regular letters and symbols on the computer keyboard. Although they are also called "smileys," they represent a wide range of feelings.

| | | | |
|---|---|---|---|
| :-) | happy | :-() | bored |
| ;-) | playful, winking | :-( | sad, unhappy, upset |
| :-< | miserable, frowning | :-D | laughing, joking |
| :-\| | indifferent, who cares? | :-X | it's a secret, lips are sealed |
| (-: | left-handed writer | %-) | cross-eyed, exhausted |
| 8-) | wearing sunglasses | ::-) | wearing regular glasses |
| B-) | wearing dark-rimmed glasses | 8:-) | girl, woman |
| :-)>== | boy, man | :-{) | has a mustache |
| :'-( | crying | :-/ | confused, not sure, skeptical |
| :-# | wearing braces | :-o | talking |
| \|-D | laughing out loud | :-O | shouting |
| :-0 | uh-oh! | :-@ | screaming |
| :-& | tongue tied | :-] | grinning |
| \|-O | yawning | :-P | sticking tongue out |
| \|-I | sleeping | :-[ | frowning, miserable |
| :-> | smirk, joking, devilish | :-{} | wearing lipstick |
| {:-) | wearing a toupee | *<:-) | Santa or partygoer |
| *.o) | clowning around | [ ] ** | hugs & kisses |
| {{{}}} | thinking it over | 0 :-) | angel, angelic |
| [:-] | robot | <:-) | dunce |
| [:-) | wearing earphones | <:3 )~ | mouse |
| 3:] | pet, cat, dog, cow | 8 :-) | wizard |
| $-) | greedy | :-* | kiss |
| @--)-- | flower, rose | <()(—)<< | fish |
| :-)X | wearing a bow tie | (:::[ ]:::) | bandaid |
| @(*0*)@ | koala bear | | |